African-American Voices in Young Adult Literature

Tradition, Transition, Transformation

Edited by
Karen Patricia Smith

The Scarecrow Press, Inc.
Lanham, Maryland, and London
2001

SCARECROW PRESS, INC.

Published in the United States of America
by Scarecrow Press, Inc.
4720 Boston Way, Lanham, Maryland 20706
www.scarecrowpress.com

4 Pleydell Gardens, Folkestone
Kent CT20 2DN, England

British Library Cataloguing in Publication Information Available

The hardback edition of this book was previously cataloged by the Library of
Congress as follows:

  African-american voices in young adult literature : tradition,
    transition, transformation / Karen Patricia Smith, editor.
      p.   cm.
  Includes bibliographical references and index.
  ISBN: 0-8108-2907-X (alk. paper)
  1.   Young adult literature, American—Afro-American
  authors—History and criticism. 2. Youth—United States—
  Books and reading. 3. Afro-American youth—Books and
  reading. 4. Afro-American youth in literature. 5. Afro-Americans in
  literature. I. Smith, Karen Patricia, 1948-
  PS153.N5A347   1994
  810.9'896073—dc20   94-13800

ISBN: 0-8108-4272-6 (paper)

Manufactured in the United States of America.

♾™ The paper used in this publication meets the minimum requirements of
American National Standard for Information Sciences—Permanence of
Paper for Printed Library Materials, ANSI/NISO Z39.48-1992.

This book is dedicated with great appreciation to
Jane Anne Hannigan

Table of Contents

Acknowledgements

I am indebted to all those who helped this project come to fruition. In particular, may I thank my family who, as always, offer me support in all of my projects, feedback when questions arise and unending encouragement in overcoming hurdles.

I am also deeply indebted to the friends and colleagues who responded to my requests to contribute their time and their expertise to write the chapters for this volume.

Grateful thanks are due to Kay E. Vandergrift who has generously offered advice and input during the evolution of *African-American Voices in Young Adult Literature*.

My heartfelt appreciation is extended to Betty Jean Parks who designed and prepared the camera-ready copy for this manuscript and also assisted with the arduous task of proofreading. She has shown tremendous patience and dedication to this project and has consistently produced copy of the highest quality.

Last, but assuredly not least, deep thanks are given to Jane Anne Hannigan who expended great efforts on behalf of this project, too numerous to list. She is an energetic and tireless individual and friend, who also enthusiastically encouraged me when one afternoon I began a phone conversation by saying, "I have an idea for a book on African-American young adult literature . . ."

Introduction

Two years ago I went to Australia on a research trip. Several days into the trip, through chance seating on an airplane, I sat next to a gentleman and his wife, whom I later discovered had strong connections to the world of literature for young people. We spent the next two hours in animated conversation about the world of books for children. As luck would have it, we discovered that my hotel was only an hour or so away from their home. Having received a very kind invitation to visit them several days later, I left my hotel with few concerns, other than that I was greatly looking forward to the evening. What I did not know was that the gentleman and his wife, in an effort to arrange a truly congenial evening, had invited several neighbors and friends for the occasion specifically to meet me, apparently one of the few African-Americans with whom they had ever come in contact. The evening began well enough, but it soon became apparent to me that one neighbor, in particular, was bent upon questioning me about "life at home" in a very peculiar manner.

As the evening progressed, I began to realize that all of the questions I was asked (and they came so thick and fast as to simulate an interrogation) had to do with what I thought and what I ate, my family, my background and, particularly, crime and danger, anxiety and fear, in short what Brent Staples in *Parallel Time: Growing Up in Black and White* implied by his reference to "the Real Negro questions."[1] Truth to tell, I had anticipated, before leaving home, that I, as an African-American traveling alone in Australia, might be the target of certain inquiries. But the intensity of the questions surprised and, needless to say, disconcerted me. The neighbor remarked on the recent Los Angeles riots (which had taken place four months previous) and asked me, a New York resident, how far I lived from Los Angeles. Recovering quickly from my amazement, I was glad to be able to think on my feet and come up with an answer which I knew would set him back on his heels a bit. "About as far," I commented, "as you do from Perth." This really did seem to catch him off guard, as he apparently had the expectation that I would say that I had been right in the thick of things. I wasn't sure if he was more amazed by the fact that I really lived no place near the scene of the riots, or by my knowledge of where we were in relationship to Perth. In any case, one thing was clear. He held a stereotyped viewpoint of African-Americans. Somehow, we weren't quite like "other" Americans. Somehow, I just didn't seem to fit in with his concept of what African-Americans were *really* like.

When the evening was ended, *I* was left with a question or two lingering in *my* mind. I wondered where exactly he had gotten his notions of African-Americans. (I also wondered why he thought it was polite or acceptable to question a stranger so very closely about her background.) After a few more nights in my hotel, looking at the evening news, it hit me with an unpleasant shock that I might understand at least part of the puzzle. There was a great deal of coverage on Australian television newscasts about America's "problems." When African-Americans were featured in such newscasts, we were pictured as poor, often angry, from broken homes—seemingly perpetuating the situation through our lifestyles. Our youth appeared to be, for the most part, without education or goals. We were certainly well outside the mainstream of middle class white America. In short, I realized that some Australians and, I am sure, many others abroad receive a distinctly negative image of African-Americans through selective newscasting.

While we often debate the kind of coverage given African-Americans within the United States, we seldom consider what images those across the Atlantic or the Pacific are receiving. Does it make a difference? Absolutely. For it is part of the general perception *received* and *maintained* by those who may never have an opportunity to visit the United States, and also those who later emigrate to this country. It is, as well, part of a perception received and maintained by those who have been born in this country. Of the impressions which may be gathered after accumulated viewing of negative portrayals of black people, in particular following the Los Angeles riots, Ronald Takaki, author of *A Different Mirror: A History of Multicultural America*, has this to say:

> The live televised images mesmerized America. The rioting and
> the murderous melee on the streets resembled the fighting in
> Beirut and the West Bank. The thousands of fires burning out of

control and the dark smoke filling the skies brought back images
of the burning oil fields of Kuwait during Desert Storm. Entire
sections of Los Angeles looked like a bombed city. "Is this America?" many shocked viewers asked.[2]

But those "shocked viewers" were just as well the "average" American
citizen as the international viewer, who saw the devastation as the tragically yet utterly fascinating outcome of the rampages of "every black,"
rather than the random violence of a few. African-Americans often
wonder how someone who may have just arrived in the country can
exhibit such obviously biased behavior towards those with whom they
have had no personal contact. Perhaps the answer may be found, at
least in part, in what individuals have seen and/or, equally importantly,
in what they have read. Such perceptions serve as a negative legacy for
all; those who struggle daily for recognition in this country, the young
who as yet have had no opportunity to make their mark upon society,
and the unborn who are totally innocent of the world into which they
have yet to enter.

This is a book about African-American young adult literature. It
offers a collection of fourteen original essays entirely devoted to this
subject and represents, to my knowledge, the first time a set of essays
on this topic has been published. The purpose of this book is to inform
teachers, librarians and other professionals working with young people
about aspects of this area, and to stimulate some further thinking about
a literature which has a great deal to communicate. Hopefully, this book
dispels some previously held notions not only about the literature, but
about the people of whom it speaks. Again, hopefully, it may get some
people thinking about the "canon," as it exists and as it should be. As
Maya Angelou has said, referring in this case to young people who are
composing pieces of writing and its relationship to literary knowledge:

> Young people today who are writing need to know the writers of
> English . . .—they need to know everybody from Chaucer to
> Nikki Giovanni. I don't think there is any real value in giving
> people one half of the solution. Sometimes half the solution will
> encourage somebody to go on to find the other half, but if you say
> this is half the solution and this is all there is of any conse-
> quence—don't ever look any further— this is terrible.[3]

Whether or not young people are engaged in the writing process or the
process of personal recreational reading, the same may be said; one

half of the solution is no solution at all.

The need or rationale for determining what becomes part of the canon cannot be separated from the fact of historical confluence. By this is meant that the circumstance of a piece of literature officially joining a canon, mainstream or otherwise, is determined by its ability to "fit in" with the established mode of thinking at the time. Cornel West has stated that: "Any attempt to expand old canons or constitute new ones presupposes particular interpretations of the historical moment at which canonization is to take place."[4] While young adult literature has had a difficult time finding its way into the curricula of elementary and secondary schools, *African-American* young adult literature has had an even more difficult time. What has occurred by necessity is the development of a *secondary* canon of young adult literature. Authors like Mildred D. Taylor, Walter Dean Myers, Virginia Hamilton, Rosa Guy and Eloise Greenfield, not to mention the many authors of non-African-American background who choose to write of the African-American experience, have assisted in adding significant works to the canon of young adult literature.

The literature speaks for itself; the people of whom it speaks are often misunderstood and their thoughts and actions are more than often misinterpreted. These considerations are, of course, what prevents the literature from gaining total acceptance. Additionally, the literature still suffers from a relative lack of distribution. According to a study done by the Cooperative Children's Book Center in 1990, out of approximately 5,000 titles in children's and young adult literature published that year, only 51 were written and/or illustrated by African-Americans.[5] The literary market is ever sensitive to the situation of the literary moment, a fact commented on by Henry Louis Gates in his essay "Tell Me, Sir, . . . What *Is* 'Black' Literature?" He observes that the past deficit of materials available in the area of black literature was due in large part to the market sensitivity of publishers wary of risk-taking. "American publishers, ever sensitive to their own predictions about market size, became reluctant to publish works in this field."[6] While the multicultural pendulum, during the late eighties and nineties to date, has swung back in favor of interest in multicultural publications, still one notes that relatively few African-American authors tend to dominate the scene, though this has been somewhat alleviated since Rudine Sims noted the scarcity of African-American authors and illustrators in her 1984 publication *Shadow and Substance: Afro-American Experience in Contemporary Children's Fiction.*[7]

A second purpose of this book will be to take a look at African-American literature with a new eye. The sub-title of this book is "Tradition, Transition, Transformation." I selected this phrase because I considered the entire spectrum of African-American young adult literature as a changing, dynamic field; always taking in the possibility of a new and perhaps thought provoking work. I was reminded of this most recently when I read Angela Johnson's just announced Coretta Scott King Award–winning work *Toning the Sweep*. Certainly different from anything I have read before, Johnson's book artfully weaves a story of intergenerational love amidst the sadness of impending death from cancer, communicated through the brilliance of a cinema verité style of writing. The story unfolds in the present active tense, as the protagonist films the last days of her grandmother's life using a camcorder. Works such as *Toning the Sweep* illustrate the creative possibilities of African-American literature, and bring home to us the fact that the genre is a living and dynamic entity and, that like all literature, but particularly that which speaks of the cultural experience of a people, it holds the promise of exciting discovery.

Some of the works discussed in this collection of essays hark back to African-American folklore, church theology or family ritual. This is the case with the chapter by Cosette Kies, which explores the debt to an aspect of African-American religious belief and folklore, and my own chapter on Mildred Taylor, which shows Taylor's ability to interweave church theology within a riveting family chronicle. Other contributions are a reflection of concerns which are primarily born of change and preoccupation with change. This focus is reflected in such pieces as those by Dianne Johnson-Feelings about the African-American middle class, and Carol Jones Collins' chapter on biographies. Still others begin to address issues that, while some of us have been aware of them for a long time, were previously those which were not spoken of because they were considered to be too painful and, perhaps, too embarrassing. And then there are those contributions which offer methods of expression which break the bonds of standard approaches, issues which are in fact reflective of the transformation of African-American literature. Such emphases are illustrated through the article on color and class by Linda Zoppa and also through that of Kay E. Vandergrift in her portrayal of the feminist approach to African-American female poetry. Taken together, the fourteen chapters in the collection share unique viewpoints about a literature which is still growing and developing and which, happily, is becoming, as Edna Reid's article shows, more widely disseminated. A brief discussion of the content of each of the chapters follows which will, I believe, whet the appetite of the reader.

In her chapter, Carol Jones Collins approaches biography as a genre which offers to African-American young people the promise of introduction, exploration and consideration of other selves. Collins argues that through the art of biography, young people can discover a fuller potential and thereby "expand the social resources accessible to them." The presentations available through the literature also afford African-Americans the opportunity to emotionally confront and deal with the racism present in American society. Through her examples, drawn from books by Lerone Bennett, James Haskins, Walter Dean Myers, Elaine Feinstein, Mary E. Lyons and Virginia Hamilton, among others, Collins demonstrates the critical importance of the genre as a literature of personal validation, hope and therefore growth in the possibilities which the future may offer to young people.

There once was a time when African-American poets were little known and little regarded. W.E.B. DuBois tells the following story recounted in his essay "Criteria of Negro Art":

> A professor in the University of Chicago read to a class that had studied literature a passage of poetry and asked them to guess the author. They guessed a goodly company from Shelley and Robert Browning down to Tennyson and Masefield. The author was Countee Cullen. Or again the English critic John Drinkwater went down to a Southern seminary, one of the sort which "finishes" young white women of the South. The students sat with their wooden faces while he tried to get some response out of them. Finally he said, "Name me some of your Southern poets." They hesitated. He said finally, "I'll start out with your best: Paul Laurence Dunbar"![8]

African-American poetry is a living and vital force in contemporary African-American literature. The female legacy, in regards the poetic art, little written about until recent times, has been formidable; names such as Phillis Wheatley, Sojourner Truth and Georgia Douglas Johnson have left a permanent mark on African-American poetry. Henry Louis Gates in his acclaimed collection *The Schomburg Library of Nineteenth-Century Black Women Writers*, consisting of thirty volumes and published in 1988 by Oxford University Press, has chronicled the legacy of such poets as Mary E. Tucker (Lambert), Adah Isaacs

Menken and Eloise Alberta Veronica Bibb. In her chapter on African-American female poets, Kay E. Vandergrift draws together some of the strongest examples of the contemporary art as it has been presented for and/or adopted by adolescents (or those who present poetry to them), and discusses the poetry within the context of a feminist approach. Vandergrift focuses upon the issue of voice and demonstrates how, over time, African-American women have expressed their unique perspectives in a multitude of voices, mirroring their hopes, fears and individual dreams. It has been said that actions speak louder than words, but indeed words can effectively mirror actions. For African-American poetry is the poetry of experience. We are also reminded of this by poet and author June Jordan, who speaks of the influence of her "ghetto" upbringing during the 1930s and 1940s upon the artist she was to become in her text *Technical Difficulties: African-American Notes on the State of the Union:*

> And from such "breeding grounds of despair," Negro men volunteered, in droves, for active duty in an army that did not want or honor them. And from such "limited" communities, Negro women, such as my mother, left their homes in every kind of weather, and at any hour, to tend to the ailing and heal the sick, regardless of their color, or ethnicity. And in such a "culturally deprived" house as that modest home created by my parents, I became an American poet.[9]

From Gwendolyn Brooks to Rita Dove, from expressions of outrage to pure exaltation, Vandergrift offers an insight-filled approach to the consideration of these artists bringing to bear both their uniqueness as artists and also as women of color.

Hilary Crew also explores the feminist perspective in relationship to mothers and daughters. Crew takes into account the approaches of both black and white feminists, illustrating the key differences between their viewpoints; black feminists stressing such issues as the entire framework of relationships inherent within the black family, "othermothers" who impact the lives of those for whom they have assumed responsibility and the encompassing and terrible legacy of slavery and the manner in which it has affected the relationships of the generations of mothers and daughters who have come after. Put another way, according to Missy Dehn Kubitschek, such an historical approach reflects the "every mother a daughter," concept.[10] White feminists on the other hand have, as Crew points out, stressed the early relationships of mothers and daughters as the cornerstones of future relationships between these young women and their mothers. Taken a step further, this framework gives rise to a form of "the child is mother of the woman." Informed by such theorists as Nancy Chodorow, Gloria I. Joseph, Carol Gilligan and Patricia Hill Collins, Crew focuses upon the role of the mother-daughter, and othermother and daughter relationships in the growing-up process experienced by adolescents within African-American texts and also, significantly, the manner in which adolescents reflect the influence of mothers and othermothers both as females and as specifically African-American females. Drawing from authors as varied as Alice Childress, Virginia Hamilton, Jacqueline Woodson and Sharon Mathis among others, Crew reveals patterns of cause and effect, impact and aftermath which direct the course of the female players in selected African-American young adult novels.

The publishing market has witnessed an increase in the number of magazines for young adults. Though the number remains small, there have been several new magazines which specifically target an audience of *African-American* young adults. In their joint chapter on periodical literature for African-American young adults, Lynn S. Cockett and Janet R. Kleinberg survey the availability of such periodicals in an attempt to raise our consciousness of a "neglected resource." Arguing that one of the major objectives of information professionals is to connect client with resource, the authors remind us not only of the power such publications exert, but also of the images they convey. Cockett and Kleinberg make reference to interviews of individuals within the publishing sector, and discuss specific magazines which target an African-American audience of young adults. They also examine "mainstream magazines" in order to determine whether or not they meet the needs of African-American youth. Particularly useful for such a subject is the content-analysis survey which was conducted of four mainstream magazines, by the authors. Categories considered in the survey were cover models, ad models, photo spreads, celebrities, human interest stories and racial issues. Their results are reflective of the fact that while the African-American presence has come a long way, it still has far to go in terms of making its influence felt within this form of media.

Until recently, to read about African-American young adult literature was to read the literature of the "underclass," leaving readers, young and old alike, with the possible lasting impression that all African-American youth grow up in one parent homes located somewhere in a ghetto, leading an impoverished existence, actively engaged in criminal activity, moving slowly yet inexorably towards a no-hope future. While it remains a fact that African-Americans often do not have the "advantages" experienced and expected by a white middle class society, the fact is also that most African-Americans, despite poor economic circumstances, are law abiding citizens. They may also be members of a growing middle class.

Negative perceptions and overgeneralizations lead to many types of inequities, among which are the oftentimes related narrations of the classic "taxi-cab story." As an adolescent, it took me some time before I finally understood the reason why white taxi-cab drivers in New York City habitually would not stop for black passengers. Just two years ago, I had the same experience when a taxi-cab refused to take me (all dressed up and waiting in front of a well respected hotel) to my sister's house located in the Hyde Park area of Chicago. I have since been amazed at the number of identical narrations offered by outraged African-Americans, many of them members of the middle class, and some of them quite well known in literary circles. Most recently, Ellis Cose in *The Rage of a Privileged Class* (1993), Cornel West in *Race Matters* (1993) and June Jordan in *Technical Difficulties: African-American Notes on the State of the Union* (1992) as well as perceptive white American Andrew Hacker in *Two Nations: Black and White, Separate, Hostile, Unequal* (1992), speaking of the indignity suffered by the African-Americans who try to hail a cab, all shared their "taxi-cab stories." It comes unfortunately as no shock, then, to read a fictionalized version of a "taxi-cab story" as part of the narrative of Walter Dean Myers' *Somewhere in the Darkness* (1992), in which the African-American protagonist Jimmy Little speaks of the difficulty of hailing a cab in an urban setting. I am beginning to believe that one could form another volume entirely devoted to such narrations—nonfiction; but it would be a very unhappy volume indeed. Jordan poignantly concluded her *Technical Difficulties* text with a quiet statement, almost a plea:

> Yes, I am exhilarated by the holiday I enjoyed with my friends, and I am proud of the intimate camaraderie we shared. But somebody, pretty soon, needs to be talking, sisterly and brotherly, with the taxi drivers of the world, as well.[11]

Dianne Johnson-Feelings' chapter, on the depiction of the middle class in African-American young adult literature, addresses an aspect of this problem of perception. She reminds us that a black middle class does indeed exist and has a presence in the literature. Through an examination of works by such authors as Rosa Guy, Walter Dean Myers and Rita Williams-Garcia, Johnson-Feelings offers illustrations of how the African-American middle class demonstrates its presence through the literature. The author has several concerns, not least among them is that of the larger issue of stereotyping which prevails in the absence of positive models.

On the other hand, realism, Johnson-Feelings points out, is also essential, for black characters must mirror real people, rather than positive "types" of individuals. She informs us of the transformational nature of the middle class focus in African-American young adult literature, a literature which "promises to be controversial, challenging and revealing." Such presentations hold the promise, as well, of helping to transform societal perspectives.

Linda J. Zoppa's article on the subject of color and class is a revealing portrayal of a subject previously deemed "taboo" for discussion outside the home of the African-American. This is a subject often reserved for dinner table debate and small gatherings where one catches up on the news of various relatives, friends and associates, but not one which African-Americans easily share with the outside world. Jill Nelson has stated that "the issue of color is one which was by and large created for us and one we adopted at our own folly."[12] The degree of impact the issue has on the daily lives of individual African-Americans may be arguable; what is not argued is the origin of the problem:

> . . .—racism. The pattern of white society's giving light-skinned blacks special privileges is as old as the peculiar institution of slavery. On plantations, dark-skinned slaves toiled in the fields while their lighter co-workers—some of them the illegitimate children of the master—had the comparatively cushy jobs of cook, seamstress and driver. These mulatto children were sometimes given their freedom, or sent to school by their masters; they went on to become the basis of the black middle class.[13]

As we read through accounts of slavery and presentations based upon actual experiences, such as the recent work by Mary E. Lyons, *Letters From a Slave Girl: The Story of Harriet E. Jacobs* (1992), based upon the life of Harriet Jacobs during the early 1800s, scenes of a scheming master ever ready to seduce young and helpless slave women and girls give credence to a reality too terrible for the contemporary African-American to contemplate. One of the results of these forced attacks would be a long-lived preoccupation with gradations of skin color. Linda Zoppa explores the issues involved in color and class in relationship to white character perceptions of black characters, skin tone color perception between and among black characters, the related factor of class, and the relationship of class and color to attitudes towards gifted and talented peers. These factors are revealed through an analysis of four novels, *Blue Tights* (Rita Williams-Garcia), *The Music of Summer* (Rosa Guy), *Come a Stranger* (Cynthia Voigt) and *The Dear One* (Jacqueline Woodson). Zoppa suggests that the literature offers us the opportunity to examine the problem in the open, but calls for a larger agenda in which such issues will be seriously considered, with positive results which will ultimately benefit both black and white members of society.

Critical approaches which offer us the opportunity to study elements either in part or in whole from an individual author's repertoire also make, I believe, a major contribution to a collection of essays. In instances where an author's output is prolific, such critiques are almost mandatory for those of us who view the literary genius as a soul in process, continually growing and developing. Walter Dean Myers is such a soul. His work, in relationship to the theme of the portrayal of the male adolescent, is critically presented by Dennis Vellucci. Black male adolescents, Vellucci points out, are "at risk" in the most basic sense of the word. He cites statistics which indicate that white males of the same age group are far less likely to be victims of homicide.

Yet, in a world filled with violence and potential violence which necessarily calls for a life philosophy of adaptation to "living on the edge," Vellucci demonstrates that it is still possible to create a convincing type of narrative having individual perseverance and moral integrity as a major theme. Vellucci examines six works by Myers in which he discusses the author's ability to create protagonists who can overcome the entanglements of hostile environments (with varying degrees of success), without becoming completely desensitized as human beings. He examines the significance of male bonding and also institutional and individual responses to the problem of standards as vehicles which may offer young people, both within the stories and in reality, opportunities for action. These opportunities, which Myers communicates to us through his works, are often lost in the shuffle, eluding those who might actually have the power to make a difference. Significantly, existing adversity is often seen as holding the potential of growth for the protagonist, who may ultimately become a stronger human being as a result of what he has undergone. Such a focus in the present day and age is imperative and can have the effect of helping to disintegrate the walls which society builds to "typecast" young black men.

But what specifically of the fathers in African-American young adult literature? Where are they in the narrations? Are all portrayals indicative of a lack of effective parenting on their part? Marcia Baghban, in her chapter on positive images of African-American fathers in young adult literature, offers a discussion of the historical background affecting the relationship of African-American fathers with their families. She further explores these relationships through the literature utilizing examples provided by such authors as Mildred Taylor, Virginia Hamilton, and Walter Dean Myers. Black fatherhood is seen as a role taken quite seriously both in reality and in the literature, but a role which is challenged on all sides by historical factors which will not die, and regenerating social factors which often act as a barrier to the "living out" of the role in its ultimate ideal. Andrew Billingsley has stated some of the difficulties which inhibit the success of African-American males:

> . . . black men are caught up in a social system which beams exceedingly contradictory signals to them. On the one hand, because they are males in a male-oriented society, they are expected to be dominant, powerful, and strong providers. They are consequently given higher status and considerably more privileges than black women. On the other hand, because they are black in a white-dominated society, they are often perceived as subservient and relatively powerless in comparison to white men, who are their role models. Consequently, they are more dependent on their women. They know and experience this contradiction keenly. They feel the unfairness of it all.[14]

Despite the presence of obstacles, Baghban demonstrates that it is still possible for black fatherhood to triumph, which it does with more regularity than members of society would have us believe. Such accounts serve as literary witnesses to the fact that it is possible to rise above one's condition, and offers African-American young adults, both males and females, a reason for pressing on while presenting white young adults a view of African-American fathers that is a little bit different from that which they have traditionally come to accept.

The saying "the past is prologue for the future" makes us mindful of the fact that there is much value in history, particularly when that history focuses upon the triumphs as well as the trials of a people. We are led to remember that whatever travails come our way, there is the promise of hope, even if the results do not quite work out immediately in the way we would anticipate or prefer. My chapter on the works of Mildred D. Taylor focuses upon Taylor's conception of her personal family chronicle cast within a fictionalized format. Set in Depression times, the six novels discussed offer a rich tapestry which interweaves the vibrant colors of one family's experiences in Mississippi. Their ability to cope and surmount the inherent difficulties indigenous to their environment stand as a banner heralding the possibilities of what could be, even in what certainly was among the worst of times for African-Americans. Nikki Giovanni refers to the resourceful nature of African-American literature, its ability to help us come to terms with the past and simultaneously prepare for the future:

> The literature of Black Americans is, in the words of Stevie Wonder, "a ribbon in the sky." We learn about and love the past because it gives us the courage to explore and take care of the future.[15]

Taylor's works are examined from the point of view of how the author balances the rage inherent in the condition of the African-American with the ability to move towards a goal which surpasses survival, and ultimately embraces triumph. The vehicles through which this is accomplished include the incorporation of spiritual belief and practice into daily living, the management of economic resources during a time when they were few, far between, or non-existent, the challenge of coping with the politics of inequitability, and the importance of the inheritance of land in the black man's quest for fair representation in an environment in which he was, at best, invisible. Mildred Taylor has demonstrated her strong ability to create a great and moving tale. Awareness, however, of the close relationship the story has with actual events from Taylor's life empowers the narratives with a sense of "historical witness" that is not often experienced by the reader within a work of pure fiction.

Often we overlook, in the concept of the "other" as it applies to the African-American, the fact that embedded *within* the black experience are further areas which are connected to our arrival from another place. The forced removal from Africa and the effect it has had is often referred to as we struggle to understand the reality of our contemporary challenges. Less often do we consider the challenges of contemporary blacks who come to America from other places. In her chapter on the African-Caribbean journey, Lucille H. Gregory examines four works by Rosa Guy, Joyce Hansen, Jamaica Kincaid and Jacqueline Roy. She offers an enlightening discussion of the uniqueness of the African-Caribbean experience, and the singular manner in which these authors convey this uniqueness through the literature. In addition to being outsiders as members of the black race, African-Caribbeans must cope with the extra burden of being *foreign* outsiders. Gregory argues that we can only fully begin to appreciate the black experience when we take into consideration all members of that experience, and when we pay attention to the individual rites of passage which its members must undergo as, often, an unfortunate introduction to American culture. Billingsley speaks of the tension which exists between African-Americans and newly arrived black Caribbean-Americans:

> Some of this tension is due to cultural differences. Some is due to the nature of racism in American society. The Caribbean people come from a region where blacks constitute a majority. They are accustomed to seeing blacks in positions of power. Consequently they are often intolerant of American racism. They sometimes seem to resent it more. Yet they do not always identify with the African-American struggle. Some have sought to avoid stigmatization from the dominant white society by distancing themselves from African-Americans. Like all such efforts, however, there can only be limited and isolated success. The Caribbean community cannot be insulated from institutionalized racism.[16]

Gregory suggests that the novels discussed can empower us in our quest to gain a greater awareness of the concerns of black Caribbeans before they emigrate to the United States; the framework of the native land consciousness does not automatically depart from one's *being* upon arrival in the United States. She calls for a "revolution" in young adult literature, one in which participants will take on the challenges of "new ideas and new perspectives" which will equip participants in more effectively overcoming the consequences of racism both within and outside the United States.

It has been pointed out that one of the aspects of African-American young adult literature is the fact that much of the literature is created by relatively few authors. Virginia Hamilton stands at the head of the list of highly respected African-American young adult authors. Her repertoire, inclusive of the genres of fiction, folktales and biography primarily, offers readers realistically communicated narrative and elegant prose. Hamilton has also experimented with the genre of, what I refer to as, science fiction–fantasy.

In her chapter on the *Justice* trilogy, Millicent Lenz examines the three works *Justice and Her Brothers*, *Dustland* and *The Gathering* in terms of their development of what is referred to as "the American Myth of the Frontier." In this, Lenz is concerned with Hamilton's ability to create a consciousness which speaks of a certain "faith in progress," a faith which Hamilton believes ultimately has the potential of offering readers the possibility of a "majestic change in the human race." Many years ago, I recall, in a conversation with Hamilton, she stated the challenge inherent in composing a story written in a non-realistic mode. I remember telling her at the time, that while I could appreciate the fact that fantasy and science fiction are difficult and demanding genres, I felt keenly not only the success inherent in these particular works as works of literature, but also that African-American youth need what fantasy and science fiction have to offer—in addition to the more realistic or informational presentations which help young people to get a "handle" on a specific event in history, or a perspective on a contemporary problem. While all literary genres make certain demands upon readers, fantasy and science fiction make special demands. When one combines the two arts, as I believe Hamilton does in the *Justice* trilogy, one must be faithful to the rules of both, while at the same time paying close attention to the natural and realistic unfolding of the story. It is a unique responsibility. As readers, we come in *after* the action; we are not present while the author grapples with his or her material. If we were, we might have an even greater respect for the creation process. Instead, we have the pleasant task of reading the work after the fact, making a decision as to whether or not it really meets our needs, and issuing a verdict of affirmation or, perhaps, condemnation.

Lenz points out that part of Hamilton's thematic structure involves the search for self; a search which must necessarily take place when one attempts to establish a sense of "frontier consciousness." A most significant part of the frontier, and perhaps one of the most exciting for young people (as exciting as the search for self is meaningful), is the protagonist's ability to survive in a hostile environment, a concept most profoundly developed in *Dustland*. However, a consciousness cannot be fully developed without the hope of delivery, an expression of hope and redemption. Lenz further develops her premise in her analysis of *The Gathering*. What Hamilton effectively does for us, Lenz argues, is to offer each of us an agenda for thought; a way of looking at the world in which we are currently living and perceiving how the things which affect us in life so deeply are really embedded in our concept of consciousness. We have in fact within us the power to change our destiny—if, that is, we so desire.

Few African-American women have chosen to make the science fiction genre an exclusive commitment. In her chapter on Octavia Butler, Janice Antczak explores the contributions of this artist to this genre. Butler's voice is one which, while not intentionally nor exclusively within the young adult mode, speaks to the *interests* of the young adult. Hers is a provocative voice; one that invites thought and requires the reader to relinquish any inhibitions he or she might have about strong language and sexuality. Race, gender and power are three themes which may be identified in Butler's work. Antczak carefully explores these through the works and suggests that while the world in which the stories are set is the world of the future, the concepts explored are indicative of a timelessness which young adults will appreciate. One of the most unique aspects of her novels is her placing of female protagonists in positions where they may act as challengers to male authority. In so doing, Butler requires that her audience leave the realm of the fantastic and deal with some important, if not uncomfortable, issues. Antczak demonstrates that the nature of the genre, an exciting and colorful one, which includes the possibilities of the unexpected, *adds to* rather than detracts from the messages to be conveyed. Young people are offered contemporary issues which they can recognize and with which they can identify, but within an atypical framework. Such a presentation allows the young adult to encounter issues of importance to him and to society, through the creative and alternative-rich world of science fiction.

While fantasy and science fiction are literatures of the imagination, some aspects of African religious practice provide us with themes which form the basis of occult presentations. In her chapter on the contributions of voodoo to the development of horror literature in this country, Cosette Kies investigates a phenomenon which has intrigued and alternately frightened white society. While many of the writers employing aspects of voodoo are white, the theme, when employed within a United States–based text, is still often associated with Africa.

Kies offers an overview of the use of this theme in writing for young adults. While voodoo, often viewed as "dark and exotic," has the effect of instantly adding an element of mystery and danger to the plot line, within this usage, it may also have the effect of *trivializing* what is taken by many Africans as a very serious religion. During the course of her discussion, Kies points out that many of the novels present voodoo as integral to their horror theme, but generally, the older works do not place emphasis upon the positive aspects of voodoo. Having carefully surveyed the literature, Kies has found that changes have begun to take place which more adequately speak of voodoo and its variants as possessing positive values rather than the potential for death and disaster. This is seen as a direct outgrowth of modern day emphasis upon sensitivity toward all people and their attendant cultures and religions. Going beyond her immediate agenda, Kies' chapter may raise some questions about our role in helping to facilitate the change to more sensitive approaches to voodoo in the literature. As a secondary outcome, it may also encourage us to more adequately explore the relationship between voodoo and horror literature as a possible sub-genre of the larger division of horror.

The chapters discussed above attempt to bring individually unique perspectives to an examination of aspects of African-American young adult literature. But this is a literature which has had to fight for recognition within the larger framework of literature, and is one which still has not found a place within the even larger concept of the canon. However, one observes that in order for a phenomenon to be truly accepted, it must first attract the attention of those possessing literary power and, secondly, it must find a consistent place in appropriate media. Edna Reid, in her chapter on the dispersion of contemporary African-American young adult literature, provides a unique look at a method of documenting the appearances of young adult authors within different on-line bibliographic databases. Reid applies a model created by her for use within the context of her research on terrorist literature, and applies that model to the young adult framework. Her findings, which include a total of 202 publications representing 18 authors, show a greatly increased amount of activity in the field during the period 1980–1989. Going beyond this finding, it seems likely that political and social factors, which during this time had begun to heavily emphasize the concept of multiculturalism and the lack of literary materials written by people of color, may account for the close to double the number of publications which appeared during this time. What does this mean for African-American young adult literature? Among the implications may be that this literature is finally beginning to be considered a vital type of literature by those interested in young adult concerns; concerns which literary artists deem to be an important vehicle for addressing American youth, particularly African-American youth. If this is the case, then those of us who care deeply about promoting the literature are currently bearing witness to the "legitimization" of a genre.

The fourteen chapters which comprise *African-American Voices in Young Adult Literature: Tradition, Transition, Transformation* present unique aspects of ways of looking at literature designed for and/or enjoyed by a particular segment of the youth populace. Each contributor has demonstrated that he or she highly values the areas and/or individuals which he or she chose to write about and has an investment in the concept of African-American young adult literature. As I write this introduction, new literary works are being created which will, it is hoped, continue to enrich a field deserving of attention, merit, discussion and, in many instances, praise. This is an energetic literature, sometimes poignant, and sometimes filled with the rage of a people who were made to wait too long (and who, many would contend, continue to wait). Through the literature, the African-American young adult, and indeed all young adults, may well find a place for beginning or extending their understanding of the experience of a people, which must necessarily take place to ensure greater racial and ethnic harmony.

NOTES

1. Brent Staples, *Parallel Time: Growing Up in Black and White* (New York: Pantheon Books, 1994), 259.
2. Ronald Takaki, *A Different Mirror: A History of Multicultural America* (Boston, MA: Little, Brown and Company, 1993), 4.
3. Maya Angelou, "An Interview with Poet, Novelist, and Playwright Maya Angelou," interview by Joe Milner, *SLATE Newsletter* (October 1993), quoted in *The Council Chronicle* (February 1994), 9.
4. Cornel West, *Keeping Faith: Philosophy and Race in America* (New York: Routledge, 1993), 33.
5. Ginny Moore Kruse and Kathleen T. Horning, *Multicultural Literature for Children and Young Adults*, Third edition (Madison, WI: Cooperative Children's Book Center, 1991), xii.

6. Henry Louis Gates, Jr., "Tell Me, Sir, . . . What *Is* 'Black' Literature?" chap. in *Loose Canons: Notes on the Culture Wars* (New York: Oxford University, 1992), 92.

7. Rudine Sims, *Shadow and Substance: Afro-American Experience in Contemporary Children's Fiction* (Urbana, IL: National Council of Teachers of English, 1984), 105.

8. W.E.B. DuBois, "Criteria of Negro Art" (1926), in *W.E.B. DuBois: A Reader*, ed. Andrew Paschal (New York: Macmillan Publishing Co., 1993), 91.

9. June Jordan, "For My American Family," chap. in *Technical Difficulties: African-American Notes on the State of the Union* (New York: Pantheon Books, 1992), 8.

10. Missy Dehn Kubitschek, "Every Mother a Daughter," chap. in *Claiming the Heritage: African-American Women Novelists and History* (Jackson, MS: University Press of Mississippi, 1991), 143.

11. Jordan, 168.

12. Vanessa E. Jones, "Colorism: Light-Skinned, Dark-Skinned: The Conflict that Divides the Black Community," *Daily News* (13 February 1994), 2.

13. Ibid.

14. Andrew Billingsley, *Climbing Jacob's Ladder: The Enduring Legacy of African-American Families* (New York: Simon and Schuster, 1992), 243.

15. Nikki Giovanni, *Racism 101* (New York: William Morrow and Company, Inc., 1994), 156.

16. Billingsley, 265.

REFERENCES

Angelou, Maya. "An Interview with Poet, Novelist, and Playwright Maya Angelou." *The Council Chronicle* (February 1994): 9.

Billingsley, Andrew. *Climbing Jacob's Ladder: The Enduring Legacy of African-American Families.* New York: Simon and Schuster, 1992.

Cose, Ellis. *The Rage of a Privileged Class.* New York: HarperCollins, 1993.

DuBois, W.E.B. "Criteria of Negro Art" (1926). In *W.E.B. DuBois: A Reader*, ed. Andrew Paschal, 86–96. New York: Macmillan Publishing Co., 1993.

Gates, Henry Louis Jr., ed. *The Schomburg Library of Nineteenth-Century Black Women Writers.* New York: Oxford University Press, 1988.

Gates, Henry Louis Jr. "Tell Me, Sir, . . . What *Is* 'Black' Literature?" Chap. in *Loose Canons: Notes on the Culture Wars.* New York: Oxford University, 1992.

Giovanni, Nikki. *Racism 101.* New York: William Morrow and Company, Inc., 1994.

Guy, Rosa. *The Music of Summer.* New York: Delacorte Press, 1992.

Hacker, Andrew. *Two Nations: Black and White, Separate, Hostile, Unequal.* New York: Charles Scribner's Sons, 1992.

Hamilton, Virginia. *Dustland.* New York: Greenwillow, 1980.

____. *The Gathering.* New York: Greenwillow, 1981.

____. *Justice and Her Brothers.* New York: Greenwillow, 1978.

Johnson, Angela. *Toning the Sweep.* New York: Orchard Books, 1993.

Jones, Vanessa E. "Colorism: Light-Skinned, Dark-Skinned: The Conflict That Divides the Black Community." *Daily News* (13 February 1994): 2–3.

Jordan, June. "For My American Family." Chap. in *Technical Difficulties: African-American Notes on the State of the Union.* New York: Pantheon Books, 1992.

Kruse, Ginny Moore and Kathleen T. Horning. *Multicultural Literature for Children and Young Adults: A Selected Listing of Books 1980–1990 By and About People of Color.* Third edition. Madison, WI: Cooperative Children's Book Center, 1991.

Kubitschek, Missy Dehn. "Every Mother a Daughter." Chap. in *Claiming the Heritage: African-American Women Novelists and History.* Jackson, MS: University Press of Mississippi, 1991.

Lyons, Mary E. *Letters from a Slave Girl: The Story of Harriet E. Jacobs.* New York: Charles Scribner's Sons, 1992.

Myers, Walter Dean. *Somewhere in the Darkness.* New York: Scholastic, 1992.

Sims, Rudine. *Shadow and Substance: Afro-American Experience in Contemporary Children's Fiction.* Urbana, IL: National Council of Teachers of English, 1984.

Staples, Brent. *Parallel Time: Growing Up in Black and White.* New York: Pantheon Books, 1994.

Takaki, Ronald. *A Different Mirror: A History of Multicultural America.* Boston, MA: Little, Brown and Company, 1993.

Voigt, Cynthia. *Come a Stranger.* New York: Fawcett Juniper, 1986.

West, Cornel. *Keeping Faith: Philosophy and Race in America.* New York: Routledge, 1993.

____. *Race Matters.* Boston, MA: Beacon Press, 1993.

Williams-Garcia, Rita. *Blue Tights.* New York: Bantam, 1988.

Woodson, Jacqueline. *The Dear One.* New York: Delacorte Press, 1991.

Notes On Contributors

JANICE ANTCZAK

Janice Antczak is Professor of Literature at Brookdale Community College. She holds a doctorate in library science from the School of Library Service, Columbia University. She is author of *Science Fiction: The Mythos of a New Romance* (1985) and has published articles in *School Library Journal, Children's Literature Association Quarterly, New Jersey Libraries, Podium*, and essays in *Twentieth-Century Young Adult Writers* (St. James Press, 1994) and *Twentieth-Century Children's Authors* (St. James Press, 1989).

MARCIA BAGHBAN

Marcia Baghban is Associate Professor of Elementary Education at Queens College of the City University of New York, where she teaches reading, language arts and children's literature. She has published numerous articles in *The Reading Teacher, Resources in Education, Reading Horizons, Focus* and *Kentucky Reading Journal*. She has been a National Endowment for Humanities Fellow (World Studies Institute), has also received a Queens College Faculty-in-Residence Award and two Appalachian Studies Fellowships, Berea College, Kentucky, among other honors.

LYNN S. COCKETT

Lynn Sharon Cockett is a graduate of the Rutgers University M.L.S. program. She is the Young Adult Librarian at Nutley Public Library, Nutley, New Jersey. She edits a column entitled "Famae" for the *Journal of the Children's Literature Council of Pennsylvania*.

CAROL JONES COLLINS

Carol Jones Collins is a middle school library media specialist at Montclair Kimberley Academy in Montclair, New Jersey. She holds a Master of Arts degree in Human Relations from New York University and an M.L.S. degree from Rutgers University. She has published "A Tool for Change: Young Adult Literature in the Lives of Young Adult African-Americans," which appeared in the Winter 1993 issue of *Library Trends*. She has also contributed to *Twentieth-Century Young Adult Writers* (St. James Press, 1994). Ms. Collins is currently doing research in the areas of ethics in children's literature, African-American biography, culture and identity and also the rhetoric of African-American leaders. She is a doctoral candidate for the Ph.D. degree at Rutgers University, School of Communication, Information and Library Studies.

HILARY S. CREW

Hilary S. Crew is a Ph.D. candidate at Rutgers University, School of Communication, Information and Library Studies. Her publications include "From Labyrinth to Celestial City: Settings and the Portrayal of the Female in Science Fiction," in *Journal of Youth Services in Libraries* (Fall 1988) and "A Feminist Paradigm for Library and Information Science," co-authored with Jane Anne Hannigan, which was published in *Wilson Library Bulletin* (October 1993). She has also written essays on Robin McKinley and Richard Peck, published in *Twentieth-Century Young Adult Writers* (St. James Press, 1994). Ms. Crew currently serves as Adjunct Instructor at Rutgers University.

LUCILLE H. GREGORY

Lucille Hernandez Gregory was born in Brooklyn, New York. She moved to Puerto Rico at the age of fifteen. After earning a B.A. in Political Science she attended the University of Puerto Rico Law School. She is author of " 'The Puerto Rican Rainbow': Distortion vs. Complexities," published in *The Children's Literature Association Quarterly* (Spring 1993). Ms. Gregory has served as co-compiler with Donnarae MacCann and William Welburn of a forthcoming publication entitled *Civil Rights Action Kit for Librarians*. She is currently working on a collection of six essays on the literature of the Spanish speaking

Caribbean and is pursuing a Ph.D. in American Studies at the University of Iowa.

DIANNE JOHNSON-FEELINGS

Dianne Johnson-Feelings earned her A.B. degree in English/Creative Writing at Princeton University, an M.A. in Afro-American Studies and Ph.D. in American Studies at Yale University. She now lives in her home state where she teaches African-American literature and children's literature at the University of South Carolina. She shares her love of literature with her husband, children's book illustrator Tom Feelings. Johnson-Feelings is the author of *Telling Tales: The Pedagogy and Promise of African American Literature for Youth* (Greenwood Press, 1990).

COSETTE N. KIES

Cosette N. Kies is currently Professor in the Department of Leadership and Educational Policy Studies at Northern Illinois University. She has served as Professor and Chair of the Department of Library and Information Studies at Northern Illinois University. She is author of *Presenting Young Adult Horror Fiction* (Twayne, 1992); *Supernatural Fiction for Teens*, 2nd edition (Libraries Unlimited, 1992) and *Presenting Lois Duncan* (Twayne, 1994). She has also written articles, essays and reviews for *VOYA, School Library Media Activities Monthly, Twentieth-Century Young Adult Writers* and has contributions in the forthcoming *St. James Guide to Fantasy Writers* (St. James Press).

JANET R. KLEINBERG

Janet R. Kleinberg is a school media specialist at the Rockaway Valley School in Boonton Township, New Jersey. She is currently a Ph.D. candidate at Rutgers University, School of Communication, Information and Library Studies.

MILLICENT LENZ

Millicent Lenz is Associate Professor, School of Information Science and Policy, State University of New York at Albany, where she teaches literature for children and young adults. She holds a doctorate in English literature from Northern Illinois University, Dekalb and an M.L.S. from the University of Wisconsin, Madison. Her publications include *Nuclear Age Literature for Youth: The Quest for a Life-Affirming Ethic* (American Library Association, 1990), and she is joint author with Ramona M. Mahood of *Young Adult Literature: Background and Criticism* (American Library Association, 1980). She has published articles in *Children's Literature Association Quarterly*. Her current research is centered on the depiction of future worlds in literature for young people.

EDNA REID

Edna Reid is Assistant Professor at Rutgers University, School of Communication, Information and Library Studies where she teaches courses in information science. She is currently on leave from Rutgers working as an Associate Professor in the Information Studies Programme at Nanyang Technological University in Singapore. She has authored several studies that highlight the value of the information professional in the analysis, synthesis, exploitation and management of information in diverse environments. Before accepting the post doctorate assignment at Berkeley, Dr. Reid spent about twelve years in several corporate and intelligence community organizations as a data analyst team leader, systems analyst, database administrator and librarian. In addition, she worked as a consultant in Ramstein, Germany and in Ghana, West Africa.

KAREN PATRICIA SMITH

Karen Patricia Smith is Assistant Professor at the Graduate School of Library and Information Studies, Queens College where she teaches courses in school library media, children's literature and research methods. She has published numerous articles and reviews in *Journal of Youth Services in Libraries, School Library Journal, Children's Literature Association Quarterly* and *The ALAN Review*. She is author of *The Fabulous Realm: A Literary-Historical Approach to British Fantasy, 1780-1990* (Scarecrow Press, 1993) and has served as editor for the *Library Trends* (Winter 1993) issue entitled "Multicultural Children's Literature in the United States." She serves as member of the Board of Directors of the Children's Literature Association. She has given numerous presentations on children's literature and young adult literature within the United States and in Australia, Spain and Sweden.

KAY E. VANDERGRIFT

Kay E. Vandergrift is Associate Professor at Rutgers University, School of Communication, Information and Library Studies. She has published widely in children's literature and school library media in such journals as *Library Trends, Children's Literature Association Quarterly, Journal of Youth Services in Libraries, English Quarterly, School Library Journal* and *School Library Media Quarterly*. Professor Vandergrift has contributed extensively in chapters to books. She is author of *Child and Story: The Literary Connection* (Neal-Schuman, 1980), *Children's Literature: Theory, Research, and Teaching* (Libraries Unlimited, 1990) and *Power Teaching: A Primary Role of the School Library Media Specialist* (American Library Association, 1994). Her current research combines feminist theory and reader-response literary criticism.

DENNIS VELLUCCI

Dennis Vellucci teaches high school in New York City. He is a graduate of Fordham University and of the University of Southern California, and holds a Master's degree in English. He has received fellowships from the National Endowment for the Humanities and from the Joseph A. Klingenstein Institute of Teachers College, Columbia University. He has published numerous book reviews in *Commonweal*. He is currently completing a Master's degree at the Graduate School of Library and Information Studies, Queens College of the City University of New York.

LINDA J. ZOPPA

Linda J. Zoppa earned her B.S. and M.A. degrees in Music Performance from New York University. She also has earned an M.L.S. degree at the Graduate School of Library and Information Studies, Queens College of the City University of New York. She is currently a middle school library media specialist in New York City and is completing an advanced course of study through the Professional Certificate Program in Library and Information Studies at Queens College. She has published numerous reviews in *The Book Report, Appraisal*, and *School Library Journal*. She currently serves as Chair of the American Association of School Librarians Cultural Diversity Committee.

ONE

African-American Young Adult Biography: In Search of the Self

Carol Jones Collins

> . . . the streets of my native city were filled with youngsters searching desperately for the limits which would tell them who they were, and create for them a challenge to which they could rise.
>
> James Baldwin, *Nobody Knows My Name*

African-American biographies for young adults have much to offer young adults in general and African-American young adults in particular. They can help black youth find a place to stand emotionally and psychologically. They can help black young people develop a sense of kinship with their black forebears, letting them know that they do not stand alone. African-American biographies can enable black youth to recognize that being black does not have to mean defeat, but can also mean triumph and achievement. And they can allow the black young adult access to all the many black people who have gone through struggles and overcome adversity. African-American young adult biography can especially provide for the black reader the opportunity to become deeply involved in the lives of other black people in ways not possible in face-to-face contact.

THE BIOGRAPHICAL DEBATE

The place of biography in literature has been disputed for years. John Dryden, considered by many to be the father of literary criticism, did not, when he was writing in the 1600s, include the biography in any of his writings.[1] Serious discussion of biography would only be opened some one hundred years later with the publication in 1791 of Boswell's *The Life of Samuel Johnson LL.D.* James Boswell has been called the first great modern biographer and the father of modern biography, and it was his life of Johnson that set the tone for the writing of biography until well into the twentieth century. In the nineteenth century, in response to Boswell's methods of using personal letters, anecdotes, and actual conversation, biography's standing was uncertain. It was lauded on the one hand because it concerned human affairs, but condemned on the other hand because it was thought to invade the subject's personal privacy and to show the subject's personal failings.

A revolution of sorts occurred in biographical writing in 1918 when Lytton Strachey used a mixture of facts, psychological analyses, and his imagination to write brief, but telling, sketches of Thomas Arnold, General Charles Gordon, Cardinal Manning, and Florence Nightingale. The publication of Strachey's *Eminent Victorians* and later *Queen Victoria* in 1921 renewed the debate about biography: Is biography fiction or non-fiction? Is it the biographer's role to create heroes or to destroy them? What are the uses of biography? What are the qualities of a good biography?

Over the course of centuries, thoughtful critics have answered these questions in various ways. But a certain broad theme seems to persist despite the passage of time. In fact, two broad themes emerge. The first is that human greatness should be preserved; the second is that actual lives as they were lived should be uncovered and revealed, a sort of melding of Boswell and Strachey.

These themes can be seen in the writings of a number of critics, starting with Plutarch, who in the first century A.D. wrote, "My design is not to write histories, but lives."[2] In the sixteenth century, Francis Bacon wrote, "lives, if wrote with care and judgement [sic], proposing to represent a person, in whom actions, both great and small, public and private, are blended together, must of necessity give a more genuine, native, and lively representation, and such as is fitter for imitation."[3] Samuel Taylor Coleridge looked at biography as a way to call attention to the great qualities in a life: "the great end of biography . . . is to fix the attention and to interest the feelings of men on those qualities and actions which have made a particular life worthy of being recorded."[4] The noted critic, Harold Nicolson, wrote that "a good biography encourages people to believe that man's mind is in truth unconquerable and that character can triumph over the most hostile circumstances."[5]

If the importance of a thing can be determined by the number of prominent people writing and thinking about it, then biography can be considered important indeed. Thomas Carlyle, George Santayana, and Virginia Woolf have all written about it. Still, the genre has yet to be fully understood. André Maurois called it art, but Virginia Woolf called it a superior craft. The literary critic and biographer Leon Edel called biography "a nascent art" and "a vulnerable art." It is his contention that the written life generates very strong emotions and, despite the writing of hundreds of biographies each year, the genre is really only just beginning to be fully explored.[6]

Leon Edel is especially important to this essay because in *Writing Lives* he sought to merge the writing of biography with Freudian psychology and with the "new science of man" as articulated by certain segments of the social sciences, particularly anthropology and sociology. Edel urged the biographer to "analyze his materials to discover certain keys to the deeper truths of his subject. . . . These belong to the truths of human behavior."[7]

Edel saw the writing of biography as the act of searching for the "figure under the carpet," of digging for the life of the subject:

> The public facade is the mask behind which a private mythology is hidden—the private self-concept that guides a given life. . . .
> The ways in which men and women handle their lives, the forms they give to their acts of living . . . their handling of human relations, their ways of wooing the world or disdaining it—all this is germane to biography, it is the very heart of a biography.[8]

Edel spoke too of the constant struggle that must exist between biographer and subject, for the biographer is far from anonymous. The danger occurs for the biographer when he or she is either dominated by or dominates the subject, for the writing of biography is "a quest for proportion." Always the biographer must shape, but not distort the life under study. At the same time, the biographer must find ways to use all the tools of history and the social sciences that are available and germane to the writing of that particular life.[9]

Edel's inclusion of the social sciences as an integral part of the writing of biography represents an important step, for it is the newer sociological and anthropological approaches to exploring lives that can change how biography is viewed. Using the term participant-observer[10] for the role of the biographer, Edel contends that biographers must become deeply involved in the lives of their subjects. He stresses that they must establish long-term and multi-sided relationships with their subjects within the context of the subjects' natural environment.

EXPRESSIONS OF SELF AND AFRICAN-AMERICAN IDENTITY

Perhaps the most significant development for the writing of biography in this postmodern age is a new concept of the self. This new concept suggests a role for the biographer that Edel argued and Woolf seemed to suggest when she wrote that "a biographer must keep pace with the development of the personality he is recreating . . . keeping pace not only with an individual but with those many selves which we are within our constituted self."[11] The "new" social sciences point the way for the discovery by biography of these selves and for defining what these selves really are. This resultant, deeper biography allows the reader of biography and the subject of biography to have a truly meaningful encounter, an encounter that has the power to change the reader's life.

It is the biographer's knowledge of this "constituted self," either through received knowledge or instinct that can create a biography that serves the best interests of African-American young adults. Yet, this "self" that Edel and Woolf target as essential to biography has come to mean something entirely different among the more radical social scientists than what it means among the traditionalists.

The traditional image of the self is of an entity that is bounded and limited and can be definitively described. This self has one true nature or set of characteristics that exist within a person. It is discoverable and measurable. In short, the self is a coherent whole and exists separate and apart from all other selves.[12] Kenneth Gergen defines the traditional concept of self as a single, autonomous individual, with the capacity for self-direction and self-reliance.[13] But, this is not the view the posttraditionalists or, as they are more frequently called, the post-modernists, hold. Gergen contends that in the postmodern view of the self, "the very concept of personal essences is thrown into doubt."[14] The notion of selves then "as possessors of real and identifiable characteristics, such as rationality, emotion, and will are dismantled."[15] Gergen argues that these old ideas about the self have been replaced by the view that "persons exist in a state of continuous construction and reconstruction."[16] For Gergen, the self is a matter now of perspective, negotiation, and constant and persistent building and rebuilding. It is relational and subjective, as opposed to being separate and objective. Jacques Lacan called the self a "locus of relationships."[17]

Gergen and others contend that the self is constructed through the effect of the reactions of others and through the incorporation of the responses of other people. In short, the self is created through social relationships.[18] Peter Berger and Thomas Luckman argue that the face-to-face encounter between persons is by far the most important social encounter:

> The most important experience of others takes place in the face-to-face situation, which is the prototypical case of social interaction. All other cases are derivations of it. . . . In the face-to-face situation the other is fully real. . . . Indeed, it may be argued that the other in the face-to-face situation is more real to me than I myself. . . . "What he is," therefore, is ongoingly available to me.[19]

Berger and Luckman further argue that the self is really a reflection of the attitudes, behaviors, and emotions of significant others.

To have an identity is to have a specific place and status in the world in relation to others. For African-American children and young adults, this process by which the self, by which the person is literally created, has tremendous significance. Within the social context of American society, the very nature of the black youth's everyday face-to-face encounters is fraught with danger. If the social construction of the self is reflective, what is all too often reflected to black youth are negative images, the rhetoric of failure, and the discourse of racism and inferiority. What is frequently reflected is blacks as victims or victimizers, as criminals and suspects, and as a problem to be either disregarded or resolved. Nearly a century ago W.E.B. Du Bois asked of black people, "How does it feel to be a problem?"[20] The question still hangs heavy in the air.

Many black youth take on this negative self and the attitudes and emotions that go with it. They take their place in the status and place assigned to them by others. The selves that they are or will be continue to be created and recreated in the eyes of a disapproving larger society. Black youth are shaped by their special and particular social context.

If the self is dependent on social interaction, then where is there hope for developing the positive and healthy selves of black young adults? The social construction theory that defined the "new" self offers the promise of help. If the self can be populated with other selves through face-to-face interaction, cannot the self also be populated with other selves through non face-to-face encounters? Gergen writes of other forces at work on the self in addition to face-to-face encounters. He lists the memory of other selves, imagined selves, and the self as represented in poetry, drama, novels, movies, speech, dreams, and fantasy as substitutes for face-to-face encounters.[21] All these other kinds of encounters also shape the self. These other selves from other sources can become models for young black people. They can set standards for behavior and can, as much as any real person, be admired, imitated, and emulated.

African-American biography is the vehicle that can provide a multitude of other selves to young adult African-Americans. Reader response theory demonstrates that there can be a deep and abiding relationship between the reader, or rather the self, and the selves made accessible to the reader through a text. Wolfgang Iser has written extensively about the relationship between reader and text. This is typical of his thinking on the subject:

> It is only as I read that I become the self whose beliefs must coincide with the author's. Regardless of my real beliefs and practices, I must subordinate my mind and heart to the book. The author creates, in short, an image of himself and another image of his reader; he makes his reader, as he makes his second self, and the most successful reading is one in which the created selves, author and reader, can find complete agreement.[22]

Iser suggests that the act of reading compels the reader's self to merge with the author's self, that the act of reading somehow creates a new self. Reading, according to Iser, is a "dynamic interaction between text and reader." Through reading, the reader's experience is changed and transformed, since reading has the same structure as experience.[23] As with face-to-face encounters, the text stimulates change in the reader's views and this continually changing view allows the reader to move beyond his or her own experience.

Louise Rosenblatt, among the first to contribute to the field of reader response theory, wrote this:

> Just as the personality and concerns of the reader are largely socially patterned, so the literary work, like language itself, is a social product. The genesis of literary techniques occurs in a social matrix . . . yet ultimately, any literary work gains its significance from the way in which the minds and emotions or particular readers respond to the verbal stimuli offered by the text.[24]

Again, what is described is a kind of merging, a meeting of the minds, to ultimately form something better. Rosenblatt has called the act of reading a performance, a transaction between reader and text, and a medium of explanation. This act of reading allows the reader to do a myriad of things, to explore who he or she is or can be, to expose untapped emotions and feelings, and to acquire a perspective on life once unavailable.

For young black readers, this interaction with another through a text is a critical act because it enriches and greatly expands the social resources accessible to them. This means that the reader can take a step beyond television and videos with their narrow portrayals of blacks as criminals, suspects, athletes, and "round the way girls." They can take a step beyond their parents and teachers, who often reflect the negative images held of blacks in the society. They can also take a step beyond their friends who may all too often reinforce and even exult in the societal image of blacks as a problem without a solution.

Through black biography, it is possible for black young adults to tap into the accumulated wisdom of countless generations and to dispel, as Maya Angelou so movingly put it, this "black ugly dream."[25] Biography can address the issue of displacement and help young black people answer the questions, Where do we belong? and How can we "make it over"?

African-American biography has another, very important task to perform. It can help young black Americans understand the racism that assaults them everyday. Sidonie Smith wrote about black autobiography, but the same role, that of helping blacks understand racism can be used as well with black biography:

> In a society where blackness is met with implicit and explicit forms of racism, the understanding of that very racism, its motivations, its effects upon the self and the society at large, is tantamount to the understanding of one's identity.[26]

Black biography for young adults capable of facilitating this level of relatedness between the reader and the text, must possess certain characteristics. Black biography should reflect the author's vision. It should reveal the many selves of the subject to the reader. It should go beneath the surface of the subject and tell the reader how the subject came to be the person he or she became. It should not merely chronicle a life, displaying the dry facts of a person's life, but should explain that life. It should engage itself deeply in the emotional life of the subject. As for the biographer, he or she should not be afraid to display emotion or passion, for this is what separates good biography from bad biography. Vision, passion, regard for the subject, lively prose, and a willingness to seek beneath the surface are all qualities of good black biography.

What follows are examples of African-American biography for young adults as they should be done. Still, no one should assume that all African-American biographies for young adults are exemplary; many, far too many, are dull and disappointing. These flawed biographies are reflective of the fact that the biographer cares little for and knows less about the subject, has little regard for the intellectual and emotional capacities of the reader, and substitutes facts and events for the "how" and "why" of the life. What results is that the reader is never engaged, in fact, has nothing with which to be engaged. A marshalling of facts, slick copy, and judicious use of photographs may make a great looking book, but they do not make a life. The life itself is essential, crucial.

MODELS OF AFRICAN-AMERICAN BIOGRAPHY FOR YOUNG ADULTS

Lerone Bennett—*What Manner of Man*

None of these things can be said of Lerone Bennett's biography of Martin Luther King, Jr., *What Manner of Man*. Any number of biographies about King have been written for children and young adults. Most are distinguished by their dullness and their inability to find the man behind the image. In these biographies, King is a plaster saint, is without flaws, is "turn-the-other cheek" peaceful. These biographies portray him as one dimensional, and what is worse, humorless and bloodless. King the man is lost within an emphasis on him as a dreamer of dreams. But this could not have been the King who galvanized millions with his courage, his words, and his actions.

What is most disturbing about these portrayals is that they tend to dilute and distort King's role in black people's struggle for equal rights in this country. A man who gave a speech in 1963 about a dream cannot long remain important to young black people in 1993. Bennett manages to counter this leaden image with a portrait of King that shows him as highly complex, with contradictions, with doubts, with fears, but also with strongly held convictions, as fearless, and as driven.

Bennett's biography is informed by his friendship with King, by his personal recollections of Morehouse College, the school both attended; and by personal interviews with King, his wife, his close friends, former classmates, and relatives. And it is clear from the text that Bennett has a high regard for King's many accomplishments, has affection for him as a person, but is not in awe of him. This position allows Bennett as biographer to engage in a relationship with King through the text and enables him to present King's many selves to the reader. Thus, Bennett explores King's childhood, his young adulthood, his experiences in college and graduate school, King as a lover and husband, King as a father, and King as a leader. In short, Bennett attempts to present King as a whole and complete person, and to show how he got to be who he eventually became.

Bennett makes use of numerous quotations from King's friends and relatives, those who "knew him when." King's mother spoke of his early fascination with words. She remembered his telling her, "you just wait and see," he said at the age of six, "I'm going to get me some big words."[27] Given King's career as a minister and activist, this recollection is certainly in keeping with the King persona. But there are other recollections that are sharply in contrast with it. King's younger brother, A.D., recalled an altercation he had with King when they were young:

I remember once that I was giving our sister Christine . . . a hard time, and he told me to cut it out. I kept on with whatever I was doing and M.L. suddenly reached over and picked up a telephone. I thought he was going to call Daddy or Mother, wherever they were, but he didn't. He conked me over the head with that phone and almost knocked my brains out.[28]

A.D. also remembered that King was quick to settle arguments when they were young by wrestling, with the one who won the wrestling match winning the argument. A.D. said that King would demand that he and whomever he was arguing with "go to the grass" when words could not settle the dispute. As a result, King "went to the grass" on many an occasion.

Bennett's picture of King was as a complex child, and he recounts two childhood events that demonstrate this. Bennett maintains that King attempted suicide twice before his thirteenth birthday. The first time occurred when his beloved grandmother was accidently knocked unconscious. King, thinking that she had been killed by the blow, ran upstairs and jumped out of the second floor window. He was unharmed, and amidst great concern and alarm from the adults in the house, calmly got up and walked away. The second attempt came when this same grandmother actually died. Upon hearing the news, he again rushed upstairs and jumped out of a second floor window. Again, he was able to walk away calmly and unharmed.

As King grew older, this fiery streak in him was subdued and controlled. Bennett points out that it took King some time to adopt and adapt Gandhi's non-violent techniques, that he had to go through a number of personal trials, not the least of which was the bombing of his home, before he fully began to accept non-violence as a powerful tool. In fact, when his home was bombed during the Montgomery bus boycott, severely damaging the house but leaving his wife and nine-month old daughter unharmed, he went to the sheriff's office with friends and applied for a gun permit. His application was denied.

Bennett was able to create a King that young adults can relate to, can accept as a person, a person with tremendous physical courage, and a person who acted on his convictions, despite the consequences. Perhaps the speech that should be remembered and referred to time and again by young black people is the first one he gave as the newly elected president of the Montgomery Improvement Association. Given during the first days of the Montgomery bus boycott, in Montgomery, Alabama, it ends with these stirring words:

> If you will protest courageously, and yet with dignity and Christian love, when the history books are written in future generations, the historians will have to pause and say, "There lived a great people—a black people—who injected new meaning and dignity into the veins of civilization."[29]

Martin Luther King, Jr., was twenty-six years old when he was thrust into leadership and thirty-nine when he died. In those thirteen years, he and his colleagues were able to change the face of America. He did this with deeds, vision, and courage, not dreams. He was complex, unique, and different. Perhaps, through *What Manner of Man*, these many aspects of the man can have some relatedness to the young reader, can mean something to him or to her, can change their lives.

James Haskins—*James Van DerZee: the Picture Takin' Man*

Many black young adults, especially those in urban areas, have not had the benefits of living with or near their grandparents. Reading James Haskins' biography of James Van DerZee has the feel of sitting at the feet of an older relative and listening to the many stories he has to tell about his life. *James Van DerZee: The Picture-Takin' Man* is stamped with Haskins' deep affection and respect for Van DerZee. In his introduction, Haskins discusses how he met the ninety-year-old Van DerZee and the friendship that developed between them. Haskins is respectful of Van DerZee's photographic skills, aware of his hardships and struggles, and concerned with Van DerZee's place in African-American history:

> Here was a man who had lived nearly a century. He had seen photography advance from a primitive process to a highly developed science and a true art form, both. He could remember when color photography was impossible, when a picture was spoiled if the subject moved, when things that are invisible to the naked eye were also invisible to the camera's age. . . . He had seen more American history and black American history than most of us ever will. He had seen Harlem change from a suburb built for the wealthy to a well-kept black community, to a teeming riot-torn slum.[30]

Haskins places Van DerZee within the framework of a century of American and African-American history. Yet, he had toiled away in Harlem for much of that time in relative obscurity, taking pictures of black American life. And he would have remained an obscure black photographer had not his photographs been discovered and combined into an exhibition at the Metropolitan Museum of Art. The exhibit was called "Harlem on My Mind." Before the exhibit, he had been poor, living from hand-to-mouth, had even been evicted for non-payment of rent from the apartment he and his wife had occupied for years. After the exhibit, sums of money poured in, and, while not making him rich, allowed him to live a little better than he had been living. At eighty-two, he also began to receive recognition for his work. So at ninety, when he spoke extensively about his life to James Haskins, he could look back over that life in relative comfort and security.

Haskins primarily uses the quotes he had accumulated in interviews with Van DerZee. It is these quotes that enable the reader to feel close to Van DerZee, almost as if in mutual conversation. The reader sees Van DerZee's life through Van DerZee's words.

Haskins begins with Van DerZee's birth in 1886 in Lenox, Massachusetts. The reader is introduced to his family, his childhood, his early education, and his early interests in singing. Photography was a secondary interest. Haskins presents Van DerZee as a man with quiet dignity, but also as a man with human failings. The conversation below, as recounted by Van DerZee, indicates the circumstances under which he and his first wife married. He was all of nineteen:

> When she said, "I believe you've ruined me," I could see all my dreams bursting like soap bubbles in the air. I said, "you say it's me, so let's get married." She said, "No, we won't get married. I'll go off and you'll never hear from me again." I said, "Why do that? You say I'm the father. Might as well get married."[31]

Well, they got married, but the marriage was never strong and fell totally apart when their daughter died. Van DerZee said of himself at that time:

> I hadn't been too long out of my own house, and I was still with my father. People had taken care of me. And I felt if I paid the landlord once or twice he oughta lay off me for awhile, but I found that every month he was right there again, wanting money.

I didn't have the sense of responsibility that went along with having my own apartment and being married.[32]

This biography is enhanced by Haskins' extensive use of Van DerZee's many family photographs. The reader gets to see his mother, his father, his brothers and sisters, and other relatives when they lived in Lenox. These photographs are remarkable because they were taken when photography was young and relatively primitive. There are photographs of life in Harlem. Van DerZee photographed Harlem socialites, soldiers, and just plain, everyday people. He also photographed athletes and entertainers. There are pictures of Joe Lewis, Jack Johnson, Florence Mills, Hazel Scott, and Bill "Bojangles" Robinson.

The photographs and the text, especially the words of Van DerZee, allow the reader to get into the flow of Van DerZee's life. The reader sees him in and out of work, learns about his difficult first marriage, and sees him struggling to survive in turn-of-the-century New York City. The book is really akin to sitting and talking to Van DerZee, similar to talking with an older relative, a grandfather perhaps or an uncle. The young reader is also exposed to black history, since he or she can read about the Harlem Renaissance, Marcus Garvey and his Universal Negro Improvement Association (UNIA), World Wars I and II, and the Great Depression.

The pictures are fascinating and there is a gentleness about this book, a gentleness in the narrative that helps the reader know Van DerZee as a person and as a black man. Haskins' affection for Van DerZee is palpable and infectious. Van DerZee has some words of wisdom to impart, although one suspects that he would never have thought himself wise. He had this to say about living life:

I'd like to live to be a hundred. There's still a lot to learn. You never stop learning, and you never stop trying to figure out what life is all about. . . . When you're small, you got small troubles. When you're big, you got big troubles. Seems like there's one thing after another. Only reason I'm hanging around is to see what is going to happen next![33]

Walter Dean Myers—*Malcolm X: By Any Means Necessary*

Malcolm X: By Any Means Necessary, by Walter Dean Myers, shows the young reader the many sides of Malcolm X. But this is not what makes this such an effective biography, since Malcolm's many transformations are well known. It is Myers' vision of Malcolm X and his place in American history that shapes this biography. Myers sets out to explore how Malcolm X became Malcolm X, and he tells Malcolm's story with a righteous anger, bordering at times on white, hot rage. He paints Malcolm's childhood as one of extreme deprivation, shadowed by racism and bigotry. Myers concentrates on the impact such a childhood had on the man, Malcolm X. At every crucial turn in Malcolm's young life, his youthful spirits were smothered and his natural academic abilities were twisted and distorted. And at a time when a child needs a mother and a father, his father was killed under suspicious circumstances, and his mother suffered a mental collapse:

> By the age of thirteen, Malcolm had seen his house burn down. He had been exposed to the violent death of his father, had known extreme hunger, had seen the slow breakdown of his mother, and had also seen brothers and sisters placed in homes.[34]

When Malcolm's father was killed in 1931, Malcolm was six years old, and he became afraid to go to sleep in the dark. It is not surprising then that Malcolm Little as Malcolm X would scare America. What did he have to lose? He had already lost his childhood to white racism and the indifference of those who should have helped him.

Myers tells the familiar story: the street life in Roxbury, Detroit, and Harlem; criminal activity, a prison term, and the sudden and complete conversion to the Black Muslim faith. Yet, Myers is able to make this story new to the reader, to inject little known details, to explain Malcolm's anger and to justify that anger. What is more, Myers gives Malcolm and the Muslims a role in the Civil Rights Movement that few would admit:

> It was Malcolm's anger, his biting wit, his dedication that put the hard edge on the movement, that provided the other side of the sword, not the handle of acceptance and nonviolence, but the blade. . . . Malcolm and the Nation of Islam drove the civil rights movement, gave it the dark side that many feared it might have.[35]

Myers fleshes out his story of Malcolm with a brief history of slavery, the beginnings of slavery in this country, a discussion of the Great Depression and its impact on black people, and a description of the Civil Rights Movement and its importance. He writes about Malcolm's intellectual abilities, his academic promise, and the ways in which white society ignored Malcolm's obvious gifts. He discusses the lure of the streets for Malcolm. If he, Malcolm, couldn't make it in the white man's world, he could make it in the black man's world. Then came the "conk," the popular 1940s hair style for black men, and the zoot suit, the last word in 1940s male sartorial splendor. The street life took Malcolm over until he made the mistake of committing a robbery with three white girls. The girls gave state's evidence and got very light sentences; Malcolm got six to eight years of hard labor at the Charlestown State Prison, across from Boston.

Myers' emphasis on Malcolm's desire to learn, to improve himself, and to grow is a very good thing. This is a message black young adults need to hear. This is a side of Malcolm, a self, that black youth need to know. Myers lists a host of books Malcolm read, more precisely, devoured, while in jail: biographies of Hannibal, Ibn Saud, Marx, Lenin, Stalin, Hitler, Rommel, Gandhi, Patrick Henry, and John Brown; and works by H.G. Wells, Will Durant, Plato, Aristotle, Spinoza, Nietzsche, and Schopenhauer. He also immersed himself, as much as it was possible from a prison library, in black history.

Myers makes an effort to describe and to understand Malcolm's devotion to Elijah Muhammad, and he calls the eventual split inevitable. He is also concerned about the F.B.I.'s role in Malcolm's life and frequently mentions its sinister presence. A chapter is devoted to Martin Luther King, Jr., and the differences, as well as the similarities, between the two men. Other chapters are devoted to Malcolm's assassination, who might have killed him, and his legacy.

Black young adults who read this biography are going to become angry. But it is better to become angry with knowledge than with ignorance. That anger may be aroused in many places in this biography, perhaps at the description of Malcolm's murder:

> Between the living, frozen for the moment in shock and grief, lay Malcolm. The white shirt was opened by dark fingers looking to help. The holes, dark in their grim pattern within the spreading stain, caused the hand to recoil.[36]

Perhaps that anger, however, might be replaced by a sense of pride and a sense of purpose when the reader reads what Malcolm left behind:

He remains because he represented, and still represents, something that other leaders, leaders as courageous as Malcolm, did not. These leaders, black and white, men and women, willing to risk their lives in the search for justice for all people, represented a courage that was right for the time. But Malcolm's words speak to today's time, and to the young people of today. . . .[37]

Elaine Feinstein—*Bessie Smith* and Mary E. Lyons— *Sorrow's Kitchen: The Life and Folklore of Zora Neale Hurston*

African-American women suffer a double tyranny, are twice oppressed, as women and as blacks. It is vital that their lives be written, since black men have not been the only achievers. How did the black woman fare in the backwoods of racism? What are her contributions? Few really good biographies for young adults have been done on black women. Elaine Feinstein's *Bessie Smith* and Mary E. Lyons' *Sorrow's Kitchen: The Life and Folklore of Zora Neale Hurston* are exceptions. Neither author glosses over or ignores the faults of her subjects. Each attempts a balanced and reasoned approach. Both succeed in portraying a black woman living her life as best she could under difficult circumstances and trying times. Smith and Hurston were down, were often out, and they suffered, but both women remained true to their art and to themselves. Bessie Smith, of course, was the great blues singer, who burst upon the music scene in the 1920s. She was a wild woman, a bisexual, a brawler, a drinker, but, most of all, she was a consummate performer who introduced America to the blues.

What shines through in *Bessie Smith* is Feinstein's admiration for Smith as a person and as a woman. The connection between these two women, Feinstein, who is white, and Smith, who was black, is Smith's music. In the book's very first chapter, Feinstein wonders how she would be perceived by Smith and speaks to the differences between them. In Feinstein's mind, what matters most is Smith's music and its ability even now to move the listener some sixty years after it was first recorded.

From her position as a white woman, Feinstein reveals Smith's life as she lived it. She looks at Smith's early life in Chattanooga, Tennessee, in the 1890s, her rise to fame but not fortune, her artistry, and her love of good times. Feinstein breathes life into Smith, brings her back in all her finery and glory. One can almost hear and touch Smith, see her strutting "her stuff" across a stage:

If I try to conjure up Bessie's presence, in wig and feathers, ready to go on stage, she rises before me, a large-framed woman, with a quick temper, used to resorting to violence when crossed. She was strong enough to fell a man; and she didn't always wait to be attacked before using her fists.[38]

Smith's work was also admired by musicians who were her contemporaries:

There's no explainin' her singing, her voice. She don't need a mike; she don't use one. . . . As she sings she moves slowly round the stage. Her head, sort of bowed. From where I'm sittin' I'm not sure whether she even has her eyes open. On and on, number after number, the same hush, the great performance, the deafening applause.[39]

Feinstein seeks not only the performer, but the Smith behind the stage image. Feinstein writes that Smith grew up in the streets, fending for herself and singing on corners for nickels. This hardscrapple life produced the woman, a confident but vulnerable woman:

Bessie carried herself as if she did not know how old she was, and felt beautiful, and liked her own size, in the same way that she wore her blackness with pride. . . .[40]

Feinstein even dispels as myth the long-accepted view that Smith bled to death in Mississippi because she was refused treatment in the whites only hospital. There is no comfort in this because she replaces it with an even more chilling version of Smith's death. Despite everything, however, what the reader is left with is a life, Smith's life, lived to the fullest and on her own terms.

The same can be said of Zora Neale Hurston. She lived her life the way she wanted and suffered the consequences. Writing at a time when black women could not expect to be accepted as writers, she preserved. When the folkways of poor southern blacks were being deprecated, she set about preserving black folklore. When a black fiction that did not raise the specter of race as an issue was being criticized, she wrote perhaps the finest book of that kind, *Their Eyes Were Watching God*. Hurston was different, unique, stubborn, irascible, herself. Of course, she died poor. But between being born poor and dying poor, she became who she wanted to become.

Lyons captures Hurston in all her many guises—as child, as student, as writer, as anthropologist, as folklorist. She does this by imaginatively using excerpts from Hurston's own works, various pictures, interviews, and by also inserting a touching piece by Alice Walker about looking for Hurston's grave.

All this works because it enables the young reader to see the whole of Hurston, even her imperfections and she had many. The reader first sees her as an independent brash kind of child:

> She was sassy and impudent, but it was clear to Lucy Hurston that Zora was also bright. Lucy was proud of her daughter's talents. . . . When she came home with wild stories about talking to birds and walking on the lake, Mama listened. . . . Zora's grandmother would "foam at the mouth" and accuse Zora of being a lying heifer. "You hear dat young'un stand up here and lie like dat? . . . Grab her! Stomp her guts out! Ruin her!"[41]

In her early youth and after her mother died, Hurston had a difficult time and held a grudge against her stepmother for keeping the family separated. Later, not one to keep her feelings to herself, Hurston beat the stepmother senseless and, in the heat of battle, threw a hatchet at the woman. Despite her temper and poverty, she managed to complete high school, graduate from college, and start graduate work in anthropology.

Ending up in Harlem, she struggled to make a living as a writer. For the most part, she succeeded. In a thirty-year writing career, she produced seven books and more than one hundred short stories, plays, essays, and articles. She has been called "a genius of the South" by Alice Walker.[42] She travelled southern backwoods collecting stories. She travelled to Haiti and New Orleans to learn voodoo ritual. In between, she went from Florida to Baltimore to Harlem to the Caribbean, each stop representing a kind of milestone in her life. She ended her days poor and alone in Florida, where she had started. But this does not mean that she had accomplished nothing, far from it:

> Despite incredible odds, Zora Neale Hurston made her own luck.
> "I shall wrassle me up a future . . . or die trying."[43]

Virginia Hamilton—*Anthony Burns: The Defeat and Triumph of a Fugitive Slave*

The life and times of the slave have been depicted, but mainly through the autobiographies of ex-slaves. Rarely has a biography been done of the slave. Virginia Hamilton's *Anthony Burns: the Defeat and Triumph of a Fugitive Slave* is one of those rare biographies. It is difficult to imagine what it must have been like to be a slave, to live on a plantation, to be uncertain and fearful most of the time—to escape from slavery and then be recaptured. Although this is a story that has not been widely told, slavery from the slave's viewpoint, it is one black young adults should know and cherish.

Hamilton has made an extraordinary effort to get into the mind of a slave, to see what he saw, and to feel what he felt. She begins with Burns' life as a child on the plantation. She recreates his life as a slave through flashbacks, since, for most of the biography, Anthony Burns is in jail in Boston, Massachusetts. To escape the horror of being jailed and possibly returned to southern slavery, Burns retreats into himself and remembers his childhood and youth.

Hamilton explores the thorny issue of Burns' self-identity. Who is he? Who is his father? The answer seems to be that Burns may be the plantation owner's son. This is never quite resolved, but it is certainly a source of confusion to Burns:

> It was true, Anthony's skin was lighter than that of most property. And his mamaw was indeed a breeder woman. She was made to have a baby each year so that he Mars would increase his holdings. Still, nobody knew for certain whether Anthony was he Mars John Suttle's second son.[44]

Hamilton paints life on the plantation as a grim one, full of fear and sudden turns; very little could be counted on:

> Mars Charles slapped him smartly on his head. Anthony rose and stood at attention before him with his eyes still downcast. He held his cap against his chest, his free hand straight at his sides. His position there before the master was one of a careful, respectful slave. . . .[45]

When the decision was made to run, Burns escaped by ship to the North. But the North of 1854 was unlike the North in the 1830s and 1840s. The Fugitive Slave Act had been enacted and now the owner of an escaped slave had a legal right to retrieve his slave even if the slave ran to a northern state. Burns was recaptured on the streets of Boston and jailed. Manacled and given nothing to eat, he is desolate and stunned by his situation:

> His head felt light. He wanted so much just to lie down. The wrist
> irons and the chain that connected them grew heavier by the
> minute. . . . He felt miserably hot in his shoulders and deathly
> cold in his legs.[46]

Hamilton explores the world of the slave from a unique vantage
point, through the eyes of one slave who actually lived, who escaped
slavery, and then was returned to it. All the feelings of terror, of frustration, of misery, and of pain are explored and revealed. Few can read
this book without feeling some kinship with Anthony Burns.

This is the effect Hamilton wanted and one she was able to
achieve. She writes of being haunted by Burns' story and her "relief
and satisfaction" at having written his life. She is concerned about the
issue of freedom, what one does with it, and how one achieves it. For
the young adult reader, there is the message that perhaps freedom
should not be taken lightly:

> All these years Anthony Burns has lived in my thoughts: this
> man, born a slave, whose painstaking and burning desire to "get
> gone" from crippling bondage was all but forgotten by history.
> By writing about him I found that he not only came to life for me
> but that he lives again for all of us. In gaining a sense of who he
> was we learn about ourselves. As long as we know he is free, we
> too are liberated.[47]

Virginia Hamilton—*W.E.B. DuBois: A Biography* and *Paul Robeson: The Life and Times of a Free Black Man*

The other biographies by Hamilton are also noteworthy, *W.E.B.
DuBois: A Biography* and *Paul Robeson: The Life and Times of a Free
Black Man*. Hamilton, in both the DuBois biography and the Robeson
biography, writes the lives of these two men from their birth to their
death. She places them in an historical context and presents them to the
young adult reader as black men who must not be forgotten or ignored.
DuBois and Robeson are linked in several, crucial ways. Each was
born into a large, closely-knit family in the North. Each was supremely
gifted intellectually. Each was highly educated. Neither man was in the
habit of compromising his beliefs or doing what was politically or
socially expedient. Each was hounded and persecuted by the United

States government, and each suffered in other ways for the many unpopular stands he took.

Hamilton writes about each man with passion and with affection and respect. Her admiration for them as strong black men is obvious. In the DuBois biography, Hamilton makes use of his own writings to give him voice. Through that voice, time melts away, and the words written or spoken ninety years ago still have power, still are important, and still have a tremendous urgency:

> As a race we are still kept in ignorance far below the average standard of this nation and of the present age, and the ideals set before our children in most cases are far below their possibilities and reasonable promise.[48]

DuBois often wrote passionately and movingly about the brutal treatment endured by blacks, particularly after a willingness to serve and die in America's foreign wars:

> We sing: This country of ours, despite all its better souls have done and dreamed, is yet a shameful land. It lynches. . . . It disfranchises its own citizens. . . . It steals from us. It insults us . . . make way for Democracy! We saved it in France, and by the Great Jehovah, we will save it in the United States of America, or know the reason why.[49]

For his beliefs, DuBois was tried as a criminal. His passport was lifted by the government, and he and his wife were not allowed to travel out of the country for several years. His manuscripts were rejected by leading publishing houses. His mail was tampered with. He was ostracized by many of his colleagues:

> But the old man never ceased his work. He did not cringe or hide. No longer able to travel abroad, he spoke out and wrote whenever he could. The Doctor and his wife adjusted as best they could to their lowered income. . . . However, for him the deepest hurt of all was that black boys and girls would no longer know his name.[50]

Through Hamilton and others, black boys and girls now have the opportunity to know his name and to know him. Silenced in his own land, he was honored and finally given shelter and comfort abroad. When the ban on his passport was lifted, DuBois left America for Africa, never to return. The Ghanaian government heaped honors upon him. It built him a house with a garden, and there he worked on his autobiography. He died in 1963, ironically, on the eve of the great March on Washington.

Hamilton thought him to be a great man, a great fighter:

> He was our great man, our keeper, and we were his dream. The distance between us was never far.[51]

In writing her biography of Paul Robeson, Hamilton pays tribute both to her father Kenneth Hamilton and Paul Robeson. She recalls a time when her father shared with his children his knowledge of the world and black achievement. He had particular regard and respect for W.E.B. DuBois and Robeson:

> . . . however he came by his knowledge of Mr. Robeson, he gave it his special rendering. So that by the time I heard of this great man, he embodied much of my father's hopes and dreams for his own children. Not fame, particularly, but attitude.[52]

Paul Robeson was prodigiously talented—an actor, a singer, an athlete, and a scholar. But he had the misfortune of being born at the wrong time, in the wrong skin. His mother died, burned to death, when he was six. His father, after losing his job as minister of a church in Princeton, took odd jobs in several New Jersey towns before settling down again as a minister in Somerville, New Jersey. Rev. Robeson died when Robeson was in college and did not see Robeson's later triumphs as a concert singer and actor. Robeson was, during the 1930s, lionized in England for his work in *Othello*, *Showboat*, and *All God's Chillun Got Wings*.

Although Robeson had suffered many indignities in America at the hands of Americans, it was an incident in Germany that made him a fighter against racial oppression. He and his wife were threatened by Nazi stormtroopers on a train platform in Berlin. The incident was frightening and ugly, but it served to politicize him as no other incident had done:

> The dangerous moments on the train platform did much to complete the changes going on inside him. The artist searching for his individual place in the world merged with the man who would never retreat from injustice. After Berlin, Paul's political point of view crystallized and he was bound to fight intolerance wherever he found it.[53]

Like DuBois, Robeson was not afraid to espouse his beliefs. Hamilton writes that "he earned hundreds of thousands of dollars—and forewent just as many thousands which he could have earned by refusing to say what people expected a member of a downtrodden race might well have said."[54] Once he recognized the full global state of injustice, he did what he had to do to guarantee a "social revolution" for racial equality and independence for colored peoples. He fought against racial injustice through concerts and speeches. He became a member of politically unpopular organizations. He stood up to intense interrogation by the House of Representatives Committee on Un-American Activities and was not intimidated.

For these acts, he was harassed by the United States government, as was DuBois, all during the 1950s. His passport was lifted, thereby depriving him of income from concerts abroad. Opportunities to work in the United States dwindled because he was branded a communist and a subversive.

Hamilton summed up Robeson's life beautifully when she wrote:

> he was more than one man, more than a symbol for blacks like my father whose dreams had been thwarted. . . . For black America, he embodied an age-old Spirit of Survival, beginning with . . . slave revolts. . . . For half a century, Paul Robeson was that Spirit for an entire race.[55]

Certainly, these eight biographies are not the only ones of African-Americans worthy of note. Others exist. *Thurgood Marshall: A Life for Justice*[56] by James Haskins is outstanding. Haskins digs beneath the surface and tries to uncover the man Thurgood Marshall. The same can be said of Elizabeth Van Steenwyk's *Ida B. Wells-Barnett: Woman of Courage.*[57] Wells-Barnett's life was written as she lived it. She was not perfect, but few could have withstood the withering attacks she had to endure from both whites and blacks, men and women, simply because she protested the lynching of blacks. Finally, James Lincoln Collier has given us *Duke Ellington.*[58] Collier places his biographical emphasis on Ellington the musician, but Ellington the man is still allowed to shine through.

CONCLUSION

This essay has discussed eight black lives as depicted in biography. All the subjects have long been dead, but each still has something special to say to young black readers. Their lives are the kind of lives that need to be shared with willing and receptive readers. But this can only be done if the biographies themselves are written with care, skill, and an understanding of the power biography can have. DuBois and Robeson still speak to us about waging battle against heart chilling injustices. They tell us not to give up, no matter what. Malcolm still has the power to jolt us out of our complacency and our ignorance. Bessie can still move us with a song and her brassy ways. And we are in the prisoner's dock with Anthony Burns awaiting the verdict: freedom or slavery.

Biography as a genre for young adults must be more carefully written, more carefully thought through. The writing of biography must be informed with three critical theories: reader response theory, social construction theory, and theory on the writing of biography. These three are indispensable to the writing of a deeper biography. Reader response theory speaks to the power of the act of reading, to what the reader brings to the text, and to what the text brings to the reader. Social construction theory lays to rest the notion of the self as a unified whole, existing within a person. It replaces it with the notion of the self as a creation of relations with others in face-to-face contact, or even through contact with the others in books, plays, dreams, or memory. Finally, critical thought on the writing of biography suggests that a life be written from the inside out, that a parade of facts as substitutes for the life makes for poor biography.

When these intellectual streams flow together, as they sometimes do, they can produce biographies such as those discussed here. And it is just this kind of biography that can provide the best exposure of African-American youth to a great variety of significant black lives. This deep biography can present to the young black reader new opportunities for growth and new ways to express themselves as whole people.

NOTES

1. James L. Clifford, ed., *Biography as an Art: Selected Criticism 1560–1960* (New York: Oxford University Press, 1962), 10.
2. Milton Lomask, *The Biographer's Craft* (New York: Harper & Row, 1986), 121.

3. Clifford, 7.
4. Ibid., 58.
5. Ibid., 250.
6. Leon Edel, *Writing Lives* (New York: W.W. Norton & Company, 1984), 21.
7. Ibid., 29.
8. Ibid., 30.
9. Ibid., 64.
10. John Lofland and Lyn H. Lofland, *Analyzing Social Settings* (Belmont, CA: Wadsworth Publishing, 1984), 12.
11. Edel, 194.
12. Jonathan Potter and Margaret Wetherell, *Discourse and Social Psychology* (London, England: Sage Publications, 1987), 95–101.
13. Kenneth Gergen, *The Saturated Self: Dilemmas of Identity in Contemporary Life* (New York: Basic Books, 1991), 8.
14. Ibid., 7.
15. Ibid.
16. Ibid.
17. Anthony Welden, "Lacan and the Discourse of the Other," in *The Language of the Self*, ed. Jacques Lacan (New York: Delta, 1975), 41.
18. Kenneth Gergen and Keith Davis, eds., *The Social Construction of the Person* (New York: Springer-Verlag, 1985), 5.
19. Peter Berger and Thomas Luckman, *The Social Construction of Reality* (New York: Doubleday, 1966), 27.
20. W.E.B. DuBois, *The Souls of Black Folk* (New York: Vintage Books, 1990), 7.
21. Gergen, 68–71.
22. Wayne Booth, *The Rhetoric of Fiction* (Chicago, IL: University of Chicago Press, 1963), 137.
23. Wolfgang Iser, *The Act of Reading: A Theory of Aesthetic Response* (Baltimore, MD: Johns Hopkins University Press, 1978), 107.
24. Louise Rosenblatt, *Literature as Exploration* (New York: Modern Language Association, 1983), 28.
25. Maya Angelou, *I Know Why the Caged Bird Sings* (New York: Random House, 1969), 4.
26. Sidonie Smith, *Where I'm Bound: Patterns of Slavery and Freedom in Black American Autobiography* (Westport, CT: Greenwood Press, 1974), 120.
27. Lerone Bennett, Jr., *What Manner of Man: A Biography of Martin Luther King, Jr.* (Chicago, IL: Johnson Publishing Company, Inc. 1976), 17.
28. Ibid., 24.
29. Ibid., 66.

30. James Haskins, *James Van DerZee: The Picture-Takin' Man* (New York: Dodd, Mead & Company, 1979), 10.
31. Ibid., 59.
32. Ibid., 69.
33. Ibid., 252.
34. Walter Dean Myers, *Malcolm X: By Any Means Necessary* (New York: Scholastic Inc., 1993), 32.
35. Ibid., x-xi.
36. Ibid., 174.
37. Ibid., xi.
38. Elaine Feinstein, *Bessie Smith Empress of the Blues* (New York: Penguin Books, 1985), 14.
39. Ibid., 80–81.
40. Ibid., 29.
41. Mary E. Lyons, *Sorrow's Kitchen: The Life and Folklore of Zora Neale Hurston* (New York: Charles Scribner's Sons, 1990), 3–4.
42. Ibid., ix.
43. Ibid., 3.
44. Virginia Hamilton, *Anthony Burns: The Defeat and Triumph of a Fugitive Slave* (New York: Alfred A. Knopf, 1988), 15.
45. Ibid., 84.
46. Ibid., 35.
47. Ibid., 180.
48. Virginia Hamilton, *W.E.B. DuBois: A Biography* (New York: Thomas Y. Crowell Company, 1972), 113.
49. Ibid., 124.
50. Ibid., 183.
51. Ibid., 197.
52. Virginia Hamilton, *Paul Robeson: The Life and Times of a Free Black Man* (New York: Dell Publishing, 1974), 12.
53. Ibid., 73.
54. Ibid., 121.
55. Ibid., 14.
56. James Haskins, *Thurgood Marshall: A Life for Justice* (New York: Henry Holt and Company, 1992).
57. Elizabeth Van Steenwyk, *Ida B. Wells-Barnett: Woman of Courage* (New York: Franklin Watts, 1992).
58. James Lincoln Collier, *Duke Ellington* (New York: Macmillan Publishing Company, 1991).

REFERENCES

Angelou, Maya. *I Know Why the Caged Bird Sings*. New York: Random House, 1969.

Baker, Houston A. *Afro-American Poetics: Revisions of Harlem and the Black Aesthetic*. Madison, WI: The University of Wisconsin Press, 1988.

Baker, Houston, and Patricia Redmond, eds. *Afro-American Study in the 1990s*. Chicago, IL: University of Chicago Press, 1989.

Baldwin, James. *Nobody Knows My Name*. New York: Dell Publishing Co., 1962.

Bennett, Lerone, Jr. *What Manner of Man*. Chicago, IL: Johnson Publishing Company, 1976.

Berger, Peter, and Thomas Luckman. *The Social Construction of Reality*. New York: Doubleday, 1966.

Booth, Wayne. *The Rhetoric of Fiction*. Chicago, IL: University of Chicago Press, 1963.

Braxton, Joanne M. *Black Women Writing Autobiography: Tradition Within a Tradition*. Philadelphia, PA: Temple University Press, 1989.

Clifford, James, ed. *Biography as an Art: Selected Criticism 1560–1960*. New York: Oxford University Press, 1962.

Cole, John, ed. *Biography & Books*. Washington, DC: Library of Congress, 1986.

Collier, James Lincoln. *Duke Ellington*. New York: Macmillan Publishing Company, 1991.

Collins, Carol Jones. "A Tool for Change: Young Adult Literature in the Lives of Young Adult African-Americans." *Library Trends* 41 (Winter 1993): 378–392.

Comer, James, and Alvin Poussaint. *Black Child Care*. New York: Simon and Schuster, 1975.

DuBois, W.E.B. *The Souls of Black Folk*. New York: Vintage Books, 1990.

Edel, Leon. *Writing Lives: Principia Biographia*. New York: W. W. Norton, 1984.

Feinstein, Elaine. *Bessie Smith Empress of the Blues*. New York: Penguin Books, 1985.

Fleming, Margaret, and Jo McGinnis, eds. *Portraits: Biography and Autobiography in the Secondary School*. Urbana, IL: NCTE, 1985.

Gergen, Kenneth J. *The Saturated Self: Dilemmas of Identity in Contemporary Life*. New York: Basic Books, 1991.

Gergen, Kenneth J., and Keith E. Davis. *The Social Construction of the Person*. New York: Springer-Verlag, 1985.

Goffman, Erving. *Interaction Ritual*. New York: Pantheon Books, 1967.

Hamilton, Virginia. *Anthony Burns: The Defeat and Triumph of a Fugitive*

Slave. New York: Alfred A. Knopf, 1988.

_____. *Paul Robeson: The Life and Times of a Free Black Man.* New York: Dell Publishing, 1974.

_____. *W.E.B. DuBois: A Biography.* New York: Thomas Y. Crowell, 1972.

Haskins, James. *James Van DerZee: The Picture-Takin' Man.* New York: Dodd, Mead & Company, 1979.

_____. *Thurgood Marshall: A Life for Justice.* New York: Henry Holt and Company, 1992.

Helms, Janet, ed. *Black and White Racial Identity: Theory Research, and Practice.* Westport, CT: Greenwood Press, Inc., 1990.

Homberger, Eric, and John Charmley, eds. *The Troubled Face of Biography.* New York: St. Martin's Press, 1988.

Iser, Wolfgang. *The Act of Reading: A Theory of Aesthetic Response.* Baltimore, MD: Johns Hopkins University Press, 1978.

Landau, Elliott, Sherrie Epstein, and Ann Stone, eds. *Child Development Through Literature.* Englewood Cliffs, NJ: Prentice-Hall, 1972.

Lofland, John, and Lyn H. Lofland. *Analyzing Social Settings.* Belmont, CA: Wadsworth Publishing, 1984.

Lomask, Milton. *The Biographer's Craft.* New York: Harper & Row, 1986.

Lyons, Mary E. *Sorrow's Kitchen: The Life and Folklore of Zora Neale Hurston.* New York: Charles Scribner's Sons, 1990.

Mead, George. *Mind, Self, and Society.* Chicago, IL: The University of Chicago Press, 1962.

Mokros, Hartmut, and Margaret Carr. "Relationally Engendered Selves." In press in S. Deetz, ed. *Communication Yearbook.*

Myers, Walter Dean. *Malcolm X: By Any Means Necessary.* New York: Scholastic, 1993.

Natov, Roni. "The Truth of Ordinary Lives: Autobiographical Fiction for Children." *Children's Literature in Education* 17 (April 1986): 112–125.

Olney, James, ed. *Autobiography: Essays Theoretical and Critical.* Princeton, NJ: Princeton University Press, 1980.

Pachter, Marc. *Telling Lives: The Biographer's Art.* Washington, DC: New Republic Books, 1979.

Potter, Jonathan, and Margaret Wetherell. *Discourse and Social Psychology.* London, England: Sage Publications, 1987.

Rosenblatt, Louise M. *Literature as Exploration.* New York: The Modern Language Association of America, 1983.

Shotter, John, and Kenneth Gergen, eds. *Texts of Identity.* London: Sage Publications, 1989.

Smith, Sidonie. *Where I'm Bound: Patterns of Slavery and Freedom in Black American Autobiography.* Westport, CT: Greenwood Press, 1974.

Suleiman, Susan, and Inge Crosman, eds. *The Reader in the Text: Essays on*

Audience and Interpretation. Princeton, NJ: Princeton University Press, 1980.

Taylor, Charles. *Sources of the Self: The Making of Modern Identity.* Cambridge, MA: Harvard University Press, 1989.

Van Steenwyk, Elizabeth. *Ida B. Wells-Barnett: Woman of Courage.* New York: Franklin Watts, 1992.

Welden, Anthony. "Lacan and the Discourse of the Other." In J. Lacan, ed. *The Language of the Self.* New York: Delta, 1975.

TWO

And Bid Her Sing: A White Feminist Reads African-American Female Poets

Kay E. Vandergrift

Young adults delight in pushing language to its outer limits. They invent words and phrases, play with pronunciation and enunciation, and deliberately *misuse* language to make it more useful for their own purposes. Often this is to declare their own individual identities or to signify a community separate from the dominant adult establishment. Each generation of young people has its own slang, song lyrics, and other unique languages which mark their time and culture. This is the poetry of youth. Few young adults think of these uses of language as poetry. In fact, if they think of poetry at all, it is probably as some esoteric or sentimental adult affectation far removed from their own lives.

ON THE NATURE OF POETRY AND YOUNG ADULTS

Poetry, like adolescence, is filled with impossible questions, wonder, rebellion, thoughtfulness, experimentation, playfulness, intense sensations, and emotional extremes. It has an energy, a vitality and a freshness of vision that can transform everyday experiences into acrobatic words and images that leap from the page with daring spontaneity. It can hold both delight and despair at the appropriate distance to provide the perspective and the strength to accept these extremes as part of the natural rhythms of life. Young people have much in common with poets, and their own lives resound with the rough-hewn poetry of slang, street-talk and rap. Too often, however, adults try to force them to reject these forms of poetry and accept what is for them artificial and alien to their personal experiences and concerns. Thus, they are more likely to ridicule than to respect poetry, and even those young adults who do, despite the odds, discover a kinship with poetic language and imagery are discouraged and may allow this relationship to atrophy and die. If poetry is to remain alive in the lives of young people; teachers, librarians, and parents must open the doors to both the unformed poetry of young people themselves and to the full range of published poetry with its harshness, pain, protest, and, yes, even sexuality and vulgarity.[1]

Much of the power of some contemporary poetry, not just that of African-Americans, is the way it forces readers to confront the language that excludes, oppresses or victimizes those outside the master narrative. This master narrative or ideological script imposed on others by white middle-class male notions of authority makes subtle use of pejorative or violent language as a weapon against others. Poets often expose this language and, by dwelling on, repeating, or even yelling words not ordinarily said aloud; they disempower them or turn them back on the victimizers. Young people need to recognize such uses of language and confront that shock of recognition when they read in powerful poetry words ordinarily written only on walls. Adults sharing contemporary poetry with young adults in schools and libraries, however, need to be aware of this language and the fact that some may object to young people reading these words, even if they do hear, even use, them in their own lives. Where this is the case, we may still select specific poems which introduce youngsters to a range of contemporary poets without the most *offensive* language. Although some of the segments of poems quoted in this chapter do contain language not sanctioned in schools and libraries; for the most part, they do not demonstrate this overt demystification of obscenities.

All young adults probably have an affinity for and a need for poetry in their lives, but it may be especially important to retain poetry in the lives of African-American youth. African-American language and culture are unusually rich in poetry. From the slave songs, spirituals, street hollers, jazz, blues, and rap, there is a wealth and intensity of language and meaning that speaks to African-American youth both of their history and of the problems and possibilities of contemporary life. All of these are oral forms, often accompanied by music and movement which is true of the real poetry of human experience. Poetry is an oral art; it comes to life in performance. Its written form is, at best, the equivalent of a musical score suggesting what might be or, at worst, an autopsy report on a once-vibrant living thing. Too often young people look at the words of a poem on the printed page without any appreciation for the sound of the human voice saying, singing, or even screaming those words. In order to demonstrate how the human voice brings life to the cold, dead page, one might look first at printed poems and then listen to recordings of those poems.[2] Of course, their own voices saying, singing, chanting, or crying the words are the best means of connecting young people with poetry.

ACCESSIBILITY OF POETRY BY AFRICAN-AMERICAN WOMEN

For some time, concerned adults have been working to assure that young African-Americans have stories in which they can recognize themselves, their culture, and their own lives. This is equally important in poetry. Some few important African-American poets have been anthologized and included in school curricula.[3] Langston Hughes, a popular poet among young adults of all cultures, is an obvious example. Certainly his voice remains one of the most powerful and most evocative in speaking to all peoples regardless of age, gender, race, ethnicity, or social class. What is clear, however, is that few contemporary African-American poets are readily available to young people in schools and libraries today. African-American women are especially notable for their absence. In spite of a strong sisterhood of poets, the same few African-American women seem to be represented over and over in collections of either women poets or African-American poets. Erlene Stetson's *Black Sister* remains the landmark collection celebrating the poetry of African-American women from colonial times to 1980.[4] This collection and others in the bibliography at the end of this chapter includes the work of a number of African-American women poets not discussed here but whose poetry is important to consider in building a collection.

Although poetry of major African-American women who have entered into the mainstream of western literary traditions is readily available, the works of many others have been lost over time. Further, many contemporary African-American female poets are published by small, sometimes even obscure, presses and are not advertised, reviewed, or sold through channels readily available to schools and libraries.[5] Often these are relatively inexpensive paperbacks available only by mail directly from the publisher or from specialized bookstores. Thus, they are virtually inaccessible to most young people and to the teachers and librarians who might purchase and share this poetry with them.

There is another kind of accessibility that must also be considered in approaching this poetry, that of the reader's ability to comprehend works outside one's own cultural context. A major difficulty in the composition of this chapter is that I, as a middle-aged white woman, cannot be fully attuned to the distinct aesthetic of these poets and the sensibilities of African-American youth. Although I have attempted to inform my own understanding and appreciation of these poets through study of African-American feminist theory and literary criticism, as well as through an immersion in the poetry itself, I am well aware that many women of color feel disconnected from feminist theory which has been dominated by females in predominantly white intellectual centers of power. White feminists who argue against hierarchical thought, nonetheless, often seem to assume a hierarchy of oppression with sexism at the top and racism as a lesser form of domination. In fact, gender is just one strand in a very complex pattern of domination including race, class, ethnicity, religion, and sexual orientation, all of which must be considered interactively.

Poetry, with its powerful language and images and its sharpness of vision, is one of the best ways to come close to comprehending the effects of such domination on human lives. White women who have felt oppression based on gender, class, or economics must feel fortunate when they compare their lives with the lives of women of color and the added brutalities and daily indignities they have had to endure. Some of this brutality comes from the power of language itself—a language embedded with images of white as good and black as evil, of golden hair and blue eyes as symbols of beauty, of dark continents and dark people who need to be brought into someone else's light. White women may resent, sometimes even rebel against, the waif-like body images the media extols; but black women have, until very recently, seldom seen themselves in the popular media, and even magazines such as *Ebony* have been filled with ads for skin lighteners and hair straighteners. Young people, both black and white, as well as those of us who share literature with them can at least begin to feel the impact of this pervasive image-making when we read many of these poems.

Readers also vicariously experience the pain and the rage felt by African-Americans who see their children shot down on what Audre Lorde called that "desert of raw gunshot wounds" which is the city.

> The policeman who shot down a 10-year-old in Queens
> stood over the boy with his cop shoes in childish blood
> and a voice said "Die you little motherfucker" and
> there are tapes to prove that. At his trial
> this policeman said in his own defense
> "I didn't notice the size or nothing else
> only the color." and
> there are tapes to prove that, too.[6]

Equally as devastating is the aftermath of that incident in which a jury of eleven white men and one black woman found the policeman innocent of any crime. The woman said

> "They convinced me" meaning
> they had dragged her 4' 10" black woman's frame
> over the hot coals of four centuries of white male approval
> until she let go the first real power she ever had
> and lined her own womb with cement
> to make a graveyard for our children.[7]

The poem ends with the contrasting response to the murder of an elderly white woman by the black speaker. Lorde writes that a Greek chorus will be singing in 3/4 time "Poor thing. She never hurt a soul. What beasts they are." Listening to a recording of Lorde's voice chanting and crying with controlled rage, those of us who are *others* to this community begin to feel the devastation in the difference between "justice had been done" and "What beasts they are."[8] With her, we sense what she has elsewhere named

> the mysterious connection
> between whom we murder
> and whom we mourn?[9]

Acknowledging that I read these poems as one outside the cultural context in which they were formed, I also deny the kind of solipsism which makes one interpret other lives as if they were lived identically to one's own. Literature, perhaps more effectively than anything else, helps us get closer to those whose lives are unlike our own and to find points of commonality of the human spirit. Thus, I approach the poetry of these African-American women as I enter into all literary engagements, acknowledging both my need to recognize and appreciate differences of experience and perspective and the fact that I may not be able to fully understand or appreciate another's work. In the process, however, I ask of myself what I ask of my students—an honest effort to navigate landscapes that differ from those we know best and to learn from the experience.

ON VOICE

One of the recurring themes in various approaches to feminist criticism is the concept of "voice." In a world in which women are considered "others," that is, outside of and defined by their differences from the norms of male society, strong female voices have been silenced or suppressed. Feminist scholars in all fields speak of finding their own authentic voices beneath the layers of male socialization. Young people too are engaged in the task of finding their own voices in a world dominated by adults, and this is especially difficult for young women who are constantly bombarded by images in the popular culture which portray females as objects rather than as subjects. Some of the discussions of female voice or voices, however, may in themselves silence women. The assumption that there is one authentic female voice or that each woman has only one authentic voice limits full human potential. bell hooks, feminist author and critic, tells of writing in both standard English and in black dialect and of the reaction of others who felt that the dialect must be her true authentic voice.[10] Are our expectations for young people also narrow and restrictive at a time when they should be encouraged to try out many voices? Are teachers and librarians too willing to pigeonhole youngsters according to gender, age, grade, class, reading level, ethnicity, or sociological or educational labels? The poetry of African-American women can speak to all regardless of these distinctions. All young people have, at one time or another, shared with these poets the self-denial of having to speak in the voices that dominate them in order to be heard.

In spite of their unique voices, there are some common characteristics of many African-American poets, threads of which can be
traced through the work of Lucy Terry and Phillis Wheatley to that of
Patricia Smith and Rita Dove. Some of these characteristics are not
gender-specific, that is, they are found in poetry of African-American
males as well as females. Many poets have incorporated aspects of the
oral traditions of African and African-American culture in their work.
At times, readers can almost hear African drum rhythms or the field
shouts or hollers with their choruses of response. The influence of
slave narratives with their religious overtones and double-entendres,
the sounds of spirituals and of sermons and later the blues, jazz, and
black urban speech are genderless and evident throughout the whole
history of African-American poetry. So too is the tradition of storytelling with a richness of language, often combining dialect or non-
standard English with more formal, even classical, language and forms
to create fresh images and a kind of immediacy that draws readers into
the work. Allusions to African and African-American culture and to
both historical and contemporary events are often very important.

The above characteristics are very much in evidence in the work
of African-American women poets, but these women also share some
additional commonalities. Their histories and the stories they tell differ
somewhat from those of their male counterparts. Their endurance of
slavery included at least the threat, if not the actuality, of sexual as well
as other forms of physical domination by their white masters. Some of
them also tolerated domination and brutalization by their own men who
exerted the power denied them in the outside world in their own homes.
Thus, these female voices became primal screams protesting both the
literal and metaphoric rapes they endured. Alternatively, their female
perspectives lead to a focus on the daily events of home, family, or
children, on the rituals of everyday life, and on the quietly resigned yet
proud and rebellious strength of their mothers. Some African-American women, especially those writing during the first half of this century, have been so intent on regaining or reclaiming the voices of these
mothers of the race that their voices were, in some sense, more collective than individual. Alice Walker reveals that this affinity with the
collective consciousness of African-American women is still present in
contemporary writers when she says "By 'herself' she of course meant
multitudes, of which she was at any given time in history a mere representative."[11] More recently, many poets have looked back to Sojourner

Truth's cry "Ain't I A Woman?" with emphasis on the *I*. While recognizing and appreciating their forebearers, each is affirming herself, declaring her own uniqueness and her own special vision of the world. This has been, at least in part, the difference between African-American and white feminists. From the beginning, white feminists have been declaring their liberation from various gender bindings while African-American women were necessarily more concerned with survival than liberation—their own personal survival and that of their mothers and daughters in a world in which they were oppressed by racial and economic barriers as well as gender.[12]

Those familiar with African-American poetry will recognize a variation of these words of Countee Cullen in the title of this chapter:

> Yet do I marvel at this curious thing:
> To make a poet black, and bid him sing![13]

If it is a curious thing to bid *him* sing, how much more curious it is to bid *her* sing. Many African-American women have reported that they suffer from a kind of double jeopardy or dual discrimination and domination, that of both race and gender from those outside their culture and of gender from those within African-American society. Working-class women of color may be the most oppressed of all peoples. Their voices have been silenced for generations; but throughout history some African-American women have overcome social and economic barriers to make themselves heard. Through poetry, African-American women have preserved the voices of those who were not heard, have maintained the identities of those whose humanity was ignored or denied and have spoken the unspeakable about their lives.

EARLY VOICES—WHISPERED MESSAGES

Probably the first known African-American woman poet was Lucy Terry (1730–1821) who, at age 16, wrote about an Indian raid on Deerfield, Massachusetts in 1746.[14] More familiar is Phillis Wheatley (ca. 1735–1784), the 18th century slave who was one of the best-known poets of her time. She was not only the first female African-American to have a book of poetry published in America, but the only female poet published in this country since Anne Bradstreet a century earlier.[15] Wheatley was treated as somewhat of a *pet* of the cultured white society of her day who admired her scholarly use of classical poetic forms without acknowledging the subtle sub-texts of the concerns of women and children, even African-American women and children.

The concept of *voice* is particularly interesting in regard to Wheatley and other early poets discussed in this chapter. Wheatley was educated in white, male, European traditions of poetry by those who purchased her as a slave and produced work that was similar in both subject and style to what she had studied. Thus, she celebrated or eulogized prominent religious or political leaders who could not even fully acknowledge her existence as a human being. She also, however, celebrated the talent of a young African painter calling him a "wond'rous youth," perhaps the first time that the young man was openly called Sapio Moorhead, painter, rather than some white owner's *boy*.[16] In addition, her deferential tributes to those considered her betters often contained subtexts expressing her feelings about her own fate as a slave as in these lines hidden within "To the Right Honorable William, Earl of Dartmouth, His Majesty's Principal Secretary of State for North America, etc.,"

> I, young in life, by seeming cruel of fate
> Was snatch'd from Afric's fancy'd happy seat.
> What pangs excruciating most molest
> What sorrows labour in my parent's breast?
> Steel'd was that soul and by no misery mov'd
> That from a father seized his babe belov'd
> Such, such my case. And can I then but pray
> Others may never feel tyrannic sway?[17]

These lines written in 1772, prior to this country's own war for freedom, expressed for Wheatley and for her readers "from whence my love of Freedom sprung." This love of freedom and a search for a place to belong in an often alien culture are themes that have persisted through two centuries of African-American women's poetry. Wheatley, and other African-American poets of her time, wrote *for* and *to* an audience of white oppressors. This was natural because, from the age of seven, Wheatley was included in the dual worlds of slavery and white literate society. In the 19th century when it became illegal for slaves to learn to read and write, African-American poetry could no longer be published for white audiences. Therefore, the content shifted to the concerns of the oppressed culture in which these poets existed. It is interesting to note that of these early poets, it is only Wheatley's poetry that is included in the canon presented to young adults,[18] perhaps because we, as a society, are still not ready to receive the messages African-American women shared with each other.

Sojourner Truth's (1797–1883) "Ain't I A Woman?" speech at the Akron, Ohio Women's Rights Convention in 1852 has been adapted into poetic form by Erlene Stetson, and its title remains a rallying cry for oppressed women everywhere.[19] Mid-19th century novelist Frances E.W. Harper (1825–1911), published nine volumes of poetry and spoke strongly for the freedom of African-Americans.[20] Harper employed a variety of poetic forms and subjects, but one of her consistent themes was that of woman as rebel. Her strong Christian consciousness led her to appeal to her white religious sisters to protest the treatment of slaves:

> When ye plead for the wrecked and fallen,
>   The exile from far-distant shores,
> Remember that men are still wasting
>   Life's crimson around your own doors.
>
> Have ye not, oh, my favored sisters,
>   Just a plea, a prayer or a tear,
> For mothers who dwell 'neath the shadows
>   Of agony, hatred and fear?[21]

Contemporary young women will still recognize what, even in Harper's day, was "A Double Standard."

> Crime has no sex and yet today
>   I wear the brand of shame;
> Whilst he amid the gay and proud
>   Still bears an honored name.
>
> Can you blame me if I've learned to think
>   Your hate of vice a sham,
> When you so coldly crushed me down,
>   And then excused the man?[22]

One of the next African-American woman to publish a volume of poetry was Georgia Douglas Johnson (1886–1966), whose *The Heart of a Woman and Other Poems* appeared in 1918.[23] This was the first of three volumes of poetry representing three stages of a woman's life—youth, motherhood, and age. Works such as the title poem and "My Little Dreams" still speak to young women of all races and cultures. Between Harper and Johnson, poems of other female African-Americans such as Angelina Weld Grimké (1880–1958), and Anne Spencer (1882–1975), were published in anthologies, but they produced no individual volumes of poetry. Grimké was one of our earliest lesbian poets,[24] and Spencer was a Black Seminole Indian. Jessie Fauset (1888–1961), a much anthologized poet, was widely read during the Harlem Renaissance of the 1920s along with her contemporary Georgia Douglas Johnson.[25] Fauset's poem "Touché,"[26] in which a young woman forgives her lover for speaking of *gold locks* while touching her black hair because of her memories of her own first dream lover and the "Blue eyes he had and such waving gold hair!" reminds one of Whoopi Goldberg's tragic-comic routine of the young girl with the long blond wig, of Toni Morrison's *The Bluest Eye* and of Patricia Smith's "Blonde White Women."[27]

Although the language and conventions of much of this 18th, 19th, and early 20th century poetry may not speak to contemporary young adults, some of it cries out with the urgency of life in those times. It is important to trace the roots of African-American female poetry for its own sake, but this work may also help young people place historical events in context. For example, along with contemporary accounts of slavery in the last century, students should hear the words of Frances E.W. Harper who lived during that time describing "The Slave Auction."

> And mothers stood with streaming eyes,
>   And saw their dearest children sold;
> Unheeded rose their bitter cries,
>   While tyrants bartered them for gold.[28]

A POWERFUL DUALITY OF VOICE

The work of Gwendolyn Brooks (1917–), is pivotal in any discussion of African-American women's poetry. Not only was she the first African-American (male or female) to win the Pulitzer Prize and the first African-American woman to be widely recognized for her poetry, Brooks' own evolution as a poet mirrored major changes in African-American art and social consciousness. Her first volume of poetry, *A Street in Bronzeville* published in 1945, revealed keen observational skills and an ear for the vernacular speech of everyday life. Her skillful combination of formal poetic conventions and the idioms and emotions of the poor people of Harlem emphasize the differences between two worlds. Her consciousness of a sense of community among those entrapped by racial and economic barriers seems to be the beginning of a search for African-American identity in spite of her integrationist philosophy and belief in the commonality of human experience.

Surely one of the most powerful poems from *A Street in Bronzeville* is "The Mother," the first two lines of which hint at its impact for contemporary youth.

> Abortions will not let you forget.
> You remember the children you got that you did not get,[29]

Annie Allen, A Ballad of Chicago Negro Life (1949) was Brooks' second volume of poetry and the one for which she won the 1950 Pulitzer Prize. In this three-part story of Annie Allen's life, from childhood to adolescence to womanhood, she experiments with a number of stylistic devices within the conventional form of the ballad to bring both an immediacy and a larger symbolic meaning to a woman's life. Unfortunately, the segment in which the adolescent girl becomes painfully aware of society's harsh treatment of African-Americans is based on the *Aeneid* and requires a knowledge of Virgil to be fully comprehended and is thus out-of-reach for many young people. The critical acclaim awarded this poetry, although celebrated by the African-American artistic community, did not protect it from the charge of being so intellectualized that it was remote from those whose lives it depicts.

Bronzeville Boys and Girls (1955) and *The Bean Eaters* (1960) brought Brooks back to the simpler language, rhythms and musical inflections which make her work accessible to a wider audience, including young people. *Bronzeville Boys and Girls* is intended for children, although its short, powerfully emotional verses may have an even greater impact on young adult and adult readers looking back at childhood. "We Real Cool" is probably the best known poem from *The Bean Eaters* and has for more than three decades spoken very directly to young people and has even been credited with preventing a number of them from joining the subjects of the poem who say "We left school." It is in this volume that one finds the beginnings of the poet's focus on civil rights and black identity.

The year 1967 was a turning point in Gwen Brooks' life and in her work. After enthusiastic, almost adoring receptions, from white middle-class audiences, she went to Fisk University where she encountered an energized group of new black writers led by Le Roi Jones (later Amiri Baraka) who acknowledged her only with a kind of cold respect. She called these new black brothers "tall walkers" and was greatly influenced by them and their work, causing her to rethink her own relationship with her people and her role as a black artist.

Although Brooks had been working on *In the Mecca* for some time, it was finally published in 1968 and is generally considered the volume in which she began to write *to* and *for* blacks rather than *about* them. Not only did the influence of the civil rights and black arts movements lead to a heightened racial consciousness, the structures of her poetry opened up to include greater use of free verse. Mecca is a tenement from which a variety of voices are heard, often through moving portraits of strong black women who live there. The primary voice is that of Mrs. Sallie Smith, who is searching the building for Pepita, one of her nine children, finally revealed to have been murdered. Sallie's other children who "ain seen her" personalize the effects of poverty on young people as they express their hate for symbols of wealth, such as a lace handkerchief, and for those who possess those symbols while, contrarily, they express their affinity for roaches and rats. The aborted search for Pepita itself symbolizes the difficulty of the search for self-discovery and for connections with others in the midst of such poverty.

In 1969, Brooks severed her relationship with Harper & Row which had published all of her books because she wanted to associate herself with the new black presses. After the assassination of Martin Luther King, Jr., there was a change in both the subjects and the style of her work, with a greater sense of immediacy and defiance expressed in freer verse forms. Even the title *Riot* (1969), her first book published by Broadside Press, expresses such change. *Family Pictures* (1970) evokes the same kinds of pleasure and pain that comes from looking through an old photo album. One of the best-known and most powerful images from those pages is that of young Lincoln West who was so ugly that even his family rejected him. Ironically it was only when a white man called him "the real thing" that he was able to think of himself as someone special in spite of the speaker's intent.

> Black, ugly, and odd. You
> can see the savagery. The blunt
> blankness. That is the real
> thing.[30]

Even more poignant is Brooks' ability to enter the mind of young Lincoln West when she ends the poem with

> When he was hurt, too much
> stared at—
> too much
> left alone—he
> thought about that. He told himself
> "After all, I'm
> the real thing."
>
> It comforted him.[31]

The *comfort* Lincoln takes from this negative statement exemplifies the kinds of distortions and reversals of reality that have enabled oppressed peoples to survive in harsh and alien environments. Such subversions of reality are evident in much of Brooks' work and in other African-American poetry.

Brooks continued to publish with, and thus lend her considerable support to, black presses from 1969 on. In 1981, *to disembark* which includes *Riot*, *Family Pictures*, and *Becomings*, all originally published by Broadside Press, plus *Boys Black* from *Ebony* magazine was released by Third World Press. During these years, she had also been actively involved in helping young writers develop their art. She conducted workshops for a Chicago street gang, offered prizes for schools and endowed the George Kent Awards which were first presented to Mari Evans and Sonia Sanchez in 1987. Brooks' life work as a poet has been a rich combination of superbly mastered classical forms and the urgency of the lives of poor, urban African-Americans. From the formal sonnet to fractured folk speech, her words have captured the lives, the hopes, the despair, and the aspirations of the disenfranchised in American society.

FAMILY VOICES AND PRAISE OF BLACK MEN

Naomi Long Madgett (1923–), teacher, publisher, and poet, has produced seven volumes of her own poetry and edited another collection of African-American women poets. She is best known for her lyric verses of personal and family life. Her *One and The Many* contains poetry about Madgett's teenage years through her marriage and divorce. "Sarah Street (St. Louis)" tells of her joy in moving from a racist high school in New Jersey to an all-black school in Missouri. Perhaps her most popular poem is one that became almost a battle cry of the civil rights movement but was often not attributed to its author. In "Midway," the universal African-American narrator says "I've prayed and slaved and waited and I've sung my song. You've bled me and you've starved me but I've still grown strong."[32] *Octavia and Other Poems* is probably the volume of Madgett's own poetry that is most appealing to young adults. In fact, this was the first book of poetry to be "required" reading in Detroit high schools. Most of this collection is a celebration of the poet's own family during the early part of the century, often in the form of free verse letters from parents to children. These poetry letters reveal the struggles they faced as in this poem from mother to son.

> I long to see the day I can rest.
> I have worked and worked till now
> I am just worked down and played out,
> but how can I bear to see my children
> have to take a back seat and come up short.[33]

The appendix, including photographs, a family tree, and brief biographies, adds to the interest in those depicted in the poems. There is a tone of genteel resignation with which these characters speak of their lives that today's young adults may not want to accept; nonetheless, the poems speak to young African-Americans of the history of their own families. The everyday exchanges about daily life are at times punctuated by the beauty of a lyrical reflection as in "Desert Song."

> Years in the desert have left me thirsty
> and alone. No oasis calls me. My mouth is full
> of the taste of sand. I am convinced I will die
> of dehydrated dreams.[34]

Madgett made a significant contribution to African-American women's poetry when, to celebrate the twentieth anniversary of Lotus Press, she collected new poems from fifty-five poets for *Adam of Ifé: Black Women in Praise of Black Men.* These positive images of strong African-American males, although written by women, are especially important for young African-American men to hear. Many of these poets are younger or relatively unknown; therefore, this is an excellent collection to introduce newer poets as well as to present positive images of African-American men. Dr. Pinkie Gordon Lane, Poet Laureate of the state of Louisiana, speaks of her brother.

> His drums
> beat a vocal message
> He "gigs" his way into
> his own world and circles
> angels, devils, with African
> telecommunications in this
> modern idiom.[35]

Or listen to Abimbola Adama tell African-American men "Don't Listen."

> From Africa to Indian land they tried
> to convince you that you
> were not all right
> not worthy
> and they
> were
> Do not listen to their lies
> for they are skilled and well versed
> in unthinkable deception[36]

VOICES OF SLAVE WOMEN

Dolores Kendrick's (1927–) *The Women of Plums: Poems in the Voices of Slave Women* gives human faces and feelings to often anonymous slave lives. The opening poem "To Market, to Market," subtitled "Arthur Mason's Shopping List, November 6, 1804," is powerful in its inclusion of "one nigger wench & child" among the list of hogs, a cow, and cups and saucers.[37] In the poems that follow, we hear the many voices of slave women, torn from their own land or born into bondage in this country, who cry for husbands and lovers and children separated from them, for food for their babies, for escape from the brutality and sexual advances of their masters or for freedom. At the same time their voices resound with echoes of the spirit of survival in impossible situations and of faith in a better world to come, if not on earth then in heaven. Kendrick uses an alternating internal and external voice in "Hattie on the Block" in which she ends with "we be sold, but we ain't bought." When Hattie is speaking to her child rather than to her inner self, her words are printed in plain text.

> Still, Carrie, be still, child. Don't cry,
>   don't let them see you cry, honey,
> there's a victory in that. Keep the tears
>   inward, outta they sight.
>
> . . .
> Evil be pretty sometimes, don't it?
>
> Money look good, even if it be for your soul.[38]

Kendrick uses italics for Harriet's inner voice as she begins the silent prayer to not be separated from her child Carrie.

> *Souls cain't be bought.*
> *I won't be of much use to anybody*
> *who buys me without my Carrie here.*
> *I be crippled, needin' crutches: who gonna*
> *pay for them? Or will I have to work*
> *the fields limpin' about with my mind*
> *catchin' butterflies, when I should be*
> *pickin' cotton, 'cause my soul be amputated*
> *when you bought me without my Carrie*
> *for a few dollars cheaper?*[39]

This collection would be especially useful in connection with reading slave narratives and modern versions of them such as Mary Lyons' telling of the Harriet Jacobs story.[40]

A UNIFYING & UNIVERSAL VOICE

The multi-talented Maya Angelou (1928–), best known for her autobiographical novels beginning with *I Know Why the Caged Bird*

Sings,[41] suffered a self-imposed silence for more than five years of her youth. In part, it was poetry that gave her back her voice; and now her own poetry is heard from such unlikely sources as the character played by Janet Jackson in the John Singleton film *Poetic Justice*, in the song "Take Time" written for Roberta Flack, and, most powerfully, in her own voice at the inauguration of President William Clinton on January 20, 1993. This inaugural poem, "On the Pulse of Morning" uses images of the rock, the river, and the tree from African-American spirituals to present a poetic vision of this nation grounded in faith yet "perpetually under siege."[42] Much of this poem is a calling of names of all the peoples who make up this great country and, by naming them, she gives them prominence in our history. Angelou tells all those who have been dominated that

> History, despite its wrenching pain,
> Cannot be unlived, but if faced
> With courage, need not be lived again.[43]

The poem ends even more optimistically.

> Here on the pulse of this new day
> You may have the grace to look up and out
> And into your sister's eyes,
> And into your brother's face,
> Your country,
> And say simply
> Very simply
> With hope–
> Good morning.[44]

If young people are asked to study this poem, as they undoubtedly will be, they should begin by listening to Angelou's tape on which she sings portions of the spirituals from which she took her inspiration before making the words of the poem come alive in the majesty and the melody of her voice.[45] Her naming of all the groups of people, even those ". . . bought/Sold, stolen, arriving on a nightmare/ Praying for a dream," lovingly includes them in the tapestry that is the United States.

In a much earlier poem, "The Calling of Names," Angelou emphasizes the importance of names as a source of identity by tracing African-American names from "nigger" to "colored" to "Negro" to "Black."[46] She also names specific historical figures in "Our Grandmothers," a tribute to African-American women throughout United States history.

> These momma faces, lemon-yellow, plum-purple,
> honey-brown, have grimaced and twisted
> down a pyramid of years.
> She is Sheba and Sojourner,
>   Harriet and Zora,
>   Mary Bethune and Angela,
>   Annie to Zenobia.[47]

This poem ends with the line from the spiritual referred to in "On the Pulse of Morning" and also used as the title of this most recent volume of her poetry—*I Shall Not Be Moved.* The final poem in this volume is entitled a series of names, "Ailey, Baldwin, Floyd, Killens, and Mayfield," and speaks of the power of great souls on the lives of others.

> And when great souls die,
> after a period peace blooms,
> slowly and always .
> irregularly. Spaces fill
> with a kind of
> soothing electric vibration.
> Our senses, restored, never
> to be the same, whisper to us.
> They existed. They existed.
> We can be. Be and be
> better. For they existed.[48]

This is the message of much of Angelou's work. In her poetry, as well as her autobiographical writings, she uses images and events both from her own life and from the history of humankind to give shape to universal experiences. In "Human Family" she writes

> I note the obvious differences
> between each sort and type,
> but we are more alike, my friends,
> than we are unalike.[49]

Although her poetry is not as well known as her novels, both her political and personal poems provide insight into emotions touched upon elsewhere in her work. What could be a more apt introduction to

I Know Why the Caged Bird Sings than the poem "Caged Bird" which compares the life of a free bird with that of a captive.

> But a caged bird stands on the grave of dreams
> his shadow shouts on a nightmare scream
> his wings are clipped and his feet are tied
> so he opens his throat to sing.

> The caged bird sings
> with a fearful trill
> of things unknown
> but longed for still
> and his tune is heard
> on the distant hill
> for the caged bird
> sings of freedom.[50]

THE COSMOPOLITAN WARRIOR VOICE

Audre Lorde (1934–1992) frequently introduced herself as an African-Caribbean American warrior feminist poet or as a black, lesbian mother in an interracial marriage; and much of her poetry addresses the reconciliation and indivisibility of these several selves. She was also a teacher, a librarian, and a political activist on the international scene. Above all else, however, she was a poet who left behind a powerful legacy of words and images that continue to haunt and ennoble readers. As a woman who defined herself in all of these ways, Lorde was constantly denying racial and sexual stereotypes from within and without the African-American community. In a preliminary note to *Chosen Poems—Old and New*, she writes, "Here are the words of some of the women I have been, am being still, will come to be. The time surrounding each poem is an unspoken image."[51] Her earliest published poetry, written when she was a teenager, was much more subdued and conventional, both in substance and in style, then the later fierce, sometimes explosive, voice which often personalized political realities.

In one of her early poems, Lorde wrote:

> and I am trying to speak
> without art or embellishment
> with bits of me flying out in all directions

```
screams    memories    old pieces of pain
struck off like dry bark
from a felled tree[52]
```

From 1961, the year this poem was written and also the year she earned her MLS from Columbia University and when Langston Hughes accepted several of her poems for *New Negro Poets, USA*, until 1992 when she finally lost a long battle with cancer, Lorde's voice did indeed speak more and more forcefully about all the things she cared about so passionately. Lorde was not only a poet, she was one of the first and most influential black feminists. In a presentation entitled "The Master's Tools Will Never Dismantle the Master's House," she said.

> Women of today are still being called upon to stretch across the gap of male ignorance and to educate men as to our existence and our needs. This is an old and primary tool of all oppressors to keep the oppressed occupied with the master's concerns. Now we hear that it is the task of women of Color to educate white women—in the face of tremendous resistance—as to our existence, our differences, our relative roles in our joint survival. This is a diversion of energies and a tragic repetition of racist patriarchal thought.[53]

One of the recurring images in Lorde's poetry is that of the mirror. Sometimes the speaker is invisible, casting no image, but at other times she sees the various personas she presents to the world, many of which are those of the outsider.

> There is a timbre of voice
> that comes from not being heard
> and knowing   you are not being
> heard   noticed only
> by others   not heard
> for the same reason.[54]

Even when she felt she was not heard, however, Lorde continued to write because

> For women, then, poetry is not a luxury. It is a vital necessity of our existence. It forms the quality of the light within which we

predicate our hopes and dreams toward survival and change, first made into language, then into ideas, then into more tangible action: Poetry is the way we help give name to the nameless so it can be thought. The farthest horizons of our hopes and fears are cobbled by our poems, carved from the rock experiences of our daily lives.[55]

For Lorde,

Being a poet is not merely a question of producing poems. Being a poet means that I have a certain way of looking at the world, involving myself in the community around me. I am committed to work, and I see myself as a poet moving through all of the things that I do.[56]

One world she looked at, and helped others see more clearly, was the world of home, family and love surviving against almost impossible odds in hostile urban landscapes laden with both racial and sexual oppression. She also draws her readers into the larger global community, especially the community of women of color throughout the world. Always her vision is unblinking, in spite of pain, rage, and disbelief at humanity's capacity for inhumanity, but her anguish and private fury are not futile. She puts a personal face on political atrocities saying

Be who you are and will be
learn to cherish
that boisterous Black Angel that drives you
up one day and down another
protecting the place where your power rises
running like hot blood
from the same source
as your pain.[57]

The life that Lorde portrayed in her poetry was not an easy one. Her voice spoke out against injustices of all kinds. There is a harshness in these poems and very little humor, but there is always hope.

But I who am bound by my mirror
as well as my bed
see cause in color
as well as sex.

and sit here wondering
which me will survive
all these liberations.[58]

Lorde was taken from the world too soon, never really having had time to survive all these liberations, but she left behind a repertoire of fresh and impassioned poems that will continue to inspire others to fight for their own liberation.

A REVOLUTIONARY VOICE

Sonia Sanchez (1934–) has often been called a poet of the revolution; and, indeed, many of her poems literally scream of injustice and militancy. It is also true, however, that she has written sensitive love poems and powerfully-packed personal haiku and tanka. In her first book, *Home Coming*, she celebrates Malcolm X and chastises the Supremes. Of the former, she says

yet this man
this dreamer,
thick-lipped with words
will never speak again
and in each winter
when the cold air cracks
with frost, i'll breathe
his breath and mourn
my gun-filled nights.[59]

Her poem about the Supremes is entitled "Memorial"

—cuz they dead. . .
the supremes
done gone
and bleached out
their blk/ness[60]

As in the work of many contemporary poets, particularly those who had their aesthetic birthing during the militant 1960s, Sanchez's poems often include language that may be offensive to some readers or listeners with common four letter words, sexually explicit images and racial epithets used most often to counter what they represent in the lives of her people. In "Nigger," for instance, she attacks that label directly.

> nigger.
> that word
> ain't shit to me
> man . . . .
> i know i am
> black.
> beautiful.[61]

In his introduction to one of her most belligerent collections of poems, Dudley Randell writes of her:

> This tiny woman with the infant's face attacks the demons of this world with the fury of a sparrow defending her fledglings in the nest. She hurls obscenities at things that are obscene. She writes directly, ignoring metaphors, similes, ambiguity, and other poetic devices. But her bare passionate speech can be very effective.[62]

The title poem, "we a baddDDD people (for gwendolyn brooks/ a fo real bad one)" uses some obscene language, but is really a kind of morality tale calling for

> . . . discipline
> of the mind.
> soul. body.   no drinken cept to celebrate
> our victories / births.
>   no smoken.   no shooten
> needles into our blk / veins
>   full of potential blk/
> gold cuz our
>   high must come from
>   thinking working
>   planning fighting loving
>   our blk / selves
>   into nationhood.[63]

A Blues Book for Blue Black Magical Women is a song of praise for generations of African-American women. At the time of its writing, she was a member of the Nation of Islam, and that philosophy is evident here, but it does not overpower the poetry. There is joy in her poem "women."

> rise up earth mother
> out of rope-strung-trees
> dancing a windless dance
> come phantom mother
> dance me a breakfast of births
> let your mouth spill me forth
> so i creak with your mornings.
> come old mother, light up my mind
> with a story bright as the sun.[64]

Some of the most powerful works in *homegirls & handgrenades* are long prose-poems, often portraits of women. In "Just Don't Never Give Up on Love," an old woman sharing a park bench tells the poet of her past loves and at the end "We hugged; then she walked her 84-year-old walk down the street. A black woman. Echoing gold. Carrying couplets from the sky to crease the ground."[65]

"Norma," who had been a "genius" in math and languages until she became pregnant and left school, is encountered on a city street.

> I heard her hello. Her voice was like stale music in barrooms. There she stood. Norma. Eyelids heavy. Woman of four children, with tracks running on her legs and arms.
>
> . . .
>
> Tongue-tied by time and drugs, she smiled a funny smile and introduced me to her girls. Four beautiful girls. Norma predicted that they would make it. They wouldn't be like their mother. They would begin with a single step, then they would jump mountains.[66]

A QUIET CELEBRATORY VOICE

Lucille Clifton (1936–) is probably best-known as a creator of children's books, but she is also a poet of extraordinary talent. Like Gwen Brooks and Audre Lorde, Clifton writes of the everyday experiences of African-American life, but her voice is quieter than those of most of her contemporaries. Although she presents brutally honest portrayals of the harsh realities of life, her work is a celebration of the spirit that allows ordinary people to survive in the most difficult circumstances. She focuses on individual human beings, often presenting brief portraits or character sketches of those who find optimism, even heroism, amidst the small tragedies of living.

Clifton's poetry is accessible to the people about whom she writes. She uses simple, economical language and concrete symbols to force readers to consider big ideas. Thus, there is a complexity in simplicity, a strong and introspective female voice that whispers truths that resound loudly in the minds and hearts of her readers.

Not all of Clifton's characters are heroic. As in the poems of many of these African-American women, it is primarily the men who lack the resiliency to triumph over tragedy. In her first book, for instance, we meet Robert who

> was born obedient
> without questions
>
> . . .
> until he died
> the color of his life
> was nigger.[67]

On the other hand, women take strength from their foremothers

> . . . I got a long memory
> and I come from a line
> of black and going on women
> who got used to making it through murdered sons[68]

And, with perhaps an ironic look at self, the final lines of this volume speak to the children of a poet.

> children
> when they ask you
> why is your mama so funny
> say
> she is a poet
> she don't have no sense[69]

Good News About the Earth, Clifton's second book of poetry combines poems about the years of the author's childhood, current events from the 1960s and 1970s, and poems with Biblical references. Once again we read of the young African-American girl "trying to be white."

I walked out quietly
mornings
in the '40s
a nice girl
not touching
trying to be white[70]

Poems about Kent State, Bobby Seale, Robert Penniman, and other people and events remind older readers of those times and could be used in studies of African-American history, but young readers may otherwise find them time-bound.

an ordinary woman is truly a celebration of the strength of and bonds between women. Clifton writes of the poet "tap dancing for my life"[71] and of her grandmother Lucille who "shot the whiteman off his horse/killing the killer of sons."[72] and even of the triumphant killing of roaches with mama until

. . . they fell
dying onto our shoulders, in our hair

. . .

and we were glad, such cleanliness was grace[73]

This book ends with the statement of an almost universal truth, one with which all women who have reached a certain age can identify. In her thirty-eighth year, the poet reflects upon her life and concludes

i had expected more than this.
i had not expected to be
an ordinary woman.[74]

Two-Headed Woman speaks of Clifton's maturation as a woman and as a poet and of her religious faith. She sings of the "green girl/ in a used poet"[75] and pays homage to her nappy hair which "the greyer she do get, good God,/ the Blacker she do be!"[76] These and many other references to the young girl still alive behind even a grandma face may help contemporary young adults bridge the gap between generations in their own families. *Next* continues to sing of Clifton's own family and her own dreams but also comments poignantly on the problems of the human family throughout the world. Referring to, among others the young people of Buchenwald, Vietnam, Johannesburg, Nagasaki, she writes:

for all that remains of the children,
their eyes,
staring at us,   amazed to see
the extraordinary evil in
ordinary men.[77]

Clifton's latest book of poetry, *The Book of Light*, continues her conversations with God, with various Biblical characters, and with Atlas who "learned to carry it/ the way a poor man learns to carry everything."[78] She also writes both to Superman and to Clark Kent, once again cutting larger than life figures down to human proportions, "not wonder woman and not superman."[79] And, as always, she writes of family and self, inviting readers:

won't you celebrate with me
what I have shaped into
a kind of life? i had no model.
born in babylon
both nonwhite and woman
what did i see to be except myself?
i made it up[80]

Young people reading Clifton's poems will find inspiration, endurance, simple pleasures, joy amidst adversity, and the confidence to make up their own lives.

THE EXPLOSIVE PERFORMER

Ntozake Shange (1948-) writes poems that are expressive and explosive, that shout and cry in their evocation of the life of an African-American woman in contemporary society. Her impassioned portrayals of the joys and sorrows of women's lives capture events and emotions in language that sometimes risks offending traditional white, western sensibilities. This language, however, is a perfect match for the stories told and emotions felt; and her unconventional spelling and punctuation reflect the sounds of human voices responding to the full range of lived experiences. Be-bop and jazz rhythms come alive in the musical beats of Shange's language. Even the placement of words on the page sometimes gives the impression of the letters and words of her poems dancing to that beat on the page. She expresses it best herself.

i live in music
     live in it
          wash in it
i cd even smell it
wear sound on my fingers
sound falls   so fulla music
ya cd make a river where yr arm is &
hold yrself
          hold yrself in a music[81]

In *for colored girls . . .*, she says "& poem is my thank-you for music."[82]

There is also controlled rage in many of Shange's poems, calling attention to the violence, violation, and oppression endured by her characters. This begins with the disappointments or rejections of a young girl who "knew I waznt sposedta/ but i ran inta the ADULT READING ROOM. . ."

TOUSSAINT L'OUVERTURE
waz the beginnin uv reality for me
in the summer contest for
who colored child can read
15 books in three weeks
i won & raved abt TOUSSAINT L'OUVERTURE
at the afternoon ceremony
waz disqualified
        cuz Toussaint
               belonged in the ADULT READING ROOM
                 & i cried
& carried dead Toussaint home in the book[83]

Shange also reminds us that the reality of everyday life can enter the spirit and become an omnipresent fear.

every 3 minutes a woman is beaten
every five minutes a
woman is raped/ every ten minutes
a lil girl is molested
yet i rode the subway today
i sat next to an old man who
may have beaten his old wife
3 minutes ago or 3 days/ 30 years ago

he might have sodomized his
daughter but i sat there
cuz the young men on the train
might beat some young women
later in the day or tomorrow
i might not shut my door fast
enuf/ pushhard enuf[84]

Shange's rage is both personal and political, in response to the daily indignities or horrors of everyday life as well as to international horrors such as apartheid. On the other hand, in some of her poems there is also the pure, exuberant joy of a young child's playful spirit and her love for her mother.

mommy can i ask you something / please
mommy can i ask you something / mommy
do you love me / oh good i'm glad mommy
i love you mommy / mommy can i ask you something
mommy i just wanna ask you one more
thing / mommy can you fly?[85]

for colored girls who have considered suicide/ when the rainbow is enuf, probably Shange's best-known work, is a "choreopoem" in which seven women speak, dance, and sing of the harsh realities of their lives.[86] The beauty of the language of this poem somehow both releases and intensifies these experiences for readers or audience while the poem/play confirms the oneness of women as the characters recognize their strength in each other. Although the published version of this work speaks powerfully to readers, it is in the sounds, the movements, the timing and the beat of its performance that the voice of the author and characters resounds most clearly. The author was bitterly attacked for her portrayal of African-American men in this work, but it has continued to speak to all women, especially those whose voices have been silenced by the oppression of the men in their lives. Near the beginning of the play, the first speaker cries out to be heard and recognized and appreciated in a voice that speaks to all oppressed women who long to be "handled warmly,"

i can't hear anythin
but maddening screams
& the soft strains of death

& you promised me
you promised me . . .
somebody/ anybody
sing a black girl's song
bring her out
to know herself
to know you
but sing her rhythms
carin/ struggle/ hard times
sing her song of life
she's been dead so long
closed in silence so long
she doesn't know the sound
of her own voice
her infinite beauty
she's half-notes scattered
without rhythm/ no tune
sing her sighs
sing the song of her possibilities
sing a righteous gospel
let her be born
let her be born
& handled warmly.[87]

Shange is an intellectual as well as an emotional poet who uses literary, socio-political, and pop culture references which require readers to be aware of worlds outside the poems in order to fully appreciate the richness of the created worlds within. *A Daughter's Geography* opens with "Mood Indigo" which refers to her own life experience of growing up in an affluent African-American family that introduced her to "men who changed the world."

it hasnt always been this way
ellington was not a street
robeson no mere memory
du bois walked up my father's stairs
hummed some tune over me
sleeping in the company of men
who changed the world[88]

In most of that volume, however, the poet's voice is angry, strident and pained, as when she writes of the murders of children in Atlanta.

cuz he's black & poor   he's gone
took a bus/ never heard from again

but somebody heard a child screaming
        & went right on ahead
children disappearing/ somewhere in the woods/ decaying
just gone/ disappeared/ in atlanta[89]

There are more personal and equally devastating poems in *The Love Space Demands (a continuing saga)* as when "crack annie" who holds her daughter down for the rapist who will supply Annie with her drugs says:

                        my
daughter / & he swore he'd give me twenty-five
dollars & a whole fifty cent of crack /
whenever/ i wanted / but you know / i'm on the pipe /
& i don't have no new pussy / & what difference /
could it
make / i mean shit/ she caint get pregnant /
shit / she only seven years old[90]

AN URBAN SONGSTRESS

Patricia Smith (1955-) is a former journalist who uses her reporter's eyes and ears to capture the flavor of urban life. In *Big Towns, Big Talk* the characters she portrays come to life in dramatic monologues which the author often performs. The opening poem "Annie Pearl Smith Discovers Moonlight" begins

My mother, the sage of Aliceville, Alabama,
didn't believe that men had landed on the moon.
"They can do anything with cameras,"
she hissed to anyone and everyone who'd listen,[91]

Young readers will recognize the combination of exasperation and protective love for a parent who resists today's reality for the assurance of a world in which

Them stars, them planets ain't ours to mess with.
The Lord woulda showed Hisself if them men
done punched a hole in my heaven.[92]

Smith shares with many of her predecessors a memory of childhood in which

> I remember striving for that breathlessness,
> toddling my five-year-old black butt around
> with a dull gray mophead covering my
> nappy hair, wishing myself golden.[93]

She ends this poem, however, with the acknowledgement that such wishes are "treachery," saying "I can find no color darker, more beautiful, than I am."[94] The poems move from celebration to a kind of weary pensiveness as the speaker wonders if her white husband really understands how she feels as the owners of a truck stop stare and speculate about her in "Heartland."

> He studied with Robert Hayden, taught at the blackest
> College in one of America's blackest cities,
> understands glass ceilings and the politics of black rage,
> but has he ever worn his bones on the outside?[95]

Many of these poems are responses to current events from the incident of the man who drove his truck through the window of a crowded restaurant and then shot and killed twenty-seven people to a new regulation for claiming bodies in the Los Angeles coroner's office to the woman who burst into a California courtroom and shot the man about to stand trial for the rape of her daughter. Two of the most chilling poems in this collection are "Skinhead" who feels he was "born to make things right"[96] and "Chinese Cucumbers" in which the narrator searches for one more "cure" for AIDS for his lover who was "dying so loud you could hear it."[97]

In spite of the seriousness of Smith's poetry, there is also a bounce to it; here are the rhythms of jazz and Motown and rock and roll. Sometimes she even uses song lyrics to structure a poem as in "On the Street Where She Lives."[98] This is poetry that will speak to today's young people.

AN ELEGANT VOICE

Rita Dove (1952-) is the most celebrated of contemporary African-American female poets. In 1993, she became Poet Laureate of the United States, the youngest person and the first African-American to be so named. Earlier, in 1987, Dove won a Pulitzer Prize for *Thomas and Beulah*, a cycle of poems about a black couple in the Midwest from 1900 through the 1960s, loosely based on her grandparent's lives.[99] In the 1993 Introduction to her *Selected Poems* which includes *The Yellow House on the Corner* (1980), *Museum* (1983), and *Thomas and Beulah* (1986), the poet speaks of her childhood experiences as reader and writer.[100] She tells of pulling Shakespeare and other great writers from the family bookshelves at an early age.

> Of course I did not understand every single word, but I was too young to know that this was supposed to be difficult; besides, no one was waiting to test me on anything, so, free from pressure, I dove in.[101]

She also says that, as a young person, she

> didn't think of writing as an activity people admitted doing. I had no living role models—a "real" writer was a long-dead white male, usually with a white beard to match.[102]

Today Dove herself demonstrates to young adults that poets come in every age, gender, race, and ethnicity and that, if adults encourage them to read without the pressure of some form of testing, young people will find poetry that speaks very personally to them. They may discover that

Sometimes

> a word is found so right it trembles
> at the slightest explanation.
> You start out with one thing, end
> up with another, and nothing's
> like it used to be, not even the future.[103]

In most of her poetry, it is not the future, but the past, Dove writes about. *The Yellow House on the Corner* contains many poems about slavery and freedom; *Museum* provides fresh views of people and events from a European perspective and a reminder of the damage done to women treated as museum objects. She continues with explorations of personal history in the beautifully lyrical verses of *Grace Notes*.[104] With keen observations and compactfully powerful language, she combines the histories of ordinary people with the history of the

United States. In *Thomas and Beulah,* for instance, readers are presented with quietly compelling images of the joys and hardships of the lives of the protagonists from youth to courtship, marriage, children, grandchildren, and inevitably death. Their stories are portrayed against the backdrop of the Depression, World War II, Civil Rights, and the rise of Black Power. Using alternative points of view of husband and wife, the poet forces readers to look twice at events, yet she somehow maintains enough distance that the events ultimately speak for themselves. The chronology at the end of the volume will help young readers understand and place these poems in context. One might well read these poems along with a study of African-American history to get a sense of the impact of national events on the lives of those seemingly far removed and occupied with just going on with their own lives. It is, however, often the little images of everyday life such as "the screens unlatched/ to let in starlight"[105] or Beulah's need, like Virginia Woolf's, for a room of her own.

> She wanted a little room for thinking:
> but she saw diapers steaming on the line,
> a doll slumped behind the door.
>
> So she lugged a chair behind the garage
> to sit out the children's naps.
>
> . . .
>
> building a palace. Later
> that night when Thomas rolled over and
> lurched into her, she would open her eyes
> and think of the place that was hers
> for an hour—where
> she was nothing
> pure nothing, in the middle of the day.[106]

Many years later, her four daughters grown, Beulah's youngest tells her

> *Mother, we're Afro-Americans now!*
> What did she know about Africa?
> . . . Where she came from
> was the past[107]

This may have been a past where "*Each hurt swallowed / is a stone.*"[108] but it was also a past of love, endurance, strength, hope, and ultimately triumph.

Dove's insight, her sharply-focused woman's vision of events in everyday life, and the beauty of her language may signal a shift in African-American female poetry as dramatic as that reflected in the work of Gwendolyn Brooks in the 1960s. For three decades, most African-American poets have worked to free themselves from traditional Western poetic structures and have reached out to their audiences with language close to the speech of everyday life. Dove's poetry is more akin to Brooks' early work with its technical accomplishment and disciplined control. Perhaps her combination of knowledge, sophistication, and technical competence, along with the eyes, the ears, and the heart of a storyteller will enable Dove, like Brooks, to reach both scholarly and popular audiences and build bridges between them. Her work itself consistently bridges opposites, connecting male and female, young and old, black and white, the past and the present. Still a young poet, Rita Dove has much yet to say to all the peoples of the world.

CONCLUSION

The few extraordinary poets included in this chapter are merely representatives of the diversity and the range of African-American female voices in this country. The segments of the poems reprinted here can only hint at the power of the totalities of the particular poems and of the body of each poet's work. Since most of these poems were written from the 1960s to the 1980s, there are similarities among the unique personal voices because they reflect, to some degree, the social consciousness of the time in which they were written.

There was a shift of social consciousness in the 1960s from an African-American integrationist aesthetic to a separatist black or Afrocentric aesthetic. In the first, those who had been excluded from the white, male traditions of Western literature spoke of the commonality of all human experience; and, in the second, African-Americans excluded others to establish unique standards for literature expressing authentic experiences of their own lives. This shift is seen clearly in the changes within the work of Gwendolyn Brooks. After three decades of emphasis on free verse forms and harsh language expressing distinct African-American experiences, Rita Dove returns to an expression of the common ancestry of women of all races and times and writes of their lives in very disciplined and technically-polished language and forms. Perhaps we have now arrived at a time when audiences of all races can recognize and appreciate poetry that celebrates both our uniquenesses and our universal human condition.

There are many more talented African-American female poets whose work speaks to young people today. The names of some may already be known to this audience because they have also published stories or poems for children and young people.[109] Some of these poets, Mari Evans, Nikki Giovanni, and Alice Walker, for example, were obviously already well established as adult authors before they wrote for children and would be included in any list of key African-American or female literary figures. Other adult poets whose work may appeal to young adults should also be shared.[110] Although some of these are older, established poets found in libraries and reference tools, others are relatively new writers whose work is available only from small presses. We need to seek out these lesser-known works or challenge young people themselves to find them. In addition, we might locate the places in our communities where poets share their work with audiences to hear the living performances of poetry.

Each of these poets has written from her own personal experience as a woman and as an African-American. Sometimes the poems are reflections of a woman's life, sometimes of a racial identity, sometimes of an American consciousness, but often they get to the heart of the human community. Young people should be encouraged to read, listen, and respond to the widest possible range of human voices. The inclusion of African-American female poets is one of many important groups of songs in the larger human chorus.

Those brought up to believe that poetry is, by its very nature, about birds and flowers and sweetness and joy will find little that meets those expectations in the work quoted in this chapter. They will, on the other hand, find a great deal about love—not an ethereal romantic love, but the kind of tough love that cries out from oppression and pain to survival. The metaphors employed are more often those of the winters of despair than of the hopeful blossomings of spring. Yet there is hope. These poets find metaphoric meanings in the harshness of the real world or even in the obscenities of the very language that both oppresses them and sets them free. These are not happiness-bound, upbeat poems, but among them are examples both of the quiet caring of pure mother love and of a bawdy, devil-may-care, in-the-moment love of a woman for a man. Mostly, there is the duality of the African-American woman's experience that answers violence, death, and even the destruction of the soul with anger, rage, sometimes even violence in return. Ultimately, however, their voices are heard singing with hopefulness, with an uplifting spirituality and with inspiration that encourages their people to not just "keep on keeping on," but to celebrate their accomplishments both of the spirit and in the real world. As Mari Evans says, in contrast to the words of Countee Cullen,

Who
can be born black
and not
sing
the wonder of it
the joy
the
challenge

Who
can be born
black
and not exult! [111]

NOTES

1. There is currently a great deal of concern about the influence of what is called "gangster rap" on young people, particularly on African-American urban teens for whom rap may be the only poetry they hear. In addition to its advocacy of violence and drug use, gangster rap is degrading to women. Young teens, however, are caught up in the sounds and say this rap "tells it like it is" for those growing up poor and black in US cities. See, for example John Leland, "Criminal Records: Gangster Rap and the Culture of Violence," *Newsweek* 112 (November 29, 1993): 60–64.

2. A good example of this is the recording of Maya Angelou reading her Inaugural poem, *On the Pulse of Morning* which adds a dimension not revealed in the printed text. Author/illustrator Ashley Bryan speaks of this need to hear poetry in a videotape interview during which he also reads poetry of other African-American poets as well as some of his own. *Meet Ashley Bryan: Storyteller, Artist, Writer* (American School Publishers, 1991), videocassette. Listening to poets Nikki Giovanni and Audre Lorde read their poetry also confirms this concept of orality and poetry.

3. Langston Hughes was the most frequently anthologized minority author as reported in Arthur N. Applebee, *Literature in the Secondary School: Studies of Curriculum and Instruction in the United States* (Urbana, IL:

National Council of Teachers of English, 1993), 104. Other African-American poets which appear in the Appendix List (pp. 236–242) include Clifton, Cullen, Johnson, Dunbar and Wheatley.

4. Erlene Stetson, ed. *Black Sister: Poetry by Black-American Women, 1746–1980* (Bloomington, IN: Indiana University Press, 1981).

5. Among the small presses that publish African-American women poets are Seal Press, Broadside Press, Third World Press, Kitchen Table: Women of Color Press, South End Press, Lotus Press, The Crossing Press, Eighth Mountain Press, Virago Press, Thunder's Mountain Press, Africa World Press, Zoland Books and Shameless Hussy Press.

6. Audre Lorde, "Power," in *The Black Unicorn* (New York: Norton, 1978), 108.

7. Ibid., 109.

8. Audre Lorde, *Shorelines.* Audiotape. Read by the author (Signature Series C–178. Washington, DC: Watershed Intermedia, 1985).

9. Audre Lorde, "Dear Joe," in *The Marvelous Arithmetics of Distance: Poems—1987–1992* (New York: Norton, 1993), 29.

10. bell hooks, *Talking Back: Thinking Feminist, Thinking Black* (Boston, MA: South End Press, 1989), 11.

11. Alice Walker, *In Search of Our Mothers' Gardens* (San Diego, CA: Harcourt Brace Jovanovich, 1984), 371.

12. Kesho Yvonne Scott, *The Habit of Surviving: Black Women's Strategies for Life* (New Brunswick, NJ: Rutgers University Press, 1991).

13. Countee Cullen, "Yet Do I Marvel," in *The Black Poets*, ed. by Dudley Randall (New York: Bantam, 1971), 100.

14. Lucy Terry, "Bar's Fight, August 28, 1746," in *The Black Poets*, 37.

15. Phillis Wheatley, *The Poems of Phillis Wheatley*, ed. with Introduction by Julian D. Mason, Jr. (Chapel Hill, NC: University of North Carolina Press, 1989).

16. Phillis Wheatley, "To S. M., A Young African Painter, On Seeing His Work," in *Black Sister*, 15–16.

17. Phillis Wheatley, "To the Right Honorable William, Earl of Dartmouth, His Majesty's Principal Secretary of State for North America, Etc.," in Joanne M. Braxton and Andree Nicola McLaughlin, eds. *Wild Women in the Whirlwind: Afra-American Culture and the Contemporary Literary Renaissance* (New Brunswick, NJ: Rutgers University Press, 1990), 30.

18. Although not in the standard textbook anthologies, Gwendolyn B. Bennett's poem "Hatred" was included in Arna Bontemps, ed., *American Negro Poetry* (New York: Hill & Wang, 1963), 73, and was very popular with many of the rebellious young people I taught during the late 1960s and early 1970s. I'm not sure that, at the time, we thought about her being an African-American woman—or what difference it would have made if we had.

19. Illona Linthwaite, ed. *Ain't I A Woman: A Book of Women's Poetry from Around the World* (New York: Wings Books, 1993).

20. See, for example, the recently published collection in the Schomburg Library of 19th Century Black Women Writers: Frances Ellen Watkins Harper, *Complete Poems of Francis E. W. Harper*, ed. by Maryemma Graham (New York: Oxford University Press, 1988).

21. Frances E. W. Harper, "An Appeal to My Countrywomen," in *Poems by Frances E. W. Harper* (Philadelphia, PA: George S. Ferguson, 1895), 194.

22. Frances E. W. Harper, "A Double Standard," in *Poems by Frances E. W. Harper*, 177.

23. Georgia Douglas Johnson, *The Heart of a Woman and Other Poems* (Boston, MA: Cornhill, 1918).

24. See, for example, the recently published collection in the Schomburg Library of 19th Century Black Women Writers: Angelina Weld Grimké, *Selected Works of Angelina Weld Grimké*, ed. by Carolivia Herron (New York: Oxford University Press, 1991).

25. Fauset was also editor for W.E.B. DuBois' *Crisis* magazine and was instrumental in publishing the poetry of Langston Hughes and Countee Cullen. She was also an editor of *The Brownies' Book*, a 1920s magazine for young African-Americans.

26. Jesse Redmon Fauset, "Touché," in *Black Sister*, 63–64.

27. Toni Morrison, *The Bluest Eye* (New York: Holt, Rinehart & Winston, 1970) and Patricia Smith, "Blonde White Women," in *Big Towns, Big Talk* (Cambridge, MA: Zoland Books, 1992), 21–23.

28. Frances E. W. Harper, "The Slave Auction," in *The Black Poets*, 39.

29. Gwendolyn Brooks, "The Mother," in *The Black Poets*, 165–66.

30. Gwendolyn Brooks, "The Life of Lincoln West," in *to disembark* (Chicago, IL: Third World Press, 1981), 28.

31. Ibid., 29.

32. Naomi Long Madgett, "Midway," in *The Black Poets*, 197; and in *Pass It On: African-American Poetry for Children*, selected by Wade Hudson, illus. by Floyd Cooper (New York: Scholastic, 1993), 21.

33. Naomi Long Madgett, "Drexel Street," in *Octavia and Other Poems* (Chicago, IL: Third World Press, 1988), 36–37.

34. Naomi Long Madgett, "Desert Song," in *Octavia and Other Poems*, 38.

35. Pinkie Gordon Lane, "Four Poems for Gordon," in Naomi Long Madgett, ed. *Adam of Ifë: Black Women in Praise of Black Men* (Detroit, MI: Lotus Press, 1992), 70.

36. Abimbola Adama, "Don't Listen," in *Adam of Ifë*, 200.

37. Dolores Kendrick, "To Market, to Market," in *The Women of Plums: Poems in the Voices of Slave Women* (New York: William Morrow, 1989), 19.

38. Dolores Kendrick, "Hattie on the Block," in *The Women of Plums*, 50.
39. Ibid.
40. See, for example: Gerder Lerner, ed. *Black Women in White America: A Documentary History* (New York: Vintage Books, 1973); John Bayliss, ed. *Black Slave Narratives* (New York: Macmillan, 1970); Linda Brent, *Incidents in the Life of a Slave Girl* (San Diego, CA: Harcourt Brace Jovanovich, 1973); and Mary E. Lyons, *Letters from a Slave Girl: The Story of Harriet Jacobs* (New York: Charles Scribner's, 1992).
41. Maya Angelou, *I Know Why the Caged Bird Sings* (New York: Random House, 1970).
42. Maya Angelou, *On the Pulse of Morning* (New York: Random House, 1993), unpaged.
43. Ibid.
44. Ibid.
45. Maya Angelou, *On the Pulse of Morning*. Read by the author. Cassette RH–292 (New York: Random House, 1993).
46. Maya Angelou, "The Calling of Names," in *Poems* (New York: Bantam, 1986), 45.
47. Maya Angelou, "Our Grandmothers," in *I Shall Not Be Moved* (New York: Bantam, 1991), 36.
48. Maya Angelou, "Ailey, Baldwin, Floyd, Killens, and Mayfield," in *I Shall Not Be Moved*, 48.
49. Maya Angelou, "Human Family," in *I Shall Not Be Moved*, 5.
50. Maya Angelou, "Caged Bird," in *Poems*, 184.
51. Audre Lorde, *Undersong: Chosen Poems—Old and New* (New York: Norton, 1992).
52. Audre Lorde, "Bloodbirth," in *Undersong*. Revised edition (New York: Norton, 1992), 19.
53. Audre Lorde, "The Master's Tools Will Never Dismantle the Master's House," in *Sister Outsider: Essays and Speeches* (Freedom, CA: Crossing Press, 1984), 113.
54. Audre Lorde, "Echoes," in *The Marvelous Arithmetics of Distance*, 7.
55. Audre Lorde, "Poetry Is Not A Luxury," in *Sister Outsider*, 37.
56. Charles H. Rowell, "Above the Wind: An Interview with Audre Lorde," *Callaloo* 14 (Winter 1991), 85.
57. Audre Lorde, "For Each of You," in *Undersong*, 80.
58. Audre Lorde, "Who Said It Was Simple," in *Undersong*, 95.
59. Sonia Sanchez, "malcolm," in *Home Coming* (Detroit, MI: Broadside Press, 1969), 16.
60. Sonia Sanchez, "Memorial," in *Home Coming*, 29.
61. Sonia Sanchez, "Nigger," in *Home Coming*, 12.
62. Dudley Randall, "Introduction," in Sonia Sanchez, *We a BaddDDD People* (Detroit, MI: Broadside Press, 1970), 9.

63. Sonia Sanchez, "we a baddDDD people (for gwendolyn brooks/ a fo real bad one)," in *We a BaddDDD People*, 53.
64. Sister Sonia Sanchez, "woman" in *A Blues Book for Blue Black Magical Women* (Detroit, MI: Broadside Press, 1974), 23.
65. Sonia Sanchez, "Just Don't Never Give Up on Love," in *homegirls & handgrenades* (New York: Thunder's Mouth Press, 1984), 13.
66. Sonia Sanchez, "Norma," in *homegirls & handgrenades*, 21.
67. Lucille Clifton, "Robert," in *Good Times* (New York: Random House, 1969), 6.
68. Lucille Clifton, "For deLawd," in *Good Times*, 18.
69. Lucille Clifton, "Admonitions," in *Good Times*, 37.
70. Lucille Clifton, "The Way It Was," in *Good News About the Earth* (New York: Random House, 1972), 3.
71. Lucille Clifton, "The Poet," in *an ordinary woman* (New York: Random House, 1974), 61.
72. Lucille Clifton, *an ordinary woman*, 73.
73. Ibid., 81.
74. Ibid., 95.
75. Lucille Clifton, "what the mirror said," in *two-headed woman* (Amherst, MA: University of Massachusetts Press, 1980), 8.
76. Lucille Clifton, "homage to my hair," in *two-headed woman*, 5.
77. Lucille Clifton, "sorrow song," in *Next* (Brockport, NY: Boa Editions, 1987), 21.
78. Lucille Clifton, "Atlas," in *The Book of Light* (Port Townsend, WA: Copper Canyon Press, 1993), 55.
79. Lucille Clifton, "final note to clark," in *The Book of Light*, 47.
80. Lucille Clifton, "won't you celebrate with me," in *The Book of Light*, 25.
81. Ntozake Shange, "i live in music," in *nappy edges** (New York: St. Martin's Press, 1991), 126.
82. Ntozake Shange, *for colored girls who have considered suicide/ when the rainbow is enuf* (New York: Collier/Macmillan, 1977), 13.
83. Ibid., 26–27.
84. Ntozake Shange, "with no immediate cause," in *nappy edges**, 114.
85. Ntozake Shange, "Who Needs A Heart," in *Ridin' the Moon in Texas: Word Paintings* (New York: St. Martin's Press, 1987), 35.
86. This work was first produced as a play at the Bacchanal, a woman's bar outside of Berkeley, California. From its California beginning in 1974 to its critical success at Joseph Papp's Public Theater and to the Broadway Booth Theater performance in 1976 which yielded the Obie Award, it has been performed in many places. Shange said of this work: ". . . the rest of the cast is enveloping almost 6,000 people a week in the words of a young black girl's growing up, her triumphs & errors, our struggle to become all that is forbidden by our environment, all that is forfeited by our gender,

all that we have forgotten." Introduction, xv.

87. Ntozake Shange, *for colored girls who have considered suicide/ when the rainbow is enuf*, 4–5.
88. Ntozake Shange, "Mood Indigo," in *A Daughter's Geography* (New York: St. Martin's Press, 1983), 13.
89. Ntozake Shange, "About Atlanta," in *A Daughter's Geography*, 45.
90. Ntozake Shange, "crack annie," in *The Love Space Demands (a continuing saga)* (New York: St. Martin's Press, 1992), 47.
91. Patricia Smith, "Annie Pearl Smith Discovers Moonlight," in *Big Towns, Big Talk*, 3.
92. Ibid., 4.
93. Patricia Smith, "Blonde White Women," in *Big Towns, Big Talk*, 21.
94. Ibid., 23.
95. Patricia Smith, "Heartland," in *Big Towns, Big Talk*, 25.
96. Patricia Smith, "Skinhead," in *Big Towns, Big Talk*, 68.
97. Patricia Smith, "Chinese Cucumbers," in *Big Towns, Big Talk*, 110.
98. Patricia Smith, "On the Street Where She Lives," in *Big Towns, Big Talk*, 113–114.
99. Rita Dove, *Thomas and Beulah* (Pittsburgh, PA: Carnegie-Mellon University Press, 1986).
100. Rita Dove, *Selected Poems* (New York: Vintage Books, 1993).
101. Ibid., xx.
102. Ibid., xxi.
103. Rita Dove, "Ö," in *Selected Poems*, 64.
104. Rita Dove, *Grace Notes* (New York: Norton, 1989).
105. Rita Dove, "A Hill of Beans," in *Thomas and Beulah*, 54.
106. Rita Dove, "Daystar," in *Thomas and Beulah*, 61.
107. Rita Dove, "Wingfoot Lake," in *Thomas and Beulah*, 72–73.
108. Rita Dove, "Promises," in *Thomas and Beulah*, 51.
109. See, for instance, the poetry of Alexis Deveaux, Mari Evans, Nikki Giovanni, Eloise Greenfield, Nikki Grimes, Cheryl Willis Hudson, June Jordan, Sharon Bell Mathis, Joyce Carol Thomas and Alice Walker.
110. Becky Birtha, Gracie Burnett, Cheryl Clarke, Jane Cortez, Gayl Jones, Irma McClaurin, Laini Mataka, May Miller, Karen Mitchell, Patricia Parker, Helen Earle Simcox, Saundra Sharpe, Nancy Travis, Margaret Walker and Sherley Anne Williams.
111. Mari Evans, *Black Women Writers: Arguments and Interviews* (London, England: Pluto Press, 1985), 200.

REFERENCES

Adoff, Arnold, ed. *Celebrations: A New Anthology of Black American Poetry.*

Chicago, IL: Follett, 1977.

Angelou, Maya. *All God's Children Need Traveling Shoes*. New York: Bantam, 1991.

_____. *Gather Together In My Name*. New York: Bantam, 1975.

_____. *The Heart of a Woman*. New York: Bantam, 1982.

_____. *I Know Why The Caged Bird Sings*. New York: Bantam, 1971.

_____. *I Shall Not Be Moved*. New York: Bantam, 1991.

_____. *On the Pulse of Morning*. New York: Random House, 1993.

_____. *On the Pulse of Morning*. Read by the author. Cassette RH–292. New York: Random House, 1993.

_____. *Poems: Just Give Me A Cool Drink of Water 'fore I Diiie; Oh Pray My Wings Are Gonna Fit Me Well; And Still I Rise; Shaker, Why Don't You Sing?* New York: Bantam, 1986.

_____. *Singin' and Swingin' and Gettin' Merry Like Christmas*. New York: Bantam, 1977.

Baker, Houston A., Jr. and Patricia Redmond, eds. *Afro-American Literary Study in the 1990s*. Chicago, IL: University of Chicago Press, 1989.

Blackshire-Belay, Carol Aisha, ed. *Language and Literature in the African American Imagination*. Westport, CT: Greenwood Press, 1992.

Braxton, Joanne M. and Andree Nicola McLaughlin, eds. *Wild Women in the Whirlwind: Afra-American Culture and the Contemporary Literary Renaissance*. New Brunswick, NJ: Rutgers University Press, 1990.

Brooks, Gwendolyn. *Beckonings*. Detroit, MI: Broadside Press, 1975.

_____. *In the Mecca*. New York: Harper & Row, 1968.

_____. *Selected Poems*. New York: Harper & Row, 1963.

_____. *to disembark*. Chicago, IL: Third World Press, 1981.

_____, comp. *Jump Bad: A New Chicago Anthology*. Detroit, MI: Broadside Press, 1971.

Brooks, Gwendolyn and others. *A Capsule Course in Black Poetry Writing*. Detroit, MI: Broadside Press, 1975.

Christian, Barbara. *Black Feminist Criticism: Perspectives on Black Women Writers*. New York: Pergamon Press, 1985.

Clifton, Lucille. *The Book of Light*. Port Townsend, WA: Copper Canyon Press, 1993.

_____. *Good News About the Earth*. New York: Random House, 1972.

_____. *Good Times*. New York: Random House, 1969.

_____. *an ordinary woman*. New York: Random House, 1974.

_____. *two-headed woman*. Amherst, MA: University of Massachusetts Press, 1980.

_____. *Next: New Poems*. Brockport, NY: Boa Editions, 1987.

Collins, Patricia Hill. *Black Feminist Thought: Knowledge, Consciousness, and the Politics of Empowerment*. New York: Routledge, 1991.

DeShazer, Mary K. *Inspiring Women: Reimagining the Muse.* New York: Pergamon Press, 1986.

Donaldson, Laura E. *Decolonizing Feminisms: Race, Gender, & Empire Building.* Chapel Hill, NC: University of North Carolina Press, 1992.

Dove, Rita. *Grace Notes.* New York: Norton, 1989.

_____. *Selected Poems.* New York: Vintage Books, 1993.

_____. *Thomas and Beulah.* Pittsburgh, PA: Carnegie-Mellon University Press, 1986.

Evans, Mari, ed. *Black Women Writers: Arguments and Interviews.* London, England: Pluto Press, 1985.

Gates, Henry Louis, Jr., ed. *Reading Black, Reading Feminist: A Critical Anthology.* New York: Meridian, 1990.

Gates, Henry Louis, Jr. and K. A. Appiah, eds. *Alice Walker: Critical Perspectives Past and Present.* New York: Amistad, 1993.

Georgoudaki, Ekaterini. *Race, Gender, and Class Perspectives in the Works of Maya Angelou, Gwendolyn Brooks, Rita Dove, Nikki Giovanni, and Audre Lorde.* Thessaloniki, Greece: Aristotle University of Thessaloniki, 1991.

Gould, Jean. *Modern American Women Poets.* New York: Dodd, Mead & Co., 1984.

Hernton, Calvin C. *The Sexual Mountain and Black Women Writers: Adventures in Sex, Literature, and Real Life.* New York: Doubleday, 1990.

Holloway, Karla F. C. *Moorings & Metaphors: Figures of Culture and Gender in Black Women's Literature.* New Brunswick, NJ: Rutgers University Press, 1992.

hooks, bell. *Ain't I A Woman: Black Women and Feminism.* Boston, MA: South End Press, 1981.

_____. *Feminist Theory From Margin to Center.* Boston, MA: South End Press, 1984.

_____. *Talking Back: Thinking Feminist, Thinking Black.* Boston, MA: South End Press, 1989.

Hudson, Wade, compiler. *Pass It On: African-American Poetry for Children.* Illus. by Floyd Cooper. New York: Scholastic, 1993.

Jackson, Blyden. *A History of Afro-American Literature: Volume I The Long Beginning, 1746–1895.* Baton Rouge, LA: Louisiana State University Press, 1989.

Kendrick, Dolores. *Now Is The Thing To Praise.* Detroit, MI: Lotus Press, 1984.

_____. *The Women of Plums: Poems in the Voices of Slave Women.* New York: Morrow, 1989.

Lee, Carol D. *Signifying As A Scaffold for Literary Interpretation: The Pedagogical Implications of an African American Discourse Genre.*

Urbana, IL: National Council of Teachers of English, 1993.

Linthwaite, Linda, ed. *Ain't I A Woman!: A Book of Women's Poetry From Around the World*. New York: Wings Books, 1990.

Lorde, Audre. *The Black Unicorn: Poems*. New York: Norton, 1978.

_____. *The Marvelous Arithmetics of Distance: Poems—1987–1992*. New York: Norton, 1993.

_____. *Shorelines*. Audiotape. Read by the author. Signature Series C–178. Washington, DC: Watershed Intermedia, 1985.

_____. *Sister Outsider: Essays and Speeches*. Freedom, CA: The Crossing Press, 1984.

_____. *Undersong: Chosen Poems Old and New*. Revised edition. New York: Norton, 1992.

_____. *Zami: A New Spelling of My Name*. Freedom, CA: The Crossing Press, 1982.

Lorde, Audre. Special Issue of *Callaloo: A Journal of African-American and African Arts and Letters*. Vol. 14, no. 1 (Winter 1991): 38–103.

Madgett, Naomi Long, *Octavia and Other Poems*. Chicago, IL: Third World Press, 1988.

_____. *Pink Ladies in the Afternoon*. New enlarged edition. Detroit, MI: Lotus Press, 1990.

_____, ed. *Adam of Ifé: Black Women in Praise of Black Men*. Detroit, MI: Lotus Press, 1992.

Malson, Micheline R. and others, eds. *Black Women in America: Social Science Perspectives*. Chicago, IL: University of Chicago Press, 1988.

Melhem, D. H. *Heroism in the New Black Poetry: Introductions & Interviews*. Lexington, KY: The University Press of Kentucky, 1990.

Moraga, Cherrie and Gloria Anzaldua, eds. *This Bridge Called My Back: Writings By Radical Women of Color*. Latham, NY: Kitchen Table: Women of Color Press, 1981.

Pearlman, Mickey and Katherine Usher Henderson. *Inter/View: Talks with America's Writing Women*. Lexington, KY: The University Press of Kentucky, 1990.

Piercy, Marge, ed. *Early Ripening: American Women's Poetry Now*. New York: Pandora, 1987.

Randall, Dudley, ed. *The Black Poets*. New York: Bantam, 1971.

Russell, Sandi. *Render Me My Song: African-American Women Writers from Slavery to the Present*. New York: St. Martin's Press, 1990.

Sanchez, Sonia. *A Blues Book for Blue Black Magical Women*. Detroit, MI: Broadside Press, 1974.

_____. *Home Coming*. Detroit, MI: Broadside Press, 1969.

_____. *homegirls & handgrenades*. New York: Thunder's Mouth Press, 1984.

_____. *I've Been A Woman*. Chicago, IL: Third World Press, 1985.

____. *Under A Soprano Sky*. Trenton, NJ: Africa World Press, 1987.

____. *We A BaddDDD People*. Detroit, MI: Broadside Press, 1970.

Scott, Kesho Yvonne. *The Habit of Surviving: Black Women's Strategies for Life*. New Brunswick, NJ: Rutgers University Press, 1991.

Shange, Ntozake. *A Daughter's Geography*. New York: St. Martin's Press, 1983.

____. *for colored girls who have considered suicide/ when the rainbow is enuf*. New York: Collier/Macmillan, 1977.

____. *The Love Space Demands (a continuing saga)*. New York: St. Martin's Press, 1992.

____. *nappy edges**. New York: St. Martin's Press, 1991.

____. *Ridin' the Moon in Texas: Word Paintings*. New York: St. Martin's Press, 1987.

____. *three pieces**. New York: St. Martin's Press, 1981.

Smith, Barbara. *Toward A Black Feminist Criticism*. Freedom, CA: Out & Out Books/The Crossing Press, 1977.

Smith, Patricia. *Big Towns, Big Talk*. Cambridge, MA: Zoland Books, 1992.

Stetson, Erlene, ed. *Black Sister: Poetry by Black American Women, 1746–1980*. Bloomington, IN: Indiana University Press, 1981.

Trimmer, Joseph and Tilly Warnock, eds. *Understanding Others: Cultural and Cross-Cultural Studies and the Teaching of Literature*. Urbana, IL: National Council of Teachers of English, 1992.

Wagner, Jean. *Black Poets of the United States: From Paul Laurence Dunbar to Langston Hughes*. Trans. by Kenneth Douglas. Urbana, IL: University of Illinois Press, 1973.

Walker, Alice. *In Search of Our Mothers' Gardens*. San Diego, CA: Harcourt Brace Jovanovich, 1984.

Wallace, Michele. *Black Macho and the Myth of the Superwoman*. London, England: Verso, 1990.

____. *Invisibility Blues: From Pop to Theory*. London, England: Verso, 1990.

THREE

Feminist Theories and the Voices of Mothers and Daughters in Selected African-American Literature for Young Adults[1]

Hilary S. Crew

In the young adult novel, *Rainbow Jordan*, written by Alice Childress and published in 1981, fourteen-year-old Rainbow narrates how she feels abandoned during her mother's frequent absences: "Truth is, what else is it but *abandon* when she walk out with a boyfriend, promise to come home soon, then don't show?"[2] Her language expresses the pain of loss she feels at her mother's absence and the import to her of her mother's life-affirming presence: "When my mother is away it feel like death; but when she's back it's like life again."[3] The love, anger, and loss that Rainbow voices in relation to her maternal mother[4] reproduces the intensity of a particular relationship imagined and constructed between an adolescent and her mother in a specific cultural context.

The increase in multicultural materials and studies in children's and young adult literature emphasizes the imperatives of respecting cultural diversity and context of texts and being aware of the issues involved in writing about, discussing, and defining those who are outside the dominant culture.[5] The focus of this chapter therefore, is to briefly discuss some of the different feminist theoretical positions from which the mother–daughter relationship has been studied in both black and white critical literary studies and the relevance and limitations of recent feminist studies on female adolescence and the mother–daughter relationship. Additionally, an analysis follows of how the mother–daughter relationship is constructed in the context of various black family structures in different settings represented in selected African-American young adult novels and adult books recommended for high school students.

THE MOTHER–DAUGHTER RELATIONSHIP AND FEMINIST THEORIES

Since Adrienne Rich's oft quoted statement that the "cathexis between mother and daughter . . . is the great unwritten story,"[6] the significance of the mother–daughter relationship has been recognized by feminist theorists from diverse theoretical approaches. No longer an unwritten story in white feminist scholarship, there is now a rich resource of interdisciplinary scholarly studies on this relationship crossing the fields of psychoanalysis, sociology, and literary criticism and which includes within its bounds the study of motherhood as an institution. White feminist literary criticism, in particular, has drawn upon feminist revisions of psychoanalytic theories as frameworks within which to study the mother–daughter relationship in literary texts.[7]

The narratives of these revisions, although from diametrically different theoretical positions, have emphasized the importance of the mother's early relationship with her daughter in shaping this relationship and the continuing working out of this relationship in adulthood.[8] The seminal work of Nancy Chodorow, *The Reproduction of Mothering* for example, argues that less distinct boundaries are drawn between mothers and daughters than between mothers and sons. Girls do not give up attachment to their mothers in forming a relationship with the father, but rather define themselves in a relational triangle with both mother and father.[9]

In calling for a specifically black feminist approach in discussing black mother–daughter relationships, Gloria I. Joseph warns against analyzing conceptions of motherhood and mother and daughter relationships from white feminist psychoanalytic theoretical perspectives without taking into account the differences of race and culture. Black females, writes Joseph, have been excluded from these studies and to discuss relationships between black mothers and daughters in the same terms as those of white mother and daughter relationships disregards black women's own explanations, interpretations, and experiences.[10] The same critique is made by Patricia Hill Collins who points out that white feminist scholars, who have written about motherhood for example, Nancy Chodorow and Jane Flax, have written from the standpoint of white middle-class women which does not address issues of black motherhood.[11]

Joseph suggests that the black mother–daughter relationship is best discussed within the context of the black family network rather than in the isolated dyad of mother and daughter which is the object of study in psychoanalytic theoretical writings.[12] Collins also stresses the centrality of the extended family and the "resilient, woman-centered networks of blood mothers and othermothers" to the concept of black motherhood and the mother–daughter relationship.[13] Other issues which are germane to the study of the black mother–daughter relationship are the sharing of a collective history of the injustice of slavery in which mothers and children (and thus daughters) were forcibly separated one from another, the continued sexism in both black and white communities, and racial inequality.[14]

In black literary criticism, studies of the mother–daughter relationship have included novels written by Toni Morrison and Paule Marshall.[15] Writing of the lack of material on black mother daughter relationships in general, Joseph refers to the novels, biographies, and poetry of black women which have served as primary source material for a study of this relationship including authors Zora Neale Hurston, Gwendolyn Brooks, Toni Morrison, and Alice Walker among others.[16] *Double Stitch* is a recent anthology of poems, essays, and fiction on the black mother–daughter relationship together with critical essays which reproduces both the diverse experiences of this relationship and its central importance in the lives of black women. The inclusion of narratives by authors Maya Angelou, Sonia Sanchez, and Alice Walker for example, makes this collection eminently accessible to high school students.

THE MOTHER–DAUGHTER RELATIONSHIP AND ADOLESCENCE

Both black and white feminist literary studies of the mother–daughter relationship have generally excluded novels marketed specifically for young adults. Young adult literature is a literature which specifically addresses itself to adolescence and at the same time constructs the experience of adolescence for the young adult reader. Often foregrounded in these novels are relationships with parents with the concomitant issues of conflict, separation, and individuation. Terri Apter in *Altered Loves: Mothers and Daughters During Adolescence* and authors in *Making Connections: The Relational Worlds of Adolescent Girls At Emma Willard School* critique the traditional theories of adolescence which have posited adolescence as a time of rebellion against parents, a time of detaching oneself from parents and turning to peers for self-validation. It is a construction of adolescence which has also been reproduced and applied to black female adolescence in which it is stated that in mid-adolescence, a teenager will push herself away from family and become more closely allied to peers. And separation and independence between a female adolescent and her parents are constructed through conflict and questions of control.[17] Feminist theorists have posited new narratives for female adolescence based on connections between adolescent girls and their mothers. Apter, who interviewed pairs of mothers and daughters, suggests for example, in *Altered Loves* that adolescent girls transform rather than abandon their relationships with their mothers and that conflict with a mother becomes a way of a daughter maintaining her relationship with her mother. "She fights with her mother because she wants, and believes she can, make her mother see and make her mother listen."[18] Conflict thus becomes a way of remaining in connection—an argument reiterated by Carol Gilligan. Disagreement between an adolescent girl and her mother accordingly, can be a sign that they are in relationship.[19] The crisis for adolescent girls, writes Gilligan, is one centered around connection not separation:

> For girls to remain responsive to themselves, they must resist the conventions of feminine goodness; to remain responsive to others, they must resist the values placed on self-sufficiency and independence in North American culture.[20]

The limitation of this research is that western white feminist perspectives on adolescent mother–daughter relationships have, in the above texts, not generally addressed racial and cultural differences in their analyses of the relationship between adolescent daughters and their mothers. The interviews with adolescent girls at the Emma Willard School, for example, are based, as Gilligan points out, on girls living "in a relatively isolated setting, in an atmosphere of privilege and promise, in an intensely female community housed in the architecture of high western culture."[21] A small group of minority students were interviewed at the Emma Willard School, but these girls are not representative of black female adolescents since they were growing-up and being educated in settings in which they were racially apart.

Janie Ward concludes from these interviews that questions of racial identity and the consciousness of the double jeopardy of being both black and female were central in the girls' answers in the interviews.[22] Joanne Braxton, in her analyses of black women's autobiographies, writes that in these texts, black women "speak of a perilously intensified adolescence, accompanied by perception of gender as well as racial difference."[23] The black mother–daughter relationship is discussed in recent scholarship within the context of race, class, and gender oppression in which mothers protect their daughters as long as they are able, while also imparting to them the necessary skills to survive.[24]

Social learning theory rather than psychoanalytic frameworks are used in analyzing this relationship in which mothers and othermothers are discussed in relation to their function as role models for their daughters.[25] The connections and affective relationships between black mothers and daughters and the independence and responsibility of black daughters are considered within socio-economic contexts. A mothers' emotional relationship with her daughter is thus considered in relation to the pressing demands of ensuring physical nurturance. "Black women's efforts to provide a physical and psychic base for their children," writes Collins, "can affect mothering styles and the emotional intensity of black mother–daughter relationships."[26]

The mother–daughter relationship has thus been studied from a number of very different theoretical perspectives. In particular, white and black feminist critics suggest different approaches in analyzing this relationship. The emphasis of black feminist scholars is placed on analyzing the mother–daughter in racial, social, and cultural contexts rather than within psychoanalytic frameworks. The white experience of adolescence is also constructed through different scripts of development. The most recent research posits connections between adolescent mothers and daughters. This different narrative of female adolescence challenges the classical psychoanalytic theories of adolescence in which attachment to the mother has been written about for example, as "an insidious dependency" by one influential male theorist.[27]

Studies of black adolescence stress the double jeopardy of being both black and female, and emphasis is placed on the role of mothers in the enculturation of daughters and the effects of this role on their relationships. Black feminist critics have thus discussed the relationship through the integration of theory and the concrete everyday actions and experiences of black mothers and daughters. The merging of abstract thought with action, Collins explains, is a theoretical stance adopted by black scholars that engenders other ways of thinking and results in different theories than can be generated by either thought or action alone.[28]

In the African-American texts discussed below, the mother–daughter relationship or grandmother–mother–daughter relationship is constructed as an important and integral part of an adolescent's growing-up. Central in determining how the mother–daughter relationships are imagined in these texts, are the questions of who is speaking—mother or daughter—from where she speaks in terms of time, place, and socio-economic context, and how she speaks. The relationship between the mother and daughter is thus analyzed within the context of family and place with an emphasis on listening to voices of mothers and daughters whether in relationship, conflict, or in separation. And essential also to these analyses are questions of how much and in what ways a female black adolescent identifies with the voice of her mother in relation to the double jeopardy of being both black and female.

THE VOICES OF MOTHER AND DAUGHTER
IN *RAINBOW JORDAN*

In Childress' *Rainbow Jordan*, the voices of teenage daughter, Rainbow, her mother Kathie, and Josephine, Rainbow's "interim" mother, who cares for Rainbow in Kathie's absence, each speak separately in separate chapters. While Rainbow speaks of her loss, abandonment, and love for her mother, the voice of Kathie, Rainbow's mother speaks from a position of economic and social powerlessness as she is "stranded outta town" in a motel with her boyfriend and promoter, Burke. Pregnant at the age of seventeen years and divorced after one year from Rainbow's father, Leroy, Kathie has struggled in limited circumstances to provide economic support for Rainbow, relying on occasional child support money from Leroy, Aid to Dependent Children checks, and earnings from her sporadic work as a go-go dancer.

Collins writes that an assumption of white perspectives of the patriarchal nuclear family has been the existence of separate gender roles for the economic provision and love and care of children, respectively. In contrast, women in African-American families have through necessity "long integrated their activities as economic providers into their mothering relationships."[29] The mother–daughter relationships in the majority of the young adult novels discussed in this chapter are noticeably constructed within a one-parent family structure in which the absence of fathers, through death, desertion, or divorce places the onus of providing and caring for a family on mothers.

In *Rainbow Jordan*, as in other novels cited in this chapter, the difficulties of a mother in meeting both the economic and affective needs of a daughter as well as her own needs, engenders a rupture in the relationship between mother and daughter. The rupture in *Rainbow Jordan* is revealed through the angry and frustrated voice of a young woman. Thrust into the responsibility of mothering situated in a context with little social and economic support, Kathie tells of the incident when five year old Rainbow, left alone in the apartment, is rescued from the burning building when some cheap wiring catches fire:

> Yes. I HAD LEFT HER ALONE. I had bein so damn good till life was no fun a-tall. Gotta go out sometime. . . . That fella had been after me to go out with him and kept sayin how he could help me. People lose interest if you never can go anywhere. He was a louse.[30]

In this passage as in others, Kathie voices her own needs for a life and identity separate from that of being a mother to her daughter and discloses her continuing dependence on men for financial and also emotional support. Kathie's voice, out-of-relationship with that of her daughter's, defines Rainbow in opposition rather than in relation to self reproducing a split between her wish for separateness and the satisfaction of her own needs and the nurturance which she attempts to give her daughter. This split is doubled in Rainbow's first-person narrative which reveals the destructive side of a relationship in which Kathie displaces her anger on Rainbow—blaming Rainbow's very existence for her entrapment. Rainbow remembers and reports her mother's frustrated outburst: "Wasn't for you I'd be somewhere. No man ever got serious . . . cause I got you!"[31]

Elided from Kathie's narrative is the physical and verbal abuse which she metes out to her daughter. The ellipses in the text signify what is not said or admitted to self as she tells how she had spent the babysitting money on new pajamas for Rainbow and had also "bought new black patent shoes with a ankle strap . . . like she had been wanting."[32] The silent spaces in Kathie's narrative are filled in by Rainbow's first person narrative in which she tells of the beating she receives from her mother for drinking the milk that Kathie was saving for the next day without permission and the new "pair-a black leather sandals" her mother had bought her with the ADC money. "Some of the best presents I ever got," Rainbow continues, "was the day after a beatin."[33]

Kathie's silence thus covers over that to which a mother cannot admit even to herself—the actual physical and verbal abuse of her daughter. Marianne Hirsch points out that to express anger as a mother is to separate herself from the expected role of a mother to care and nurture others. Not only is this culturally unacceptable but it also does not allow a mother's self-interest to be taken into account along with caring for others. Hirsch writes that this is a "pervasive general cultural taboo to which all women whether white or black, are subject."[34] Kathie's voice reveals her anger, but it is in the daughter's narrative that the abuse which is the result of maternal anger is exposed. Kathie's threat (reported in Rainbow's narrative) that she is "gonna beat all the black of you, Rainbow!" reproduces the terrible anger of being both black and poor, and a young mother. Her daughter's blackness, literally and metaphorically, signifies the powerlessness of this position.

Kathie is one of the few mothers in adolescent literature, who has agency in the sense that she speaks as a subject through taking up an unmediated "I" position in the text. She thus directly expresses both her own thoughts and feelings about her daughter, their relationship, and her anger from her perspective. Her first-person narrative, however, reveals her entrapment and actual lack of agency in a relationship with a man who abuses her, upon whom she is dependent, and her position in a situation she cannot control. As she unsuccessfully struggles to sew dresses for Rainbow, her desperation is revealed in her cry that she is "gonna be a good mother if it kills" her.[35] Little more than an adolescent herself, Kathie's powerlessness, and her voice of anger and self-interest are thus constructed in opposition to the expected role model a black mother is expected to be for her teenage daughter.[36]

Rainbow's voice reveals her own love and loyalty for her mother with whom she attempts to stay in relationship: "I love her even now while I'm puttin her down."[37] Rainbow finally realizes that she cannot "count" on her mother, and only then does she acknowledge the lacuna between her desire for connection and the reality of her mother's lack of attachment to her as she tells Josephine that her mother has never loved her as she has loved her—"and never will."[38]

THE DIFFERENT VOICES OF MOTHERS AND DAUGHTERS

The intense need for the love and presence of their working mothers is also expressed by adolescent daughters in Virginia Hamilton's *Sweet Whispers, Brother Rush* and Jacqueline Woodson's *The Dear One*. The voice and language of fifteen-year-old Tree, in Virginia Hamilton's *Sweet Whispers, Brother Rush*, speaks, like Rainbow, of her love and loss for her absent working mother.

> Muh Vy, spoken M'Vy, with the softest sighing to mean,
> Miss you, Mama; Love you, Mama. All the tenderness and grief
> she and her brother Dab felt at the thought of her when they were
> so alone sometimes without her."[39]

Left alone to care for her retarded brother, Tree accepts the need for her mother to be absent in order to provide for herself and Dab. "M'Vy had to be somewhere else so she and Dab and M'Vy, too, could have all the things they had to have."[40] Placed in economic circumstances in which they must provide economic support to their families, mothers excuse and explain their choices to their daughters. The voice of Tree's mother, faced with the illness and death of Dab, reproduces the guilt and blame of a mother who has had to choose between providing nurturance and economic sustenance as she admits to Tree that she had made a mistake and should have "taken less money and stayed" with Tree and Dab.[41]

However, when twelve-year-old Afeni in *The Dear One* accuses her mother, an attorney, of allowing her career to prevent her from spending time with Afeni, her mother's voice is firm as she spells out to her daughter that her love is shown through that which she provides:

> Don't you ever let me hear you say I don't love you, because if I'm not showing it in words, I'm showing it with actions! I didn't grow up saying it, so I can't start now. But I love you is in every meal you eat, every piece of clothing you wear, and every clean sheet you sleep on![42]

Afeni's mother's refusal to accept blame for her style of mothering consciously reproduces in this more recent novel, both an awareness and a refusal of a culturally prescripted ideal of mothering and of a mother–daughter relationship that does not allow for differing circumstances and different kinds of relationships. Afeni realizes that her one-parent family is not represented by "some TV family where everything was perfect all the time." Her father was absent, and even if other girls had close relationships with their mothers, she and her mother were not, perhaps because of their personalities as loners.[43] In this young adult novel, as in *Sweet Whispers, Brother Rush* and some other young adult novels, the mother does not represent the limiting and stereotypical image of the "strong black mother" for her daughter.[44] Afeni's mother, though described as "strong," has had a drinking problem and has made "mistakes." Reproduced in these novels is the schism between the "idealized versions of maternal love extant in popular culture" and the kind of love and care that can be provided by mothers whose own lives are less than perfect.[45]

A tone of cynicism and defeat is heard in the voice of Didi's mother in *Motown and Didi* set in Harlem in the 1980s, when Didi is upset at the news that she has not been offered a full scholarship. "It wasn't everything, because the sun kept burning and the earth kept turning—that's what she was fixing her mouth to say," but Didi's mother suppresses her words when she sees the "pain and hurt twisting Didi's face into an ugly mask."[46] Seventeen-year-old Didi voices her strong need to "forget who she was and where she came from" by obtaining a scholarship at a college far from Harlem with its environment of drugs and poverty, and the need to get away from her mother whose "fragile hands" she had been "holding" for "too long."[47]

The manipulating voice of her mother reveals her need for her daughter. She does not see her daughter's need to go so far away to college, and when she recovers from a stroke tells her daughter that the doctor said if she has "another accident" she may not live. She would then not "need" her daughter as much.[48] Her mother's need for her, although perceived by Didi as real is also perceived by her as a "trap." The conflict between providing sustenance to her mother in which Didi "would have to give more of herself" and give up her own dreams for college and other choices in life reproduces the tension between an adolescent daughter's voiced need to move away to find a different life for self and the moral responsibilities she has towards the "flesh and blood" of family. In this particular situation and context, Didi's voice clearly reproduces the dilemma of the cost of staying in relationship with those she cares about: "For any person she cared for, any brick in the squatting buildings that she touched, any rhythm she walked to in the streets would help to trap her in Harlem."[49]

Throughout the novel, however, her choices have reproduced a valorization of care and commitment to relationships—to her mother, to a brother hooked on drugs, and to the welfare and safety of Motown, a young man who saved her from an attempted assault. Didi's wish to go away is associated with her wish to "lead her family out of the poverty that sucked on them, night and day."[50] In the 1980s urban setting of *Motown and Didi*, there is a lack of an extended family network to whom mother and daughter may turn for support. Collins refers to the breakdown of "community structure of blood mothers and other-mothers in many inner-city neighborhoods" because of illegal drugs.[51] In this novel, as in *Rainbow Jordan*, the relationship between mother and daughter is constructed within a structure of disintegrating family and community networks in which the absence of the daughter's father is conspicuous.[52]

Listening to the voices of female adolescents, Gilligan and others note the tensions and shifts in the language of young women as they define their meanings of independence and talk about issues of separation, connections, and relationships in association with their own needs and the needs of others.[53] In these and other African-American young adult novels discussed in this chapter, a tension is constructed between the voices of those mothers who struggle for physical and emotional survival in difficult circumstances and the voices of their adolescent daughters. Daughters voice their own needs for love, support, and autonomy yet are expected to take on responsibilities both on-behalf and for their mothers.

In *Listen For the Fig Tree* by Sharon Mathis, the voice of twelve-year-old Muffin reveals the ambivalence she experiences between feeling responsible for her mother, who is distraught with grief on the anniversary of her husband's brutal murder on Christmas day, and the sacrificing of her own plans for enjoying the celebration of Kwanza. Accused by her friend, Ernie, of not "seeing" clearly in relation to her mother's problems, Muffin (who is literally blind) wishes Ernie to understand:

> that saying she wasn't going to worry about her mother anymore didn't mean she really wasn't going to worry. It just meant that she was going to think only about the good things that happened.[54]

At one point, losing patience with her mother, who has turned to alcohol to bury her pain, Muffin tells Ernie that she is going to Kwanza "no matter what!" And she places her own needs over those of her mother the day she arrives home to find her mother lying asleep in her own vomit—deciding to go ahead with what she had planned to do that day rather than focusing on the care of her mother.

The hiatus and misunderstandings constructed between the voices of mother and daughter are increased by Leona, whose voice is out-of-relationship with her daughter. She accuses Muffin of blocking her "way" as she goes out to drink and states that Muffin's "being embarrassed" means "*nothing*" to her.[55] She has defined herself in relation to her husband rather than Muffin: "Mainly it was just me and that man." She had told him that without him she "just" did not "count."[56]

The less powerful voices of mothers' are constructed in opposition to the stronger voices of daughters in several of these young adult novels. Muffin's mother tells her daughter not to give up after Muffin has been assaulted. "I give up. You can't give up. You young!"[57] Muffin eventually understands that she can give her mother the "strength" she needs to survive. In this novel, as in *Motown and Didi*, the strength of the daughter's voice reverses the power relation between mother and daughter. Muffin's mother ineffectually reminds her daughter and others that she and not Muffin is the mother. Didi wonders: "Was she the daughter? The child? Perhaps there had been a mistake, and it wasn't Darlene that wasn't 'right' but Didi, and she was the mother."[58]

Subverted also by these daughters is the powerlessness which is handed down to them by their mothers. Metaphors constructed around seeing and blindness denote their daughters' clearer visions. Muffin's mother speaks of herself as being "bad luck" to her daughter and of the legacy of blindness that has been handed down to Muffin from her family. The blind daughter however, sees more than the mother who "don't want no eyes." As Govan points out, the voice and vision of Rainbow in *Rainbow Jordan* is more perceptive than either Kathie, her mother, or Josephine, who cares for her in her mother's absence.[59] Tree, the adolescent daughter in *Sweet Whispers, Brother Rush* sees the "*mystery*" which her mother has never seen and thus gains insight and understanding of her mother's past which her mother has hidden from Tree—a past which has its own inheritance of "blood and sickness."

A DAUGHTER'S IDENTITY WITH HER MOTHER

Didi's perception in *Motown and Didi* that her mother is vulnerable because she is a woman alerts her to the vulnerability of her "own womanhood."[60] The vulnerability of mothers and the awareness of the double jeopardy of being both black and female alert daughters to their own positions. In *The Dear One* is reproduced the consciousness of the power relationships of gender and race as well as the inequality of parent and child. Twelve-year-old Afeni tells her mother that:

> There's always going to be someone deciding what I can
> and can't do. If it's not because I am a kid, it'll be because I'm a
> woman. If it's not because I'm a woman, it'll be because I'm
> black.[61]

A raised consciousness engenders its own strength in that these daughters are aware of the danger of becoming subjected to the same oppressive patriarchal and racial structures that their mothers have endured and in which they are positioned. Afeni's mother tells her with "something like fear" in her voice to never "feel like you don't have power, Feni."[62] In this novel however, Afeni's voice is strengthened by her mother and her friends—a female bonding through which Afeni is taught both the values of responsibility and caring for others and to regard and take pride in the strengths and values of the black community.

The voices of daughters constructed in some of these novels are caught between their rejection or repetition of their mothers' histories and their loyalty, attachment, and identity with their mothers—mothers, who have also often shown themselves to be strong, despite their mistakes and weaknesses. Afeni's mother expresses concern that her friend's daughter, Rebecca, pregnant at fifteen, is repeating her mother's past.[63] Rebecca, whose grandmother and great grandmother were also pregnant in their early teens, comments that she "don't want to be like my moms. She had to leave school because of me."[64] She affirms her identity separate from that of her mother, whom she resembles. "But I'm not Clair, I'm Rebecca!" she insists.[65]

Reproduced in *Sweet Whispers, Brother Rush*, is the shifting double consciousness of being both daughter and mother as Tree moves between present and present, taking her mother's place in caring for Dab in the former, and in the latter becoming her mother as she observes her mother whipping Dab. "Tree was there, seeing, but felt herself fading. She was the woman, her gorge rising. She was the girl child, seeing pictures, shapes."[66] When Dab dies, Tree, who had rejected identification with the mother who abuses her brother, blames her mother in terrible pain and anger for her treatment of Dab. She would put a "kitchen knife" through her mother or herself to "bleed out the hate and the love."[67] There is in these novels, a consciousness of the shifting, blurred boundaries between wishing to both identify and disidentify themselves from their mothers. While daughters disassociate themselves from and blame their mothers' weaknesses, they can also acknowledge their strengths. Afeni affirms her mother's strength to Rebecca in *The Dear One* and in *Sweet Whispers, Brother Rush*, the toughness and determination that Tree had always known, shows in her mother's face.

When mothers fail to enable their daughters to move beyond their limitations, reproduced in the voices of their daughters is the fear of being subordinated and trapped within the same circumstances. In Kristin Hunter's *Lou in the Limelight* Lou finally separates from her mother, whose strength is used only to keep her daughter from that which she fears and which lies outside the boundaries she knows. Only by separating from the confining strictures and values of her mother, whom Lou and her brother perceive as wanting to "*stay* down" can Lou move out and upwards. Community and religious values constitute identity with mother in *Lou in the Limelight* and Higginson and

Bolden's *Mama, I Want To Sing*. They are the basis for conflict between mothers and daughters in these novels as daughters move outwards from the inside environment of family, community, and church to the outside as they insist on establishing their own lives and identities separate and different from that of their mothers. The anger of mothers is expressed at what they focalize as their daughters' rejection of the values they have instilled in their daughters and therefore a rejection of themselves as mothers. In both of these last mentioned novels, narrative plots are constructed in which daughters wish to sing "worldly" music outside the bounds of home and to separate their talented voices from the disapproving voices of their mothers in order to create songs of their own. Lou's angry blues composition "Talk 'Bout Yo' Mama" sums up her attitude that her mother "only knows about her life" but not what is "best" for her daughter.

A NETWORK OF OTHERMOTHERS

While daughters may find their voices out-of-relationship through conflict with mothers, voices may stay in relationship with women who become othermothers. Reproduced in several of young adult African-American novels are the networks of othermothers which supplement the mother and adolescent daughter relationship. They substitute for a lack and absence that is missing to the daughter from her maternal mother and are additional to the maternal mother's emotional and physical nurturance of a teenage daughter. Alternative relationships are constructed between these othermothers and adolescent daughters in which voices of these supplementary voices take a mediating position between a maternal mother and daughter in situations of conflict. They represent for the daughter alternative values and roles for the young woman struggling to extricate herself from what she perceives as the confining strictures of her mother. Without the boundaries of the confines of the maternal, these othermothers nurture, train, and provide practical support to young women. They help daughters to traverse the boundaries of the inside to the culture and power of the outside while maintaining those connections to family and values that contribute to empowering the adolescent female.

THE DIFFERENCE OF OTHERMOTHERS

Pivotal to the construction of othermothers in these texts are their differences from maternal mothers and the different relationships constructed between them and their proxy daughters. This difference is constructed through the opposition of gender in *Listen For the Fig Tree*, as a circle of male nurturers protect Muffin and her mother. Muffin's mother is displaced by the gentle Mr. Dale, who offers the young girl love, protection, and tutelage—in effect engages in the practice of mothering—subverting stereotypical sexist assumptions of masculinity. The male voices reproduced in this novel are ones that embody caring for others in relationship—a caring that is absent now from the maternal voice of Leona.

Differences from the maternal mother in other novels are reproduced through traversing class and socio-economic boundaries. The constructions of other, alternative world views through the agency of othermothers contribute to both the liberation and liberalization of adolescent daughters. The presence of a network of othermothers and their differences from the maternal mother is constructed in *Lou in the Limelight* in which a succession of different women provide care and sustenance to Lou. Julia, the cousin who adopts Lou is described as: "Wonderfully different" and a "law unto herself." Surrounded by books, art, and music, Julia, a gifted musician, is eager to share her life of culture and travel with Lou. Julia's house makes Lou feel as though "she was in Paradise."[68] Sister Carrie, is described as a "second mother" to Doris in the novel, *Mama, I Want To Sing*. A former blues singer, she breaks down for Doris the oppositions between the inside culture of church and community and the outside world of fashion and show business.

In *The Dear One*, fifteen-year-old Rebecca moves from the poverty of her home in Harlem to the black suburb of middle-class professionals, where Afeni's mother and her lesbian friends give her support during the last months of her pregnancy and for the birth of her baby. They are there for her, Marion tells Rebecca, to give her "space and quiet," to spend "time" with her—to prevent her slipping through "the cracks."[69] Rebecca confronts her prejudices towards lesbianism and Afeni her negative attitude towards sharing her home with a pregnant young woman as they form connections across barriers of socioeconomic differences. In this young adult novel, written from a feminist perspective, the voices of othermothers affirm the care for others in their relationships and are constructed as exemplars for the adolescent daughters.

The adoptive mothers in these novels mostly speak from networks of connections and relationships in the black community, for example, the protective mothering circles in *Listen For the Fig Tree* and *The Dear One*, and Julia in *Lou in the Limelight*. Their relationships with these female adolescents are however, predicated on the distances constructed between them. Mr. Dale is always "Mr. Dale" to Muffin. Othermothers do not supplant the maternal mother by reforming the maternal bond between mother and daughter. Daughters acknowledge the difference. Doris in *Mama, I Want to Sing* "knew no one could replace her mother" using words and images to describe their relationship that emphasize the maternal, nurturing body of the mother.[70] Jerutha, who defines herself to Lou and the Soul Brothers as their "mama away from home" in *Lou in the Limelight* reassures Lou's mother that she "wouldn't dream of coming between mother and daughter."[71] Underlying these connections with a difference in these latter two novels are assumptions about the conflicting relationships between adolescent daughters and mothers structured around the daughters' needs to individuate and the resulting clash of values. An assumption also reproduced in *Lou in the Limelight* is that the intensity of Lou's relationship and the love they have for each other prevents them, as Aunt Jerutha suggests, from getting along. "Of course you love her, I know that. She knows it too. And she loves you. That seems to be why the two of you can't get along."[72] And Aunt Jerutha, as othermother, mediates by separating Lou from her mother. Collins writes that othermothers "often help to defuse the emotional intensity between bloodmothers and their daughters."[73] Distance thus seems to be a necessary corollary for an adolescent daughter's good relationship with an othermother in these novels. Maintained however, are the unequal power relationships between an othermother and daughter.

OTHERMOTHERS AND THE PRACTICE OF MOTHERING

While an othermother may mediate between a maternal mother and her teenager, she also may take on a disciplinary role in relation to the daughter thus showing her responsibility to the young woman and legitimizing her position as a surrogate mother—a member of a larger protective circle extant to the girl's home. In *Lou in the Limelight*, Tina, an employee of the casino in Las Vegas where Lou and the Soul

Brothers are working, warns Lou against the prostitution indigenous to performing in the corrupt milieu of show business at the casino. She gives Lou a "stinging slap" when she forces Lou to utter the word "prostitution." And Lou understands that the slap was "like one of her mother's, and meant that Tina was treating her like one of her children."[74] In the voice of an admonishing mother, Tina tells Lou: "I'm talking to you like a mother, that's why I won't stand for any lying from you."[75]

Reproduced in this novel and *Mama, I Want To Sing* is the maintenance of traditional family, community, and religious values that are still to be valued and maintained by the adolescent daughter away from home and her maternal mother which are enforced by the voice of an othermother. Aunt Jerutha, in *Lou in the Limelight* subdues Lou's singing group partners, who are high on drugs at the casino, by reintroducing religious values into their environment through the recitation of prayers and the group singing of hymns. Jerutha's injunction to Lou: "Don't forget who you are and where you come from"[76] is repeated almost word for word in Sister Carrie's warning to Doris in *Mama, I Want to Sing* that she "keep in touch" with herself, that she remember who she is and where she comes from, and to remember her "house training."[77]

The central role that othermothers play in the lives of adolescent daughters as role mothers is thus reproduced in several young adult novels. And othermothers, rather than maternal mothers, are constructed as the strong mothers in these young adult novels, without however, being constructed through stereotypical images of the good mother. Othermothers would thus seem to engage in the practice of different kinds of mothering in specific contexts—a mothering separated from the maternal bodies of mothers.[78] Collins explains the concept of othermothers as one in which:

> community othermothers work on behalf of the black community
> by expressing ethics of care and personal accountability which
> embrace conceptions of transformative power and mutuality.[79]

In *Water Girl*, by Joyce Carol Thomas, Amber's adoptive mother gives her the love that Amber realizes legitimizes her as her mother: "A mother is the one who loves you."[80] The painful absence of the maternal mother is described by Amber in terms of abandonment—the language used by Rainbow to describe feelings about her mother's absence.

THE MOTHER–DAUGHTER RELATIONSHIP
AND THE FEMALE SLAVE NARRATIVE

The anguish of separation of maternal mothers from their daughters is recorded in the social and historical context of the female slave narrative. Perhaps the most difficult relationships to comprehend and give testament to are those constituted out of the oppression and injustice of slavery itself—connections instituted between white women who are described as like mothers to young black slave girls. These connections were predicated on the very crux of those power relations which sexually abused and oppressed black mothers, whose daughters were sometimes forcibly separated from them.

In the oral histories of North Carolina slave women narrated in *My Folks Don't Want Me To Talk About Slavery*, daughters give voice to the separations between mothers and daughters that were enforced through the institution of slavery. The voice of Patsy Mitchner reports how her mother was sold and with her sister and brother "were shipped to the Mississippi bottoms in a boxcar." The separation from her mother was irrevocable. "I never heard from my mother any more," she reports.[81] Sarah Debroh tells how she was taken from her mother's cabin to be trained as a housemaid and how her "mammy cried, 'cause she knew I would never be allowed to live at the cabin with her no more."[82]

Set during Reconstruction in the piedmont area of North Carolina, Belinda Hurmence's young adult novel, *Tancy* constructs the parallel narrative of the adolescent Tancy's emancipation from Miss Puddin, within the larger historical and social context of Emancipation. Tancy's subsequent search for her "real mother," writes Hurmence, parallels the "innumerable ex-slaves who set out to find their families after the Civil War."[83] Throughout the novel, the language of independence and freedom is used to construct Tancy's position as adolescent and that of black mulatto slave girl as she realizes that she is free both as slave maid and surrogate daughter to the white woman who, with Mas Gaither, her father, has "meant everything to Tancy, everything," for she "had never known a mother or father."[84]

Tancy's relationship to Miss Puddin has been constructed around the sexual exploitation of Tancy's mother and the forced separation of mother and daughter when Tancy is only a nursing baby. Tancy is taken into the house by Miss Puddin "to be a constant reproach to the master." Tancy's attachment to the woman she refers to as "like a mother" and "more like a mother to us than a mistress," and the affection that is reproduced between Miss Puddin and Tancy is constructed, however, through a violation of relationships. White mother as other-mother is invested with a dominance and inequality based on slavery over and above the unequal power relationship between mother and child, which necessarily distorts and falsifies a relationship with a young black slave girl taken into her home.

In the double voice of adolescent and slave girl, Tancy voices resistance to ownership and inequality. She resists Miss Puddin's efforts to deny her the knowledge that she is free and independent and Miss Puddin's threat to "reclaim" her. She resists the sexual violation of Billy, her stepbrother. The injustice that unites Tancy and her maternal mother, Lucy, is that they are placed within a system of sexual abuse. Tancy, herself the blood daughter of a white slave owner, is exposed to sexual assault, a common occurrence for many young black female slaves.[85] The false family relationship constituted through slavery is unmasked as Julie, the cook, tells Tancy: "No such thing as brothers and sisters between white folks and black. You and Billy got the same daddy, is all."[86] And Tancy, when she uncovers the facts about her black mother, comments that: "No matter how Miss Puddin expressed it, she was *not* Tancy's mother. Lucy was; Lucy who resided as Lulu in Mas Gaither's ledger, real, taken note of."[87]

Only through the forbidden act of reading anything other than the Bible had Tancy learned of her slave mother in an entry in the plantation ledger: "6/16/48—Lulu lying in. 6/17/48—Lulu delivered of Tancy. Both well."[88] The record of the alteration of Tancy's name from the name given to her by her mother and the various names by which her mother is known—Lulu, Lucy, Lucinda, Sin—reproduce the loss of identity and forced separation between mother and daughter. The search for Tancy's mother ends with her location of Sin, now mistress to a former slave owner, and charging rent to black families living in the huts and hovels of Shantytown from land procured from her white lover. Tancy recoils from the old woman who does not represent the idealized mother of her dreams:

> Sin, Lucinda. Oh, Mother, Tancy grieved already yearning for the lost mother of her dreams. How could she give up the Lulu she had fashioned in her mind—soft, sweet Lulu, beloved of Mas Gaither?"[89]

The de-idealization of the mother is constructed within the historical and social denigration of black women under slavery. "Lulu was a bad woman," Tancy is told, the "kind of woman" who was sold to speculators in the slave trade. Blamed for the sexual exploitation of her masters, her name Sin, the symbol of "female evil and sexual lust," Tancy's black mother is constructed against the purer white mother, Miss Puddin with her "smooth and golden and shining" hair.[90]

Subverting archetypes of an idealized and strong black mother, Sin is nevertheless accepted by Tancy as her mother for whom she is— a survivor of forced labor and sexual exploitation. Rejected by her sons and their wives, Sin is reunited with her daughter, who is determined now to stay with her mother and not lose her again. In this novel, a narrative plot which reproduces connections with a maternal mother is a reversal of those narrative plots in young adult novels in which adolescent girls move away from their maternal mothers to achieve independence or, are in relationship with replacement, or surrogate mothers in lieu of their mothers. Tancy's emancipation is achieved in conjunction with the search for her maternal mother:

> It was not emancipation that had freed her, she realized; she had to do that for herself, and she debated whether or not she would have struck out at all, had she not gone looking for her mother.[91]

Hurmence writes that "Tancy's yearning and searching parallels what many young people experience today, looking for some ideal, or 'mother' on the way to discovering themselves."[92] Independence for a black adolescent female as constructed in the social and historical context of this novel is the freedom to search for lost connections that have denied her the worth of her black identity and identity with her black mother. Sin tells Tancy that there is no "mistake"—that she is indeed her mother as she links racial identity with identification of the maternal mother. "Look at her eyes, no whites to them, just like mine."[93] Tancy's emancipation and re-connection with her maternal mother is thus constructed within the collective history of the severing of the bonds of black mothers and daughters in slavery—a severance that denied black daughters ownership of their rightful name, maternal mother, and racial identity.

The fictional narrative *Tancy*, though narrated by an anonymous narrator, is analogous to the female slave narrative, which tells not only of the "journey from slavery to freedom" but tells also of the black woman's experience as a slave from her perspective. In this novel, as in Mary Lyons's young adult novel, *Letters From A Slave Girl*, the focus is on the abuses suffered by black women and on the separation of families generally left out of male slave narratives.[94] In *Tancy*, the loss and re-connection formulated around the absence and presence of the mother—a central figure in this novel—is doubled in a sub-plot in which Tancy experiences the anguish of giving up a child she has cared for to his rightful mother. In *Letters from A Slave Girl*, Harriet, a black slave mother, is separated from her own daughter for the years she is in hiding before she can escape and they are eventually re-united in the North. In both novels, the stories of mothers and daughters—often an unwritten story—are especially documented.

In the young adult novel, *Letters from A Slave Girl*, a fictionalized version of the slave narrative, *Incidents in the Life of A Slave Girl*, oy Harriet Jacobs, published in 1861, Lyons chooses to reproduce Harriet's loss of her own mother and her need to still feel connected to her through the use of a narrative style in the form of letters that Harriet as a young girl, addresses to her dead mother, one of several addressees. "Mama," she writes, "I am not so lonesome if I can talk to you in my Book."[95] And to an absent mother she recounts in an intimate voice her feelings and experiences as she grows up, her first dance, her first beau, and then as she grows older, the vulnerability of a young black slave girl to the sexual exploitation of a slave owner.

She tells of the betrayal of her mother's mistress, who had left eleven-year-old Harriet to be sold in her will, despite the promise made to her mother that she would take care of Harriet. She admits to the love that she feels for her mistress who had "been almost a mother" to her since her maternal mother's death: "I love her like I love you. It might hurt you to hear that, but I can't help it."[96] The relationship had seemed especially strong to Harriet since her grandmother had nursed her mistress, and her mother had grown up and played with her like a sister before they understood that "the white girl be owning the black one."[97]

The attachments and connections reproduced between white mothers and their black slave girls are necessarily based in a system of betrayal and ownership and formed in the absence and lack of the maternal mother. Yet in *Tancy*, the connection and mother–daughter tie that exists between them is acknowledged when Tancy pays Miss Puddin a visit, once she is secure in her knowledge of freedom and independence. Miss Puddin claims that she was "more of a mother than ever" Tancy's mother was. Tancy admits to the truth of this and is sensitive to the "mother-tie [that] twanged between them like a strummed chord."[98]

Tancy's symbolic journey as a daughter from ownership and the unequal power relationship of a white mother to emancipation and a rediscovery of her own black roots and mother parallels the historical moment in which the novel is set. Tancy's journey however, resolves neither the contradictions and ambiguities between mother(s) and daughter nor racial difference. As Tancy comments, "everything was never *worked* out. Not with Miss Puddin, not with Sin."[99] Attachments between mothers and daughters, whether maternal, othermothers, or between surrogate mothers are thus structured across distance, contradictions, and differences.

A WHITE MOTHER AND BLACK DAUGHTER NARRATIVE WITH A DIFFERENCE

A more recent adult novel recommended for young adults also reproduces a mother–daughter relationship situated across racial difference. In Dori Sander's *Clover*, set in recent times in South Carolina, ten-year-old Clover and her white stepmother, who barely know each other, struggle to cross the racial and cultural differences and oppositions that divide them, after Clover's father is killed. Sara Kate, focalized by Clover as "strange," is objectified and criticized as one of those "white women" by Clover's family. The perceptive voice of Clover, aware of prejudice and difference, focalizes the distance that separates them at the beginning of their relationship:

> So here we are. Two strangers in a house. I think of all the things I think I'd like to say to her. Think of all the things I think she'd like to say to me. I do believe if we could bring ourselves to say those things it would close the wide gap between us and draw us closer together.[100]

Wishing for their voices to be in relationship and for them to "learn something from each other," Clover's voice reveals her need for attachment and love from a mother. The day Sara Kate calls her her daughter is for Clover "really something." The difference that will always be between them is humorously noted by Clover as she comments that:

> They say when two people live together, they start to look alike. Well, Sara Kate and I have been living together for a long time and there is no way we will ever look alike.[101]

GRANDMOTHERS, MOTHERS, AND DAUGHTERS

In *Black Women Writing Autobiography*, Braxton writes of "the importance of female bonding especially between the narrator, her grandmother, and her daughter" in the female slave narrative, *Incidents in the Life of A Slave Girl*.[102] The bonds of grandmothers, mothers, and daughters are also reproduced in Maya Angelou's autobiography, *I Know Why the Caged Bird Sings* and in the adult novel, Ntozake Shange's *Betsey Browne*. In Angelou's biography, particularly, the voice of the grandmother is strong, as she disciplines and protects her granddaughter in the face of racial inequality. In both of these texts set in the historical and social context of racial prejudice, the grandmothers are central figures in the family structures of the adolescent daughters.

Loving bonds between grandmothers and granddaughters are reproduced in young adult novels. The voice of the grandmother has been an important and strong one to Afeni in *The Dear One*. In Woodson's *Maizon at Blue Hill*, Maizon's grandmother has raised her granddaughter whom she encourages to move beyond the bounds of Brooklyn. The strength of the lineage of grandmothers, mothers, and daughters is celebrated in the poetry, autobiographical writings, and essays of black women in *Double Stitch* including for example, Alice Walker's essay, "In Search of Our Mothers' Gardens." Reproduced in both young adult and adult texts is the vital importance and emotional intensity of the mother–daughter relationship.

CROSS-CULTURAL DIFFERENCES AND SIMILARITIES

The diversity of these relationships constructed and imagined within different socio-economic contexts and time-frames emphasize the pluralities of black mother–daughter relationships and the differing experiences of black female adolescents as constructed in these texts. With the recent focus on the mother–daughter relationship, both in the field of scholarship and literary works, more young adult and adult novels are available in which this relationship is situated within different racial and ethnic contexts. A question to be raised is what commonalities and differences are there in relation to those mother–daughter relationships reproduced in other cultural contexts in young adult literature, particularly?

Limiting discussion to white American mother–daughter relationships reproduced in various contexts in young adult novels, and conscious that different theoretical perspectives produce different kinds of knowledge, some preliminary questions may be raised and some preliminary brief overall comparisons made with the African-American young adult novels discussed in this chapter. One might ask, for example, what different assumptions are made and what different narratives are written about adolescent development cross-culturally, which would affect the kind of mother and adolescent daughter relationships imagined and constructed in these texts?

The assumption that adolescence is a time of individuation and separation when the adolescent daughter separates from her mother with hostility and turns toward her father within the patriarchal nuclear family will provide a different script for a narrative plot of the mother–daughter relationship for example, than the assumption that adolescent daughters remain in relationship with their mothers. The question of what is valorized—an adolescent daughter's coming to maturity through attaining self-sufficiency and independence or through maintaining connections and being responsive to a mother while retaining a unique sense of self—will affect the the kind of mother–daughter relationship constructed within a particular narrative plot. A linear plot, for example, may construct a daughter's move towards independence by separation from her maternal mother. A plot more circular in conception may construct a daughter's connections and re-connections with a maternal or othermother.

The question may also be raised how different socio-economic contexts and assumptions of family structures and mothering affect the construction of this relationship? Assumptions that a mother and adolescent–daughter relationship is situated in the separate gendered spheres centered around the patriarchal nuclear family will provide a different narrative script perhaps, than the alternative reality that mother–daughter relationships are situated in contexts in which the mothers provide economic sustenance in one-parent families. The absence of the father particularly, may engender a different narrative plot in which mother, father, and daughter form a triangular relationship within the nuclear family, as scripted by Chodorow. In the small selection of African-American novels discussed in this chapter, the absence of the father is particularly noticeable.

Reproduced in the mother–daughter relationships in the specific novels discussed in this chapter, is a valorization of an adolescent daughter's attachment or re-connection to a mother, although not necessarily a maternal mother. The presence of a network of othermothers in some African-American young adult novels discussed, for example, in the novels, *The Dear One*, *Listen For the Fig Tree*, and *Lou in the Limelight*, emphasizes a community role of mothering—a concept which seems generally absent from young adult novels in which relationships between white mothers and adolescent daughters are constructed. Alternative mothers constructed in some of these latter relationships are more apt to be replacement mothers, whose connections to an adolescent girl are predicated on a maternal mother's permanent absence. Or, an alternative role mother may be the mother of the daughter's friend in a contrasting and separate sub-plot of a mother–daughter relationship. The questions then to be raised are: is this a difference that would hold true across a larger comparative study and how much do different social constructions of mothering affect the kind of mother–daughter relationships created in young adult literature?

The voices of adolescent daughters in several African-American young adult novels shift between the needs and responsibilities of self and those of their mothers—those of Muffin in *Listen For the Fig Tree* and Didi in *Motown and Didi*, for example. The absence of the patriarchal nuclear family and the mother's struggle to be both economic provider and affective nurturer is noticeable in the narrative plots in which this relationship is constructed. The construction of the mother–daughter relationship in these novels are in contrast to several constructed relationships of white mothers and adolescent daughters in the narrative plots of some young adult novels in which the separation of the daughter's voice from that of the mother's is culturally assumed and valorized.

In considering how this relationship is constructed and imagined

in young adult novels, one might also raise the question of how much
the formulaic conventions of young adult literature might also structure
this relationship across cultures? The voices of adolescent daughter
protagonists, with whom readers are more likely to identify, would
sometimes appear to be stronger and more perceptive than the more
fragile voices of their maternal mothers in relationships constructed
between both black maternal mothers and their daughters and white
maternal mothers and adolescent daughters. In this selection of African-American novels, the voices of Rainbow, Didi, and Muffin are
particularly strong, for example. In the relationships formulated
between maternal mothers and adolescent daughters in young adult
novels, there would appear to be an absence of the archetypal white
maternal mother or maternal "strong black mother," in comparison for
example, to Angelou's autobiography *I Know Why the Caged Bird
Sings*. Adolescent daughters may sometimes, Didi and Muffin for
example, be rescuers of less strong mothers thus subverting the powerlessness that is handed down from mother to daughter, whether the
mother be white or black.

In these African-American young adult novels, the awareness of
the vulnerability of being both black and female is often reproduced
in the voices of adolescent daughters in relation to their relationship
with their mothers. It is present in the voices of Didi and Afeni, for
example. The voice of Muffin speaks from a position of strength and
pride in her racial identity: "To be black was to be strong, to have
courage, to survive. And it wasn't an alone thing. It was family . . . It
was her mother."[103] Questions of power and powerlessness and racial
identity would thus seem integral to the construction of the black
mother and adolescent relationship in these novels.

In the majority of young adult novels, in which both black and
white mother and adolescent daughter relationships are constructed,
the mother is not a narrating agent in that she does not take up an "I"
position in the text and thus does not relate her thoughts and feelings
about the relationship from a subject position in the text. Focalized by
the daughter and other characters, she is most frequently an object in
the text, whether a black or a white mother; a mother who is spoken of
and spoken for by others, especially by a daughter. The formulaic conventions of young adult literature may thus cut across cultural differences to some extent in constructing particular kinds of narrative plots
and representations of mothers in which mother–daughter relationships

are reproduced and in which daughters must be represented as strong adolescent protagonists.

THEORETICAL ISSUES

I have listened to the voices in these texts as a white woman. Aware of the different theoretical positions of black and white feminism(s) in analyzing the mother–daughter relationship, I nevertheless, ask whether there are some points of intersection. How relevant, for example, are recent feminist revisions of female adolescents and their relationships with mothers by Gilligan and others to black female adolescents? The voices of daughters in these young adult novels strongly maintain connections with difference to either maternal mothers and othermothers for example, in different historical and socio-economic contexts. Their voices also struggle with the issues of independence, separation and their own needs in conjunction with meeting the needs and responsibilities of mothers. While Gilligan's research and others exclude black adolescents, for the most part in texts quoted in this chapter, are there yet points of connection here which may be useful in talking about the black mother and adolescent daughter relationship?

In affirming the attachments between African-American women, Collins refers to the mother–daughter relationship as "one fundamental relationship among black women."[104] Central to the different constructions of mother–daughter relationships in young adult novels, whether white or black, are the feelings of love, anger, and loss that daughters experience in relation to their mothers, which would affirm the centrality of the relationship in both black and white mother–daughter relationships. And while the theoretical perspectives of black and white feminists are diverse and are posited from very different positions, there is a convergence at least in the affirmation of the importance of the connections and continuities of the mother–daughter relationship which would appear to cross different cultures and theories.

bell hooks writes of the value of a "cross-ethnic feminist scholarship."[105] Cross-culturally, there would appear to be commonalities and interesting cultural differences in the structure of mother–daughter relationships in young adult novels. The work of Nancy Scheper Hughes for example, emphasizes the different social constructions of mothering and mother–daughter relationships in her research in Brazil.[106] Certainly, I have found insights from both black and white feminist theories useful in listening to the voices of black mothers and daughters in a literature in which cultural assumptions of adolescence and their parental relationships are scripted in books marketed for black and white adolescents alike.

The study of mother–daughter relationships in young adult literature emphasizes the importance of noting the multiplicity and diversity of this relationship in different social, cultural, and racial contexts. It also emphasizes the need to take into account revised narratives of female adolescent development which differ from a monolithic traditional adolescent psychology—in which the development of girls and their relationship with their mothers have been subsumed under a white male development narrative as an other unwritten story.

NOTES

1. Portions of this chapter are from Hilary S. Crew, "A Narrative Analysis of the Mother–Daughter Relationship in Selected Young Adult Novels" (Ph.D diss. in progress. Rutgers, The State University of New Jersey).
2. Alice Childress, *Rainbow Jordan* (New York: Coward, McCann & Geoghegan, 1981), 7.
3. Ibid., 58.
4. The term "maternal mother" is used throughout the text to define a daughter's biological mother.
5. See for example, Kay Vandergrift, "A Feminist Perspective on Multicultural Children's Literature in the Middle Years of the Twentieth Century," *Library Trends* 41, no. 3 (1993): 354–377.
6. Adrienne Rich, *Of Woman Born* (New York: W. W. Norton, 1976), 225.
7. See, for example, literary studies of the mother–daughter relationship from a white feminist perspective in novels published for adults recommended for high school students: Roni Natov, "Mothers and Daughters: Jamaica Kincaid's Pre-Oedipal Narrative," *Annual of the Modern Language Association Division on Children's Literature and The Children's Literature Association* 18 (1990): 1–16; Jeanne Gerlach, "Mother Daughter Relationships in Lois Duncan's *Daughters of Eve*," *The ALAN Review* 19, no. 1 (1991): 36–38.
8. Marianne Hirsch, *The Mother/Daughter Plot: Narrative, Psychoanalysis, Feminism* (Bloomington, IN: Indiana University Press, 1989), 132.
9. Nancy Chodorow, *The Reproduction of Mothering* (Berkeley, CA: University of California Press, 1978), 167.
10. Gloria I. Joseph, "Black Mothers and Daughters: Their Roles and Func-

tion in American Society," in *Common Differences: Conflicts in Black and White Feminist Perspectives*, by Gloria I. Joseph and Jill Lewis (Boston, MA: South End Press, 1986), 76–81.

11. Patricia Hill Collins, *Black Feminist Thought: Knowledge, Consciousness, and the Politics of Empowerment* (New York: Routledge, 1991), 116.

12. Joseph, 76.

13. Patricia Hill Collins, "The Meaning of Motherhood in Black Culture and Black Mother–Daughter Relationships," in *Double Stitch: Black Women Write About Mothers and Daughters*, ed. Patricia Bell-Scott et al. (New York: HarperPerennial, 1993), 47 & 53.

14. Johnetta Cole, "Preface," in *Double Stitch*, ed. Bell-Scott et al., xiii–xiv.

15. For example, Carmen Subryan, "Circles: Mother and Daughter Relationships in Toni Morrison's *Song of Solomon*," *Sage* V, no. 1 (Summer 1988): 34–36; Rosalie Riegle Troester, "Turbulence and Tenderness: Mothers, Daughters, and 'Othermothers' in Paule Marshall's *Brown Girl, Brownstones*", in *Double Stitch*, ed. Bell-Scott et al., 163–172.

16. Joseph, 80.

17. Mary C. Lewis, *Herstory: Black Female Rites of Passage* (Chicago: IL: African-American Images, 1988), 7.

18. Terri Apter, *Altered Loves: Mothers and Daughters During Adolescence* (New York: St. Martin's Press, 1990), 77.

19. Carol Gilligan, "Preface," in *Making Connections: The Relational Worlds of Adolescent Girls at Emma Willard School*, ed. Carol Gilligan et al. (Cambridge, MA: Harvard University Press, 1990), 20.

20. Ibid., 10.

21. Ibid., 5.

22. Janie Ward, "Racial Identity Formation and Transformation," in *Making Connections*, ed. Gilligan et al., 220.

23. Joanne Braxton, *Black Women Writing Autobiography: A Tradition Within A Tradition* (Philadelphia, PA: Temple University Press, 1989), 205.

24. Collins, "The Meaning of Motherhood in Black Culture and Black Mother–Daughter Relationships," in *Double Stitch*, ed. Bell-Scott et al., 55.

25. Ibid., 54–57.

26. Collins, *Black Feminist Thought*, 127.

27. Peter Blos, "Modifications in the Traditional Psychoanalytic Theory of Female Adolescent Development," *Adolescent Psychiatry* 8 (1980): 16–17.

28. Collins, *Black Feminist Thought*, 29.

29. Collins, "The Meaning of Motherhood in Black Culture," in *Double*

Stitch, ed. Bell-Scott et al., 48.

30. Childress, 26.
31. Ibid., 11.
32. Ibid., 26.
33. Ibid., 12.
34. Hirsch, 170 & 194.
35. Childress, 30.
36. Joseph writes of the tradition in which black mothers "have served as role models for their daughters" and the special difficulties of adolescent mothers in fulfilling this role. See "Black Mothers and Daughters" in *Double Stitch*, ed. Bell-Scott et al., 101–102.
37. Childress, 9.
38. Childress, 138.
39. Virginia Hamilton, *Sweet Whispers, Brother Rush* (New York: Philomel, 1982), 12.
40. Ibid., 17.
41. Ibid., 211.
42. Jacqueline Woodson, *The Dear One* (New York: Delacorte, 1991; Dell, 1993, 84).
43. Ibid., 85–86.
44. Barbara Christian writes about the "domineering mother [which] has been so much a part of black mythology," see *Black Feminist Criticism: Perspectives on Black Women Writers* (New York: Pergamon Press, 1985), 17; Collins writes about the "controlling images" of black motherhood and the need to unmask the images of the "matriarch" and "superstrong black mother," see *Black Feminist Thought*, 117.
45. Collins, *Black Feminist Thought*, 127.
46. Walter Dean Myers, *Motown and Didi: A Love Story* (New York: Viking Kestrel, 1984), 10.
47. Ibid., 13.
48. Ibid., 90.
49. Ibid., 73.
50. Ibid., 17.
51. Collins, *Black Feminist Thought*, 122.
52. Sandra Govan writes of the lack of the "usual or traditional community support structures typically illustrative of Afro-American life and culture" in "Alice Childress's *Rainbow Jordan*: The Black Aesthetic Returns Dressed in Adolescent Fiction," ChLA Quarterly 13 (Summer 1988): 70–74.
53. See Carol Gilligan and others in *Making Connections*; also, Carol Gilligan, *In A Different Voice* (Cambridge, MA: Harvard University Press, 1982).

54. Sharon Bell Mathis, *Listen For the Fig Tree* (New York: Viking Press, 1974), 84.
55. Ibid., 10.
56. Ibid., 113.
57. Ibid., 153.
58. Myers, 13.
59. Govan, 72.
60. Myers, 13.
61. Woodson, 31.
62. Ibid.
63. Ibid., 13.
64. Ibid., 69.
65. Ibid., 62.
66. Hamilton, 69.
67. Ibid., 173.
68. Kristin Hunter, *Lou in the Limelight* (New York: Scribner's), 291.
69. Woodson, *The Dear One*, 60.
70. Vy Higginson with Tonya Bolden, *Mama, I Want To Sing* (New York: Scholastic, 1992), 48.
71. Hunter, 213.
72. Ibid.
73. Collins, *Black Feminist Thought*, 128.
74. Hunter, 121.
75. Ibid., 122.
76. Ibid., 135.
77. Higginson with Bolden, 176.
78. Sara Ruddick writes of the concept of "maternal practice" separated from that of the biological mother which "begins in a response to the reality of a biological child in a particular social world," see (*Maternal Thinking: Toward A Politics of Peace*. New York: Ballantine Books, 1989), 17.
79. Collins, *Black Feminist Thought*, 132.
80. Joyce Carol Thomas, *Water Girl* (New York: Avon Books, 1986), 106.
81. Belinda Hurmence, ed., *My Folks Don't Want Me To Talk About Slavery: Twenty-one Oral Histories of Former North Carolina Slaves* (Winston-Salem, NC: John F. Blair, 1984), 76.
82. Ibid., 56.
83. Belinda Hurmence, *Tancy* (New York: Clarion Books, 1984), 203.
84. Ibid., 2.
85. bell hooks, *Ain't I A Woman: Black Women and Feminism* (Boston, MA: South End Press, 1981), 24.
86. Hurmence, *Tancy*, 27.
87. Ibid., 30.

88. Ibid., 11.
89. Ibid., 158.
90. bell hooks writes of the "sexist ideology" of the 19th century, in which black women were denigrated "as the originator of sexual sin" and constructed as the "embodiment of female evil and lust" in opposition to the "glorified de-sexualized identity" of white women, see *Ain't I A Woman*, 31 & 33.
91. Hurmence, *Tancy*, 182.
92. Ibid., 203.
93. Ibid., 158.
94. Valerie Smith writes of the differences between male and female slave narratives in the "Introduction," in *Incidents in the Life of A Slave Girl: Harriet Jacobs* (New York: Oxford University Press, 1988), xxvii–xl.
95. Mary E. Lyons, *Letters From A Slave Girl* (New York: Scribner's, 1992), 4.
96. Ibid.
97. Ibid., 10.
98. Hurmence, *Tancy*, 194.
99. Ibid., 201.
100. Dori Sanders, *Clover* (New York: Fawcett Columbine, 1991), 100.
101. Ibid., 130.
102. Braxton, *Black Women Writing Autobiography*, 38.
103. Mathis, *Listen For The Fig Tree*, 170.
104. Collins, *Black Feminist Thought*, 96.
105. bell hooks, *Talking Back: Thinking Feminist, Thinking Black* (Boston, MA: South End Press, 1989), 48.
106. Nancy Scheper-Hughes' research shows, for example, that alienation and distance between mothers and daughters are regarded as an "aberration" in the community of Alto women in the northeastern region of Brazil, and that the community of the Alto is clustered around "intergenerational female-centered households," see *Death Without Weeping: The Violation of Everyday Life in Brazil* (Berkeley, CA: University of California Press, 1992), 310.

REFERENCES

Angelou, Maya. *I Know Why the Caged Bird Sings*. New York: Bantam, 1971.
Apter, Terri. *Altered Loves: Mothers and Daughters During Adolescence*. New York: St. Martin's Press, 1990.
Bell-Scott, Patricia and others, eds. *Double Stitch: Black Women Write About Mothers and Daughters*. New York: HarperPerennial, 1993.
Blos, Peter. "Modifications in the Traditional Psychoanalytic Theory of Fe-

male Adolescent Development." *Adolescent Psychiatry.* Vol. 8. Chicago, IL: University of Chicago Press, 1980: 8–24.

Braxton, Joanne M. *Black Women Writing Autobiography: A Tradition Within A Tradition.* Philadelphia, PA: Temple University Press, 1989.

Childress, Alice. *Rainbow Jordan.* New York: Coward, McCann & Geoghegan, 1981.

Chodorow, Nancy. *The Reproduction of Mothering.* Berkeley, CA: University of California Press, 1978.

Christian, Barbara. *Black Feminist Criticism: Perspectives on Black Women Writers.* New York: Pergamon Press, 1985.

Cole, Johnetta. "Preface." In *Double Stitch: Black Women Write About Mothers and Daughters,* ed. Patricia Bell-Scott et al., xiii–v. New York: Harper-Perennial, 1993.

Collins, Patricia Hill. *Black Feminist Thought: Knowledge, Consciousness, and the Politics of Empowerment.* New York: Routledge, 1991.

Collins, Patricia Hill. "The Meaning of Motherhood in Black Culture and Black Mother–Daughter Relationships." In *Double Stitch: Black Women Write About Mothers and Daughters.* ed. Patricia Bell-Scott et al., 42–60. New York: HarperPerennial, 1993.

Crew, Hilary, "A Narrative Analysis of the Mother–Daughter Relationship in Selected Young Adult Novels." Ph.D. diss. in progress, Rutgers, The State University of New Jersey.

Gerlach, Jeanne. "Mother Daughter Relationships in Lois Duncan's *Daughters of Eve.*" *The ALAN Review* 19, no. 1 (Fall 1991): 36–38.

Gilligan, Carol. *In A Different Voice: Psychological Theory and Women's Development.* Cambridge, MA: Harvard University Press, 1982.

Gilligan Carol and others, eds. *Making Connections: The Relational Worlds of Adolescent Girls at Emma Willard School.* Cambridge, MA: Harvard University Press, 1990.

Govan, Sandra Y. "Alice Childress's *Rainbow Jordan*: The Black Aesthetic Returns Dressed in Adolescent Fiction." *Children's Literature Association Quarterly* 13, no.1 (Summer 1988): 70–74.

Hamilton, Virginia. *Sweet Whispers, Brother Rush.* New York: Philomel, 1982.

Higginson, Vy with Tonya Bolden. *Mama, I Want To Sing.* New York: Scholastic, 1992.

Hirsch, Marianne. *The Mother/Daughter Plot: Narrative, Psychoanalysis, Feminism.* Bloomington, IN: Indiana University Press, 1989.

hooks, bell. *Ain't I A Woman: Black Women and Feminism.* Boston, MA: South End Press, 1981.

_____. *Talking Back: Thinking Feminist, Thinking Black.* Boston, MA: South End Press, 1989.

Hunter, Kristin. *Lou in the Limelight*. New York: Scribner's, 1981.

Hurmence, Belinda, ed. *My Folks Don't Want Me To Talk About Slavery: Twenty-one Oral Histories of Former North Carolina Slaves*. Winston-Salem, NC: John F. Blair, 1984.

Hurmence, Belinda. *Tancy*. New York: Clarion Books, 1984.

Jacobs, Harriet. *Incidents in the Life of A Slave Girl*. New York: Oxford University Press, 1988.

Joseph, Gloria I. "Black Mothers and Daughters: Their Roles and Function in American Society." In *Common Differences: Conflicts in Black and White Feminist Perspectives*, by Gloria I. Joseph and Jill Lewis, 75–126. Boston, MA: South End Press, 1986.

Joseph, Gloria I. and Jill Lewis. *Common Differences: Conflicts in Black and White Feminist Perspectives*. Boston, MA: South End Press, 1986.

Lewis, Mary C. *Herstory: Black Female Rites of Passage*. Chicago, IL: African American Images, 1988.

Lyons, Mary E. *Letters From A Slave Girl: The Story of Harriet Jacobs*. New York: Scribner's, 1992.

Mathis, Sharon Bell. *Listen For The Fig Tree*. New York: Viking Press, 1974.

Myers, Walter Dean. *Motown and Didi: A Love Story*. New York: Viking Kestrel, 1984.

Natov, Roni. "Mothers and Daughters: Jamaica Kincaid's Pre-Oedipal Narrative." *Annual of the Modern Language Association Division on Children's Literature and The Children's Literature Association* 18 (1990): 1–16.

Rich, Adrienne. *Of Woman Born: Motherhood as Experience and Institution*. New York: W. W. Norton, 1976.

Ruddick, Sara. *Maternal Thinking: Toward A Politics of Peace*. New York: Ballantine Books, 1985.

Sanders, Dori. *Clover*. New York: Fawcett Columbine, 1990.

Scheper-Hughes, Nancy. *Death Without Weeping: The Violence of Everyday Life in Brazil*. Berkeley, CA: University of California Press, 1992.

Shange, Ntozake. *Betsey Brown*. New York: St. Martin's Press, 1985.

Subryan, Carmen. "Circles: Mother and Daughter Relationships in Toni Morrison's *Song of Solomon*," *Sage* 5, no.1 (Summer 1988): 34–36.

Thomas, Joyce Carol. *Water Girl*. New York: Avon Books, 1986.

Vandergrift, Kay. "A Feminist Perspective on Multicultural Children's Literature in the Middle Years of the Twentieth Century." *Library Trends* 41, no. 3 (1993): 354–377.

Ward, Janie. "Racial Identity Formation and Transformation." In *Making Connections: The Relational Worlds of Adolescent Girls at Emma Willard School*, ed. Carol Gilligan et al., 215–232. Cambridge, MA: Harvard University Press, 1990.

Woodson, Jacqueline. *The Dear One*. New York: Dell, 1993.
Woodson, Jacqueline. *Maizon at Blue Hill*. New York: Delacorte, 1992.

FOUR

Periodical Literature for African-American Young Adults: A Neglected Resource

Lynn S. Cockett and Janet R. Kleinberg

The purpose of this chapter is twofold. First, it is an examination of the young adult magazine publishing industry. Specific attention is given to the relevance of magazines to African-American teens throughout history. Second, and perhaps more important to those who work with young adults, is the appended bibliography of magazines. The annotations cite those magazines that seem to best suit the needs of African-American teens, and also to succeed in selling well enough to satisfy a very competitive market.

In order to thoroughly understand the processes involved in magazine writing, editing, and publishing, we have talked with people in those positions at a variety of magazines for young adults. We are especially grateful to the staff at *Black Beat, Sassy, Seventeen, Young and Modern*, and *Young Sisters and Brothers*, all of whom were extremely helpful, and who each added an interesting perspective to our research and our continually developing philosophy of reaching young adults.

Reaching young adults and connecting them with information is the most important goal that each of us in this field holds. All librarians and information professionals approach this objective through unique and distinct means. It has become increasingly evident, based upon library circulation statistics and unobtrusive observation, that teens spend a considerable amount of their reading time involved with magazines. It is for this reason we believe that each person interested in service to young adults must familiarize him/herself with this continually growing genre. Regardless of individual biases among librarians, magazine use is a given in the field of work with young adults. Illiteracy is still a societal problem in the United States; however, a more subtle issue is that of aliteracy. Most adolescents know how to read, but many choose not to read. Teens often claim lack of time as the main reason that they no longer read books for pleasure once they reach high school. Magazines offer easy reading, short articles, the most current information, and the appeal of powerful graphics. Peer pressure dictates that a teenager with a hardcover book must somehow not fit into the norm. Magazines are an accepted, indeed preferred, form of print for this age group.

Lee Kravitz, Editorial Director of Scholastic's three social studies periodicals, has said that, "The purpose of magazines is to connect kids to the world. In order to make magazines as compelling as possible, they must speak directly to teens in a language they consider authentic."[1] Authenticity is perhaps the most important characteristic of a voice that speaks to youth. Whether that voice is the voice of a classroom teacher, a librarian, or a publication, it must be true. Often, the best intentions sound saccharine, and young adults are astute at recognizing and rejecting patronizing voices.

OVERVIEW

In order to accomplish our twofold task of examining and recommending magazines, we will first provide a context for understanding magazines in the 90s by reviewing magazine publishing for youth through history. In this section of the chapter, we are concerned with the definitions of youth and the changing attitudes of adults toward children and young adults throughout distinct periods of history.

Next, we examine the current crop of magazines marketed directly to young adults. In this section we are most concerned with those magazines that seem to be the blockbusters in sales and marketing. The focus is upon general interest, lifestyle periodicals.

Finally, we look closely at the few magazines marketed specifically for an African-American audience. In doing so, we compare the magazines marketed to the general, mainstream public with those for black youths. This section of the chapter asks questions about mainstream magazines, and whether or not they meet the needs of African-

American teens—or if they even attempt to do so.

Unfortunately, many good magazines for youth, specifically minority youth, have failed. From 1921 to 1922, W.E.B. DuBois, eminent black leader in education, published a magazine called *The Brownies' Book*. This periodical's short life is testament to the problem of sustaining magazines for minority youth audiences. A more recent example of the same unfortunate phenomenon is the (1986) demise of *Ebony Jr.!* These magazines will be discussed in greater detail later in the chapter.

MAGAZINE PUBLISHING FOR YOUTH: A BRIEF HISTORY

Magazines for children and young adults have long been a part of the publishing industry. A retrospective examination of periodicals for youth provides a window on the changes in society's perception of childhood and young adulthood. "Throughout the 19th century, there was much debate over the nature of the child. Older notions of innate depravity yielded to more benign definitions. Concepts of children's books and magazines shifted to accommodate, and even to champion the newer attitudes."[2]

The Youth's Companion

Early magazines for children, such as *The Youth's Companion*, whose first edition appeared on June 6, 1827, were didactic and prescriptive. The transition that took place in the mid-nineteenth century included a shift in thought away from viewing children as merely small adults. Society was moving toward a perception of childhood as a distinct developmental stage, with its own socialization skills and a need for literature that reflected the characteristics of children.

Over time, *The Youth's Companion* changed in tone, shifting its emphasis to reflect these social changes. Editors recognized the need to include amusements such as puzzles, word plays, and more cheerful graphics. It moved away from moralistic stories to stories of adventure and fun. In 1860 anonymity of authorship was abandoned. Such well-known authors as Louisa May Alcott and Frances Hodgson Burnett were given bylines for their fiction, signalling a change in the magazine's tone. The magazine began to de-emphasize didacticism and emphasize literary quality. By the late nineteenth century it included better illustrations, puzzles, and more fiction.

Radencich writes that the 1840s and 1850s were a time of energetic literary development in America. The country saw a burgeoning of its own literature, including magazines for youth. A preponderance of these magazines were religious in nature; they were intended to instruct and elevate rather than to entertain.[3] This emerging American literature was not truly democratic in its representation. While it was distinctly American, it was not inclusive of all of America's people. African-Americans, still under the yoke of slavery, remained disenfranchised and ignored by mainstream presses. The belief that democracy depended upon an informed citizenry resulted in a flourishing system of public education and free public libraries. Blacks, however, as slaves were alienated from this system. They were, ". . . systematically excluded from full participation in the 'American dream.' "[4] Their rich oral tradition was not validated in print until many years later.

St. Nicholas Magazine

St. Nicholas Magazine began its illustrious reign during the 1870s. It joined and eventually superseded *The Youth's Companion* as the most popular and widely circulated magazine for children. *St. Nicholas* was not rooted in the same religious ethos as its older rival. Its stated goal was to, "make the spirit of St. Nicholas (Santa Claus) bright in each boy and girl in good, pleasant and helpful ways, and to clear away clouds that sometimes shut it out."[5]

The girls and boys to whom this magazine addressed its message and iconography were white. Black children, when included, were depicted as dehumanized caricatures. This problem was obvious to W.E.B. DuBois, who in 1919 decided to create a magazine which would edify the black child. At the time, DuBois was editor of *The Crisis*, the NAACP's publication. DuBois' first idea was to publish a "Children's Number" under the auspices of *The Crisis*. Plans changed, and a full-blown children's magazine was born: *The Brownies' Book*.

The Brownies' Book

From January 1920 to December 1921, exactly twenty-four issues of *The Brownies' Book* were published. DuBois established seven goals for the publication. The first was to engender black pride. One way in which the magazine accomplished this task was through the use of photographs of black children engaged in all the activities of childhood. These were included in order to validate the experience of the African-American child.

A second objective was to teach black history. A column entitled "As the Crow Flies" chronicled and summarized developments in black advancement toward equality. Historical narratives taught children about their ancestors and heritage.

Third, the magazine featured biographical sketches of prominent black leaders in order to teach children that people of color could and should hold important political and community positions. Among DuBois' contemporaries were two black leaders of stature equal to his: Booker T. Washington and Marcus Garvey. Washington's philosophy of gradual integration without focusing on first attaining political rights was antithetical to DuBois' passionate belief in "The Talented Tenth," the idea that blacks should be educated to become leaders. Because of the philosophical schism between the two men, Booker T. Washington never graced the pages of *The Brownies' Book*. Neither were children encouraged to embrace Marcus Gravey's back-to-Africa philosophy. This was simply at odds with DuBois' faith in the ability of blacks to maintain their cultural heritage while achieving success in America.

The Brownies' Book's remaining goals, as stated, were: "To teach …a code of honor and action in their relations with white children.… To turn their little hurts and resentments into emulation, ambition and love of their own homes and companions. . . . To point out the best amusements and joys and worthwhile things of life. . . . And to inspire them to prepare for definite occupations and duties with a broad spirit of sacrifice."[6] Another objective, according to Morah, included furthering the education of black children. The magazine also published reader mail, thus creating a forum for the exchange of ideas and information.

Financial difficulties forced *The Brownies' Book* to feature a bold statement on its December 1921 cover, addressing its readers directly: "And now the month has come to say goodbye. We are sorry—much sorrier than any of you, for it has all been such fun. . . ."[7]

Although its life was brief, *The Brownies' Book* was no small accomplishment. It was the first magazine published specifically for black youth (its audience was six- to sixteen-year-olds). It was not until

1973 that another publication with similar goals appeared. That magazine was *Ebony Jr.!*

Ebony Jr.!

Despite a gap of more than fifty years between them, *The Brownies' Book* and *Ebony Jr.!* shared many common values and characteristics, both stated and implied. Each of them stressed racial awareness. Readers were encouraged to perceive socio-economic class and geographic origins vis-à-vis their race. African and African-American heritage were emphasized. Family loyalty, gender roles and racial unity were also important subjects.[8] In *The Brownies' Book*, values which reflected the Biblical "fruits of the spirit" included gentleness, goodness, kindness, and self-control. *Ebony Jr.!* also taught values, but with less emphasis on things spiritual and more on things practical such as hard work and honesty. We will see later that current young adult magazines continue to communicate values reflective of the 1990s.

Ebony Jr.! claimed to have an audience of children through the age of fourteen. Nevertheless, the style and content of the magazine seem to have been geared toward a younger audience. Similar in appearance and format to *Highlights for Children Magazine*, *Ebony Jr.!* included many cartoon-like illustrations, puzzles, and juvenile stories. The biographical sketches so important to the pages of *The Brownies' Book* were also important to *Ebony Jr.!* However, while *The Brownies' Book*'s sketches were about prominent leaders and figures of interest to adults as well as children, *Ebony Jr.!* featured many black Americans whose work was of particular interest to younger children. A typical biographical sketch featured the work and a few facts about people who wrote children's literature, Eloise Greenfield, for example.

Like its predecessor, *Ebony Jr.!* filled a great need for literature by, for, and about African-Americans. It also served, as did *The Brownies' Book*, to empower young black people with a sense of pride in themselves and their culture.

CONTEMPORARY MAGAZINES FOR YOUNG ADULTS

Setting The Context

Teens are choosing magazines as their sources of information and entertainment. Circulation statistics (1992) from the Nathan Straus Young Adult Library in New York City indicate that each non-fiction book in the young adult collection circulated only .72 times, while each of its circulating magazines was borrowed 4.33 times. This mandates that librarians and information specialists concerned with the needs of young patrons examine those magazines. Our mission in this section of the chapter is to give readers an overview of the types of periodicals being produced for teenagers. We understand that much of this section is not focused primarily on African-American youth or publications specifically for them; it is nevertheless necessary to provide a context in which to examine the emergence of special audience magazines.

We are, therefore, attempting to select and describe the magazines against which specialized publications are competing for a share of the market. Our criteria are based upon format and content and the way in which each of these magazines treats self-esteem and other current issues of importance to teens.

Zines

Our research does not examine special interest magazines, current event periodicals, or educational magazines such as those published by Scholastic Press. Neither does it examine independent "zines." "Zine" is a generic term for a variety of alternative press publications. The advent of desktop publishing has provided a forum in which zines flourish.[10] Zines are very small publications, usually seen by fewer than one thousand people per issue, which address esoteric topics. Readers of zines comprise a geographically diverse network of like-minded persons.

Zines cover a multitude of topics ranging from food to art to Satanism. Ephemeral in nature, many zines publish only one or two issues before they disappear. One elder statesman of this genre is *The Realist*, which began publishing in the 1960s. Back in publication after a long hiatus, it takes a satirical look at all aspects of American life and politics, mixing fact and fiction. Music zines appeal to hardcore fans of many varieties. Teenagers, as major music consumers, are attracted to publications such as *Metal Curse*, with its focus on heavy metal music and current reviews. *The Teen Scene* focuses on modern pop music. Ubiquitous fanzines are published for lovers of Madonna, Jimi Hendrix, and the Beatles, to name just a few. Zines should not be dismissed when building a YA collection. Some attention may be given them simply by including reviews of zines. An excellent zine review is *Factsheet 5*; it is listed in the sources consulted.

Four Mass Market Publications:
Sassy, Seventeen, Teen & YM

Magazines for young adult women also address current sociological issues, such as AIDS and abortion, and topics which are approached from a more political perspective including the environment and political correctness. The most widely read magazines in this category are *YM* (*Young and Modern*), *Teen*, *Seventeen*, and *Sassy*. *YM*, with its polished look and emphasis on fashion, beauty, and self-help quizzes, reaches over 1.25 million readers each month. *Sassy*, whose initial circulation was 500,000, has recently jumped to an impressive 750,000 readers per month.

The circulation of this relatively new magazine grew dramatically during its first four or five years and has reached a plateau. Marjorie Ingall, one of *Sassy*'s three staff writers, explained that this leveling off in growth should not be construed as negative, pointing out that the magazine is willing to forego wider circulation in favor of maintaining its focus and unique journalistic style.[11]

YM's content is reader-driven; it relies on reader mail and focus groups. Editors at *YM* are committed to providing teenagers with information that they ask for and expect. Groups of teens are invited to the magazine's offices in order for editors and writers to interview them and glean information to plan future issues.

Unlike *YM*, *Sassy*'s content is determined by editorial decisions based upon staff perceptions of information teens need to know or have. The editorial ethos is to make these issues accessible to teens who might not be aware of or interested in them prior to reading the magazine.

Today's teenagers favor a television format for its slickness and brevity. The MTV generation wants information fast with a minimum of effort.[12] The magazine industry accomplishes a similar style with colorful graphics and short articles punctuated with the most current teen slang. Some magazines employ the use of this vernacular better than others.

Sassy maintains a chatty, intimate style, described by writer

Marjorie Ingall as similar to a letter from a best friend.[13] Writers and editors at *Sassy* "take great pains within this conversational tone to make sure that everything is grammatically correct. When [they] use the word *like*, [they] always set it off by commas. The copy editor also checks every bit of copy against a *Sassy* style guide."[14] This style is effective in drawing readers into the content because it reads the way teenagers' conversations sound. A similar approach is employed at *Young Sisters and Brothers*, which will be discussed in greater detail in the next section of this chapter.

All four of these lifestyle magazines, *Sassy, Seventeen, Teen*, and *YM*, are obviously marketed and written for female audiences. Among the diverse field of general interest magazines for young adults, there is only one written specifically for young men. This is *Dirt*. Published quarterly, with no immediate plans for greater frequency, *Dirt*'s subtitle offers "fuel for young men."

Common to these popular mainstream magazines are fashion layouts, advice columns, Hollywood celebrity profiles, some fiction and reviews, and the ubiquitous self-help quizzes. The differentiating characteristic of each of these magazines is its own perspective and the position each one takes on the issues that they all address. *Teen, Seventeen*, and *YM* tend to take a mainstream approach, while *Sassy*'s context is somewhat more feminist and anti-establishment. For this reason, *Sassy* is perceived by some of its competitors as an alternative magazine. Readers of *YM, Seventeen*, and *Teen* are seen as heading toward *Mademoiselle* and *Cosmopolitan*, while *Sassy* readers may find themselves moving on to alternative zines or magazines such as *Harper's* and *The New Yorker*, whose perspectives are more politically left of center.[15]

All of these magazines reflect and therefore validate the young adult experience. The volatile world of teens is one in which advocates are needed and welcomed. Through their advice columns and their published reader mail, periodicals for teens provide a forum for interchange among teen readers as well as with their adult role models. As mainstream publications, they succeed because they do indeed reflect the concerns and interests of mainstream teens.

Content Analysis of Four Mainstream Magazines

Of significant note is the absence to any meaningful degree of

African-Americans in the pages of *Sassy, Seventeen, Teen* and *YM*. Close scrutiny of their pages yielded noteworthy results. The units of analysis for this section of the study were twelve issues of each magazine from the publication years 1992 and 1993. We chose six variables: first, the use of cover models of color; second, the frequency of advertisements featuring or including African-Americans; third, feature photo spreads in which black models appeared; fourth, the inclusion of African-American celebrities; fifth, feature articles on racial issues; and sixth, human interest stories about African-Americans. The table below shows the results, noting the number of times in twelve issues each magazine contained models of color or stories relating to African-American issues. Approximate percentages are explained in the following text.

**Content Analysis of Four Mainstream Magazines
In Relation to African-American Issues**

Categories	Mass Market Magazines			
	Sassy	*Seventeen*	*Teen*	*YM*
Cover Models	1	2	0	0
Ad Models	23	29	21	29
Photo Spreads	12	37	13	20
Celebrities	16	45	12	18
Human Interest Stories	12	14	11	13
Racial Issues	1	1	0	1

Cover Models

Out of the forty-eight magazines studied, black cover models appeared only three times in two of the publications. Of these three covers, both of those from *Seventeen Magazine* featured celebrities. Will Smith of television's *The Fresh Prince of Bel Air* graced the cover of the July 1992 issue, and the December 1992 cover featured the female vocal group En Vogue. Interestingly, the one issue of *Sassy*

Magazine which featured an African-American on its cover, December 1992, was its annual reader-produced issue. The model used for that cover was not a professional but rather a young woman from the Bronx, New York.

Advertisement Models

The second variable, the use of advertisements including people of color, is relatively similar for each of the magazines. Using the numbers in the table, we calculated a percentage based on the total number of advertisements in each magazine. These percentages ranged from a low of *Seventeen*'s 5.6% to a high of *Teen Magazine*'s 9.2%. When asked if its advertising department makes conscious decisions to include advertisements with black models, *Seventeen* editor Catherine Cavender replied that while there are some advertisements that are unacceptable at *Seventeen* as at *YM*, the editorial staff does not really have any input.[16] Companies choose their own models. However, if an advertiser were to ask about how to target the *Seventeen* market, Catherine would try to encourage them to use ethnically diverse models. Given the fact that the content of advertisements is completely up to the manufacturer's discretion, it appears that Madison Avenue's executives are beginning to recognize the importance of diversity.

Photo Spreads

Third, we examined photo spreads. Our criterion for this variable was that the photo spreads needed to be included in a full-length article or fashion lay-out. We counted only the number of photo spreads which included African-American models, not the number of models. In this series of numbers, *Seventeen* scored highest at 38.5%. This was followed by *Teen* at 18%, *YM* at 15%, and *Sassy* at 9%.

Celebrities

Fourth, we studied the number of times each magazine included either photo spreads or articles about African-American celebrities. It is surprising to see that *Teen* did not lead the group, since it is generally regarded as more celebrity oriented than its competitors. This could be the result of a deliberate decision by the *Teen* editorial staff to appeal to a specific demographic group, namely white female teen-agers. *Sassy* consistently includes fewer celebrities than its competi-tors, emphasizing the fact that a celebrity is not a hero.[17] When *Sassy* does include celebrities, the percentage of people of color is much higher (at 44%), than its competitors. *Seventeen*'s percentage of African-American celebrities is 13.4, *Teen*'s is four, and *YM*'s is three.

Human Interest Stories

The fifth variable, human interest stories about or including Afri-can-Americans, appears at first glance to have been well-developed in each of these magazines. We were quite flexible regarding inclusion in this category. Many of the young people who appeared in these maga-zines and are therefore represented in this statistic are young African-American men whose opinions were cited in regular features such as *Sassy*'s now defunct "What He Said," *Seventeen*'s "Guy Talk," and *YM*'s "What Guys Think." Former *YM* editor Catherine Cavender stated that specific editorial instructions were given to the "What Guys Think" writers and photographers to seek out young men from various ethnic groups, particularly African-Americans. From our study, it appears as though similar instructions are incorporated into the produc-tion of each of these columns. A percentage calculation is not neces-sary for this variable, since all four magazines generally include similar numbers of such material.

Articles About Racial Issues

The results of the final criterion, articles specifically devoted to racial topics, were a disappointment. The dearth of photographs includ-ing African-Americans foreshadows these findings. In forty-eight dif-ferent magazines, there were only three articles specifically addressing race and African-Americans. The first article, *Seventeen Magazine*'s January, 1992 "It's Not Black and White" is about interracial dating.[18] It focuses on many teens and their feelings and experiences. African-Americans are included among the many ethnic groups represented, but are not the sole topic of the article. It covers important aspects of interracial dating and young adulthood, addressing topics relative to parents, peers, and outsiders. Most of the examples are about young white women who date outside of their race, and, therefore, the article seems addressed to them, even though the photo spreads all feature a young African-American woman and a young white man. Still, it is a significant piece about a major issue of concern to young adults.

The second article regarding racial matters appeared in the November 1992 issue of *YM*. This piece about the 1992 Los Angeles riots following the Rodney King verdict recounts the story told by a young African-American woman. She describes the looting and violence in the streets of her own neighborhood, and wonders why people acted out their anger in such destructive ways.[19] While the article addressed an important, timely topic, it might have been better had it included the perspective of those involved in the riots. This article seems to have been *YM*'s clear choice of an African-American woman with politically correct but not necessarily representative feelings about the riots.

The third article was found in the December 1992 issue of *Sassy*. Once again, it is interesting to note that the article under consideration, "Why Black Unity In South Africa Is Not Happening" appears in *Sassy*'s 1992 reader-produced issue.[20] Written by sixteen-year-old Samantha Shapiro, it gives a clear and cogent analysis of the two black factions in opposition to apartheid. Through telephone interviews with representatives of both the African National Congress and the Inkatha Freedom Party, Samantha was able to clarify for teen readers the roots of hostile feelings that exist within the black population of South Africa. This young reporter dispels myths created by the popular press which label the roots of this internecine conflict as tribal.

ANALYSIS

These numbers are significant and valid. They are worth noting because the very act of flipping through the pages of a magazine and recognizing people who look like oneself validates one's experience and feelings. That shock of recognition is especially important to minority teenagers, who rarely see others like themselves in the mass media. However, these numbers alone do not tell the whole story.

Each of the four periodicals studied has its own personality. *Teen* is directed toward a somewhat younger audience than its three competitors. In a comparison of representative articles, *Teen*'s sexuality issues deal with more superficial matters such as "Guy-Rated Looks," a February 1993 article. *Seventeen*, *Sassy*, and *YM* focus on more substantive matters such as young men's opinions of sexually active girls and AIDS related issues.

Not only do these periodicals differ in the seriousness of their content, but they also diverge from one another on the basis of being more or less inclusive in tone. *Seventeen, YM,* and *Teen* are variations on a theme. These publishers are marketing their magazines to the segment of the teen population with the largest disposable income—white, suburban, and middle-class females.

Perhaps because of its progressive fashion layouts and its deliberate use of models with unconventional good looks, *Sassy* communicates a sense of inclusion. Although the numerical data seems to tell a different story, *Sassy*'s message is that there is room for individual differences, that one monolithic standard of beauty does not apply. Cultural diversity is celebrated. Of the four publications studied, *Sassy* offers the greatest diversity among its pages.

CURRENT MAGAZINES FOR AFRICAN-AMERICAN YOUNG ADULTS

Setting The Context

America's libraries show great interest in and concern for their youngest patrons. Publications and programs for babies and preschoolers are everywhere. Children's departments have their own budgets and professional librarians with age appropriate specializations to manage the collections and programs of service. Unfortunately, the same does not hold true for young adults.

Young people are well-served in libraries until they reach preadolescence, the very onset of the at-risk age group. "A great deal of falling behind in school occurs at an early age for black and Hispanic students. . . . As children move from the six- to eight-year-old age group into the nine- to eleven-year-old group, their rate of enrollment below appropriate grade . . . increases by 5% for whites, 11% for blacks, and 14% for Hispanics."[21] With well-established, busy schedules of toddler and pre-school programs, children's librarians, whose responsibilities and job descriptions often encompass young patrons from birth through age eighteen, cannot possibly begin to develop new programs of service to the at-risk YA population. They rarely have the time or the resources.

Major Metropolitan Libraries

A broad geographical survey of libraries substantiated the above. The Philadelphia Free Library, whose Office of Work With Children is one of the country's oldest and most well-respected children's services departments, has no young adult division. Philadelphia's children, who are so well-served from birth through grade six, must at eleven years of age navigate their way through adult collections unaided.

The public library system of the city of Los Angeles no longer has a young adult department. Many of its branches have young adult librarians who must function without the support of a centralized administrative office.

The circulation statistics quoted earlier from the New York Public Library are testament to the fact that young adults will read when given the appropriate materials. Even within this system which recognizes the presence of young adult patrons and their proclivity to read magazines, budget constraints have until recently prohibited many branch libraries from collecting and circulating magazines specifically published for this population. As a result, reference librarians who typically serve adult information seekers perceive that because teenagers use magazines like *Time* and *Newsweek* to complete homework assignments, these periodicals and others like them are sufficient to satisfy their educational and recreational reading needs.

The Librarian's Bias and The Value of Magazines

Many librarians need to recognize that as information specialists we have a bias towards books and scholarly materials. We may still think of periodicals as ephemera and, therefore, not worth the investment of ever-shrinking library budget dollars. Often librarians argue against the acquisition of popular periodicals because they are frequently lost or stolen. But magazines are inexpensive. Young adult magazine subscriptions cost approximately $12.00 a year. With a twelve issue per year publication schedule, each issue costs only $1.00. If it circulates over four times a year, as at the New York Public Library, this clearly shows the value of such an investment.

Content of Magazines for Black Teens

Although they represent 25% of library patrons, the above information indicates that teenagers are not being represented proportionately within library collections and services.[22] Within the small genre of young adult lifestyle magazines, there are even fewer directed specifically toward African-American teenagers. Census data and common sense within a marketing framework help us to understand why so few companies would want to take the risk of starting a young adult lifestyle magazine for African-Americans.

History tells us that the demise of *The Brownies' Book* and *Ebony Jr.!* had much to do with the fact that neither of them carried advertisements. They had to depend solely upon subscriptions for survival and simply could not do it. Magazines, like network television shows, exist to sell products. They are supported by their advertisers, not their subscribers. Magazines must target consumers with disposable income. Data from the 1990 census shows that the median income of black families was $21,420.00 as opposed to white families whose median income was $36,920.00. "In 1990, Black median family income was 58% of white median family income, a gap statistically unchanged from 1967."[23] Since it follows that black teenagers have smaller discretionary incomes than their white counterparts, publishers may well be reluctant to invest in new magazines geared toward this narrow segment of an already small market.

Among those magazines created specifically for the African-American young adult market, there is a proliferation of fanzines and music magazines. *Young Sisters and Brothers* (*YSB*), a general interest lifestyle magazine for both young men and women is the only one of its kind receiving significant attention. Black teens who have an interest in reading periodicals with an African-American focus must look to adult publications such as *Ebony*, *Essence*, and *Jet*.

While these are markedly well-established and excellent periodicals, they are written for an adult audience. This creates a two-fold problem. First, young readers are exposed to advertisements for cigarettes, alcohol, and other products which are not accepted by young adult magazines. Giving teenagers advertisements that positively reinforce adult behaviors such as drinking and smoking only serves to encourage them to participate in such behaviors.

Second, articles in adult publications treat topics from an adult perspective. Frequently that perspective is at odds with the information that young people need and is antithetical to that which parents and teachers promote. An example is the manner in which sexual issues are handled. Adult magazines tend to explore sexuality based upon the assumption that readers are already sexually active and are informed and mature. Teen magazines treat sex from a position of advocacy for readers. They help teens look critically at the issues of pregnancy, sexually transmitted diseases, peer pressure, and protection. As advocates, they provide contextual factors teens need to consider in order to make informed decisions. Family, religious beliefs, and peer pressure are just a few.

The development of self-esteem among black children and adolescents occurs under extremely difficult circumstances. Researchers and psychologists are interested, therefore, in learning how African-American young people develop self-esteem, and often score higher on tests in this area than their white counterparts. All magazines marketed for young adults claim to attribute special significance to promoting self-esteem. This is particularly true for *Young Sisters and Brothers*.

Young Sisters and Brothers (*YSB*)

This magazine, which began publishing in 1991, is helping young African-Americans to feel that they are a part of a valued cultural community. Serge Madhere writes about the importance of collective efficacy, noting that groups of people sharing common cultural mores and beliefs can solve problems through collective efforts.[24] *YSB* founder, Bob Johnson, established his magazine specifically to address the self-esteem needs and concerns of African-American young adults.

YSB reflects a mix of interests. It contains articles that are light as well as those which are serious and socially relevant. At least 50% of its stories are written by teens. In fact, *YSB* has established a writing workshop for teens in its offices. The magazine's language is a mix of colloquial and standard English. When writers and editors employ slang, they set it off in quotation marks or italics, maintaining grammatical integrity. Slang is filtered throughout the text in order to validate the language used by teens themselves.

The magazine's tone is strong and Afrocentric with historical and cultural references. For example, in one issue the origin of the terms "homeboy" and "homegirl" was explained. The root of these words dates back to the black northward migration of the 1920s. When new residents of the North referred to friends they had left behind in the South, they remembered them as their homeboys and homegirls.

The Use of Black Vernacular English in *YSB*

Just as *Sassy*'s casual writing mirrors the linguistic style of its readers, *YSB* strives to authenticate its readers' experiences. Research shows that most African-Americans employ the use of one or more forms of English. These include standard English, black English, and Black Vernacular English, also known as black slang.

"Black English is increasingly recognized as a systemic, 'rule-governed' form of language . . . like any other."[25] Black slang is an ever-changing invention of words and phrases used primarily between friends. By incorporating terms from both black English and black slang into its text, *YSB* enables teens to move back and forth from one dialect to another within a larger text written in standard English. Using the black vernacular gives African-Americans of all ages a sense of solidarity, community, and identity.[26] This works to reinforce positive self-esteem.

Through its rich linguistic mix, *YSB* acknowledges the difficult nature of straddling two disparate cultures. Black English has historically been deemed substandard by the white majority. However, it has achieved a certain prestige through the popularity of various forms of black music.[27] African-American teens, who find themselves in the middle of this paradox, must sort out rules that are at best ambiguous. This difficulty is further compounded by the fact that these young adults have largely been ignored by the publishers of lifestyle and general interest magazines. References made earlier to the mature nature of the advertising in adult periodicals testify to the fact that black teens straddle not only two dialects but also two sets of age-related standards.

The Continuing Tradition:
YSB's Similarities to *The Brownies' Book* and *Ebony Jr.!*

In the history section of this chapter, we cited Tanya Morah, whose examination of *The Brownies' Book* and *Ebony Jr.!* revealed a number of important content-related similarities. As stated previously these are: racial awareness; African and African-American heritage and history; and family loyalty and gender roles. We have applied Morah's themes to *YSB*, and have found that a majority of these principles are being used to address a new generation of African-Americans, and for the first time, that generation is specifically young adult.

Racial Awareness and Black Pride

YSB is infused with references to racial awareness and black pride. In its April 1993 issue, the "Bookin" column, a regular feature, highlighted a new book by Derek Bell, *Faces at the Bottom of the Well: The Permanence of Racism*. This same column gave readers a number of references to consult for more information about the topic, taking the opportunity to educate rather than simply review one book. The May 1992 issue's theme focused on remembering Malcolm X and his legacy.

African and African-American Heritage and History

Scattered throughout each issue of *YSB* are sidebars making reference to facts about African and African-American history and culture. Typical examples include "did you know . . . the light you are using to read *YSB* was pioneered by a Black man, Lewis Latimer. . . ."[28] "Did you know . . . the ancestors of most African-Americans came from the region of West Africa, once known as Western Sudan. . . ."[29] The magazine's music columns treat everything from Rhythm & Blues to Hip Hop, from Gospel to Rap, all with a historical perspective. It also reviews African music.

Family Loyalty and Gender Roles

Family loyalty and gender roles are explored in *YSB*. Open letters from young adults to their mothers comprise the text of a May 1992 article entitled "Dear Ma." "Reflections," a regular feature which appears on the last page, highlights the life experiences of African-Americans from many walks of life. In the June/July 1993 issue, a young man wrote about his feelings concerning the transition from boyhood to manhood. He was raised by his mother and missed the presence of a male role model. In his narrative he tells of reaching out to and being rejected by significant men in his family. He explores the pain and ambivalence this situation has caused him. While he continues to struggle with questions about his family responsibilities, this young man exemplifies maturity and insight. This article and others like it are particularly important and appropriate because they reflect the life experience of many African-American children who are growing up in homes without fathers.[30]

Racial Unity

Emphasis on racial unity is evidenced throughout the magazine, both implicitly, by its use of the vernacular and models of all hues; and explicitly with articles about the topic. The June/July 1993 issue ran a lengthy feature article about life in Los Angeles since the 1992 riots. It featured many thoughtful statements from Los Angeles residents about how peace and prosperity could be achieved. The major focus of a large part of the article is that rebuilding the city of Los Angeles can only happen if the people of its African-American community work together for a common good.[31]

Values for a Contemporary Generation

In addition to these continuing concerns among writers for a black youth audience, *YSB* has successfully brought the magazine to a 90s generation and its concerns. Of particular interest to all of society are questions regarding teen pregnancy and AIDS. Both issues are regularly addressed with sensitivity in this magazine, whose mission is particularly difficult to achieve since it is attempting to reach both young men and women.

Black Beat

Although *YSB* is one of very few lifestyle magazines for African-American teens, it is surrounded by an abundant number of special interest magazines, many of which are music oriented. These periodicals exert a strong influence and reflect the culture of black teens today. One of the most popular of these is *Black Beat*. Editor Yvette Noel-Schure has said that she perceives herself to be not only an editor but also a teacher.[32] *Black Beat* insists upon well-researched articles and in-depth interviews. Editors are very careful about the kinds of artists their magazine highlights and the nature of their lyrics. Other magazines popular with black teens are listed in the annotated bibliography in Appendix A.

CONCLUSION

Magazines for teens exist to entertain, enlighten, and inform.

Among the wide variety of publications available to the young adult market, few lifestyle magazines address the black population. Only one, *Colors*, embraces a multicultural perspective as part of its continuing editorial policy. "*Colors* is about the cultural differences that make the world exciting. And how savoring those differences (rather than killing each other over them) could make the world a little less crazy."[33] This semiannual magazine, published by Benetton, the Italian clothing manufacturer, has only begun what promises to be a provocative, if not controversial, history for itself.

Colors

The magazine's format is different each time it is published. Size varies. For instance, the Spring/Summer 1993 issue is very large scale; the Fall 1993 issue is closer to standard magazine size. This periodical is sold at Benetton stores everywhere and on a small number of newsstands. It is published in five different bilingual editions and distributed around the world. It is unfortunate that the magazine's message of cultural diversity reaches only a small number of teens, namely, those who can afford to shop at an upscale boutique.

Obviously, the primary goal of a magazine published by a clothing manufacturer and retail chain is that of promoting, advertising, and selling its newest line of clothes. This is made clear within the confines of *Colors*, since the magazine is packaged with bound Benetton catalogs. The second goal of this magazine is clearly communicated in its pages. The manufacturer has for a number of years celebrated diversity through its advertising slogan, "The United Colors of Benetton," with models of different skin colors from varied cultures. Each issue of *Colors* is centered on a theme which is always carried out from a multicultural perspective. *Colors* exudes an ethos of inclusion and diversity.

The magazine's format, layout, stories, photo spreads, copy, and humor make diversity and multiculturalism seem enjoyable and fun. Hardly a person can look at the pages of *Colors* and not be impressed with the multi-lingual approach it takes. Each page is written in both English and Spanish.

If it has not already, *Colors* will soon find itself in censorship battles, or at least in arguments from less liberal readers or their parents. The Fall 1993 issue of the magazine is dedicated to celebrating the united colors of the world, and to AIDS prevention. One of the most powerful pieces about diversity is a multi-page photo spread of people, both men and women, standing at attention, completely undressed. All that is written is the home of each person. Some models are very dark skinned, some light, some Asian. This is an excellent means of communicating *Colors'* multicultural message. The shock of frontal nudity, and the spare text heighten the message that all over the world each person is different from all others, yet shares characteristics common to all human beings.

SUMMARY

All teens deal with the difficulties of adolescence. Black teens must view the issues through the lens of color. Magazines such as *Sassy, Seventeen, Teen,* and *YM* could be more sensitive to the needs of minority teens; however, they will remain mainstream magazines targeting a mostly white readership. We believe that it would be in the best interest of African-American young adults if there were more general interest magazines published for them.

Census data indicates that the African-American population in the United States will increase by 50% by the year 2030.[34] Perhaps this projection will inspire publishers to create new magazines for this growing market. In an age of multicultural awareness and a heightened attitude of inclusion, existing publications must take pains to include articles, photo layouts, and columns addressing the interests of a much broader and more varied audience.

APPENDIX A

Annotated Bibliography of Magazines for African-American Young Adults[35]

The Art Form. Bi-monthly. $20.00 yearly. J–93 Tenbytown, Delran, New Jersey 08075. Subtitled "A Hip-Hop Publication Wit De Hardcore Flava" this large format magazine features interviews with musicians and record reviews.

Black Beat. Monthly. $22.00 yearly. 355 Lexington Avenue, New York, New York 10017. Rap, Hip-Hop, R&B, Reggae, Jazz. Feature articles and interviews reflecting the range of black music.

Black Collegian. Four issues per year. $10.00 yearly. 1240 South Broad

Avenue, New Orleans, Louisiana 70125. A career and self-development for African-American students which includes book reviews, career information, and articles about contemporary issues.

Black Excellence. Five issues published September–June. $15.00 yearly. 400 b12th Street, N.E. Washington, D.C. 20002. College life and information for high school seniors.

Colors. Published twice yearly. $3.00 per issue. 50 West 17th Street, New York, New York 10011. A magazine featuring bold design and iconoclastic editorial content. It celebrates diversity around the world while addressing issues significant to teens.

Fly! Bi-monthly. $2.95 each issue. 807 Vivian Court, Baldwin, New York 11151. This fanzine features the top stars of rap and Hip-Hop; also includes posters and pin-ups.

Fresh. Every 3 weeks. $20.00 yearly. 19341 Business Center Drive, Northridge, California 91324. Rap musicians and other celebrities, interviews, and color pin-ups.

Girlfriend. Quarterly. $10.95 yearly. 610–T–Street, NW, Washington, D.C. 20001. Premier issues of this magazine feature articles that give information on positive images for young African-American females.

Hype Hair. Quarterly. $2.95 per issue. 63 Grand Avenue, Suite 230, River Edge, New Jersey 07661. The hip hairstyles of young African-American celebrities, as well as the styles of non-celebrities are featured here with braids, dreads, twists, extensions, perms, curls, and razor cuts. For young men and young women.

Rap Pages. Bi-monthly. $9.95 yearly. 9171 Wilshire Boulevard, Suite 300, Beverly Hills, California 90210. Extended interviews with today's rap artists, including reviews and color pin-ups.

Rap Sheet. 9 issues a year. $9.95 yearly. 2270 Centinela Avenue, Box B-4, Los Angeles, California 90064. As its title suggests, Rap is the featured music in this large format newspaper with interviews with the stars and reviews of the music.

Rapmasters. Monthly. $24.00 yearly. 63 Grand Avenue, Suite 230, River Edge, New Jersey 07761. Interviews and pin-ups featuring the stars of Rap, Hip-Hop, and House music.

Right On. Monthly. $20.00 yearly. 355 Lexington Avenue, New York, New York 10017. A veteran publication featuring Rap stars and other African-American entertainers in interviews and color pin-ups.

The Source. Monthly. $19.95 yearly. 594 Broadway, Suite 510, New York, New York 10012. The Rap, Hip-Hop industry as profiled by insiders with feature articles and interviews.

Spice! Monthly. $17.50 yearly. 475 Park Avenue South, New York, New York 10016. Fashion, beauty, celebrity interviews and more for young women of African descent.

2 Hype. Bi-monthly. $13.50 yearly. 63 Grand Avenue, Suite 230, River Edge, New Jersey 07661. Rap, Hip-Hop, urban fashions, puzzles, contests, interviews, and color pin-ups.

Vibe. $12.00 yearly. 25 West 43rd Street, Suite 1100, New York, New York 10036. The premier issue features the Hip-Hop culture in music, literature, fashion, and reviews with contributions by many of the nation's most notable African-American cultural writers and observers.

Word Up! Monthly. $24.00 yearly. 63 Grand Avenue, Suite 230 River Edge, New Jersey 07661. The stars of Rap music featured in interviews and color pin-ups.

Yo! Monthly. $20.00 yearly. P.O. Box 88427, Los Angeles, California 90009. Rap, Hip-Hop and its stars featured in interviews and color pin-ups.

YES—Youth Excited About Success. 10 issues a year. $15.00 yearly. 144 North Avenue, Plainfield, New Jersey 07060. The premier issues feature African-American teens on the East Coast who are achieving excellence. Also featured are current young celebrities, music reviews, advice, fashion, and sports.

YSB—Young Sisters and Brothers. Monthly. $14.95 yearly. 3109M Street, N.W., 2nd Floor, Washington, D.C. 20007. Beauty, fashion, music, interviews, contemporary issues, and advice directed specifically towards young women and men of African descent.

African-American Adult Magazines
With Particular Appeal to Young Adults

Ebony. Monthly. $16.00 yearly. 820 South Michigan Avenue, Chicago, Illinois 60605. One of the major forces in the field of magazines for African-American adults, *Ebony* is read widely by young adults.

Emerge. Monthly. (combined issues Jan/Feb and July/Aug) $16.97 yearly. P.O. Box 7127, Red Oak, Iowa 51591–0127. This magazine calls itself black America's news magazine, and although marketed to an adult audience, it is accessible to teens.

Essence. Monthly. $16.00 yearly. 1500 Broadway, New York, New York 10036. Celebrity interviews and articles, health, and fashion dominate this, the most popular magazine for women of African descent.

NOTES

1. Lee Kravitz, Comments made during panel discussion at Young Adult Library Services Association's "Magazines for Teens," American Library Association Annual Conference, New Orleans, LA, 28 June 1993.

2. R. Gordon Kelly, *Mother Was a Lady* (Westport, CT: Greenwood Press, 1974), quoted in Marguerite Radencich, "Two Centuries of U.S. Magazines for Youth," *Journal of Reading* (March 1986): 496.
3. Marguerite Radencich, "Two Centuries of U.S. Magazines for Youth," *Journal of Reading* (March 1986): 496.
4. Tanya M. Morah, "Times Out of Joint: The Life and Death of 'The Brownies' Book.'" Paper presented at the Annual Meeting of the Association for Education in Journalism and Mass Communication, Norman, OK, 3–6 August 1986, Dialog, ERIC, ED 271779.
5. Elinor Desverney Sinnette, "The Brownies' Book: A Pioneer Publication for Children," *Freedomways* 5 (Winter 1965): 134, quoted in Tanya M. Morah, "Times Out of Joint: The Life and Death of 'The Brownies' Book.'" Paper presented at the Annual Meeting of the Association for Education in Journalism and Mass Communication, Norman, OK, 3–6 August 1986, Dialog, ERIC, ED 271779.
6. W.E.B. DuBois, "The True Brownies," *The Crisis* 18 (October 1919): 286, quoted in Courtney Vaughn-Roberson and Brenda Hill, "*The Brownies' Book* and *Ebony Jr.!*: Literature as a Mirror of the Afro-American Experience," *The Journal of Negro Education* 58 (Fall 1989): 498.
7. Morah, 3.
8. Courtney Vaughn-Roberson and Brenda Hill, "*The Brownies' Book* and *Ebony Jr.!*: Literature as a Mirror of the Afro-American Experience," *The Journal of Negro Education* 58 (Fall 1989): 494.
9. This statistic was determined using information supplied by Joanne Rosario at the Nathan Straus Young Adult Library in the Donnell Library Center, 20 W. 53 St., New York, NY, interview by Lynn S. Cockett, 29 June 1993. According to 1992 statistics, the library houses 10,800 YA non-fiction circulating titles, and 13 circulating magazines (a total of 154 magazines by the end of a year). The total non-fiction circulation for 1992 was 7780 items; the total magazine circulation was 668. This number does not include in-library use of books or of the 48 non-circulating magazine titles the library houses.
10. Mike Gunderloy and Cary Goldberg Janice. *The World of Zines* (New York: Penguin Books, 1992), 3.
11. Marjorie Ingall, Senior Writer, *Sassy*. Interview by Lynn S. Cockett and Janet R. Kleinberg, 29 June 1993.
12. Jane Pratt, "Magazine Publishing: The *Sassy* Approach," *Journal of Youth Services in Libraries* 4 (Summer 1991): 384.
13. Marjorie Ingall, Senior Writer, *Sassy*. Interview by Lynn S. Cockett and Janet R. Kleinberg, 29 June 1993.
14. Jane Pratt, "Magazine Publishing: The *Sassy* Approach," *Journal of Youth Services in Libraries* 4 (Summer 1991): 384.

15. Catherine Cavender, then editor of *YM* (now at *Seventeen*). Interview by Janet R. Kleinberg, 15 July 1993.
16. Catherine Cavender is the Executive Editor at *Seventeen*. She recently moved there from a similar position at *YM*.
17. For a representative *Sassy* article about the above subject, see Christina Kelly, "Why all the Celebrity Worship?" *Sassy* (June 1992): 54.
18. Sara Nelson, "It's Not Black and White," *Seventeen* (January 1992): 80.
19. Sutorious Paige and Jeanne Gordon, "I Was Trapped in the L.A. Riots," *YM* (November 1992): 59.
20. Samantha Shapiro, "Why Unity in South Africa Is Not Happening," *Sassy* (December 1992): 62.
21. *Census and You* (August 1992), Dialog, CENDATA.
22. Patrick Jones, *Connecting Young Adults and Libraries: A How To Do It Manual* (New York: Neal-Schuman Publishers, Inc., 1992), 7.
23. *Black Population of Metropolitan Areas: 1990 and 1980, By 1990 Black Population Rank.* Defined by Office of Management and Budget, June 30, 1990. Dialog, CENDATA.
24. Serge Madhere, "Self-Esteem of African American Preadolescents: Theoretical And Practical Considerations," *Journal of Negro Education* 60 (Winter 1992): 47.
25. Mary Rhodes Hoover, "Community Attitudes Toward Black English," *Language in Society* 7 (April 1978): 65.
26. John Baugh, "Hypocorrection: Mistakes in Production of Vernacular African-American English as a Second Dialect," *Language and Communication* 12 (January 1992): 317.
27. Ibid., 322.
28. Marcia Caster and Tonya Monteiro, "Did You Know?" *YSB* 2 (April 1993): 20.
29. Jimi Mass, "Did You Know?" *YSB* 1 (May 1992): 22.
30. The percentage of black families maintained by women with no husband present doubled between 1970 and 1980. Married couple families declined from 78% of all black families in 1950 to 48% in 1991. A little over one in three (36%) black children lived with two parents in 1991. The figure for white children is 79%. This data is from *Black Americans: A Profile* (April 22, 1993), Dialog CENDATA.
31. Raoul Dennis and Frank Dexter Brown, "Rebellion, Rebuilding and Race," *YSB* 2 (June/July 1993): 66.
32. Yvette Noel-Schure, Editor, *Black Beat*. Interview by Janet R. Kleinberg, 14 July 1993.
33. *Colors* 3 (Fall/Winter 1993): Back cover.
34. Press Release, Census Bureau Public Information Office, February 1989, Dialog CENDATA.

35. Some of the annotations used in this bibliography are cited from *Magazines for Young Adults, 1993*. A List Selected By: The Media Selection and Usage Committee, American Library Association, Young Adult Library Services Association (YALSA).

REFERENCES

Baugh, John. "Hypocorrection: Mistakes in Production of Vernacular African-American English as a Second Dialect." *Language and Communication* 12 (January 1992): 317–326.

Black Americans: A Profile. 22 April 1993. Dialog CENDATA.

Black Population of Metropolitan Areas: 1990 and 1980, By 1990 Black Population Rank. Washington, DC: Office of Management and Budget, 30 June 1990. Dialog CENDATA.

Caster, Marcia and Tonya Monteiro. "Did You Know?" *YSB* 2 (April 1993): 20.

Cavender, Catherine. Interview by Janet R. Kleinberg, 15 July 1993, Mountain Lakes, NJ.

Census and You. August 1992. Dialog CENDATA.

Colors: A Magazine About the Rest of the World 2 (Spring/Summer 1993).

Colors: A Magazine About the Rest of the World 3 (Fall/Winter 1993).

Dennis, Raoul and Frank Dexter Brown. "Rebellion, Rebuilding and Race." *YSB* 2 (June/July 1993): 66–75.

Factsheet 5: The Definitive Guide to the Zine Revolution. P.O. Box 170099, San Francisco, CA 94117.

Gunderloy, Mike and Cary Goldberg Janice. *The World of Zines.* New York: Penguin, 1992.

Ingall, Marjorie. Interview by Lynn S. Cockett and Janet R. Kleinberg. 29 June 1993, New Orleans, LA.

Jones, Patrick. *Connecting Young Adults and Libraries: A How to Do It Manual.* New York: Neal-Schuman Publishers, Inc., 1992.

Kelly, Christina. "Why all the Celebrity Worship?" *Sassy* (June 1992): 54–55, 80.

Kravitz, Lee. Panel Discussion at the Young Adult Library Services Association's *Magazines for Young Adults* Program, Annual Conference, American Library Association, New Orleans, LA. 28 June 1993.

Madhere, Serge. "Self-Esteem of African American Preadolescents: Theoretical and Practical Considerations." *Journal of Negro Education* 60 (Winter 1992): 47–61.

Mass, Jimi. "Did You Know?" *YSB* 1 (May 1992): 22.

Metal Curse. P.O. Box 302, Elkhart, IN 46515–0302.

Morah, Tanya. "Times Out of Joint: The Life and Death of 'The Brownies'

Book.'" Paper presented at the Annual Meeting of the Association for Education in Journalism and Mass Communication, Norman, OK, 3–6 August 1986. Dialog, ERIC, ED 271779, 30 p.

Nelson, Sara. "It's Not Black and White." *Seventeen* (January 1992): 80–83.

Noel-Schure, Yvette. Interviewed by Janet R. Kleinberg. 14 July 1993, Mountain Lakes, NJ.

Paige, Sutorious, and Jeanne Gordon. "I Was Trapped in the L.A. Riots." *YM* (November 1992): 58–61.

Pratt, Jane. "Magazine Publishing: The *Sassy* Approach." *Journal of Youth Services in Libraries* 4 (Summer 1991): 384–388.

Press Release. Washington, DC, Census Bureau Public Information Office. February 1989. Dialog CENDATA.

Radencich, Marguerite. "Two Centuries of U.S. Magazines for Youth." *Journal of Reading* (March 1986): 496–505.

The Realist. Box 1230, Venice, CA 90294.

Rhodes Hoover, Mary. "Community Attitudes Toward Black English." *Language in Society* 7 (April 1978): 65–87.

Rosario, Joanne. Interviews by Lynn S. Cockett: 29 June 1993, New Orleans, LA; 15 July 1993, Mountain Lakes, NJ.

Sassy. Sassy Publishers Inc., 230 Park Avenue, New York, NY 10169.

Seventeen Magazine. K-III Magazine Corporation, 850 Third Avenue, New York, NY 10022.

Shapiro, Samantha. "Why Unity in South Africa Is Not Happening." *Sassy* (December 1992): 62.

Teen. Peterson Publishing Co., 8490 Sunset Boulevard, Los Angeles, CA 90069.

The Teen Scene. P.O. Box 3483, Secaucus, NJ 07096–3483.

Vaughn-Roberson, Courtney and Brenda Hill, "*The Brownies' Book* and *Ebony Jr.!*: Literature as a Mirror of the Afro-American Experience." *The Journal of Negro Education* 58 (Fall 1989): 494–510.

YM (Young & Modern). Gruner + Jahr USA Publishing, 685 Third Avenue, New York, NY 10017.

FIVE

The New Seed: Depictions of the Middle Class in Recent African-American Young Adult Literature

Dianne Johnson-Feelings

Most critical work in the field of children's and young adult literature relating to African-Americans has, to date, focused on the ideas of race and misrepresentation. This emphasis is understandable because of the extent to which African-Americans have been negatively stereotyped as a group in mainstream children's literature. As well, a significant amount of energy has, and still is going towards reconstructing the very history of African-American literature for young people.

It is very important, when talking about African-American children's literature, to be clear about how the category is being defined. The term "children's literature" refers to the primary audience of the literature. The term "African-American literature" refers to the ethnic background of the writers. Yet, when the two are combined into "African-American children's literature" the parameters are not clear at all. This is not merely a philosophical issue, but a real problem when set in the context of the publishing world.

One difficulty is that, historically, white authors have been accepted not only as the creators of literature about or aimed at black youth, but, moreover, have been encouraged to fill this role. The implications of this history are many and demand attention outside the scope of this chapter. However, for the purposes of this chapter, the definition of African-American young adult literature is that literature written by African-American authors primarily for a young adult audience.[1]

Because the issue of race has been the obvious, primary concern of scholarship on the subject, some other issues remain to be fully explored. Or, viewed from another perspective, some issues have not been considered "issues." One of these issues is class. The assumption of many critics and readers has been that all African-Americans are part of a monolithic group in every respect. At the most, the only distinction has been between the rural experience and the urban experience. But all are grouped, in general terms, as working class. It would be fair to say that in the popular consciousness of the United States, at least until recently, black culture has been equated with poverty. This misconception impacts upon readers, critics, and writers themselves.

There are good reasons why writers have not, historically, offered many representations of the middle class in literature for young people.[2] Part of the mission, as it were, of African-American writers for youth has been, historically, to educate and re-educate in response to the miseducation that has gone on for so long. Thus, the literature is not created merely for entertainment, but for education about and documentation of certain experiences. In reality, for much of the history of the literature, there has not been a sizeable middle class. For whatever reasons, what has taken precedence is the remembrance of life in the South and negotiation of life in the North. Much of this takes the form of books about the slavery era (Julius Lester's *This Strange New Feeling*, for example), life in the rural South (Brenda Wilkinson's *Ludell* series), and life in the gritty urban North (Alice Childress' *A Hero Ain't Nothin' But a Sandwich*).

There are some exceptions to the tendency until recently, of the negligence of the middle class. Notably, the history of African-American young adult literature abounds with biographies, mostly of famous black people, who were, in fact, middle class (James Haskins is probably the most prolific African-American biographer for young adult readers). There are a disproportionate number of biographies for various reasons. One explanation is related to W.E.B. DuBois' concern that young people be educated to believe that black people could, in fact, be "great, heroic or beautiful."[3] What this translates into, then and now, is a somewhat disproportionate concentration on the biography as a medium of reconstructing history. The negative side of this is that young people are sometimes not exposed to an encompassing vision of history. They may get the idea that the only people who have made contributions to society are truly exceptional people, rather that realizing that it is the *masses* as well as the leaders that shape the world. Biographies written specifically for young readers can be misused by misguided educators also to suggest that those black people who are "successful" are somehow exceptions to the rest of the members of their communities; to suggest that if one, as an individual, possesses the requisite "gumption" and determination, *anything* is possible. This approach ignores the existence and effects of institutional racism.

Institutionalized racism is a focus in many books, among them Lorenz Graham's *North Town* (sequel to *South Town*). This book is part of a genre that might be labeled "integrationist literature"—in the most positive sense. Published in 1965, *North Town* is about the struggle of a young man to obtain an education and establish a career in a largely segregated society. It is one of the most well written and inspiring stories of the lone black teenager making his or her way in the white world. Though this literature had a proper and productive place, the major class issue here remains black versus white, rather than issues of class *within* black communities themselves (to the extent that the two spheres can be separated).

But even in the earliest literature, it is clear that, indeed, there have always been suppressed class issues in African-American society. Questions need to be posed: How are issues of economic (or socio-economic class) manifested in the literature? Are class divisions based solely on economic status? Why do depictions of middle class African-Americans appear when they do in the history of the literature? These are some of the questions that I can raise and in some cases only begin to explore in this short chapter through looking at recent young adult novels by respected African-American writers in which class is a major theme, explicitly or implicitly.

A STARTING POINT:
THE BROWNIES' BOOK MAGAZINE

I trace the beginnings of African-American children's and young adult literature as well, back to at least January 1920 through December 1921 when W.E.B. DuBois, August Granville Dill, and Jessie Fauset edited and published *The Brownies' Book* magazine. For the purposes of this chapter, it is significant that DuBois and Fauset, the main editors, are upper middle-class, Ivy League educated, light-skinned, and in some ways, privileged people. At the same time that they promoted a pan-African perspective on African-American experience, they also struggled with the class and caste divisions in these communities and the contradictions in their own thinking and editing.[4] *The Brownies' Book* manifests these tensions, sometimes in a negative, sometimes in a neutral way.

Consider the following, rather extended excerpt from the column entitled "The Judge" (written, in fact, by Jessie Fauset). In it, the Judge responds to young Wilhelmina's reasoning about buying new clothes and her complaints of being treated like a child by her parents. The Judge replies by questioning her about the basis upon which she chooses this particular hat and whether or not it is attractive on her, highlighting her figure and complexion. The Judge goes on:

> Or—and here I have a deep suspicion—do you choose it because Katie Brown has one like it and the Ladies of Avenue K, and—but hold! Who are K.B. and the L. of A.K.? Are they persons of taste, or simply of power? Do you imitate them for love, or fear? Does the choice of this hat represent your freedom of thoughtful taste, or your slavery to what the flamboyant Kitty does or to what rich white folk wear?
>
> Mind you, I'm not answering these questions—I'm just asking. We will assume that the hat is becoming and suits you and you want it. Now comes that awkward question of Money? Simply this: Of the 1,000 ways of spending this dollar, which is the best for me, for mother, for the family, for my people, for the world? If the "best" way of spending it for you makes mother starve, or the family lose the home, or colored folk be ridiculed, or the world look silly—why, then, no such hat for you, and that, too, by your own dear Judgment.[5]

I quote this passage at length for several reasons. First, it is a forceful example of the tone of the magazine. It is weighty, to say the least. What saves it from being almost demoralizing is that the reader realizes that s/he has choices and can exercise individual judgment.

The emphasis of the passage is on the *interconnectedness* of the actions and decisions of countless individuals. Specifically, this inter-relatedness is couched in terms of economic relationships—the class

implications are clear. Not only does the passage invoke ideas of freedom of taste (or choice) and power (in relationship to both black and
white people), but mentions Wilhelmina's skin color at one point. Such
issues, which appear petty in one way, are related to larger issues. One
other passage from *The Brownies' Book* contributes to this discussion.
In a story entitled "Impossible Kathleen," author Augusta Bird writes
that

> Crystal was much the prettier of the two girls. She was just about
> two shades lighter than Kathleen. . . . Kathleen also knew she was
> a darker hue than any of the girls in her clique, but she knew she
> was slenderly built, looked well in all her clothes. . . .[6]

Physical appearance emerges as an issue too often to be ignored. Consider one of the advertisements that ran repeatedly: "The Gift of the
Good Fairy." Her mission was to "make beautiful those unfortunate
ones whom nature had not given long, wavy hair and a smooth, lovely
complexion."[7] Youngsters were taught, to some degree, to compensate
for their "negroness" with their personal attributes.

Taken together, these two passages are very interesting. In the
former, the young lady in question has money; it is clear that she is part
of a middle class family, a family with disposable income.[8] All in all, it
is a very positive piece because of its emphasis on responsibility. But it
also raises some troubling issues. One of these is the idea of imitating
white people in their aesthetic tastes in an effort to be accepted in
larger American society. Related is the question of whether or not Wilhelmina's clothes "set off" her brown skin. On one hand, this sentence
can be interpreted in a positive way—her brown skin is considered
attractive. On the other hand, however remotely, for some African-
American readers, it recalls the confusion of being a young black girl
being told not to wear certain bright colors against your dark skin.

This idea is, in turn, related to that of contributing to the ridicule
of colored folk, whether by one's manner of dress or one's professional
choices. Herein is at least one other answer to why some black writers
and critics have kept some distance from intra-group class issues. It is
embarrassing, in some ways, to reveal "family business" or "dirty little
secrets" through the public venue of books. Moreover, such issues are
considered by some to be inappropriate for young readers.[9] This is one
explanation for why class issues are, in general, more clearly delin-

eated in the adult literature than in the children's/young adult.

Color stratification has to rank near the top of the list of taboo subjects. But this was not always so, cases in point being "Impossible Kathleen" and "The Gift of the Good Fairy" advertisement. But what is intriguing is the writers' lack of consciousness about the insidious nature of these advertisements. The message embodied in these instances is that light skin is, for whatever reasons, somehow better, or more desirable, than dark skin. Crystal's beauty is linked, directly, with the exact shade of her skin. One manifestation of being "unfortunate" is looking African; having kinky hair.

Though neither DuBois or Fauset is responsible for the examples in question, more than a few occur during the two-year life of the magazine of their own struggles with class related issues both in writing and in editing decisions. Someone had to make the decision to accept "Impossible Kathleen" for publication. Of course, DuBois and Fauset needed the advertisements to help finance the costs of business. Too, they had an audience to appeal to. But their audience was not a monolithic one. Luckily, it was the readers themselves who sometimes had to aid the editors and writers in critiquing the material and thinking through various problems.

Young Alice Martin was one of those readers. She offered these shrewd comments on issues of physical appearance, with implications for questions of how histories are constructed, how images and stereotypes are established and subsequently, abused. Of her school geography book, she says the following:

> . . . all the pictures are pretty, nice-looking men and women, except the Africans. They always look so ugly. I don't mean to make fun of them, for I am not pretty myself; but I know not all colored people look like me. I see lots of ugly white people too; but not all white people look like them, and they are not the ones they put in the geography.[10]

These are the observations of someone who understood a set of interconnected dynamics, with the issue of beauty somehow at the center. But what is special about these observations is that they helped the magazine to make a step forward from uncritically putting forth such problematic material. Thus, they set a precedent for all future discussion of the interconnectedness among education, books, the politics of the publishing industry, and images, visual and otherwise. Young

Alice Martin helps us to reconsider the value of the gift of the good fairy; she prods us to reconsider our true gifts as members of African-American communities.

A CONTEMPORARY CONTRAST:
ROSA GUY'S *THE MUSIC OF SUMMER*

Writer Toni Morrison also understands this constellation of dynamics. In her novel, *The Bluest Eye*, she identified the very idea of physical beauty as one of the most destructive ideas ever.[11]* The characters in this story acknowledge, explicitly, the connection between skin color and economic class. A case in point is the passage below from *The Music of Summer*, which follows the observation that despite Cathy's and her friend's negative attitudes about white people, the participation of those same white students added to the so-called success of their social functions. The passage continues:

> They, the Banning school's colored elite, had banded together with nothing in common except that they were middle class and light skinned—an answer to Banning's white students who kept them out of their inner circles. In turn they kept their darker-skinned sisters on the outside looking in.[12]

What raises this story above the level of a story such as "Impossible Kathleen" is that it places the concern of skin color within a larger context. Not only does it raise race related issues and issues of power—victim victimizing others—but it addresses the need of teenagers for social acceptance of any and every kind.

Sarah Richardson, the protagonist of *The Music of Summer*, finds out during the course of her summer that there are different kinds of acceptance, including acceptance of self. But for most of the narrative, she is concerned only with acceptance by the group referred to in the excerpt above; the group which revolves around Cathy Johnson of the "smoky blue mischievous laughing eyes. One sensed the devil at work in them."[13]

---

*Twenty-two years later, author Rosa Guy would demonstrate an appreciation for this insight by weaving reference to *The Bluest Eye* into the fabric of her young adult novel, *The Music of Summer*. Here, *The Bluest Eye* is mentioned as the main character's summer reading which she shares with others.

Sarah and Cathy are longtime friends who have grown apart, as have their mothers, who were once very close. Cathy sees Sarah only when she needs her help with something like preparing for a test at school. When Sarah decides to go to Cathy's home to confront her about not inviting her to her tea, Sarah's mother, not knowing the real reason for the visit, has a strong response, stated in strong language. What her stance is, essentially, is that Cathy owes Sarah for the time she's spent with her, and that Cathy has been treating her "like you're her goddamn slave."[14] It is no accident, of course, that Guy chooses the word "slave" rather than servant or some other term. What she accomplishes by invoking the most extreme example of historical class relationship ever to be found in this country—white masters/black slaves—is to place the tension between Sarah and Cathy within a useful context. She is reminding the reader that the source of the pain is socio-historical, and is manifested ultimately in the lives of individuals. What these socio-historical circumstances mean to Sarah's mother, Lottie, is that darker skinned Americans have always had to be goal-oriented in a world that she conceptualizes as "one mighty sea" which they had to be talented swimmers to negotiate."[15] Examples of rough waters are numerous.

One incident involves Lottie suing the management of an apartment building which didn't want her presence—"Until then, the occupants of the building had been light-skinned men and women and black men who handled big money."[16]

Yet another passage explains a long-standing misunderstanding between the two mothers, resulting in Lottie thinking that she is unwelcome, unconditionally, at the home of Mrs. Johnson (decorated with "paintings by modern black artists") or at her job. Mrs. Johnson tries to explain:

> "Don't make it sound as though I committed a crime, Sarah," Mrs. Johnson said. "With all the hoopla of what a great city we live in, we all know that there are places blacks can't go. I wouldn't have been hired if my boss had known that I was black. And the Lord knows I worked and studied hard to earn the right to my profession. Still, I can't have my friends hanging around my job. Lottie knows these things. . . ."[17]

Class stratification based upon skin color has implications not only for housing and employment, but for romantic relationships and families.

Jean Pierre, Sarah's West Indian "love interest" in the novel, confesses to her how his own father's color consciousness (supported by the weight of a whole culture) has impacted his life and the life of his mother, Madame Armand. His analysis is that an education is all that his father had to give to him, and that furthermore, he wants nothing else from his father. He does not consider his father a good or decent man, but characterizes him mainly as a man who has internalized colonial values. He does acknowledge that his father loves him, perhaps because he is his only son. Finally, however, he reasons that his father "loves my mother and did not marry her because of the color of her skin."[18]

And again there is the ultimate, if only figurative, color stratification—Europe versus Africa. Embodied in this relationship is the most extreme manifestation of the relationship between color and economic class status. When Sarah, discussing Africa with Jean Pierre, mentions Africa's poverty, he responds, in short, that Africa, in fact, is wealthy and that it is her people who are poor. Sarah's question, then, is whether or not Africa is rich in the same way that Europe and the United States are rich. His retort is simply that the West is rich because of Africa's wealth. Her answer, uttered as she thinks, is:

"And—so the people are poor."[19]

This passage is central to the story for many reasons. First, Jean Pierre's description of Africa's riches is similar to a later passage describing Sarah's beauty—a beauty which he contends is secretly recognized and envied by pale Cathy just as Africa's richness (both material and cultural) is both denied and coveted by Europeans.

Another thought underlying this passage is the reality that the educated middle class of the African diaspora, personified in Jean Pierre, is in a unique position, precisely because of the education factor, to understand and deal with the problem of intra-group class tension within a broad framework. As Jean Pierre devotes his life to the fields of agronomy and forestry in Africa, others can live their lives in a manner which demonstrates that upward mobility is not equivalent to "acting white" or forsaking one's identity.

Many of the black middle class are also in a unique position, in relationship to the idea of class consciousness, because, in many cases, economic status is tenuous. They have experienced being both working class and middle class. As one character warns:

> . . . Dad believes in old money. The only way to have old money is to build a structure. A class structure. *That* we don't have.[20]

The same is true for other characters as well. One particularly poignant scene involves Cathy's circle of friends teasing Sarah about her dark skin color. Fred, whom Sarah was once attracted to, is silent. Afterwards, she thinks back to that point in time when his father, while a medical student, worked as a school custodian,

> and she had fought Fred's battles. Yet when she had needed him he hadn't come to her defense.[21]

Rosa Guy's characterizations are brilliant. One of the wonderful things about the novel is that the characters span a wide age range. It is significant, for instance, that Jean Pierre is in his early thirties, still young but old enough to have more life experience than Sarah and the other eighteen-year-olds. Sarah, though mature, is still working through some of the contradictions in her own thinking. While she would condemn Fred's behavior, and the behavior of young people who are patronizing to anyone in a service position, she is not completely honest about or comfortable with her own class background. At one point, for example, she vehemently denies that her mother has ever scrubbed floors to support her. True enough. But Lottie Richardson and Sarah were supported for a long period of time by Lottie's aunt and uncle, who were a domestic worker and a janitor. In reaction to her own behavior, she realizes that "her tears had nothing to do with the others, and everything to do with the shock of finding out she had more of them in her than she had admitted."[22]

Realistically enough, however, the older characters possess varying degrees of insight. Sarah's mother must come to terms, too, with her own condescending attitudes towards her aunt and uncle. But Mama Dear, the character who most powerfully represents the generation of elders is, indeed, a character who is full of wisdom and knowing and understanding. It is at her comfortable upper middle class home that most of the novel takes place. It is here that the teenagers congregate with her granddaughter, Cathy; Mrs. Johnson, who invites Sarah; and Madame Armand and her son, Jean Pierre, who visit from the islands. It is she who always finds a way to restore balance to the lives of those whom she respects and cares about:

> Mama Dear had lived so long that she had become a fairy god-mother or a witch. How else could she read so clearly the thoughts and sentiments that went flittering around the old house?[23]

She is, in any case, a clear and instructive contrast to the Good Fairy who dispenses the gift of long, wavy hair and light skin. Mama Dear's home is a place of struggle but of resolution too. Likewise, throughout her career, Rosa Guy has made her novels for young adults sites where they can safely examine their own attitudes about awkward, complex issues such as class.[24]

MIDDLE CLASS STATUS TAKEN FOR GRANTED: WALTER MYERS' *18 PINE ST.*

Walter Dean Myers' name is the name that appears on the front of each book in the *18 Pine St.* series. Only when readers open to the title page do they discover that the writer is Stacie Johnson and discover that the series is "created by" Walter Dean Myers. What this indicates, in part, is that Myers is among the upper class in the world of children's and young adult publishing—publishers know that his name alone will sell any book, whether written by him or not. Myers, of course, has earned this status over the course of a prolific and accomplished career. A few others have attained similar status and power. Eloise Greenfield, for instance, has it written into her contracts that only African-Americans can be chosen as illustrators for her work. The larger point is that though others, too, are deserving of this kind of authority, few are accorded it. The road to upper middle class status in the world of publishing has been a long one for African-American writers.

In Stacie Johnson's *Sort of Sisters*, the first book in the *18 Pine St.* series, the characters, for the most part, take being middle class for granted. Eighteen Pine Street is the address of a local pizzeria which is a popular gathering spot for this group of teenagers. They are introduced in short biographies prior to the text proper. One description in particular gives a clue to their lifestyles:

> Jennifer Wilson is the poor little rich girl. Her parents are divorced, and all the charge cards and clothes in the world can't make up for it. Jennifer's tall and thin, with cocoa-colored skin and a body that's made for all those designer clothes she wears.[25]

Jennifer and the others are used to driving Mercedes sedans and black Corvettes. And their normal problems revolve around personal relationships and family disputes. None of them have drug problems, teenage pregnancies or drop out of school. They and their parents play chess and bridge. And Tasha, Sarah's cousin and "sort of sister" plays soccer and is a vegetarian. The one blatantly racist scene involves two of the characters being shown a restaurant menu before they are seated when the waiter assumes that they won't be able to afford the prices.[26]

The "heart and soul of the group" is Sarah Gordon, who is described as "pretty, with a great smile and a warm, caring attitude."[27] But like other teenagers, she is sometimes thoughtless about some important things, such as parents and money:

> They had always been there for her, sometimes in ways that she wasn't aware of, like paying the bills, but now they were always asking her questions about what schools she was going to apply to, what she wanted to do with her life.[28]

The adults in the book do, and have done, a variety of things with their lives. Mrs. Gordon is an accomplished lawyer and mother: "Despite her heavy workload, she always managed to be around for the important things."[29] One minor character is a record producer. Another is "a big-deal public relations guy."[30] Sarah's grandmother was once a Broadway actress who refuses to accept the role of a maid. During the course of the story she resumes her career, this time on television. Jennifer's "mother and grandmother both had gone to prestigious black women's colleges in the South."[31] Mr. Gordon, Sarah's father, is the principal of a high school.

Attaining a formal education is a strong theme throughout the book. Claims Kwame:

> "With my A average I'll get a full scholarship to Howard, become a lawyer or a physicist . . . marry Sarah, have three point five kids, and live happily ever after."[32]

He goes on to joke that if he doesn't get a scholarship, then Sarah will put him through school. Her response:

> "Dream on, child." Sarah shook her head. "This woman is not going to work and support some man while he is in school. When you get your degree you can give me a call to see if I'm still available."[33]

Definitely a 90s attitude. What is not a 90s scenario is David Hunter's ambition to finance his college career through the help of a basketball scholarship. What is refreshing about the scenario is that Dave maintains an A average.

Johnson and Myers play with other stereotypes as well. There are the stereotypes about beauty and who is considered attractive. Tasha is described as light skinned with long hair—sexy, smart, exotic. But the author describes others with a different kind of good looks: "Different textures of hair and a rainbow of skin colors and clothing blossomed in the halls of Murphy High."[34] Cindy Phillips "is petite, with dark, radiant skin and a cute nose. She wears her black hair in braids"[35] as does Sarah's little sister Allison. Dave, who has "tightly curled hair" and "dark skin" doesn't consider himself attractive though many girls do.[36] In contrast is the overly self-confident Roy, who seems to have no insecurities about his looks, described in terms of his "dark-chocolate skin . . . stretched tautly over his bony face, which reminded Sarah of an African sculpture she had once seen in a museum."[37]

The African diaspora is a part of the consciousness of these young people, if only in small ways. They listen to Bob Marley music. They know that Egypt is part of Africa. They wear clothes made of Kente cloth. And Kwame's name, of course, comes from an African language. Even these small things denote a change in the nature of the middle class from generations before theirs. Kwame actually has a growing collection of books about African-American history, something that would have been difficult, or impossible, for his forebears because the books did not exist.

Johnson also tackles stereotypes associated with low-achieving students. One of the book's sub-plots involves students who are labeled in that way. One of them, Kiki, analyzes the problem when she admits, "We get reputations as either bad kids or kids who aren't serious and then we have to live with that the rest of our lives."[38] Their problem in this story is not that they are tracked into the low achievement groups within mainstream schools, but that they are assigned to a separate school of their own. Explains Mr. Gordon, their principal:

> "Well, Murphy High is a school for the bright, deserving kids in this city that don't need that much help making it from day to day. . . . But a lot of students who I think are equally bright and equally deserving were falling through the cracks at Murphy. Hamilton is the place for those kids. Some are academically in trouble, some are learning-disabled, and some just need a little more caring for."[39]

What Mr. Gordon, through the author, never says is that some don't come from families with the economic resources to support their academic efforts fully. What Johnson does do is introduce a few minor characters who once attended Hamilton back when it was called Vocational High School. Mr. Grimsby, one such person, assures Kiki that "A lot of guys, no girls then, did real well from my class. Some were plumbers, some were painters or repairmen. Some even went on to college and did okay."[40]

One of the dilemmas that the author does pose through the story line is the question of how the African-American middle class should fulfill its responsibility to the rest of the black community, if they have any responsibility at all. One character, a school board member who is not in favor of a special fund-raising project to benefit Hamilton High is criticized by Mr. Gordon for his contempt for the lower class: "If you give him half a chance he'll give you the whole story about how he 'pulled himself up by his bootstraps' and never needed a helping hand."[41]

On the other hand, Mr. Gordon does not foster friendships between his students and his children: "Aside from a few kids who dropped by the Gordon home occasionally, Sarah didn't know any students from Hamilton."[42] When she heads up the fund-raising project, Tasha thinks that her attitude is patronizing and that it is inappropriate for Murphy High students to take a leadership role: "I think that maybe we can offer them some ideas, but I don't think we should do it for them. They're not a charity, you know."[43] Difficult issues such as these are not examined in depth in *Sort of Sisters*.

In all fairness, books such as the *18 Pine St.* series are not the place to expect this. The main story line, in the first book, really revolves around Sarah and cousin Tasha negotiating their own relationship. So in some respects, it is admirable that Johnson weaves so many serious issues into the form in which she is working. This form, that of teenage series books,[44] is not art in the way that some writing is, but it has its own strengths. For example, authors have the opportunity, over time, to develop characters in a way that is not possible with one-volume stories. In turn, they can develop followings of young readers who somehow identify with the characters. It will be interesting to watch the progression of this series to see whether or not the author will develop not only the characters, but various issues as well.

The series does, in fact, have a multi-racial cast of characters. Though most are black, there is at least one white girl and one Latino young man, who are not important in *Sort of Sisters*. But their presence leaves room for the exploration of topics such as inter-racial friendships and romantic relationships, interactions amongst their parents, Afro-Hispanic culture, "reverse racism," and more.

The very existence of the *18 Pine St.* series is a big step in reversing for countless young adult readers of all ethnic groups the stereotype that African-American experience is monolithic. It compels young African-American readers of whatever socio-economic class, to not take that status and the attendant stereotypes for granted.

THE NEW SEED: RITA WILLIAMS-GARCIA'S *FAST TALK ON A SLOW TRACK*

The summary on the copyright page of this novel characterizes it this way:

> Black honors student Denzel Watson spends his last summer before college selling candy door-to-door in New York, competing on many levels with the charismatic Mello, and discovering how to motivate and apply himself.[45]

"Blurbs" such as this are insignificant and significant too. They are significant because potential readers (or parents, or educators) use them to help make decisions about what to purchase. This one is interesting not because of what it says, but because of what it does not say. The important information that it imparts is that the main character is African-American, that he is an honors student, and that he develops self-motivation.

What it does not address, for whatever reason, is the fact that he is from a middle class family and that he is an honors student though he does not know how to apply himself. He describes his own success in these terms: "I had made an art of achieving the most while expending the least."[46] During the summer, Denzel does, in fact, learn the meaning of motivation and applying oneself. But these discoveries have very little to do with Mello. To Denzel, Mello is simply "someone who could never truly step into my world, go places I could go, be who I could be."[47] Mello's unfortunate socio-economic status is important only to the extent that it helps Denzel to appreciate what "[his] world" really is and means. Just as importantly, he comes to realize his parents' part in shaping that world.

Denzel's given name is Dinizulu—"my father's contribution to my eternal embarrassment. An African name."[48] He expounds, explaining, basically, that everyone was choosing a new name in the "roots" era. He continues:

> Now, I ask you. If I went back to Zululand and found my long lost cousins, would they say welcome? All this to thwart the establishment, shock Nana Dee into an early heart attack, and embarrass me, his only son. Did Dad change his name? No. He was still Vernon Everett Watson.
> Kerri was lucky. When she was born the roots syndrome had died.[49]

Dinizulu is not alone in his disdain for his name. It was after seeing Denzel Washington (in a play about Malcolm X) that he changed his name, "which was a relief to the relatives who all called me son."[50]

Problematic too, is the way in which Denzel uses the names in various situations, depending on which name suits his present purposes. For example, to help him sell cookies, he assumes the persona of a "foreign exchange student from Zululand, saving my people from de flood or de famine."[51] Not only is he self-centered and not interested in his African or African-American heritage, but he's willing to make "colored folk be ridiculed."[52] It is only after matriculating at Princeton University that he realizes the extent to which white Americans revere their own ancestry. His roommate Niels "loved Medieval everything. He was going to trace his family's tribe and castle one day. Would I dare tell him about my father's search for our roots?"[53]

Vernon Watson's "search for his roots" is protracted and sincere.

When in college, he was a member of the Students for Racial Equality[54]—a "revolutionary Black thorn in White America's side."[55] He refuses to work for a corporation that would not employ black people in South Africa. Denzel blames this decision on his family, who is comfortably middle class, not having "everything and then some."[56] But Vernon Watson does make sure that his family has certain things; his daughter has a computer as well as a "collection of blue-black dolls."[57] Denzel accuses his father of wanting him to attend Princeton so that he can brag to white co-workers. And yes, he wants Dinizulu to have the resources and other advantages that Princeton offers. But he is very pleased that they offer African Studies and African American Studies.[58]

Religion is yet another point of contention. Denzel talks about his father's disdain for European religions, Christianity in particular, which he connects to the origins of European imperialism in Africa.[59] The contention is not only between Denzel and his father, however. Denzel's mother, Lydia, is the daughter of an African Methodist Episcopal reverend. Denzel describes her as "a walking monument to the Perfect Negro in America, everything Dad hated."[60] When he questions his father about choosing his mother as a mate, his father's answer is that he married her because he loved her and always will love her.[61] It should be instructive to Denzel that these two people, whose ideas are not identical, can still respect and live with each other. Instead, he dwells on the fact that his father does not accompany the rest of the family to church where they always arrive

> in time to blend in with the "first families" of Allen [AME Church]. . . . The Callendars. "First" black family to successfully move into Rosedale without being bombed out, row six, left pew. The Duncans. First family to hold membership at some country club out on the Island, row five, center pew. . . . "We were a first family of some sort, though I wasn't quite sure of what."[62]

But no matter how much he makes fun of his mother and her social agenda, he adores her too. After noting how she carries herself, he thinks, "If I did get married, my wife would have to be a queen and know it."[63]

In Williams-Garcia's multi-layered novel, interracial relationships are also the subject of Denzel's musing. Not only does he question his father about his relationship with his mother, but they speak too, however shallowly, about his father's long-ago sexual liaison with a white woman. In Denzel's estimation, the white woman "was nothing more than a revolutionary sacrifice to my father, who was then looking for yet another means of getting back at 'honky.'"[64] Denzel's father would prefer that his son take a black girl to the prom rather than his white female buddy. But Denzel contrasts the facelessness and namelessness of his father's white "fling" to Wendy, his own friend: "Wendy wasn't a them. Wendy was a girl with wild red hair and no fashion sense, who was my academic rival since kindergarten."[65]

His relationship with Wendy is not a romantic one, except for a one-time episode: "She even asked me to break her in so she would know what it was like. I did. She said, 'Oh,' and that was that."[66] But this disturbing passage, and the topic of teenage sexuality as portrayed in the literature, deserve a separate examination. For the present discussion, what is important about his relationship with Wendy is that eventually, it disintegrates, partly because she is white and Denzel is black. As it turns out, he decides not to take her to the prom for reasons unrelated to race. But she thinks that had he in fact taken her, as they talked about for years beforehand, it might have been only "to get at your old man."[67]

Even more importantly, she reveals that she has long resented him, feeling as though she's been "in the great Denzel's shadow for twelve years because I'm white and you're Black." Irate over his being named valedictorian, she contends:

> We got the same grades. The same. But they gave you an eighth of a point over me because the parents would raise the roof if they gave it to me, a white girl. Sure. You're more charismatic. But I always worked harder. I gave correct answers while you were being credited for dressing it up with your big words and your big talk.[68]

This is the crux of the newly acknowledged tension in their relationship—the new tendency of white people to feel what they term "reverse discrimination." Williams-Garcia must be one of the first authors to address this issue in young adult literature. And part of what this charge of reverse discrimination creates is a certain kind of insecurity on the parts of some middle class black people.

In *Fast Talk on a Slow Track*, Denzel does admit that "everything I said was fast talk on a slow track."[69] But part of why he behaves this way is because he is insecure about his own abilities after a forceful series of events: spending a few weeks at Princeton's summer orientation program, not doing as well as he expected, feeling like a failure, then coming home, sharing all of this with Wendy, and hearing her honest response. What Williams-Garcia has put up for question is the huge issue of what Denzel calls "some minority program," which he perceives as an "obvious insult"[70] and remedial in nature. It doesn't occur to him after he decides to matriculate in the fall that another way in which to regard the program is as a period of adjustment to a new environment and a challenge. And he finds, in fact, that many of the regular courses are not nearly as "hard" as the program; he was initiated by fire.

Part of what Denzel does not understand is the concept of institutionalized racism. He does not understand that if a society becomes what it is by deliberate measures, it must change by deliberate measures. He does not yet understand that he does not have to apologize for the circumstances under which he is admitted to Princeton. He does not, truly, appreciate his own words when he confronts a potential cookie customer, an African-American girl who brags about her full academic scholarship to Yale. He reasons that it doesn't really matter under what circumstances he was admitted to Princeton. Without understanding it fully, he invokes Malcolm X's famous phrase, "by any means necessary," and goes on:

> "So what does it matter if I get to Princeton on a full scholarship, or by selling cookies, or with an M-16 in my hand? The point is that I'll get there." Hearing Vernon's words fire from my mouth cut short my gloating. I was amazed and sickened by the realization that Vernon's propaganda was glued to my subconscious.[71]

And lastly, Denzel does not appreciate, at this point, the value of his father's "propaganda"—what home is, what it is that parents give to their children. He *has* passed the point of thinking that "Vernon and Lydia owed me the world because they brought me into it. That's the way it should be."[72] These are some of the many and complex issues explored in this challenging novel, sometimes successfully, sometimes not; sometimes coming to a resolution, often not. Rita Williams-Garcia says that she wrote this novel for the intelligent young men with whom she went to school; young men who were unaccustomed to failure. How did they handle this? According to Garcia, those with "half a chance," some preparation, confronted it squarely. "The others are still running."[73]

Denzel Watson has more than half a chance. For what he does not remember, when insecurities begin to flood his mind, and when Wendy denigrates him, is that he has all of the ability that he needs to accomplish whatever goals he sets for himself. And the characterization that Williams-Garcia constructs offers promise that he will, at some point, understand fully that "any means necessary" includes education as well as self-defense, and everything between. He comes to understand too that regardless of what parents do or do not owe to children, children must take on responsibility too; children owe something to themselves—integrity, self-knowledge, honesty.

After getting back his first economics examination, Denzel eagerly anticipates showing it to his parents. He is proud not of his grade or of the contents of his essay or even of the promise that his examination demonstrates, indicating a real capacity for synthesizing his own thoughts with other information. Instead, he is proud that he worked and really thought, that the essay is not simply "hype." He is excited about showing his examination to his parents because

> There was no better way to sign the honor statement at the end of the exam than in my given name, Dinizulu.[74]

And there is no better way of negotiating this life, for African-American young people, than to honor their own ancestry while at the same time not being apologetic for demanding the opportunities necessary to enjoy the fruits that this country has to offer. This is the challenge of the generation Dinizulu's mother calls "the new seed."[75] *Fast Talk on a Slow Track* makes this statement forcefully.

CONCLUSION

The issue of class and how it is manifested in African-American young adult literature (as well as picture books) is complicated and multi-faceted. *The Brownies' Book* examples give only a hint of how deep and historically rooted the issue is. And because the present piece focuses upon recent literature, so much is neglected: what comes to mind is Virginia Hamilton's long track record of writing about middle class characters. One particularly relevant example is her *The House of*

Dies Drear, constructed around the family of a black college professor. In the field of picture books, Elizabeth Fitzgerald Howard is creating a memorable body of work which includes *Aunt Flossie's Hats (and Crab Cakes Later)*, the story of the memories that accompany each of Aunt Flossie's hats. What is clear is that this chapter is merely a preliminary examination of a subject that properly requires a book length investigation.

This issue is an interesting one, too, because it does not have clearly defined stages. For example, color stratification continues to be a problem. There are black republicans as well as black democrats. There are those who would define themselves as African-Americans and those who would define themselves as Americans, period. There are black middle class families who are building "class structures" and those who are experiencing downward mobility. Simply put, just as there is class stratification among black Americans, there is variation within the black middle class as well. All of the foregoing informs the literature that is created.

One of the most refreshing recent books is Angela Johnson's *Toning the Sweep*. It is not concerned explicitly with issues of class. It is concerned with family coming to appreciate one another. It is about Emmie, a young woman who gets "sent home early today because I wouldn't stand up and say the Pledge of Allegiance."[76] It is about her coming to know her mother, a woman hurt in a most personal way by the pre-civil rights era south. And it is about Emmie appreciating her unconventional, dreadlocked Grandmother:

> I can't imagine Ola knitting me anything. She does send me pamphlets on world hunger and the environment. And she sent me a T-shirt from Jamaica when she went there to a reggae festival. Ola has sent me beads from Africa and incense from India, even a case of olives from Greece 'cause she remembered that I hadn't tried them.[77]

Her emphasis is not on conspicuous consumption or appearances or conforming to social norms. Rather, her philosophy is to use her financial means in an effort to experience the world in all its facets—its textures, its climates, its sounds, its people. Most importantly, what her granddaughter remembers is: "You have to try everything if you really want to live in this world" is what she always says.[78]

The African-American middle class, as represented in young

adult literature, is still trying everything.[79] The literature and criticism exploring the evolution and unfolding of this process promises to be controversial, challenging, and revealing.

NOTES

1. For a more thorough discussion of the historical background of African-American children's literature, see Dianne Johnson's *Telling Tales: The Pedagogy and Promise of African American Literature for Youth*, Westport, CT: Greenwood Press, 1990.
2. This is not the case with African-American literature, especially from the "Harlem Renaissance" period. It is beyond the scope of this chapter however, to do an adequate comparison between the histories of adult literature and literature for the young.
3. W.E.B. DuBois, ed., *The Brownies' Book* no. 2 (1921): 63.
4. See *Telling Tales* for a detailed discussion of class issues in *The Brownies' Book* magazine.
5. W.E.B. DuBois, ed., *The Brownies' Book* no. 6 (1920): 178.
6. Ibid., no. 10, 300.
7. Ibid., back cover.
8. There is no definitive evidence about who the readers of the magazine were. A good guess is that they were the children of middle class members of the NAACP who subscribed also to the *Crisis*.
9. See *Telling Tales* for a discussion of how, in my estimation, *Ebony Jr!* contributed to its own demise partly by its restrictions on the subject matter that could be explored by contributing authors.
10. W.E.B. DuBois, ed., *The Brownies' Book* no. 6 (1920): 178.
11. Toni Morrison, *The Bluest Eye* (New York: Washington Square Press, 1970), 97.
12. Rosa Guy, *The Music of Summer* (New York: Delacorte, 1992), 16.
13. Ibid., 6.
14. Ibid., 2.
15. Ibid., 7.
16. Ibid., 8.
17. Ibid., 169.
18. Ibid., 136.
19. Ibid., 112.
20. Ibid., 70.
21. Ibid., 91.
22. Ibid., 74.
23. Ibid., 127.
24. In particular, see Guy's *The Friends*, which deals with conflict between

upwardly mobile West Indian immigrants to New York City and African-Americans, and *And I Heard a Bird Sing* of her Imamu Jones mystery series. This book examines the issue of class with fully developed black characters and white characters of various economic classes.

25. Walter Dean Myers, creator and Stacie Johnson, author, *Sort of Sisters* (New York: Bantam Books, 1992), unpaginated.
26. Ibid., 55.
27. Ibid., unpaginated.
28. Ibid., 12.
29. Ibid., 17.
30. Ibid., 114.
31. Ibid., 39.
32. Ibid., 2.
33. Ibid.
34. Ibid., 25.
35. Ibid., unpaginated.
36. Ibid., 23.
37. Ibid., 44.
38. Ibid., 111.
39. Ibid., 27.
40. Ibid., 130.
41. Ibid., 33.
42. Ibid., 5.
43. Ibid., 46.
44. It is problematic, of course, for me to place the literature in a hierarchy. Is the novel comparable to the film and the adolescent series to the soap opera? And of course, there are literary as well as "pop" series. Though I have made distinctions, I do acknowledge that there is value in various forms.
45. Rita Williams-Garcia, *Fast Talk on a Slow Track* (New York: Lodestar Books, 1991), unpaginated.
46. Ibid., 158.
47. Ibid.
48. Ibid., 39.
49. Ibid.
50. Ibid., 40.
51. Ibid., 39.
52. W.E.B. DuBois, ed. *The Brownies' Book* no. 1 (1920): 12–13.
53. Rita Williams-Garcia, 168.
54. Ibid., 9.
55. Ibid., 179.
56. Ibid., 12.

57. Ibid., 20.
58. Ibid., 167.
59. Ibid.
60. Ibid., 65.
61. Ibid.
62. Ibid., 69.
63. Ibid., 67.
64. Ibid., 23.
65. Ibid., 24.
66. Ibid.
67. Ibid., 30.
68. Ibid., 31.
69. Ibid., 47.
70. Ibid., 3.
71. Ibid., 97–98.
72. Ibid., 107.
73. Ibid., 183.
74. Ibid., 182.
75. Ibid., 22.
76. Angela Johnson, *Toning the Sweep* (New York: Orchard Books, 1993), 1.
77. Ibid.
78. Ibid., 11.
79. Authors and publishers, as well, are trying everything. For a very raw straightforward depiction of middle class African-American young adults see Joseph E. Green's *Pseudo Cool*, published in 1988 by the non-mainstream Holloway House Publishing Company. As announced on the cover, the characters are "black, wealthy and privileged" and tell stories that won't be assigned in most high school classrooms.

REFERENCES

Childress, Alice. *A Hero Ain't Nothin' But a Sandwich*. New York: Coward, McCann and Geoghegan, 1973.
DuBois, W.E.B., ed. *The Brownies' Book* (magazine). New York: DuBois and Dill, Publishers, 1920–1921.
Graham, Lorenz. *North Town*. New York: Signet Books, 1965.
Guy, Rosa. *The Music of Summer*. New York: Delacorte, 1992.
Hamilton, Virginia. *The House of Dies Drear*. New York: Macmillan, 1968.
Howard, Elizabeth Fitzgerald. *Aunt Flossie's Hats (and Crab Cakes Later)*. New York: Clarion Books, 1991.
Johnson, Angela. *Toning the Sweep*. New York: Orchard Books, 1993.
Johnson, Dianne. *Telling Tales: The Pedagogy and Promise of African Ameri-*

can Literature for Youth. Westport, CT: Greenwood Press, 1990.

Lester, Julius. *This Strange New Feeling.* New York: Scholastic, 1981.

Morrison, Toni. *The Bluest Eye.* New York: Washington Square Press, 1970.

Myers, Walter Dean, creator and Stacie Johnson, author. *Sort of Sisters* (of the *18 Pine St.* series). New York: Bantam Books, 1992.

Wilkinson, Brenda. *Ludell.* New York: Harper and Row, 1975.

Williams-Garcia, Rita. *Fast Talk on a Slow Track.* New York: Lodestar Books, 1991.

SIX

Color and Class: An Exploration of Responses in Four African-American Coming-of-Age Novels

Linda J. Zoppa

Unlike any other period in literature, the 1990s have created a genre in young adult literature that addresses, without hesitation, the realistic nature of society. Requiring honesty, authenticity, and the ability to internalize the problems and solutions presented, African-American young adults can experience a literature they have for so long demanded. In this chapter, with an historical perspective, four black young adult novels will be explored: *Blue Tights* by Rita Williams-Garcia,[1] *The Music of Summer* by Rosa Guy,[2] *Come a Stranger* by Cynthia Voigt,[3] and Jacqueline Woodson's *The Dear One*.[4] The treatment of color and class within these novels will be discussed, as well as the protagonists' response to these issues.

Literature addressing the problems of current society is best understood when the concerns of history are presented. Since the eighteenth century, the United States welcomed immigrants from many countries with diverse cultures, occupations, and ideas. As the intercultural community has grown the methods by which individuals interact with each other have become more complicated. Observing the behavior of members within a society has caused political scientists and sociologists to make certain inferences concerning how individuals survive in a multicultural environment. Historian, Marcus Hansen states that unlike their first and second generation counterparts, third generation immigrants identify more with the elements of their roots, thus creating a "new hyphenated" designation.[5] Social, economic, and political pressures have also caused third generation hyphenated-Americans to seek membership within organizations that assist them in holding onto elements of their native culture.

The process of acculturation by racial and ethnic group affiliation takes place at different rates of speed and with different levels of success.[6] Both speed and success are determined by the degree to which those already in the host society find newcomers acceptable and that to which their traditions can be merged with that of the host culture without altering its features already in existence.[7] For example, the Chinese-Americans have achieved acculturation; their coming to America has also caused them to experience differences between eastern and western values. Although American society's antagonism prevented development of a hyphenated Chinese-American culture prior to World War II, changes in attitude since then have allowed for a growth of this new community over a relatively short period of time.[8] However, despite our efforts to find and trace a common pattern of cultural change among ethnic groups over a period of time, history has taught us that no two ethnic groups have experienced the same treatment once arriving in the United States.

ACCULTURATION OF AFRICAN-AMERICANS

While some ethnic groups have successfully become part of the mainstream of American culture; others have experienced major difficulties. The acculturation process of African-Americans, the focus of this chapter, has been the most complex of all groups in the United States. Numerically, African-Americans constitute the largest single group in this country, while the time span of their interaction with American society is far greater than any other, except for Native Americans. No other single group of Americans has aspired to acculturation and assimilation with more perseverance over such a prolonged period of time, only to experience rejection and varied levels of racism. Bernard Makhoseswe Magubane contends that an African-American is fundamentally "an American who is not accepted as an American, hence a kind of negative American."[9] A century of struggling for acculturation and assimilation by the late 1960s left many African-

American leaders questioning if conformity to Anglo-American values and culture norms was too high a price to pay for the integration they had so faithfully and vainly pursued. Utilizing the philosophy of W.E.B. Dubois, the modern African-American sought a way to be both American and Negro without having to "bleach his Negro soul in a flood of white Americanism."[10] However, the societal disturbances of the 1960s caused blacks to explore their connection with the African continent. They discovered that "black" was more than just a color.

As many African-Americans learned about, and took pride in their African heritage, the stereotypes about native Africans persisted. Through the visual media Africa was perceived as an alien place filled with unusual wildlife surrounded by exotic plant life and "primitive savages." Popular culture provided additional stimulus toward creating negative stereotypes by consistently portraying white characters as leaders and black characters as followers both within the entertainment media and literature. Thus, as African-Americans attempted to understand their "Americanness" and their "Africanness," they were assaulted by conflicting views of Africa.

The birth of the Civil Rights Movement led many blacks to believe that they would finally be accepted into society as Americans. When it became clear that "acceptance" was either non-existent or ambiguous in context, black feelings of alienation intensified. Many black-American activists also soon discovered that they could not totally identify with Africa, either. However, by the early 1970s, the earlier enthusiasm once surrounding identification with Africa was reactivated as the black population desired knowledge of their roots. This reawakened interest and activities resulted in intensified Afro-centrism.

Despite the efforts of black Americans to both seek their roots and adjust within mainstream American culture, they are repeatedly victimized by the negative opinions and perceptions Americans have held concerning Africa and Africans. The concept of "blackness" and notions associated with being black have historically perpetuated damaging images.[11] Prior to the sixteenth century, the *Oxford English Dictionary* defined "black" as "deeply stained with dirt; soiled, . . . foul. . . . Having dark or deadly purposes malignant; pertaining to or involving death, deadly; baneful, disastrous, sinister. . . . Foul, iniquitous, atrocious, horrible, wicked."[12] When compared, white and black implied, respectively, "purity and filthiness, virginity and sin, virtue and baseness, beauty and ugliness, beneficence and evil, God and devil."[13] Upon seeing the first African people, the English projected these feelings about dark-skinned people. English settlers carried their negative views of Africans and their descendants with them when they colonized America. With the passage of time, white Americans embellished and perpetuated these notions. Many whites ascribed such characteristics as laziness, stupidity, immorality, and sexual excess to Africans and African-Americans.[14] These attitudes further perpetuated feelings of alienation experienced by both African-American adults and teenagers.

PERCEPTIONS OF COLOR

Relationships with whites are not the only racial struggle facing black Americans. Challenges exist as today's African-Americans interact with each other regarding shades of skin color: a painful encounter especially for the young adult who seeks inclusion and acceptability within this culturally diverse American society. For the African-American, slave heritage is more a symbol of shame than of pride.[15] Dark-skinned emigrants from the Caribbean distanced themselves from the African-American population for fear that there would be an association with elements of their history such as slavery, not-so-pleasant thoughts of Africa, the South, Emancipation, and northern migration. Furthermore, within the African-American community, beneath a surface appearance of black solidarity, lies a matrix of attitudes concerning skin color and other physical features such as hair texture, the shape of one's nose, and the color of one's eyes. Within the black American community, these physical characteristics help determine degrees of friendship and a person's status among members of peer groups.[16]

That persons with lighter skin tone were thought of as more intelligent and possessed more ability is not a new phenomenon. In 1918, sociologist, Edward Reuter, discovered that mulattoes "outdistanced darker blacks economically and socially"[17] because of their lighter skin tone. Several scholars had completed studies during the 1920s through the 1960s, all resulting in similar findings.[18] The most significant study since Reuter was performed by Joel Williamson, in 1980. His findings supported those above, with additional information indicating that the mulatto's treatment had improved over time.[19]

PERCEPTIONS OF CLASS

In addition to skin color, class designation within society has also affected the African-American's treatment in mainstream America. The same stereotyped notions and attitudes individuals harbored toward African-Americans concerning skin color, are also responsible for developing perspectives regarding class structure and worth in society.

During the recent decades, social scientists have addressed issues concerning the qualitative and quantitative definitions of class within American society. Although differences of opinion exist regarding this topic, there is more unity among researchers in declaring that blacks are victimized by society's memories of history past. A goal among social scientists has been to define whether racial discrimination is a factor in determining a group's class position within society. Another question raised is what additional characteristics are there in defining class structure and one's position within it. Adam Smith, David Ricardo, and Karl Marx define class according to one's economics.[20] Wilson explains that for blacks, race relations have improved during recent years, thus, "economics are more important than day-to-day encounters with whites" when determining class position for African-Americans in the United States. These theories however, seem to dismiss the reality that racial discrimination exists. Boston offers a more realistic method of determining class in today's society. He contends that one's position in society is based upon a combination of occupation, income, *and* power relations.[21] Boston further states that "historically, racial subjugation has created a unique class stratification, reflecting the inferior economic position blacks have been forced to occupy."[22] DeMott presents a more recent theory regarding the definition of class structure, and believes that our society is not comprised of classes but of individuals who have a desire to continually improve. This population, the majority in number, are defined as the "striving middle,"[23] of which the very rich and very poor wish to become a part.[24] Because there exist social scientists and researchers who fail to acknowledge that racial discrimination is a component in defining class structure, it is necessary to continue to confront this matter. One has only to consult recent statistics concerning the African-American's plight in America for further clarification. Nationwide, blacks constitute 10.1% of the work force, but receive only 7.8% of all the earnings of the work force.[25] The 1990 census reveals that the black family's median income was $21,423, compared to whites, whose median income was $36,915.[26] Furthermore, subjected to substandard housing, medical care, and educational systems, 39.8% of African-American families receive federally sponsored Aid for Dependent Children.[27] Unemployment remains high among the blue collar working force, which is composed of mostly black members. These and other related data clearly indicate the grim realities concerning the unfair system of determining class position within society. Among those mainstream members of society unable to separate African-Americans from the negative connotations associated with slavery, blacks continue to be considered as individuals who possess physical, not mental, skills and capacities inferior to other members of society.[28]

STEREOTYPICAL PERCEPTIONS OF THE AFRICAN-AMERICAN

Thus far, the discussion has been centered around the restricted opportunities granted to African-Americans because of their color and imposed class position within society. Negative stereotypes associated with skin color and class have made their way into the fundamental thought patterns of individuals who characterize blacks as being violent, lazy, unintelligent, and generally uncivilized. Historically, black men captured as slaves were portrayed by their owners as the contented Sambo stereotype, but simultaneously were revered as "brutal savages."[29] More damaging was the statement expressed by William Drayton, a nineteenth century advocate of slavery, that slavery controlled the "wild frenzy of revenge, and the savage lust of blood" inherent in Africans.[30] Constructing methods and rationale to support control of the black man's "uncivilized behavior," the white population created the term "nigger," implying a creature representing stupidity and indolence; the "lowest level of humanity."[31] Decades after the publication of this statement, the entertainment media further reiterated the negative image of the black population by the production of the film, "The Birth of a Nation," released in 1915. Underscoring its impact upon the African-American image, Ralph Ellison voiced his evaluation of the film:

> One answer was to deny the Negro's humanity—a pattern set long before 1915. But with the release of "The Birth of a Nation" the spread of images of Negroes as subhumans became finan-

cially and dramatically profitable. The Negro as scapegoat could be sold as entertainment, could even be exported. If the film became the main manipulator of the American dream, for Negroes that dream contained a strong dose of such stuff as nightmares are made of.[32]

While one has to agree that the number of negative images of blacks has been reduced since the early 1900s, such connotations are still prevalent within American society. The 1990s have introduced efforts towards being "politically correct" and "culturally sensitive," causing individuals to avoid conversations and written comments that would intimate racial and ethnic prejudice. Society however, utilizes a more sophisticated and subtler approach to reinforce negative concepts of African-American character. Among members of the white community, African-Americans are viewed as non-conformists—people difficult to comprehend, requiring constant scrutinizing for the purpose of understanding their culture and needs. Fearing that they would cause physical injury or property damage, whites generally associate African-Americans with illegal activity, thus causing "law-abiding blacks to be perceived as possible criminals."[33] The list of misconceptions are never ending.

African-Americans continue to endure the affects of white America's misconceptions concerning their character and behavior. Alice Walker expresses the feelings of a subjugated community:

I believe that the worst part of being in an oppressed culture—primarily because it controls the production and dispersal of images in the media—[is that it] can so easily make us feel ashamed of ourselves, of our sayings, our doings, and our ways. And it doesn't matter whether these sayings, doings, or ways are good or bad. What is bad about them and, therefore, worthy of shame, is that they belong to us.[34]

In many ways, it appears that Americans of African descent have come full circle. National laws have changed, but the ambiguity remains. Perhaps, we depend too much upon government and public policies to effect changes, when we as a society should seek alternative methods of abandoning prejudice. African-Americans are still wrestling with the same basic issues that plagued their ancestors; they are extinguishing the same fires. According to political scientist, Andrew

Hacker, America has never "opened its doors to black America,"[35] thus, preventing black Americans from becoming full citizens. As an ethnic group, African-Americans have been expected to essentially disown their culture for that of mainstream America. In order to achieve success in many areas such as literature, music, and the arts, gifted blacks have had to adopt western European culture and skills. But ironically, even for many of those who have embraced American culture, the doors have remained closed.

Feelings of alienation among the black American population then are not without validity. Author, Ellis Cose, contends that changing attitudes towards blacks could possibly be accomplished by implementing appropriate laws to govern our society.[36] Unfortunately, such laws do not change attitudes. Author, Ben Wattenberg has stated significantly that we need to make our diversity a virtue; only then can America become the world's first "universal Nation."[37]

IMPORTANCE OF YOUNG ADULT AFRICAN-AMERICAN LITERATURE

Through the vehicle of literature it is possible that both black and white young adults will be able to transcend prejudice and racism. Internalizing the problems re-enacted by fictional characters within the novels can help the young adult reader gain a better understanding of what occurs when one enters into adulthood in a changing society. Authors of today's young adult realistic novels appear to make every attempt to utilize themes to which adolescents can relate and in which they are interested. Subjects such as premarital sex, family problems, abuse, race relations, alternative life styles, and the general dissatisfaction with a materialistic society, once prohibited in earlier children's books, are prevalent in today's young adult novels. Through the protagonists, the young adult reader also safely becomes involved with vicarious experiences without personally suffering the consequences of wrong decisions. Within the privacy of the book, readers can test their beliefs and values against those revealed in the storyline. Indeed, adolescents need to see themselves within the novels they read. Marie Frankson states that literature inclusive of black-American characters in a non-stereotypical role provides an opportunity for African-American teenagers "to develop a positive image of their roles as valuable members of society; minority youth need to see themselves represented in good literature, both in their classrooms and on their library shelves."[38] The relative paucity of realistic, modern day black experience young adult novels, coupled with the existence of a larger number of books with only white characters, sends the message to African-American teenagers that members of their ethnic group are not worthy of representation within novels. Romero and Zancanella stated that "indigenous literature—that which arises from the students' own culture and locale—allows readers to make powerful connections to works that draw on what they already know and to validate the importance of that knowledge."[39] Among today's minority writers, African-Americans have the strongest voice; perhaps, through this voice, a better understanding of humanity will be gained. Until recently, there has been little in the body of American literature for young adults with which members of the African-American community can identify as reflecting, for them, a realistic experience of life in America.

WHITE CHARACTER PERCEPTIONS OF BLACK CHARACTERS

The white characters within the four novels under discussion by Voigt, Garcia, Woodson, and Guy present several challenges for their African-American peers, and in so doing, major concerns for their young adult readers. In Cynthia Voigt's *Come a Stranger*, gifted dancer, Mina Smiths, spends two summers at a camp specializing in the study of dance. Living in the inner city, Mina's home emphasizes close family ties and strong religious teaching. Protected from the problems of her immediate locale, Mina has not yet experienced the prejudice awaiting her in the real world.

During Mina's first visit to ballet camp, she becomes so involved in the beauty of her surroundings, and the experience of what she was learning and enjoying, it prevents her from noticing the exchanged glances and quiet conversations shared about her among the white students. Having won a full scholarship, Mina is surrounded with students who attend private schools in the suburbs and are accustomed to a lifestyle unknown to her. However, in spite of their subtle behavior, Mina tolerates their haughty attitudes while remaining unaware of their prejudice towards her. In fact, when her father arrives to drive her home from her first summer in attendance at the camp, Mina is asked if she is the only African-American dancer. Her father's inquiry and her subsequent affirmative response causes a realization, for the first time, that she is the only person of color studying at the camp site. It is at this moment that Mina, recalling the events of the past weeks, first realizes what her white dance instructor was implying when she previously described Mina as "undisciplined,"[40] further stating that she possessed a "certain rude grace."[41] When she is cast by her instructor to perform as Tarkaan in an original ballet offered during the term, Mina's naivete prevents her from thoroughly understanding the motivation of her instructor. She has not internalized that the character Tarkaan, requiring the use of a mask, is an evil and foreboding figure.

Not until her second summer at the camp does Mina become aware of how she is perceived by the white dance students and the instructor. Upon her arrival, she is assigned to a private room, while other students living in the dormitory are assigned roommates. During her first week in attendance she discovers that although the other dancers treat her kindly and include her in most of their activities, they have chosen not to room with her and often exchange glances in her presence. Discerning that "they were seeing the outside of her,"[42] and responding to words and behaviors historically characterized as stereotypical black behavior, Mina felt "trapped within her skin."[43]

The many quiet moments Mina spends alone allows her to gain a perspective of her true feelings and the experiences accompanying them. Confusion arises as she begins to consider whether the other students are merely treating her "nicely" on the surface to avoid problems with a black person or because they truly like her as a person. Mina compares herself to a dryad—a tree creature.[44] Looking toward nature for comfort, Mina rationalizes that trees, creations of nature, do not judge a person by their color.[45] Feeling tendencies toward identifying with anything other than her black culture, Mina, in thought, ironically acknowledges that dryads, in Greek myths, "belonged to the white world."[46] A deeper anger develops within her upon discovering that this imaginary world cannot be hers; she is black, and cannot truly claim anything that is part of the white world.

In Williams-Garcia's *Blue Tights*, fifteen-year-old protagonist, Joyce Collins, a gifted dancer, experiences similar treatment. Commenting about Joyce's large derriere, the public school white dance instructor verbalizes that "It wouldn't look right on stage . . . dancers should never have too much of anything."[47] Referring to her instructor as an "old white witch,"[48] Joyce is angered when she is told not to audition for a dance showcase soon to be performed at her school. Further embellishing her stereotypical perceptions towards blacks, the dance instructor describes Joyce as "too lazy,"[49] the "least disciplined,"[50] and often addresses Joyce in class as "blue tights, big butt."[51]

Similar feelings are experienced by Afeni Harris in Woodson's *The Dear One*. Attending a private school of mainly white students, Afeni mentions that the only person with whom she is able to communicate is Caesar, a student of Native American-Black descent. Often called names by some of the white students, Afeni aspires to the high academic standards upheld by the school, but has never found acceptance by the populace at large. Afeni learns to accommodate herself to the archaic, stereotyped teaching perceptions manifested by members of the teaching faculty. She develops the ability to discriminate between fact and fiction concerning information presented within her subject classes. Inaccurate historical details are dismissed soon after the subject test is given. When told by her history teacher that "a pilgrim gave a Native American a turkey,"[52] Afeni exchanges smiles with Caesar, knowing full well that "pilgrims gave Native Americans blankets with smallpox on them."[53]

While Afeni never voices a desire to identify with characteristics of the white world for the purpose of gaining acceptance of her white peers, her attending the private school and attaining superior grades are perceived by others as an attempt at white bonding. Considering the similar situations experienced by both Mina Smiths and Afeni Roberts, each character chooses her own strategies in order to cope with peer prejudice. The aspirations of these young people to acquire white world characteristics is not an uncommon or unrealistic behavior. James Banks indicates that very often, gifted, high achieving black youth in an all-white environment are in conflict concerning whether they should "support the dominant or parent culture."[54] Behaviors such as "speaking standard English,"[55] applying oneself to the fullest, and attaining high educational goals and the "equality of opportunity"[56] are considered, historically, exclusive to the white population. Further, Fordham explains that the high achieving, gifted adolescent in a predominantly white environment is forced to adopt a "raceless"[57] identity, a behavior requiring that the individual refrain from exhibiting even *approval* of African-American characteristics.

Contrary to Voigt and Woodson's above mentioned protagonists, Williams-Garcia's Joyce Collins in *Blue Tights* rejects any appearance of identification with white peers. Defining the white population as those who "had to have tans during the winter, had to touch her hair, [and] had to know exactly what she meant by this or that,"[58] Joyce was not discouraged by her lack of acceptance by the white population. In fact, her level of black pride and her awareness of her African-American culture increases as a result of her experiences. Removing herself from the possibility of future negative encounters, she arranges to have her schedule changed at school. Having been assigned to the predominantly white, gifted track, Joyce is reassigned to the averaged-ability, more culturally integrated program of classes. She is not interested in aspiring to what is perceived as white world characteristics.

SKIN TONE COLOR PERCEPTION
BETWEEN AND AMONG BLACK CHARACTERS

Varying degrees of skin color are indeed an issue among black characters within the four novels examined here. The protagonists, however, choose diverse methods in reacting to attitudes and responses concerning either their or other characters' variations in skin tone.

Afeni Harris, in *The Dear One*, is coerced by her mother, a mulatto, to join both the Jack and Jill and White Gloves and Manners clubs. Mrs. Harris is aware that Afeni identifies strongly with the ideals represented within these exclusive clubs. Although Afeni verbally criticizes her peers within the membership of the organizations for being snobs, she is, indeed, proud of her lighter skin tone and her high intellectual achievement. In spite of Afeni's possession of characteristics historically considered as belonging to the white population, she is unable to gain acceptance by her white peers. Her inner conflict concerning which culture to identify with is intensified as Afeni encounters rejection from both the white and black populations.

The problem blacks encounter concerning skin tone is most obvious in Guy's *The Music of Summer*. Having been close friends since childhood, both Sarah Richardson and Cathy Johnson find themselves separated and distanced during their teenaged years because of their different skin tones. Sarah, the darker-skinned young woman, finds difficulty understanding why Cathy and her lighter-skinned friends reject her repeatedly. During a summer spent with Cathy and her private-school acquaintances, Sarah discovers that indeed, physical differences such as skin color, can cause irrevocable separation between childhood friends.

As adolescence approached, Cathy developed a desire to surround herself with white and lighter-skinned black individuals. Attending an exclusive private school that has its own "colored elite"[59] consisting of middle-class and lighter-skinned blacks, Cathy and her friends, belonging to this clique, are careful to describe their skin tone as "golden"[60] or "golden brown."[61] Acknowledging that darker-skinned sisters and brothers are not welcomed among the elite social gatherings, Cathy informs Sarah "we're admitted wherever we go—without having to beg or being insulted. We're accepted, Sarah Richardson—so long as you're not tagging along."[62] Although Sarah considers Cathy's friends to be "phonies"[63] and "dull,"[64] she still yearns for the friendship they once shared during their childhood.

Many experiences during this summer convince Sarah that Cathy's rejection of her is primarily because of her darker skin tone and other physical features characteristic of African-Americans. While lying on the beach with Cathy and her elite friends, Sarah overhears one of the girls explain her boyfriend's hair texture: "Milt's hair's kinky, but his mother's white. I have good hair, so maybe our kid will not do too bad."[65] Further references to Sarah's darker skin color are made by Cathy, who states while sun-tanning on the beach, "Before I leave this summer I intend to be as black as Sarah."[66] It is evident that Cathy and her select group of friends do not attempt to spare Sarah's feelings; they openly verbalize their hostile thoughts toward her, almost awaiting a response.

PERCEPTIONS OF CLASS

Class status and position within the American class structure is of concern to the African-American protagonists within the novels. Black characters acutely are aware of their status and the stratification levels of their peers. Surrounded by students who attend private schools and whose parents hold professional positions requiring higher level education, Mina, in *Come a Stranger*, could not have attended summer camp without having received a scholarship. Mina learns, in addition, the bitter reality of the power structure in America concerning minorities and class position. Upon returning home from her shortened camp visit, her father explains that:

> Being a minority has only part to do with numbers. It has a lot to
> do with who has power, maybe more to do with that than any-
> thing else, or money. And if you're black, you've got to under-
> stand that. You've got to accept the limits.[67]

Woodson's Afeni has become accustomed to the comforts and
opportunities that her mother, a prosecuting attorney, is able to provide
for her. They live in a small, black suburban community "surrounded
by mountains. . . . The Victorian houses stand far apart from each
other, and the people who live in them are doctors and lawyers and
bankers."[68] Identifying with the values that are imposed upon her both
at home and through the elite private education she receives, Afeni
associates certain behaviors with middle/upper-middle class standards.
The differences between upper and lower class African-American behavior, as perceived by Afeni, becomes apparent when her mother
invites an unwed pregnant teenager, Rebecca Roberts, into her home.
Coming from the poorer section of a nearby city, Rebecca is as impressed with Afeni's life style as Afeni is alarmed by hers. Exhibiting
the contents of her unpacked suitcase, Rebecca could not help but
notice what Afeni was thinking: "There were two or three dingy-look-
ing pairs of underwear, a white sweatshirt, and a pair of jeans that had
been cut in the front and restitched with elastic."[69] Ashamed that
Rebecca would be sleeping in her T-shirt, Afeni fixed her eyes upon
Rebecca—not sure of how to respond. Rebecca quickly replied, "Do
you always stare like that? Because if you do, you're rude."[70]

Afeni dislikes sharing her room with a teenaged girl not aspiring
to her educational, social, and moral goals. Tension between the two
girls increases as behavioral lifestyle differences surface. This mutual
discomfort increases as Afeni engages in correcting Rebecca's gram-
mar as often as Afeni feels, is needed. Afeni, however, also receives
verbal correction as well by her street-wise visitor:

> Learn the language already. . . . You're black. Talk like it. . . . I
> know you want to ask me all kinds of questions about this baby,
> but you too polite. Rich people don't do that, do they? They wait
> until someone offers up the information.[71]

Joyce Collins, in *Blue Tights*, is also aware of class status, or the
lack of it among her peers. Growing up in the poorer section of a large
city, Joyce's mother and her abusive step-father, work long hours to

earn what is needed to survive. Unable to receive financial support for the dance instruction she desires, Joyce seeks dance programs, outside the public school, that allow her free admission. Her passion for dance coupled with her home chores cause Joyce to not dwell much on issues involving the class status of her peers; she is, however, aware that such a system exists.

Thinking about her West Indian friends, Cindi and Jay-Jay, Joyce is reminded that popularity is defined by becoming accepted by this select population.

> Joyce looked at Cindi and Jay-Jay and hungered for their popularity. She had to be part of their crew. Once she was associated with them, life at Cardozo [high school] would be fat cake.[72]

Despite Joyce's desire for acceptance among the West Indian population, she is aware that they will not include their African-American peers in many of their activities. Further emphasizing the West Indians' rejection of African-American company, Joyce explains Jay-Jay's behavior when she is among her peers: "her Island blood surface[d] and [was] submerge[d] at given moments. When Jay-Jay was with her West Indian friends she was that, when she was with her stateside friends she became that—she couldn't help that."[73] Joyce is reminded of differences between her South Jamaica, New York, neighborhood and the area of the city where Jay-Jay and Cindi reside:

> [There are] no projects. No three liquor stores to a block. No four Tabernacle Houses of Prayer to every other block. No boarded storefronts. No rib shacks. No Cadillacs. Instead there were little brown housewives trimming hedges. Sturdy brick cottages stood on green lawns, and midsized sedans boasting college stickers sat along the curbs.[74]

Guy's Sarah Richardson is reminded during her summer vacation that she is not a member of the selected elite. In addition to experiencing rejection because of her darker skin tone, Sarah is verbally abused by her peers, because her family members have been employed in blue collar positions. In an altercation, Sarah is asked, "What do you know about anything, you with an uncle who's a janitor and a mother who scrubs floors to make a living?"[75]

While Sarah finds solace in identifying Cathy's friends as "shallow,"[76] she is cognizant of the fact that her family's social and financial position, unlike Cathy's, exists because of the lack of opportunities offered to generations past. Sarah's family dreams of the day when her musical abilities will lead her to stardom; she understands, however, that this dream is grounded in "their shared experience: poverty."[77]

In each of the above situations, the African-American protagonists react to their peers while being consciously aware of the existing class stratification within present day America. Within these four contemporary novels, the characters are realistic members of today's American society, responding to a class stratification system. Thomas Boston argues that "class is defined primarily by status,"[78] and status can only be gained if opportunities are present, allowing individuals within a society means to procure them.

Each of the major protagonists discussed also possesses an innate talent or gift. Developing skills leading to success within the areas of dance or musical performance requires study and a significant financial investment. Acknowledging that only the skilled enjoy success in such endeavors, opportunities for success among those not as financially able are severely limited and practically non-existent.

ATTITUDES PROJECTED BY AFRICAN-AMERICAN YOUNG ADULTS TOWARD GIFTED AND TALENTED PEERS

Prejudice, resentment, and jealousy are among the feelings projected by black teenagers toward their intellectually gifted and talented peers within the novels examined. In reality, studies performed by psychologists and sociologists indicate similar responses by black young adults toward gifted peers. Lindstrom and San Vant argue that many gifted black adolescents are "between a rock and a hard place."[79] Although they desire to bond with the community individuals who aspire to higher goals and levels of achievement, they choose not to separate themselves from peers unsympathetic to their gifts and talents. In some situations, high achievement in a predominantly white environment is interpreted as a rejection of black culture, causing a conflict among black gifted teenagers as to which culture to support.[80] In a predominantly black environment, the gifted African-American teenager is left to encounter another difficulty not always discussed, but experienced repeatedly within generations of family members. Historically, blacks perceived the academic or social success of one individual to be an achievement for the collective black population.[81] Ford-Harris, Schuerger, and Harris argue that, nowadays, "Blacks have been less apt to view the achievements of individual Blacks as progress for all Blacks."[82] Within the novels examined, the talented and gifted individual is rarely embraced or encouraged by her black peers, implying that the above statement still has validity.

Intellectually gifted, Afeni Harris, identifies with the goals and aspirations of the Jack and Jill and White Gloves and Manners clubs. However, the lack of support and acceptance she receives from these exclusive black-populated clubs causes her frustration. She describes the clubs' membership to her mother:

> Being proud is one thing, but being out-and-out snobs is a pain. They sit around and talk about how they're going to run the world. I don't have any interest in running anybody's world. I don't care about what shades of makeup go with my skin or what sorority I'm pledging when I get to college. I'm not even in high school.[83]

In addition to not being able to commiserate with her club members, Afeni is constantly harassed by Rebecca, her un-wed house guest. Perceiving Afeni as rich and selfish, Rebecca communicates her feelings concerning Afeni's intelligence:

> Look! Just 'cause I'm in your ritzy little house, doesn't mean you gonna teach me how to talk and tell me what to do. . . . You think you special or something, but I know all about you Feni Harris. Your mama says you don't talk to nobody and you don't have any friends.[84]

While there are factors, concerning both class and moral issues, surrounding the tension between Afeni and Rebecca, the strongest barrier preventing their ability to totally communicate is Afeni's giftedness. It serves as a constant reminder to Rebecca that she is a high school drop-out and has not been given the opportunities afforded to Afeni. Rebecca ironically considers Afeni also to be a "drop-out," but a drop-out from the mainstream of black culture: an individual who chooses to identify with the white, dominant culture or pseudo-black culture reserved for a privileged population, and not with the black culture as currently perceived by American society.

Williams-Garcia's talented protagonist experiences somewhat similar treatment. Once Joyce Collins discovers her niche within an African dance ensemble consisting of only black dancers, she begins to internalize the feelings of jealousy and resentment that are meant for her. As Joyce is both complimented for her dancing abilities and cast in solo roles by the ensemble director, the envy among the other female dancers becomes more intense. Beginning to feel accepted by some members of the dance group, Joyce is admonished by one of the other female participants:

> Joyce. There are a lot of girls who have been coming here for years working their tails off hoping to be noticed. You come in off the street, out of the blue, and you're already Hassan's girl. Now, we're not particularly vicious, but break your leg and see how fast we jump for your part. Sure, there's some jealousy, but you have to deal with it.[85]

Guy's Cathy Johnson is unable to display approval or support for Sarah's musical talents or intellectual gifts. Her feelings toward Sarah are intensified as Cathy's mother constantly praises Sarah's character, educational accomplishments, and musical gift. In one of the few conversations shared by the two protagonists, Cathy expresses her feelings towards Sarah and her talents:

> Child genius. The great talent. God, how I detest seeing you blush and grin every time someone says, 'Look at that sweet, talented Sarah. How hard she works.' Overdoing, overdoing. My God, don't you ever get tired?[86]

QUESTIONS, CONCERNS, AND CONSIDERATIONS

The exploration of color and class within the addressed novels raises further issues and concerns both for our black youth, their peers, family, and society. To what degree do members of a family structure influence a teenager's concern for the importance of skin tone and/or one's class position in society? Protagonist, Joyce Collins, is told repeatedly by her mother to wear clothes to school that were different from her torn and faded jeans and T-shirts; clothing more reflective of those worn by the students coming from more affluent homes. Similarly, Afeni Harris joins exclusive-elite clubs as a result of her mother's coercion. Guy's Cathy Johnson cannot help but exude abhorrence toward darker-skinned peers knowing that her mother, not too long ago, first rejected Sarah's family because of their darker skin.[87] Perhaps, the characters mentioned would not have been so concerned about differences in skin color without some prodding and subtle (and not so subtle) re-affirmation from their parents.

Further questions need to be addressed as well. What components in our society can be altered in order to provide talented and gifted youngsters of color with the opportunities they deserve? And, finally, to what degree, if any, does talent help young people of color cope with the prejudice they endure? Teenagers can find, within their literature, reflections of, as well as answers and solutions to difficulties they will encounter in their daily lives. In her recently published article, Carol Jones Collins states that today's African-American young adult literature "can help [teenagers] overcome entrenched personal problems,"[88] and "eliminate whatever sense of isolation or alienation they may have."[89] It is possible as well that the literature can assist in more effectively raising the consciousness level and degree of proactive response of and from all members of a society too long immersed in the vestiges, results, and realities of racism.

NOTES

1. Rita Williams-Garcia, *Blue Tights* (New York: Bantam, 1988).
2. Rosa Guy, *The Music of Summer* (New York: Delacorte Press, 1992).
3. Cynthia Voigt, *Come a Stranger* (New York: Fawcett Juniper, 1986).
4. Jacqueline Woodson, *The Dear One* (New York: Delacorte Press, 1991).
5. John D. Buenker and Lorman A. Ratner, *Multiculturalism in the United States: A Comparative Guide to Acculturation and Ethnicity* (New York: Greenwood Press, 1992).
6. Harmon George, *American Race Relations Theory: A Review of Four Models* (New York: University Press of America, 1984), 2.
7. Ibid.
8. Buenker and Ratner, 5.
9. Bernard M. Magubane, *The Ties That Bind: African-American Consciousness of Africa* (Boston, MA: Little, Brown, 1987), 3.
10. W.E.B. DuBois, *The Souls of Black Folk* (New York: Citadel, 1969), 45.
11. Andrew Hacker, *Two Nations: Black and White, Separate, Hostile, Unequal* (New York: Charles Scribner's Sons, 1992), 31.

12. Winthrop Jordan, *White Over Black: Attitudes Toward the Negro, 1550–1812* (New York: Random House, 1968), 7.
13. Ibid., 8.
14. Hacker, 28, 38.
15. Derrick Bell, *Faces at the Bottom of the Well: The Permanence of Racism* (New York: Basic Books, 1992), 1.
16. Kathy Russell, Midge Wilson and Ronald Hall, *The Color Complex: The Politics of Skin Color Among African Americans* (New York: Harcourt Brace Jovanovich, 1992), 2.
17. James O. Horton, *Free People of Color: Inside the African-American Community* (Washington, DC: Smithsonian Institute Press, 1993), 123.
18. Ibid.
19. Ibid., 124.
20. Thomas Boston, *Race, Class and Conservatism* (Boston, MA: Unwin Hyman, 1988), 9.
21. Ibid., 6.
22. Ibid., 4.
23. Benjamin DeMott, *The Imperial Middle: Why Americans Can't Think Straight About Class* (New York: William Morrow, 1990), 46.
24. Ibid.
25. Hacker, 95.
26. Ibid.
27. Carol Jones Collins, "A Tool for Change: Young Adult Literature in the Lives of Young Adult African-Americans," *Library Trends* 41 no. 3 (Winter 1993): 379.
28. Hacker, 14.
29. Horton, 82.
30. George M. Fredrickson, *The Black Image in the White Mind* (New York: Harper & Row, 1971), 54.
31. Hacker, 61.
32. Carl Grant, "Desegregation, Racial Attitudes, And Intergroup Contact: A Discussion of Change." *Phi Delta Kappan* 72 (September 1990): 26.
33. Hacker, 56.
34. Alice Walker, *Living By the Word: Selected Writings 1973–1987* (New York: Harcourt Brace Jovanovich, 1988), 32.
35. Hacker, 23.
36. Ellis Cose, *A Nation of Strangers: Prejudice, Politics, and the Populating of America* (New York: William Morrow, 1992), 218.
37. Ben Wattenberg, *The First Universal Nation* (New York: The Free Press, 1990), 33.
38. Marie Frankson, *Adolescent Psychology: A Contemporary View* (New York: Holt, 1987), 70.

39. Patricia Romero and Dan Zancanella, "Expanding the Circle: Hispanic Voices in American Literature," *English Journal* 79 (January 1990): 27.
40. Voigt, 21.
41. Ibid.
42. Ibid., 56.
43. Ibid., 58.
44. Ibid., 60.
45. Ibid.
46. Ibid.
47. Williams-Garcia, 4.
48. Ibid., 11.
49. Ibid., 28.
50. Ibid.
51. Ibid.
52. Woodson, 18.
53. Ibid.
54. Donna Y. Ford-Harris, James M. Schuerger, and J. John Harris III, "Meeting the Psychological Needs of Gifted Black Students: A Cultural Perspective," *Journal of Counseling and Development* 69 (July–August 1991): 578.
55. Ibid.
56. S. Fordham, "Racelessness As a Factor in Black Students' School Success: Pragmatic Strategy or Pyrrhic Victory?" *Harvard Educational Review* 58 no. 1 (1988): 55.
57. Ibid.
58. Williams-Garcia, 90.
59. Guy, 16.
60. Ibid., 67.
61. Ibid., 15.
62. Ibid., 123.
63. Ibid., 16.
64. Ibid.
65. Ibid., 64.
66. Ibid., 67.
67. Voigt, 128.
68. Woodson, 43.
69. Ibid., 49.
70. Ibid.
71. Ibid., 68.
72. Williams-Garcia, 24.
73. Ibid.
74. Ibid., 126.

75. Guy, 71.
76. Ibid., 68.
77. Ibid., 27.
78. Boston, 6.
79. R. R. Lindstrom and S. San Vant, "Special Issues in Working With Gifted Minority Adolescents," *Journal of Counseling and Development* 64 (1986): 584.
80. Ford-Harris, Schuerger, and Harris III, 577.
81. Ibid.
82. Ibid.
83. Woodson, 12.
84. Ibid., 45.
85. Williams-Garcia, 76.
86. Guy, 122–123.
87. Ibid., 168–169.
88. Collins, 381.
89. Ibid.

REFERENCES

Bell, Derrick. *Faces at the Bottom of the Well: The Permanence of Racism.* New York: Basic Books, 1992.
Boston, Thomas. *Race, Class and Conservatism.* Boston, MA: Unwin Hyman, 1988.
Buenker, John D. and Lorman A Ratner. *Multiculturalism in the United States: A Comparative Guide to Acculturation and Ethnicity.* New York: Greenwood Press, 1992.
Collins, Carol Jones. "A Tool for Change: Young Adult Literature in the Lives of Young Adult African-Americans." *Library Trends* 41 no. 3 (Winter 1993): 378–392.
Cose, Ellis. *A Nation of Strangers: Prejudice, Politics, and the Populating of America.* New York: William Morrow, 1992.
DeMott, Benjamin. *The Imperial Middle: Why Americans Can't Think Straight About Class.* New York: William Morrow, 1990.
DuBois, W.E.B. *The Souls of Black Folk.* New York: Citadel, 1969.
Fordham, S. "Racelessness As a Factor in Black Students' School Success: Pragmatic Strategy or Pyrrhic Victory?" *Harvard Educational Review* 58 no. 1 (February 1988): 54–84.
Ford-Harris, Donna Y., James M. Schuerger, and J. John Harris III. "Meeting the Psychological Needs of Gifted Black Students: A Cultural Perspective." *Journal of Counseling and Development* 69 (July–August 1991): 577–580.

Frankson, Marie. *Adolescent Psychology: A Contemporary View*. New York: Holt, 1987.

Fredrickson, George M. *The Black Image in the White Mind*. New York: Harper & Row, 1971.

George, Harmon. *American Race Relations Theory: A Review of Four Models*. New York: University Press of America, 1984.

Grant, Carl. "Desegregation, Racial Attitudes, and Intergroup Contact: A Discussion of Change." *Phi Delta Kappan* 72 (September 1990): 25–32.

Guy, Rosa. *The Music of Summer*. New York: Delacorte Press, 1992.

Hacker, Andrew. *Two Nations: Black and White, Separate, Hostile, Unequal*. New York: Charles Scribner's Sons, 1992.

Horton, James O. *Free People of Color: Inside the African-American Community*. Washington, DC: Smithsonian Institute Press, 1993.

Jordan, Winthrop. *White Over Black: Attitudes Toward the Negro, 1550–1812*. New York: Random House, 1968.

Lindstrom, R. R., and S. San Vant. "Special Issues in Working With Gifted Minority Adolescents." *Journal of Counseling and Development* 64 (1986): 583–586.

Magubane, Bernard M. *The Ties That Bind: African-American Consciousness of Africa*. Boston, MA: Little, Brown, 1987.

Romero, Patricia, and Dan Zancanella. "Expanding the Circle: Hispanic Voices in American Literature." *English Journal* 79 (January 1990): 24–29.

Russell, Kathy, Midge Wilson, and Ronald Hall. *The Color Complex: The Politics of Skin Color Among African Americans*. New York: Harcourt Brace Jovanovich, 1992.

Voigt, Cynthia. *Come a Stranger*. New York: Fawcett Juniper, 1986.

Walker, Alice. *Living by the Word: Selected Writings 1973–1987*. New York: Harcourt Brace Jovanovich, 1988.

Wattenberg, Ben. *The First Universal Nation*. New York: The Free Press, 1990.

Williams-Garcia, Rita. *Blue Tights*. New York: Bantam, 1988.

Woodson, Jacqueline. *The Dear One*. New York: Delacorte Press, 1991.

SEVEN

Man to Man: Portraits of the Male Adolescent in the Novels of Walter Dean Myers

Dennis Vellucci

In the twenty-four years since the publication of Walter Dean Myers's first book, *Where Does the Day Go?*, Myers has proven himself to be as versatile a writer as he has been prolific, with some thirty-two titles to his credit. His work includes picture books; adventure stories for children and young adults; gritty, realistic young adult novels that depict the concerns of and pressures on adolescents in an urban setting; and non-fiction about the African-American experience in America, most recently *Now Is Your Time: The African American Struggle for Freedom* (1991) and *Malcolm X: By Any Means Necessary* (1993). The subjects of his young adult novels include war (*Fallen Angels*), teen pregnancy (*Sweet Illusions*), and gangs (*Scorpions*). In her book-length study of Myers for the Twayne United States Authors series, Rudine Sims Bishop has identified Myers as "the only black male currently and consistently publishing young adult novels"[1] and cites him as one of the few writers who seeks to redress "the serious lack of books about African-American children and their life experience."[2]

Certainly the most prominent and successful of black male writers catering to the young adult market, Myers writes most often from the perspective of young black males, a group that is frequently labeled as being "at risk," victimized by broken families and single-parent households, inadequate, inflexible, unresponsive systems of education, lack of economic opportunity, and the prejudice, both overt and subtle, that seems so deeply ingrained a part of American life, so intricately woven into its fabric. Myers has occasionally ventured into the perspective of young black women—in *Crystal* (1987), the eponymous heroine is a sixteen-year-old who finds herself in a modeling career—but clearly Crystal's situation is extraordinary. Myers's male protagonists, by contrast, come from ordinary though all too often daunting and potentially debilitating circumstances. Theirs is not the world of high-powered careers like Crystal's, but the world of Harlem's streets, gang fights and drug dealers, or, in the case of Richie Perry of *Fallen Angels*, the jungles of Vietnam. The struggles these characters face are more universal than Crystal's struggle; they are representative of their generation, their race, their culture. Psychologists and sociologists report:

> The statistics show a clear disadvantage to being born black and male in America: Black males have higher rates than white males on mental disorders, unemployment, poverty, injuries, accidents . . . homicide and suicide, drug and alcohol abuse, imprisonment and criminality; they have poorer incomes, life expectancy, access to health care, and education.[3]

National statistics suggest that more than six times as many black males between the ages of fourteen and twenty-five are likely to be victims of homicide than white men the same age.[4]

What makes Myers's characters remarkable, however, is the degree to which they are able to maintain a significant measure of personal and moral integrity in environments that are relentlessly inimical to such integrity. In six of Myers's novels written between 1981 and 1992—*Hoops* (1981), *The Outside Shot* (1984), *Motown and Didi* (1984), *Scorpions* (1988), *Fallen Angels* (1988), and *Somewhere in the Darkness* (1992)—protagonists ranging in age from twelve to twenty-two are faced with crises that challenge their decency at every turn, that threaten to thwart their personal development and moral growth. Yet each of them manages—though sometimes just barely—to retain an innate sensitivity that sets him apart and to avoid or reject the gang membership, violent behavior, and illegal activity that sociologist Ronald L. Taylor sees as a manifestation of "the culture of disengagement" that characterizes segments of black inner city youth, a consequence of "disintegrating community institutions."[5] Through his response to the obstacles that confront him, each of Myers's characters discovers truths about himself, and each approaches greater maturity. While it may be hyperbolic to say that in every case these characters transcend the limitations of their environment, neither are they defeated by them. Myers is both optimist and realist;[6] his protagonists may not always triumph, but they do survive. Conflict in Myers's serious young adult novels is never easily resolved, but it at least results in the self-knowledge and self-awareness that are the foundations of strength and resiliency.

THE SIGNIFICANCE OF MALE BONDING

The endurance of spirit in Myers's work is often the result of a meaningful and significant relationship the protagonist has with another male character, sometimes older, sometimes younger, sometimes a peer. It is this "male bonding" that becomes the most constant and reliable source of the protagonist's strength and that elicits what is most noble in his character. Bishop has observed in Myers's earliest young adult novels, *Fast Sam, Cool Clyde, and Stuff* (1975), *Mojo and the Russians* (1977), as well as in *Won't Know Till I Get There* (1982), the common motif of

> boys trying to understand their relationships with their fathers, all
> of whom have achieved some measure of success after overcom-
> ing odds [and who] are determined to see that their boys are well
> brought up and make something of themselves.[7]

Fathers in *Crystal* and *It Ain't All for Nothing* (1978) are depicted sympathetically.[8] But in the later novels featuring adolescent male protagonists, fathers are virtually an extinct species. (Statistically, more black children grow up in households without a father than grow up in households with a father.)[9] Motown's father is dead; the fathers of Lonnie Jackson (*Hoops*; *The Outside Shot*) and Richie Perry (*Fallen Angels*) deserted their families when their sons were young. When absent fathers do reappear, as they do briefly for Jamal Hicks in *Scorpions* and, more centrally to the plot, for Jimmy Little in *Somewhere in the Darkness*, they are distant, vaguely menacing figures who evoke not admiration or even much respect from their sons, but well-warranted resentment. If it is true that a son can see in his father a reflection of the man he is to become and discover himself in his father's image, Myers's characters must seek their identity elsewhere.

This element in Myers's work, paradoxically, both links it with and, at the same time, distinguishes it from, classic African-American novels of male adolescent initiation. Fourteen-year-old John Grimes in James Baldwin's *Go Tell It On The Mountain* is oppressed by his self-righteous stepfather, Gabriel, whom he regards as a hypocrite, abusive and unloving. In Richard Wright's *Black Boy*, the father is "always a stranger . . . always somehow remote and alien,"[10] and the uncles who replace Richard's father once Richard's father leaves and his mother becomes too ill to care for him, are cruel to Richard, contemptuous of his ambition, and leave him feeling so isolated from his family that he must flee them, their church, and their south in order to attain a sense of identity and self-worth.

The natural father of Ralph Ellison's nameless young narrator in *Invisible Man* is barely mentioned, but the many father figures the narrator encounters on his odyssey, both black (Bledsoe, Lucius Brockway, Ras) and white (Mr. Norton, Brother Jack) are inevitably patronizing, duplicitous, self-serving. With every bond he forms resulting in failure and betrayal, Ellison's narrator is rendered "invisible" and driven underground into isolation and seclusion. What David L. Dudley has written of African-American men's autobiography—that "black men tend to view themselves as isolated characters striving to make their way in life"[11]—is no less true of the depiction of manhood in much African-American fiction. While Myers's characters, too, are denied the bonds of father-son kinship, and suffer, as a result, from a kind of rootlessness, Myers breaks with typical representations of African-American male adolescence by giving most of his characters some positive male figure in their lives from whom they can learn or gain a significant measure of self-esteem.

In an essay on Ernest Gaines, Frank W. Shelton has suggested that, perhaps as a consequence of "the paralysis inherited by the black man from slavery," male characters in African-American literature have been unable to forge any kind of meaningful bonds because they are often portrayed as "lacking commitment . . . a willingness to give of self to another and assume responsibility for another. Black males, even supposedly enlightened ones, seem unable to achieve full maturity."[12] Myers's male characters overcome this inability and the hopelessness it portends precisely through the personal commitment, the giving of self, that they willingly undertake. Dudley maintains that intergenerational bonding is typical of literature by black women, while intergenerational conflict is typical of work by black men,[13] but despite the failure of natural fathers, this is not the case in Myers's work; Myers may be seen as something of a trailblazer in his portrayal of nurturing and supportive relationships among black men. Indeed, one of the most significant kinds of male bonding that occurs in Myers's serious young adult novels is what Rudine Sims Bishop has identified as "surrogate parenting."[14] In *Hoops*, Coach Cal Jones acts as a surrogate father for young Lonnie Jackson, exasperating Lonnie sometimes, disappointing him at other times, but ultimately giving Lonnie a sense of self-worth that his friends in the novel lack. In *Motown and Didi*, a mildly eccentric character known as "The Professor," by trade a bookseller with a shop on Lenox Avenue, offers Motown direction and advice, opening Motown's inner world not just through the reading material he supplies for Motown but through the ideology of racial pride that he imparts.

A second type of male bonding transpires when the fatherless adolescent becomes himself a father figure, a role model and surrogate parent to someone younger and from this relationship derives meaning and purpose. What keeps Richie Perry emotionally whole in Vietnam is the recurring thought of his younger brother Kenny at home. Richie knows that he is a source of pride and inspiration to Kenny, and he takes seriously the responsibilities that come with being an older brother in a home without a father. In *The Outside Shot*, Lonnie Jackson (the same character in *Hoops*, but now transported from Harlem to the Indiana campus of Montclare College) derives as much fulfillment from his work at the university hospital with an autistic boy, Eddie, as Eddie himself clearly derives. Eddie's increasing self-confidence throughout the novel reflects Lonnie's ability to adapt to his new environment.

The third type of bonding occurs when, in the absence of an older male to offer guidance or a younger male for whom he can serve as role model, the protagonist, beset by pressure and confronted by hostility, seeks comfort from a contemporary whose friendship becomes his most vital support under the circumstances. In *Scorpions*, twelve-year-old Jamal Hicks has no one to turn to when he is urged to assume his imprisoned older brother's role in a local gang except to Tito, a faithful and concerned friend who shares Jamal's suffering and confusion and who ultimately compromises his own values for Jamal. In *Fallen Angels*, Richie Perry develops the kind of friendship that is a staple of war novels with Peewee Gates, a wise cracking child of the slums of Chicago whose humor and insight help to sustain Richie.

These man-to-man relationships—father-to-son, brother-to-brother, friend-to-friend—relationships that are so much at the heart of the male adolescent experience, lie at the heart of the six novels under consideration here. This is not to suggest, of course, that women do not play an equally important role in the experience of male adolescents. But in these novels, all told from a young man's perspective, women function either as girlfriend or mother. Didi introduces Motown to romance; Mary-Ann in *Hoops* and Sherry in *The Outside Shot* provide love interests for Lonnie Jackson. They are, to some degree, positive influences, but they also bring to Motown and Lonnie uncertainty and conflict; especially in the early stages of the relationship, they make the protagonist self-conscious and cause him to question his self-worth. These relationships do not always bring out the best in the protagonists; Didi, in fact, seeking revenge upon a drug dealer whom she holds responsible for her brother's death, compels Motown to uncharacteristic violence and nearly ruins his future. Mothers, particularly in *Hoops* and *Scorpions*, but to a lesser degree in *Fallen Angels* as well, may be self-sacrificing and well-intentioned, but they are ultimately ineffectual as they attempt to instill values or to keep their family together. Myers has written, "I have always felt that young black people must have role models with which they can identify";[15] it seems natural that the men in these novels identify with men.

THE INFLUENCE OF LITERARY NATURALISM

Myers has cited Emile Zola as one of the classic novelists whose works inspired him.[16] In his bleak, vivid descriptions of ghetto life, the literary naturalism that Zola pioneered in late nineteenth century France is apparent. As Zola wrote in uncompromising terms about the French underclass, making the downtrodden and impoverished his heroes, portraying their surroundings as squalid and oppressive, inevitably shaping and conditioning the individual, binding him, enclosing him, always challenging his dignity, so too does Myers, a century later, write of the individual in modern urban America. Setting is rendered graphically in Myers's novels and it serves as a vehicle of social criticism. Motown observes sardonically the pictures the city has painted on the galvanized tin that covers the missing windows of abandoned buildings in an attempt to make the buildings seem occupied and inhabitable, and he is wary of the "winos and junkies" who, he knows, "might burn up [his] bedding or leave their wastes on it in anger"[17] if they do not find the few dollars he has stashed away in the vacant building where he makes his furtive residence. In *Somewhere in the Darkness*, fifteen-year-old Jimmy makes as much noise as he can climbing the stairs inside his tenement so as not to surprise junkies who may be hidden under the stairwell shooting up or dealing drugs. *Scorpions* begins with young Jamal observing an addict having no end of difficulty maintaining an upright posture by a lamppost, and he carefully avoids the video parlor that he knows doubles as a crack house. In his review of *Scorpions*, Robert E. Unsworth hints of the influence of literary naturalism on Myers when he comments on "the black child about to be sucked inevitably into the world of gang violence," and on "the smell of the streets where Jamal and Tito can be innocents no longer."[18] The environment, sinister and threatening, cannot easily be overcome.

INSTITUTIONAL AND INDIVIDUAL RESPONSES TO THE PROBLEM OF STANDARDS

"What you need in the community," Myers once said in an interview, "are people to set standards."[19] The communities portrayed in his novels are bereft of standards because the traditional institutions—family, school, police—have abdicated their responsibility. Families are broken and rarely exist intact. Police are cynical and indifferent; in *Motown and Didi*, their dismissal of Didi's request that they arrest her brother's drug contact and her brother as well makes Didi feel "almost dirty, ashamed of herself," and disillusioned in her expectation that "the law would protect her."[20] The Professor skeptically wonders why, if child addicts can locate drug pushers, the police cannot, but the police remain apathetic. Even in Myers's earlier novels he has been critical of the police; in both *Fast Sam, Cool Clyde, and Stuff* and in *The Young Landlords* (1979), the police regard black teenagers with suspicion and treat them with "unnecessary roughness."[21] In these later novels, the police are not overtly antagonistic towards Myers's young characters, but they are not cooperative either; they neither insure the safety of these young people, nor do they set and enforce community standards.

School officials are even worse—insensitive, manipulative, duplicitous. In *Somewhere in the Darkness*, the principal, on the day of a standardized reading test, invents trumped up infractions that he claims merit disciplinary action simply as a pretext to keep students he knows will do poorly out of class, while he allows Jimmy, who has been truant, back to class because he knows Jimmy will score well. Jimmy is a dreamer; when he tells the school psychologist of his fantasies filled with imaginary heroes who fight dragons and rescue those in trouble, sharing a deep and private part of himself, he is chided for being too old to be dreaming of imaginary creatures. Only Richie Perry of *Fallen Angels* can recall an affirming academic experience: a high school English teacher, Mrs. Liebow, encouraged his ultimately unfulfilled ambition "to go to college and write like James Baldwin,"[22] and taught him a lesson that not only serves him well in Vietnam but that serves all of Myers's adolescent protagonists well—the lesson that "what separates heroes from humans [is] the not giving in."[23] But never for Myers's other characters does school offer the structure and support needed especially in the inner city. In *Scorpions*, Myers derides all school authority. Mrs. Roberts, the school nurse, misdiagnoses Jamal's constant state of distraction and inattention as hyperactivity and attempts to drug him into submission, and the principal borders on villainous caricature, smug in his assumption that Jamal's mother cares as little about Jamal's education as Jamal himself seems to, predicting with contemptuous certainty that, sooner or later, Jamal will do something to merit expulsion.

MOTOWN AND DIDI AND *HOOPS*

It is not surprising that with the failure of family, law, and the educational system to promote values, characters turn to other sources for example and direction—Motown in *Motown and Didi* and Lonnie in *Hoops* to older men in their community. The Professor, Oliver Harris, frankly expresses his affection for Motown to Didi after Didi has exhorted Motown to kill a local drug dealer:

> I don't want to see that boy hurt. I love him as if he was my own
> son. No, I love him more. I love him the way an old man loves

his only son. When I am gone, all that will be left of me are the
few books that I've given away and a few wild thoughts that I
have planted in that young man's mind.[24]

Some of those "wild thoughts" include a sense of racial pride and an
identification with what the Professor refers to as "the tribe." To the
Professor, the young men swaggering down Harlem's streets are "not
just youngbloods but warriors walking along the edges of their tribal
lands, exalting their manhood."[25] Yet he laments the lack of respect
these young "warriors" have for themselves or for one another and
attributes it to their ignorance of their shared history, their shared heritage. He grieves that young black men feel compelled to prove their
manhood "fighting and killing their own," rather than "in the stock
market, on the job, in politics,"[26] as he claims white men do. Motown,
the Professor believes, can be saved; though whenever Motown leaves
his bookshop, the Professor worries that he is "failing the boy somehow,"[27] he finds in Motown a receptivity to the values he advocates.

Orphaned when his parents were killed in a fire, Motown, reared
in foster homes, has formed no strong or lasting attachments and has
remained very much the loner. Now, at seventeen, he lives, except for
his visits to the Professor, in relative solitude. Occasionally selling his
blood to make nine dollars from the blood bank, Motown eschews
messenger jobs as being too dangerous; unable to find the kind of job
the Professor urges him to get—one from which he will learn something—Motown reads the books the Professor gives him and gets by
on very little. Yet, despite the deprivations Motown suffers, he never
loses his conviction that "he is made for better things."[28] He first encounters Didi when she is being attacked by her brother's partners after
her futile appeal to the police. An unwilling hero who knows his best
chances for survival lie in minding his own business and staying out of
other people's trouble, Motown nevertheless comes to Didi's defense
and disperses her assailants. Later, he saves Didi's brother in two
ways: first, he throws the dope Tony is about to take down an incinera-
tor, an act that suggests he has taken the Professor's philosophy to
heart and has internalized the value the Professor has sought to pass on
to him—namely, that each member of the tribe is responsible for the
welfare of the others. This action also saves Tony from detectives waiting to make a drug bust.

When Didi comes to the empty room Motown inhabits to thank

him, Motown is shy and embarrassed. Defensive and self-conscious about his humble dwelling, he senses Didi's disapproval and wishes he had left his books out, visible so that Didi might have seen what makes him different from the other men his age in the neighborhood, men who have not had the advantage of the Professor as their mentor. Later, when his relationship with Didi blossoms, Motown solicits the Professor's approval and introduces her to him much as a young man would introduce his girlfriend to his parents. (A similar scene occurs in *Hoops* when Lonnie Jackson introduces Mary-Ann to his coach, Cal.) That Motown, for all his independence and self-sufficiency, craves a father is illustrated in a daydream he has, a flight of imagination unusual for the generally practical, down-to-earth Motown:

> Perhaps he would be walking down . . . Lenox Avenue, and he'd see a tall man, black as Motown, no, blacker still, as black as the ebony statues that stood on the shelves in the back of the Professor's shop . . . guarding the knowledge of Africa that sprawled about them. . . . "I've been looking for you all these years. . . . I am your father and you are my son."[29]

The chain of associations in Motown's fantasy of father with the Professor's shop with blackness with Africa implies that the Professor offers him both a personal identity and a cultural awareness, a connectedness to a people Motown might never otherwise have felt.

It is Motown's sensitivity that makes his acquiescence to Didi's request for vengeance at the end of the novel surprising and, perhaps, not entirely credible. A reluctant hero early in the novel, he is a reluctant avenger at the end. Level-headed and not by nature quick to violence, Motown first recommends to Didi that they go to the police, but Didi's earlier experience causes her to dismiss the suggestion. She challenges Motown to prove himself by killing Touchy Jenkins, and, reaching for a steak knife, threatens to do it herself. Still resistant, and against his better judgement, Motown nevertheless accedes to her persistence, and, in violation of his own character and values, purchases a weapon even as he "tries not to think about killing . . . or about what would happen after he had."[30] Throughout the novel, Motown realizes the importance of maintaining strength. He subjects himself to a rigorous physical workout each night in his room because he believes, "You couldn't be weak in this world and let people know it."[31] Yet his moral strength wavers, momentarily, but with potentially disastrous consequences; he has not yet acquired what Myers has called "the strength to turn away from disaster."[32] The Professor, apprised of what has happened, convinces Didi that Motown should not "throw his life away after what is already gone,"[33] and intervenes just in time to save Motown, if not from death or injury, certainly from arrest and imprisonment. Motown, who has acted as savior to Didi and to Tony, is in turn saved by the person who has functioned as father for him throughout.

An analogous relationship exists between Lonnie Jackson and Cal Jones in *Hoops*. Lonnie, two years younger than Motown, lacks Motown's maturity and his innate nobility of character. Lonnie is the kind of teenager who takes advantage of a liquor store hold-up to squirrel away a case of Johnny Walker that he hopes to sell at five dollars a bottle. His volatile temper erupts when Cal shows up in the locker room after Lonnie concludes Cal has swindled team members of the money they gave him for team uniforms. Lonnie pulls a .32 pistol from his locker, and though Myers handles the scene comically— Lonnie winds up giving himself a superficial wound that, when washed out with whiskey, "hurt as much as the shot did"[34]—it establishes Lonnie as impetuous and irresponsible. Lonnie lacks Motown's self-awareness; when he loses a basketball game, he rationalizes that had he "been playing the sucker seriously," Lonnie "would have wiped him off the court."[35] In contrast to Motown's respect for Didi, Lonnie, at least in the early part of the novel, is contemptuous of women. He sleeps with Mary Ann but flees from her declarations of love, and he boasts that he "can't see getting next to a broad but one way."[36] Unlike Motown, Lonnie has no daydream of his real father ever re-appearing, but he recalls vividly the night his father left, and it is obvious that much of Lonnie's attitude—his distrust, his temper, the emotional distance he puts between himself and others—is rooted in this painful recollection:

> It was me laying on my bed in my room, listening to my mother and father in the kitchen. She was begging and crying, and I was laying there, holding my breath, waiting for his answer. When he said he couldn't, when he had left and the door was closed and the only sound was Mama's crying in the kitchen, I started hitting the wall with my fist. I hit it and hit it until I couldn't feel the pain anymore."[37]

As an adolescent, Lonnie is still metaphorically "hitting the wall," striking out as his only means of survival.

Lonnie's skill on the basketball court and his relationship with his coach, a relationship that progresses from suspicion and resentment, to pity and respect, to affection and gratitude, help Lonnie mature until he eventually accepts an athletic scholarship and goes on to play for Montclare College, a story that Myers continues in the sequel to *Hoops*, *The Outside Shot*. Cal hones Lonnie's athletic talent but, more important, he re-sensitizes Lonnie. By confiding in Lonnie and sharing his own tragic experience, Cal enables Lonnie to "feel the pain" of another person's suffering. Cal, Lonnie discovers, had once played professional basketball but was banished from the NBA for his complicity in a gambling scheme after he had shaved points from a game. Cal's life is a series of regrets. Denied his career and insufficiently skilled to establish himself in another profession, he is briefly supported by his wife. Finally able to find a job, he works for less than a week when he returns home one day to find fire engines at his apartment building. His infant son, Jeffrey, whom Cal had left in the care of a baby sitter, perishes in the blaze, and soon, his wife leaves him. Cal has descended to the level of neighborhood "character" who drinks too much wine and who is known for his eccentricity.

In noting the father-son relationship between Cal and Lonnie, Rudine Sims Bishop has observed that "Lonnie represents a second chance for [Cal]."[38] Lonnie is the means by which Cal, himself estranged from his father, can re-enter the world of basketball, relive vicariously his former glory, regain his self-respect, and atone for the mistakes of his past. Lonnie is both a younger version of Cal and an older version of Jeffrey, the adolescent son Jeffrey did not live to become, the child Cal needs to replace. And Lonnie needs a substitute for his father. It is no wonder, then, that he and Cal are well-suited. Above all else, Cal's goal is to keep Lonnie honest so that Lonnie does not fall into the same traps that ruined Cal's life and career. He warns Lonnie against the false hopes fed to young athletes by college recruiters and teaches Lonnie to be wary of supporters who seem too altruistic. Initially resentful of Cal for being "always on [his] case,"[39] Lonnie comes to appreciate the transformation that Cal affects in him, and his self-esteem grows; he begins to "feel good" that his game "is a little deeper than a lot of other guys' games."[40] When Lonnie invites Mary-Ann to meet Cal, she is at first disdainful and calls Cal a wino. Lonnie feigns indifference and protests that Cal isn't his father, but Mary-Ann can see how sensitive Lonnie has become about Cal, and her apology does little to assuage the offense Lonnie takes on Cal's behalf. Later, Lonnie defends Cal against the suggestion made by O'Donnel, the arrogant, self-important promoter of the tournament in which Lonnie's team is to play, that, because of his tarnished reputation, Cal step down as coach. Lonnie's compassion for Cal becomes his acknowledgement of the role Cal has played in his adolescence.

In her *Booklist* review of *Hoops*, Stephanie Zvirin commented that the story "evolves a sharply etched picture of Harlem, where sex and violence emerge naturally as part of the setting."[41] During the course of the novel, welfare recipients routinely have their checks stolen from their mailboxes, teenage girls are brutalized by their boyfriends, Cal is blackmailed, bullied, and beaten. One character, against her will, is injected with heroine until she almost dies of an overdose; another is stabbed to death. Again, the environment is hostile, grim, fraught with peril, but Lonnie's athletic gift is his means of escape. In an interview, Myers once said, "It's an absolute lie that a child can get out of the ghetto through sports,"[42] yet this is precisely what happens to Lonnie Jackson. Myers ends this novel making clear the metaphor of Lonnie's basketball game for Lonnie's life; his protagonist knows that he "can't win all the time," but that if he can "keep [his] game together . . . at least [he'll] have a chance."[43] This insight, this confidence, and the opportunity Lonnie has to make a new life for himself far from the ghetto, are all parts of Cal's legacy to him.

SCORPIONS

Motown and Lonnie are blessed to have the Professor and Cal, respectively, helping them to define their place in the world. Twelve-year-old Jamal Hicks of *Scorpions* has no such figure. The role models he might have had—his father, Jevon, and his seventeen-year-old brother, Randy—have each, in a different way, failed him. Jamal is bitter that Randy has caused his mother so much grief and has remained so completely unrepentant about it. He recalls Randy's insouciance as a jury finds Randy guilty of killing the owner of a delicatessen in a robbery, and thinks to himself, "You weren't supposed to be looking cool when you made your mother cry."[44] He expresses the hope that Randy never get out of jail and is sure that, were Randy to be released, it would not be long before he courted trouble again. When his mother learns how Jamal feels, she cries again and evokes in her son so much guilt that he feels coerced to find a part-time job to earn money for Randy's appeal. Jamal knows he has little in common with his brother; where Randy is brash and defiant, Jamal is sensitive and reserved. Before going to jail, Randy advises Jamal about being "man of the house," and he urges Jamal to "take care of business" in the gang.[45] But Jamal is reluctant to undertake the gang leadership that Randy's friends, especially Mack, try to impose upon him—it is simply not in his nature—though he is tempted by the promise of money for Randy's appeal, a prospect that he regards with ambivalence, but one that his mother prays for. His father, Jevon, links Jamal's responsibility for financing an appeal to Jamal's becoming a man and leaves Jamal little choice but to betray his own best instincts.

Manhood appears to Jamal to be an unreachable goal because he is always made to feel "small inside and weak."[46] A furniture salesman who berates his mother, a patronizing school principal who has already written Jamal off as a lost cause, teachers who humiliate him for mistakes he makes in class or for homework he has not done, classmates whom Jamal perceives as tougher than he and who taunt him and mock him—all these trigger Jamal's impression of himself as powerless and helpless. His father, an infrequent visitor, also makes him feel this way by half-joking, half-threatening, "You don't want me to have to take my belt off and straighten you out." Jamal's eyes "sting with tears" not just at his father's arrogance and his lack of respect for Jamal, but also because his father is rarely present "to talk to him or help him or anything."[47] And he feels small and weak when he learns that Randy has been stabbed in a prison fight.

Jamal, like Motown, knows it is important for him to be strong— it is a lesson he learns from his mother—but, also like Motown, he has not yet acquired "the strength to turn away from disaster." When he tries on his brother's Scorpions jacket, he finds it "a little too big for him, but not by much."[48] For Jamal to grow into his brother's jacket, to follow the bad example Randy has set for him, would represent a tragic diminution of his character, but in the absence of the kind of father figure Motown and Lonnie have, Jamal's moral decline seems inevitable.

It begins when Mack gives him a gun. To Jamal, the gun has a life of its own; he fears it will discharge of its own volition, and he considers throwing the thing away as his best friend Tito advises him, but he cannot. The gun, he believes, confers upon him the strength and the maturity that he lacks and that he knows are essential for his survival. The gun will compel people to respect him. This aspect of *Scorpions* seems indebted to Richard Wright's classic story of adolescent initiation, "Almos' a Man," in which seventeen-year-old Dave Glover acquires a gun to prove his manhood and accidentally kills a mule belonging to a local landowner. His desperate attempts to cover up his crime provide amusement for the townspeople, but immeasurable embarrassment and humiliation for Dave. Sentenced to work for the landowner to remunerate him for the dead animal, and faced with his parents' wrath at home, Dave flees his small town, but takes the gun, which he tells his parents he has thrown away, with him. Dave learns nothing from his misadventure; he leaves still clinging to the gun as an emblem of his manhood despite the considerable havoc it has wrought and the chagrin it has brought him.

For Jamal, in Harlem, the stakes are higher than a dead mule. Again disregarding Tito's advice, Jamal brings the gun to school where he intends to intimidate Dwayne, the class bully who has regularly taunted Jamal and who has challenged him to a fight. An essentially harmless schoolboy dispute thus escalates into a potentially fatal confrontation; even Jamal, as he rationalizes that, "It wasn't right, Dwayne laughing at people,"[49] seems aware that his solution to the conflict is disproportionate to Dwayne's offense.

Dwayne *is* frightened by the gun; at first he doubts it is real, but once he cowers as Jamal had hoped, Jamal takes advantage, kicking the trembling Dwayne "once, twice, harder, harder."[50] But this violation of his own character does nothing to ameliorate Jamal's sense of himself as small and weak. Now he worries that Dwayne will notify authorities and that he himself will be dispatched to a youth home. Too frightened to keep the gun, but too insecure to throw it away, Jamal prevails upon Tito to hide it for him.

Without any older male to trust or confide in, Jamal comes to rely on Tito whose good and sensible counsel he has hitherto ignored. It is Jamal's friendship with Tito, a physically weak boy who suffers from asthma, but a morally strong boy who has willingly embraced the values of the religious grandmother who has raised him, that offers Jamal the possibility of redemption. Tito envisions himself as a savior; he contemplates being a fireman so that he can "save people,"[51] and he attempts to keep Jamal from the lure of the Scorpions. When Jamal remains unmoved, Tito suggests that perhaps, together, they can "get [the Scorpions] to do some good things, too."[52] Ultimately, Tito saves Jamal's life, but at great personal sacrifice: Tito fires Jamal's gun, killing a gang member as he is about to stab Jamal.

All Tito can do is cry. To Jamal's grateful, "You saved my life," Tito can only respond, "I didn't want to shoot nobody."[53] Tito suggests that perhaps, the next day, he can visit Jamal and they "can read comic books or something,"[54] but he knows that, for him, the trappings of childhood have lost their relevance and that his innocence has been spent. Chastened, Jamal realizes that Tito "had been wounded in a place [Jamal] couldn't see,"[55] but there is nothing he can sacrifice to save Tito from his psychic and spiritual wound as Tito has saved him from probable death upon the point of a knife. Tito becomes a recluse and soon leaves with his grieving and distraught grandmother for Puerto Rico, his friendship with Jamal a bittersweet memory.

The bond that exists between Tito and Jamal is a genuine one; his friendship with Tito is the most meaningful and nurturing relationship Jamal has. Without Tito, Jamal might have been sucked into the world of the Scorpions with less hesitation and fewer misgivings; without Tito, Jamal would have become another statistic, another victim of gang violence. But perhaps because Tito is Jamal's peer, his contemporary, only a child himself, he cannot have upon Jamal, despite his good intentions, his gentleness, and a wisdom that belies his youth, quite the redemptive effect that the Professor has upon Motown or Cal Jones has upon Lonnie. *Scorpions*, like *Motown and Didi*, ends in gunfire that saves the protagonist and destroys the villain; in both cases, the agent of the villain's death is in no danger of being prosecuted. Yet, the resolution of *Scorpions* is hardly a happy one; the moral ambiguity of taking a life to save a life, of resorting to violence even in the service of a just cause, of conforming to the hostility of the environment rather than challenging it or attempting to transcend it, is rendered in all of its complexity.

SOMEWHERE IN THE DARKNESS

Rudine Sims Bishop has suggested that *Scorpions* reflects an increasing darkness in Myers's vision.[56] *Somewhere in the Darkness*, Myers's most recent serious young adult novel represents, in some ways, a darker vision still. Here, the young protagonist, Jimmy Little, does have a father present, a father who suddenly appears on Jimmy's doorstep after nine years in prison to take Jimmy away from Mama Jean, the woman who has raised him and who has been to Jimmy "all that he needed, companion and friend, mother and father,"[57] so that he might travel around the country with Jimmy in an attempt to prove to his son his innocence of the murder for which he was convicted. Escaped from the prison hospital and dying of a kidney ailment, Crab Little hopes to convince a son who does not know him that while he may have been a thief, he has never been a killer.

Jimmy, like Motown and Lonnie and Jamal, has a distinct and innate sensitivity; he also seems to have been less corrupted or damaged by the neighborhood in which he has grown up than do any of the aforementioned characters. He routinely defends Mr. Johnson, the block's resident inebriate, from the taunts and projectiles of schoolboys younger than he. He is devoted to Mama Jean who has cared for Jimmy since his mother died many years before, and though he is an indifferent student who has trouble getting himself to school every morning, he often finds himself motivated by his knowledge of how hurt and disappointed Mama Jean would be if he did not go.

When asked about his father by a school psychologist, Jimmy lies that his father works as a mechanic on city buses; in general, his father does not occupy his thoughts and he has only a vague understanding of the robbery attempt that led to his father's murder conviction. Uncomfortable and uncertain at Crab's sudden arrival, Jimmy is taciturn; he denies having ever wondered about his father, but now his curiosity is aroused. He imagines standing beside Crab in front of a mirror, not just to verify this stranger's identity, but to see himself reflected in the man who calls himself his father. Jimmy is surprised to find himself wondering how much Crab thought about him in prison, and before long, his initial fear and distrust of Crab turn into a need for Crab's approval. He offers Crab the fifty dollars Mama Jean had given him in case of emergency, and he nurses Crab when Crab's illness attacks, finding the times that Crab is weakest the easiest times to be with him. Eventually, he tries, without much success, to assuage Crab's anger and disappointment when Rydell Dupuis, the man that Crab tracks to Memphis hoping that Rydell will tell the truth about the robbery and "make things right" between Crab and Jimmy, not only refuses to acknowledge Crab's innocence, but notifies the police, who soon catch up with Crab.

In Cleveland, Jimmy meets Frank, the son of an old friend of Crab's, whose ambition is to enter the Golden Gloves. As Crab and Jimmy watch Frank workout in a local gym, Jimmy feels weak, inadequate, and he wonders if Crab wants him to be more like Frank. Jimmy takes some comfort learning that Frank is a year older than he is, but he is daunted by Frank's swagger and confidence, by the way Frank has of "looking at [Jimmy], sizing him up,"[59] by the bravado Frank puts into the workout, "grunting as he threw punches,"[60] all, apparently, to extract awe and fear from Jimmy. Later, Frank verbally intimidates Jimmy, who responds simply by looking into Frank's eyes, not backing down, but not accepting the challenge either, and the moment passes. Jimmy does not tell Crab about the incident until much later; sensing that Crab associates manhood with toughness, he is afraid it will make him seem weak to Crab, unable to defend himself. When Jimmy does eventually relate his encounter with Frank to Crab, Crab offers to teach Jimmy to fight—"You got to want to hurt somebody before they hurt you," Crab cautions—and Jimmy agrees, "figuring that was what Crab wanted to hear."[61] But Jimmy has no enthusiasm for the proposition; he is simply trying to fulfill Crab's expectations of what a son should be. In an article examining male adolescence in young adult literature, Allan A. Cuseo and Barbara Williams Kerns have written, "All too often the pubescent male receives conflicting messages—be sensitive/be macho—and feels as if he is floundering in a sea of confusion."[62] This characterizes precisely Jimmy Little's dilemma in *Somewhere in the Darkness*: the message to be macho comes from Crab and the milieu into which Crab introduces Jimmy; the urge to be sensitive comes from what is best and deepest within himself.

Crab's motive in forcing Jimmy on this journey with him is dubious. Ostensibly, he wants to repair a severed relationship; he does not want "a kid that hated [him] because [he] killed somebody."[63] And he hopes that Jimmy's respect will bring him self-respect. But Crab has a score to settle with Dupuis, and he suspects that the police who might be after him will be less suspicious of a man traveling with a boy who is obviously his son than they would be of a man traveling alone. Further, Jimmy's presence gives the ailing Crab the strength to confront Dupuis, his former partner in crime. A conjure man that Crab consults for his back pain marvels at Crab's strength and wonders at its source. Clearly, Crab derives strength from having his son with him.

During the course of their journey, Jimmy begins to feel affection for Crab, albeit tempered and qualified. Early in the book, Jimmy says to Crab, "I don't love you";[64] later, he says, "I don't hate you,"[65] hinting at some progress, however limited, in their relationship. But ultimately, the values that Jimmy has apparently gained from Mama Jean lead him to reject Crab, regardless of how genuine Crab's need for Jimmy's respect might be. Jimmy is appalled when Crab rents a car with a stolen credit card, for example. Crab's world is crime, and it seems more natural for him to break the law than to obey it. His philosophy—"It don't matter how I get what I need"[66]—is one that Jimmy cannot accept, and he frankly questions his father. Not having killed someone, Jimmy explains, does not make Crab innocent if Crab still attempted robbery. Crab's fond recollection of his own father encouraging Crab to drink to prove his manhood shows Jimmy just how shallow Crab's concepts of fatherhood and manhood are. Jimmy searches for someone he loves in Crab, but all he can see is Crab's "darkness,"[67] and when Crab touches his shoulder, Jimmy jerks it away. Jimmy recoils from Crab both physically and emotionally; their odyssey finally results in the "terrible" shared knowledge that "Crab did not indeed know how to be a father."[68] Crab is the embodiment of the stereotype that sociologist Ronald L. Taylor believes has come to represent the public image of the black male: the symbolically emasculated man, who, has failed to reach "full emotional maturity," and, consequently, "tends to be a poor . . . father."[69]

Unlike many of Myers's other protagonists, Jimmy functions well enough without a role model; he feels safer on the Harlem streets that are familiar to him and that he has learned to negotiate than he feels on the road with Crab. His father's unannounced appearance and virtual abduction of Jimmy bring conflict, but they also result in Jimmy's greater maturity and self-assurance. The novel ends with a long, poignant passage wherein Jimmy imagines someday having a son of his own:

> It seemed so far off, like something that could never happen but somehow would. . . . He would tell him all the secrets he knew, looking right into his eyes and telling him nothing but the truth so

that every time they were together they would know about each other. There would be a connection, he thought, something that would be there even when they weren't together. He would know just how he was like his son, and how they were different, and where their souls touched, and where they didn't. He knew that if he ever had a son he would have to do it . . . all the time, because sooner or later, there wouldn't be enough days left to fit the meaning in.[70]

Perhaps Jimmy's difficult and unhappy experience with Crab, then, has a beneficial effect on him after all. If Jimmy is representative, the next generation of fathers will not be fated to repeat the mistakes of past generations, and the cycle of broken families, of distant or anonymous fathers, of sons left too young to their own resources might be broken. Jimmy has learned the importance of the father-son bond through its absence in his own life; his reflections at the end of the book promise that, sensitive and responsible, he will one day be for someone an exemplary guide.

FALLEN ANGELS

Many of Myers's adolescent heroes—Motown, Jamal, Jimmy Little—share a similar sensibility; they seek to reconcile gentleness with strength and try, with varying degrees of success, to endure without compromising their humanity. Put any of these characters in Vietnam and the result will be a hero very much like Richie Perry, the narrator of Myers's most adult "young adult" novel, *Fallen Angels*. Richie joins the army at seventeen; his story is told retrospectively as he is leaving Vietnam some years later, having been wounded twice, an adolescent no longer. At home, Richie had felt "the loneliness . . . of not belonging to the life that teemed around [him]."[71] A good student, but weary of not having even clothes enough for high school, Richie decides not to go on to City College, but to enlist instead. At first, Richie is unafraid. Rumors of imminent peace, persistent but ultimately false, lull Richie into the belief that a truce will soon be signed. Army life for Richie consists of little more than "standing around waiting for something to happen."[72] Richie has no strong political conviction, no impassioned belief in the rightness of America's involvement in Vietnam. He describes himself as "not gung-ho or anything, but ready to do [his] part."[73] Asked by a television news crew why he is fighting, Richie, like his comrades, speaks in the language of patriotic cliché—"I said that we either defended our country abroad or that we would be forced to fight in the streets of America"—that he has likely given little serious thought to, but that he is pleased to observe, "everybody seemed to like."[74]

Soon, of course, the experience of combat touches Richie and leads him to an honest, if disturbing appraisal of himself. Richie is confused at his response to the death of the first soldier in his unit to fall, Jenkins. "I didn't know what to feel," he reflects; as much as he regrets and grieves Jenkins's death, Richie admits to "a small voice inside" relieved that it was a friend and not himself who had been killed.[75] He is more affected by the death of Lieutenant Carroll, whom Richie praises in a letter to Carroll's wife as "a gentle man."[76] In battle, Richie is sickened by "the sight of all the bodies lying around, the smell of blood and puke and urine";[77] he remains haunted by vivid images of slaughter. Above all, he is frightened. As he awaits the choppers that will lift him high above the battle, he "trembles in fear" and "runs in near panic."[78] Richie had thought of himself as "a middle of the road kind of guy, not too brave, but not too scared either,"[79] but war teaches him that his knowledge of himself is incomplete. As skirmish erupts after skirmish, the war becomes for Richie "hours of boredom, seconds of terror."[80]

Richie also does not think of himself as a killer; he is, he believes, an emissary on a mission of peace. "We, the Americans were the good guys," Richie says. "Otherwise, it didn't make the kind of sense I wanted it to make."[81] It is natural that Richie's first kill forces him to re-evaluate himself. Gazing at photographs on the wall of what he thinks is an empty hut after a Viet Cong attack, Richie turns to see the muzzle of a gun pointed at his chest. But his would-be assailant cannot get the gun to work. Momentarily paralyzed, immobile, Richie finally stirs himself to empty the clip of an M-16 into his enemy's face. Myers's description, meant to convey Jimmy's horror, is especially graphic:

> There was no face. Just an angry mass of red flesh where the face had been. Part of an eyeball dangled from one side of the head. At the top there were masses of different colored flesh. The white parts were the worst. There was a tooth, a bit of skull.[82]

By the time of Richie's second kill, he has become a different person. Richie recognizes in the face of a teenager he is about to kill his own fear, his own weariness, but he pulls the trigger anyway and then simply sits on the ground to rest without remorse. There is little description, little emotional investment in the act; Richie has learned to distance himself. The title of the book is a reference to innocent young men who fall in battle, but Richie is a "fallen angel," too—battle has begun to numb him spiritually, emotionally, and it is as much of an effort for him to maintain his humanity in his environment as it is for Motown and Jamal in theirs. Two relationships help Richie to endure; one with his younger brother Kenny who is rarely far from Richie's thoughts, and the other with the soldier who becomes his best friend in Vietnam, Peewee Gates.

Richie is the kind of older brother Jamal Hicks might have wished Randy to be—solicitous, thoughtful, someone to look up to. "It was good having Kenny need me," Richie admits. "I had been a sort of father to him . . . and I know he missed me."[83] Richie wants to impress Kenny with his contribution to the war effort; he wants to inspire in Kenny some of the toughness that he knows Kenny will need growing up in Harlem but that he worries Kenny lacks. Yet when Richie, who in his unit has earned a reputation and even attracted the favorable attention of his superiors as an eloquent writer of letters, tries to write Kenny of the "good job" Richie had done killing, the words won't come.[84] Instead, he writes to Kenny of the rumors of peace, he sends Kenny souvenirs, including the medal he is awarded after being wounded, and he carries with him the last thing Kenny says to him as Kenny drifts off to sleep the night before Richie leaves—"When you get to Vietnam, I hope you guys win."[85] It is clear that Richie is a positive influence in Kenny's life, but it is equally true that Kenny gives much to Richie in return, "something to hold on to," as Richie says.[86] Kenny gives Richie the blessing of knowing that Richie is needed, admired and loved. With a father who has left and a mother who, it is insinuated, has had problems with alcohol, Richie and Kenny are mutually dependent, even when one of them is on the other side of the world.

Other soldiers in Richie's unit who come from more traditional backgrounds and who have fathers to write home to, find, like Jimmy Little, that their father more often creates conflict than provides support. Jenkins is bullied by his father, a former colonel whose "game plan"[87] for his son was for Jenkins to join the infantry and then go on to officers' training school. Jenkins is the first casualty. Lobel, a movie fanatic who copes with the horror of war by pretending he is an actor in a film, joined the army so that his father "would stop thinking [Lobel] was a faggot";[88] now, his father has grown sympathetic to the anti-war movement and criticizes his son's involvement in the military. Even Carroll, whose relationship with his father is close, tells his men twice how proud his father is of Carroll's being an officer "like [Carroll] didn't know what to make of it."[89] Not even for Myers's minor characters is the father/son relationship a constructive one. Kenny thus seems all the more fortunate in his relationship with Richie.

Richie's friendship with Peewee Gates also sustains him in Vietnam. Peewee is a colorful figure who often functions as the agent of comic relief, but it is also Peewee whose hand Richie holds on their way back home. At first glance, Peewee appears superficial—his three ambitions in life are to drink wine from a corked bottle, to make love to a foreign woman, and to smoke a cigar—but it is he who makes the connection between the violence of Vietnam and the dangers of urban America most apparent, and thus he serves as spokesman for Myers's social criticism. Peewee sees the military as the great equalizer. He facetiously claims to like the army because he has the same uniform, the same equipment, the same food and accommodations as the other soldiers have; for the first time in his life, no one has more or less than he does. He half-humorously suggests that "them suckers from the projects"[90] would be ruthless and efficient killers in Vietnam. When Monaco, a fellow soldier, expresses a variation on the "war is hell" cliché, Peewee retorts that the dangers of Vietnam are not dissimilar to those in Chicago. Richie, too, acknowledges a link between Vietnam and Harlem. At the sight of a dead soldier, he recalls an incident on Manhattan Avenue in which a gang member about the soldier's age lay dead, and in soldiers who are excited by the anticipation of battle, Richie recognizes "a kid on 119th Street"[91] with similar bloodlust.

Flying home, Richie finds that his mind keeps returning to Vietnam as he attempts to assess the effect of his experience. Whatever the physical injuries he has suffered, whatever the psychological scars yet to be healed, whatever the unpleasant truths he has confronted about his own character, Richie comes out of Vietnam with a sense of belonging. The loneliness he had known as an adolescent in Harlem, the perception of not being connected to the life outside him, is replaced by the camaraderie forged by men at war. He understands that Peewee, along with the other men in his squad, has taught him—more than anything in his experience before Vietnam with the exception of Kenny ever had—about love. "I had never been in love before," Richie muses as he thinks about his comrades-in-arms. "I hoped this was what it was like."[92] It is brotherhood that has sustained him. His final prayer is for "God to care for them, to keep them whole,"[93] as they have kept him whole through conditions that might otherwise have broken him.

RISK, SUCCESS, AND THE MAKING OF A HERO

The tree lined, tranquil campus of Montclare College in Indiana obviously does not hold for Lonnie Jackson the hazards that Vietnam holds for Richie Perry, but it does offer a different kind of risk, and it is as foreign a place, as far removed from Harlem to Lonnie as Southeast Asia is to Richie. "Montclare is not the world I knew," Lonnie confides, "and I felt it wasn't the world I belonged to either. But I knew it was a world that had something in it that I wanted."[94] For many of Lonnie's friends back home, college was a dream that they never really expected to realize. Through basketball, Lonnie does find opportunity, an escape from the milieu he has known all his life, and personal fulfillment. On a basketball court, Lonnie can "feel full of power," as if "some crazy kind of magic was happening to [him]."[95] Ironically, Lonnie jeopardizes his athletic and academic career by nearly falling into the same trap that snared his mentor from *Hoops*, Cal Jones. A local gambler known as "Fat Man" takes a liking to Lonnie because he sees in Lonnie a naive youth who might easily be manipulated. Lonnie is instinctively suspicious of Fat Man; yet, his association with him subjects Lonnie to suspension from the game and investigation by college athletic officials. Eventually, Lonnie is vindicated and, his innocence affirmed, he is restored to his place on the team. Through his ordeal, Lonnie finds empathy and support from his roommate, Colin, the son of an Indiana farmer, whose poverty surprises Lonnie because Colin is white and because Lonnie had always associated the ownership of property with financial security. "Back in Harlem, we used to see this as the perfect kind of life,"[96] Lonnie says on a visit to Colin's farm. Poverty and basketball create such a bond between these two that the issue of race never emerges.

The relationship that gives Lonnie the taste of being a hero, though, and the one that, in some ways, is analogous to Richie's with Kenny, is the one he forms with young Eddie Brignole, an autistic child with whom Lonnie, somewhat improbably, makes almost instant contact where trained therapists have failed, and whose mother, considered overbearing and overprotective by hospital staff, is easily won over by Lonnie despite some initial grumbling. Eddie responds to Lonnie's relaxed, self-deprecating manner; he becomes responsive and completely at ease with Lonnie, who offers to continue working with Eddie even after Eddie's father pulls Eddie out of the hospital program for which Lonnie works. Like many of Myers's other characters, Eddie, a child of divorced parents, is easily intimidated by his father's visits. Carl Brignole, a one time football player for Tulane, is a thoughtless, but not a malicious bully. Lonnie describes him as "the kind of guy who shook your hand like the harder they squeezed, the more of a man it made them."[97] His domineering personality has sent his only child retreating into a shell, withdrawing into a private world. Lonnie coaxes Eddie out, and, in the process of becoming a role model to a boy desperately in need of one, learns of gifts he has beyond athletics. Lonnie, who has a surrogate father in *Hoops*, becomes a surrogate father—or, perhaps more accurately, big brother—in *The Outside Shot*. Like Richie Perry, he is sustained in a world that is unfamiliar to him by the admiration of a boy and by the empathy of a contemporary.

FEMALE INFLUENCES ON MALE CHARACTERS

Lonnie also develops a relationship in *The Outside Shot* with Sherry, a serious, independent, self-assured young woman at Montclare on a track scholarship. But women rarely occupy central roles in the novels Myers has written from male points of view—even *Motown and Didi* has been regarded by critics to be "more Motown's story than Didi's"[98]—because they are not central to the experience of these characters, another deprivation that is a function of the environment. (Jimmy Little of *Somewhere in the Darkness* doesn't think very much about girls, though he is fifteen, and Richie Perry, who reveals so much of his life before Vietnam in *Fallen Angels*, never even suggests any kind of previous involvement in a romantic relationship.) Lonnie tries to understand why he is so uncertain around Sherry, why so many of their early encounters end in misunderstanding, and he concludes, "I wasn't used to dealing with girls outside a man-woman thing. I didn't know how to just hang out and rap or do casual things."[99] His girl-friend in *Hoops* observes that Lonnie resists emotional intimacy; even as he lies in bed with Mary-Ann, Lonnie cannot bring himself to tell her that he loves her because he is unsure of his capacity for love. What his relationships with Cal in *Hoops* and with Eddie in *The Outside Shot* show Lonnie is that he is, indeed, capable of forming an emotional attachment, just as Motown learns first from the Professor and then from Didi, and as Richie Perry learns through Kenny and Peewee.

Like many adolescent males, Myers's characters are especially uncommunicative with their mothers. When Lonnie calls his mother from campus, he cannot tell her that he misses her or that he misses home because "that kind of thing was still hard for [him] to say,"[100] and because he does not want to worry her. The mother is to be protected; she is to be spared anxiety. This is the basis of Jamal's anger at his brother Randy in *Scorpions*. This is why Jimmy does not call Mama Jean while he is on the road with Crab, even though he thinks of her often and would like to contact her. This is why Richie Perry destroys the letter he writes to his mother after Jenkins's death; he is afraid it will upset her. And Richie's mother is equally uncommunicative; she writes to Peewee to say that she loves Richie, but she cannot express that love to Richie himself.

CONCLUSION

It seems, then, that Myers's male adolescent protagonists learn to be most fully themselves through their associations with other men. These are the relationships that disclose to them the strengths and weaknesses of their character, that nurture their emotional growth and development, that teach them of responsibility—in short, that transform these boys into men. Lonnie Jackson of *Hoops* and Motown of *Motown and Didi* find surrogate fathers to offer them advice, protection, and the wisdom of their experience, but even in as strained a father-son relationship as that between Jimmy Little and Crab in *Somewhere in the Darkness*, Jimmy discovers much that is honorable about himself. His odyssey transforms him; Crab's negative example and his dependence upon Jimmy confer upon his son a maturity, a depth of understanding and responsibility, that he did not have before his journey began. Lonnie in *The Outside Shot* and Richie Perry in *Fallen*

Angels, both sons of fathers who have deserted their families and both emigres from the ghetto that has been their only home, discover that their adjustment to new, and in very different ways, challenging surroundings is eased by peer relationships that are especially reassuring as they face hostile circumstances, and by the responsibility they accept to younger boys who look to them as role models and sources of inspiration. Jamal Hicks of *Scorpions* seeks solace and support in a peer relationship as well, and though he places too great a burden on Tito for the friendship to endure, his experience teaches him about loyalty and sacrifice and disabuses him of the false notion that respect can be earned and manhood proven with a gun.

In a recent interview, Henry Louis Gates, Jr. said, "Learning to be black in this society . . . happens through the tutelage of one's parents and relatives, through the examples of one's friends, and, particularly in adolescence, through the written examples provided by people of color. . . ."[101] While there is much in Myers's serious young adult novels to appeal to all male adolescents regardless of race—male bonding is an essential part of the male adolescent experience—it is clear that Myers's work has particular appeal and can serve a distinct purpose for young black males, city bred, streetwise, challenged by poverty, racism, and sometimes circumstance to hold fast to values and maintain a sense of self worth. In Myers's characters they see their own concerns explored and struggles resolved, and recognize the value of the kinds of relationships Myers portrays as the means by which they might grow strong and survive.

NOTES

1. Rudine Sims Bishop, *Presenting Walter Dean Myers*, Twayne's United States Authors Series (Boston, MA: G. K. Hall and Co., 1990), 24.
2. Ibid., 16.
3. "Rescuing the Black Male," *The Futurist* 26 (September–October 1992): 50.
4. Carrell Peterson Horton and Jessie Carney Smith, eds., *Statistical Record of Black America* (Detroit, MI: Gale Research Co., 1990), 653.
5. Ronald L. Taylor, "Black Youth in America: the Endangered Generation," *Youth and Society* 22 (September 1990): 8.
6. Bishop, 45.
7. Ibid., 34.
8. Ibid., 50.

9. Horton and Smith, 263.
10. Richard Wright, *Black Boy* (New York: Perennial Library, 1989), 42.
11. David L. Dudley, *My Father's Shadow: Intergenerational Conflict in African American Men's Autobiography* (Philadelphia, PA: University of Pennsylvania Press, 1991), 5.
12. Frank W. Shelton, "*In My Father's House*: Ernest Gaines After Jane Pittman," *Southern Review* 17 (April 1981): 344.
13. Dudley, 5.
14. Bishop, 49.
15. Adele Sarkissian, ed., "Walter Dean Myers," in *Something About the Author*, vol. 2 (Detroit, MI: Gale Research Co., 1986), 147.
16. Ibid., 148.
17. Walter Dean Myers, *Motown and Didi* (New York: Viking, 1984; Dell, 1987), 4.
18. Robert E. Unsworth, review of *Scorpions*, by Walter Dean Myers, in *School Library Journal* 35 (September 1988): 35.
19. Walter Dean Myers, interview by Amanda Smith, in *Publishers Weekly* 239 (20 July 1992): 217.
20. Myers, *Motown and Didi*, 33.
21. Bishop, 29.
22. Walter Dean Myers, *Fallen Angels* (New York: Scholastic, 1988), 15.
23. Ibid., 36.
24. Walter Dean Myers, *Motown and Didi*, 142.
25. Ibid., 5.
26. Ibid., 122.
27. Ibid., 55.
28. Ibid., 36.
29. Ibid., 84.
30. Ibid., 162.
31. Ibid., 31.
32. Sarkissian, 155.
33. Myers, *Motown and Didi*, 167.
34. Walter Dean Myers, *Hoops* (New York: Delacorte, 1981; Dell, 1983), 34.
35. Ibid., 20.
36. Ibid., 55.
37. Ibid., 158.
38. Bishop, 58.
39. Myers, *Hoops*, 28.
40. Ibid., 43.
41. Stephanie Zvirin, review of *Hoops*, by Walter Dean Myers, in *Booklist* 78 (15 September 1981): 98.
42. Walter Dean Myers, interview by Stephanie Zvirin, in *Booklist* 86 (15

February 1990): 1153.
43. Myers, *Hoops*, 183.
44. Walter Dean Myers, *Scorpions* (New York: Harper, 1988; Harper Keypoint, 1990), 39.
45. Ibid., 38.
46. Ibid., 22.
47. Ibid., 93.
48. Ibid., 74.
49. Ibid., 101.
50. Ibid., 107.
51. Ibid., 86.
52. Ibid., 78.
53. Ibid., 196.
54. Ibid., 201.
55. Ibid., 209.
56. Bishop, 46.
57. Walter Dean Myers, *Somewhere in the Darkness* (New York: Scholastic, 1992), 74.
58. Ibid., 152.
59. Ibid., 64.
60. Ibid., 67.
61. Ibid., 90.
62. Allan A. Cuseo and Barbara Williams Kerns, "Growing Up Male," *VOYA* 7 (October 1984): 155.
63. Myers, *Somewhere in the Darkness*, 98.
64. Ibid., 52.
65. Ibid., 98.
66. Ibid., 99.
67. Ibid., 154.
68. Ibid., 156.
69. Ronald L. Taylor, "Socialization to the Black Male Role," *The Black Male in America: Perspectives on His Status in Contemporary Society*, ed. Doris Y. Wilkinson and Ronald L. Taylor (Chicago, IL: Nelson-Hall, 1977), 1.
70. Myers, *Somewhere in the Darkness*, 167.
71. Myers, *Fallen Angels*, 35.
72. Ibid., 28.
73. Ibid., 20.
74. Ibid., 77.
75. Ibid., 46.
76. Ibid., 132.
77. Ibid., 177.

78. Ibid., 167.
79. Ibid., 50.
80. Ibid., 132.
81. Ibid., 112.
82. Ibid., 181.
83. Ibid., 117.
84. Ibid., 190.
85. Ibid., 14.
86. Ibid., 187.
87. Ibid., 28.
88. Ibid., 117.
89. Ibid., 60.
90. Ibid., 24.
91. Ibid., 198.
92. Ibid., 301.
93. Ibid., 309.
94. Walter Dean Myers, *The Outside Shot* (New York: Delacorte, 1984; Dell, 1987), 136.
95. Ibid.
96. Ibid., 105.
97. Ibid., 127.
98. Gale Jackson, review of *Motown and Didi*, by Walter Dean Myers, in *School Library Journal* 31 (March 1985): 180.
99. Myers, *The Outside Shot*, 52.
100. Ibid., 77.
101. Henry Louis Gates, Jr., interview by Jerry W. Ward, Jr., in *New Literary History* 22 (Autumn 1991): 929.

REFERENCES

Bishop, Rudine Sims. *Presenting Walter Dean Myers*. Twayne's United States Authors Series. Boston, MA: G. K. Hall and Co., 1990.

Cuseo, Allan A. and Barbara Williams Kerns. "Growing Up Male." *VOYA* 7 (October 1984): 155–6.

Dudley, David L. *My Father's Shadow: Intergenerational Conflict in African American Men's Autobiography*. Philadelphia, PA: University of Pennsylvania Press, 1991.

Gates, Henry Louis, Jr. Interview by Jerry W. Ward, Jr. In *New Literary History* 22 (Autumn 1991): 927–35.

Horton, Carrell Peterson and Jessie Carney Smith, eds. *Statistical Record of Black America*. Detroit, MI: Gale Research Co., 1990.

Jackson, Gale. Review of *Motown and Didi*, by Walter Dean Myers. In *School*

Library Journal 31 (March 1985): 180.

Myers, Walter Dean. *Crystal.* New York: Viking, 1987.

____. *Fallen Angels.* New York: Scholastic, 1988.

____. *Fast Sam, Cool Clyde, and Stuff.* New York: Viking, 1975; Penguin, 1988.

____. *Hoops.* New York: Delacorte, 1981; Dell, 1983.

____. *It Ain't All For Nothin'.* New York: Viking, 1978; Avon, 1985.

____. *Malcolm X: By Any Means Necessary.* New York: Scholastic, 1993.

____. *Mojo and the Russians.* New York: Viking, 1977; Avon, 1979.

____. *Motown and Didi.* New York: Viking, 1984; Dell, 1987.

____. *Now Is Your Time: The African American Struggle for Freedom.* New York: Harper Collins, 1991.

____. *The Outside Shot.* New York: Delacorte, 1984; Dell, 1987.

____. *Scorpions.* New York: Harper, 1988; Harper Keypoint, 1990.

____. *Somewhere in the Darkness.* New York: Scholastic, 1992.

____. *Sweet Illusions.* New York: Teachers and Writers Collaborative, 1986.

____. *Where Does the Day Go?* (illustrated by Leo Carty). New York: Parents Magazine Press, 1969.

____. *Won't Know Till I Get There.* New York: Viking, 1982; Penguin, 1988.

____. *The Young Landlords.* New York: Viking, 1979.

____. Interview by Stephanie Zvirin. In *Booklist* 86 (15 February 1990): 1153.

____. Interview by Amanda Smith. In *Publishers Weekly* 239 (20 July 1992): 217.

"Rescuing the Black Male." The Futurist 26 (September–October 1992): 50–51.

Sarkissian, Adele, ed. "Walter Dean Myers." In *Something About the Author*, vol. 2. Detroit, MI: Gale Research Co., 1986, 143–155.

Shelton, Frank W. "*In My Father's House*: Ernest Gaines After Jane Pittman." *Southern Review* 17 (April 1981): 340–5.

Taylor, Ronald L. "Black Youth in America: the Endangered Generation." *Youth and Society* 22 (September 1990): 4–11.

____. "Socialization to the Black Male Role." *The Black Male in America: Perspectives on His Status in Contemporary Society.* Edited by Doris Y. Wilkinson and Ronald L. Taylor. Chicago, IL: Nelson-Hall, 1977.

Unsworth, Robert E. Review of *Scorpions*, by Walter Dean Myers. In *School Library Journal* 35 (September 1988): 35.

Wright, Richard. *Black Boy.* New York: Perennial Library, 1989.

Zvirin, Stephanie. Review of *Hoops*, by Walter Dean Myers. In *Booklist* 78 (15 September 1981): 98.

EIGHT

Through a Glass Clearly: Positive Images of African-American Fathers in Young Adult Literature

Marcia Baghban

T he image of the African-American father in contemporary young adult literature is grounded in the historical reality of slavery and its aftermath. The experience of slavery, the irony of subsequent emancipation, and the influence of industrialization provide significant contexts for the pervasive negative images of the African-American male in the literature. These images are in the state of transformation. As more African-Americans enter the literary scene and as more non African-Americans with social and political consciousness portray well-rounded, introspective, and realistic images of African-American males, positive pictures of fathers appear in the literature. Even under the most adverse circumstances, African-American male characters exert positive influences upon their sons and daughters. Until recently writers let white fathers demonstrate this behavior, but they hid it in works that featured African-Americans.

The first part of this chapter discusses the historical factors that have influenced the images of African-American males in the literature. The second part reviews recent works which portray positive images of African-American fathers in a variety of socioeconomic circumstances.

SLAVERY, FORCED RESTRUCTURING AND AFRICAN-AMERICAN RESPONSE

Slavery in America destroyed the sense of community that Africans had derived from their tribal lives and extended family ties. Slave owners developed strategies to suppress disorder and to maintain the labor force on the plantations. The masters selected only a few slaves from the same tribe so that the slaves would be less able to communicate, and they assigned males to females. They assigned one man to one woman or to several women. When the men outnumbered the women, they assigned several men to one woman.[1] Under the white patriarchy, male and female slaves were property and children. This view "equalized" male and female slaves.[2] Both worked in the fields and houses, and there was little difference in the kinds of work men and women did. However, the slave owner, unlike a father, had the choice of any female under his authority as a sexual partner and he bought or sold males and females at will.

Despite constant disorder, a communal way of life among the slaves re-emerged. Because the misbehavior of one slave endangered them all, slaves developed techniques to survive as a group. They raised most of their own food, cared for their sick, housed their homeless children, and buried their dead. Fathers took great risks and made sacrifices to free their wives and children from bondage. Some men physically rescued them while others purchased them.[3] Thomas Ducket, a runaway slave, testified to his loyalty and love:

> . . . i long to hear from my family how the ar geten along you will ples to let me no how the ar geten along . . . for god sake let me hear from you all my wife and children are not out of my mine nor night.[4]

Before long, slaves had not only a similar plight but also one language and one god. In traditional African society, they were Moslem or polytheistic but in the white-dominated culture, they melded traditional beliefs with Christianity. In worshipping, they had both an emotional outlet and an opportunity to solidify their group identity. They identified with one another or with white people while trying to maintain some identification with fading memories of Africa.

EMANCIPATION

The Civil War disrupted the family life of African-Americans and whites. After the war, many former slaves traveled around the country searching for relatives and making their marriages legal. The Freeman's Bureau tried to decide who belonged with whom. Some former slaves wound up with several spouses and several sets of children. When two or more families came together, the Bureau had to decide with which family the former slave would live. The Bureau's activities and the military protection of former slaves in the South marked the beginning of government intervention in African-American family life. The help the Bureau gave out barely alleviated the wretched condition of African-Americans.* To survive, families organized around kinship bonds and strengthened extended families. While share-cropping was a different kind of enslavement, it enabled extended families to stay intact. Large families meant more people to work the land and more money for the family. Large families also meant a high infant mortality rate and death to many young women. Initially, men tried to keep women from working in the fields, but the labor shortage forced them back into farm work.

African-Americans set up support systems to aid needy rural families as well as schools and churches. In cities like Philadelphia, which had the largest African-American population outside the South prior to the Civil War, African-Americans established their own social service agencies for the elderly, the sick, children, and the poor often under the umbrella of the church.[5]

African-American men and women had been "equal" so long that male-dominated two-partner households did not easily take hold. The man was expected to play the role of stabilizer. He was to see that the family had a home, food, and some protection. The woman was expected to have the role of organizer and to run the household. However, the success of the *man's* role depended on circumstances beyond his control. Racist practices exploited the African-American man. He was part of an agricultural society which was becoming mechanized. Jobs became fewer in rural areas as America became industrialized. To work

---

*The economic order in which African-Americans had a clear place now became an economic disorder in which African-Americans suffered not only overt racism but also ambiguous and subtle discrimination.

at all, many African-American families would have to adjust to an industrial urban way of life.

INDUSTRIALIZATION

African-Americans began to migrate in large numbers to urban centers. The men had few opportunities to become businessmen. While they often lived within walking distance of factories, the labor unions barred the men from working there. Less than one half of one percent worked in factories.[6] The women were less of a threat to white males in powerful positions. Their labor, if kept limited and low-paid, proved useful. For example, in the southern tobacco industry in the early 20th century, Janiewski found that factory managers considered African-American females their property and consistently gave them inferior work assignments and lower pay, maintaining the women as the lowest paid personnel in the industry. Clark-Lewis examines the transition from live-in domestics to day work for African-American women in Washington, D.C. from 1900–1926. Through oral histories she documents the importance of wages earned in the North to the economic survival of rural family members and the critical role of kin in providing childcare for absent parents working in urban centers. Nevertheless, in Harlem in 1925, more than six out of seven African-American homes had two parents.[7]

After World War I, African-Americans slowly and painfully were assimilated into industrial society, and since World War II more industries have opened up to African-Americans. Between 1950 and 1970, four million African-Americans moved to U.S. urban areas. By 1975, 75% of all African-Americans lived in metropolitan areas, 55% in inner cities.[8] In 1960, more than 80% of African-Americans were married and lived together.[9] However, this migration, combined with increased unemployment and underemployment in urban areas, caused female-headed households with more than one child to become an increasingly important family form.

The government stance towards female-headed households during "The Great Society" and "The War on Poverty" in the 1960s and early 1970s relied heavily for its information on Senator Daniel Patrick Moynihan's *The Negro Family: A Case for National Action*. This report, released in 1965, incorporated Oscar Lewis' culture of poverty to suggest that there is a deficient subculture of poverty with its own structure, rationale, and way of life. From this perspective, Moynihan characterized the African-American family as a female-headed "tangle of pathology." He used government statistics to imply that the increasing gap between African-American and white populations in academic achievement, delinquency rates, and various social ills derived from the crumbling of the Negro family. He recommended that government intervention establish a stable patriarchal Negro family to socialize the poor to mainstream middle class values. Moynihan ignored the literature which supported that African-American families had historically been two-parent families. He blamed family structure rather than inequality as the cause of poverty.

The Moynihan report proved useful, however, in generating inquiry into the history of African-American family life, the causes of poverty, and the survival strategies among the poor. Valentine, Hannerz, Leacock, and Stack examined the lifestyles of poor African-American families from the perspective of on-going conditions of poverty and the necessary adaptive strategies for survival. They emphasized that in the process of carrying out daily life, people experience some of the most serious effects of unequal access to society's goods, services, and information.

A popular stereotype emphasizes that African-American families historically have been female-headed and that families receiving public assistance, particularly those receiving aid to families with dependent children, compose a stagnant, permanently unemployed population that does not seek employment. In reality, the majority of African-American families have been two-parent families.[10] Fifty percent of the people who receive aid to dependent children leave the rolls within two years, and 85% leave within eight years.[11] Furthermore, many people receiving public assistance either mix these benefits with low paying jobs or vacillate between public assistance and work. Most jobs are in the secondary labor sector which is characterized by low job security, low wages, few opportunities for advancement, and limited work-related benefits. Therefore, although there might not be radical changes in the percentage of people receiving public assistance at a given time, there is a high turnover of the people on the welfare rolls.[12]

The lack of adequate employment for semi-educated African-American males forces them to take jobs in the secondary labor force. Because these jobs are insecure, they are frequently laid off. Dehavenon notes that the structure of state subsidies is such that poor men may see their children better taken care of if they absent themselves.[13] Ironically, to survive, the family members cannot live together.

WHERE DO THE YOUNG MEN GO?

The migration of primarily young adults to urban areas during the two decades from 1950 to 1970 had a dramatic effect on African-American marriage pools. The Northeast gained two African-American men for every three African-American women.[14] Moreover, faced with young adulthood, the African-American woman finds most eligible males locked in prison or away in the military. By the time she reaches thirty years of age, there will be ten less African-American men for every 100 African-American women. At forty and beyond, the numbers decrease severely.[15]

Unfortunately, the informal income pursuits of African-American males are more dangerous than those of white males. Between the ages of fifteen and forty-four, more minority males are likely to be in prison, in the military, or homeless, or dying from AIDS, homicide, drug dependency, or cirrhosis.[16]

Between 1980 and 1985, 44,428 African-American males were murdered in the United States. This death toll exceeds the number of American soldiers killed in Korea (34,000) and nearly equals the number of American soldiers killed in Vietnam (47,000). If this pace continues, by the end of the first decade of the twenty-first century, the deaths will surpass the number of American soldiers killed during World War II (292,000).[17] Ed Pitt, former Director of Health and Environmental Services of the National Urban league, states, ". . . without young men to start and maintain our families, we can have no future on this continent."[18] In addition, in most groups at all ages, males have higher death rates than females. There are higher mortality rates for African-American men than white men, particularly at the adult ages when children are conceived, born, and enculturated. Inferior maternal care and lack of access to quality health care result in higher rates of mortality for African-American male infants, children, and adolescents than for white males at the same ages.[19] African-American men in Harlem have a lower life expectancy than men in Bangladesh, one of the world's poorest countries.[20]

BLACK FATHERHOOD

There has always been wide diversity in how American families, as kinship units, and households, as residential units, are organized. In spite of important anthropological contributions to the study of family life, most contemporary public policy is based on outdated social theory which defines the nuclear family as the unique, minimal unit of social organization. Moreover, there is variation in attitude and lifestyle among the people who belong to the same socioeconomic categories in the same way that there are variations among people who belong to the same culture. We need to consider these realities when we examine any member's role in family dynamics, and we need to re-examine our national ideal models of family life in the light of these realities.[21]

For example, adequate attention has not been given to the role of the fathers of children in female-headed households with incomes of $20,000 and below. Given real contexts, it is not accurate to label many of these men "absent fathers." While the men may be absent from the household or residence, they are not absent from the family or kinship group. Leibow in his study of low income African-American men in Washington, D.C. discusses the marginal economic situation of these men. He demonstrates that although they are unable to contribute regularly to their children's financial support, they help when they are able. Leibow also notes that some men have other than economic relationships with their children. Stack finds that not only fathers but the fathers' relatives are active in the lives of the household. Okongwu shows that fathers consistently maintain relationships with their children. She also emphasizes that while low and marginally middle income fathers are unable to give regular financial help, there are crucial instances when fathers provide financial help and direct their children's lives.

Myths sometimes become the only reality. Some African-American men do desert their families, but so do some white men. They make babies they don't take care of, but so do some white men. They join gangs and commit acts of violence. They die young from drugs, alcohol, and disease. This reality is only part of the story. More than 50% of African-American fathers do stay in the home.[22] They sacrifice under difficult circumstances to provide for their families. African-American two-parent families have realized higher levels of poverty despite the labor of the wives. In 1986, the median income of two-

parent African-American families was $26,583. During this same
period, the median income for whites was $33,809.[23] They overcome
great obstacles to build strong relationships with their loved ones.
Sadly, this side of reality gets little publicity.[24]

Where are the how-to books for the young African-American
man, with or without a role model at home, who would like to know
more about being a good father to his child? Certainly Bill Cosby's
books on fatherhood are humorous looks at fatherhood but do not deal
with African-American fatherhood in particular. Earl Ofari Hutchinson
interviews six men who tell what it means to be an African-American
father in America. *Black Fatherhood* is not ". . . a book about defeat-
ism and despair. It is a book about optimism and hope. It is a book
about success. It is a book that finally lifts the cloak of invisibility from
black fathers."[25] This non-fiction book stands alone describing positive
portrayals of African-American fathers. To continue our reflections, let
us now turn to young people's fiction.

POSITIVE PORTRAYALS

"Any man can make a baby, but only a father can raise a baby" is
common advice to young males in folk wisdom. But what then does it
mean to be a father? In the jargon of the day we say, "He's there for
me." But is he there from day to day or at a time of crisis? And what
kind of support does his being there mean? Does he also have to be
strong, good, smart, kind, honest, honorable? So many outstanding
qualities would indeed be burdensome for mortals of any color. And
indeed, which qualities do children remember, for it truly is in the eyes
of their children that fathers can evaluate themselves.

Mildred Taylor describes her father as a master storyteller in the
"Author's Note" to *Roll of Thunder, Hear My Cry*. Without his words,
her words would not have been. She writes that from him she learned
to respect her heritage and herself. The quality that made him tower
above other men was his rare strength that sustained the family and all
that leaned upon his wisdom.

> He was a complex person, yet he taught me many simple
> things, things important for a child to know: how to ride a horse
> and how to skate; how to blow soap bubbles and how to tie a kite
> knot that met the challenge of the March winds; how to bathe a

huge faithful mongrel dog named Tiny. In time, he taught me the complex things. He taught me of myself, of life. He taught me of hopes and dreams. And he taught me the love of words.[26]

Taylor's father died the week before she wrote this note. She dedicates her book to her father ". . . who was in essence the man David."

DAVID LOGAN

David Logan appears first in *Song of the Trees*. He is in Louisiana while his family works their farm in Mississippi. The Depression brings his family hard times. Someone removes ten dollars from a letter he mails them, his wife is sick and has no money for medicine, and white men force $65 on his mother to cut down an unlimited number of the family's trees. His wife sends their oldest son to bring David from Louisiana. He comes home ready to dynamite the forest rather than to let the men cut down any more of their trees or carry away trees already cut. David's courage wins. The forest remains half-cut. In the sequel *Roll of Thunder, Hear My Cry*, the narrator, Cassie, refers to the injured trees several times and praises her father's integrity.

David Logan is a strong man with a powerful sense of family. Yet he is a father who is not always at home. He must leave periodically to earn money by laying railroad track in Louisiana so the family can continue to pay the mortgage on their land. They are the only African-American family who owns their land in Depression-era Mississippi. Sold to David's father by a Northerner during the Reconstruction, the land not only maintains the family physically but also binds them emotionally. In *Roll of Thunder, Hear My Cry*, Cassie does not understand the sacrifices which the family makes to keep the land.

> For it Papa would work the long, hot summer pounding steel; Mama would teach and run the farm; Big Ma, in her sixties, would work like a woman of twenty in the fields and keep the house; and the boys and I would wear threadbare cloth washed to dishwater color; but always, the taxes and the mortgage would be paid. Papa said that one day I would understand. I wondered.[27]

David Logan knows that, no matter the differences, the love of the land unites African-Americans and whites. A white family in the community, already angry at David's family for his wife's organized boycott of their store, threatens a neighboring sharecropper's family after a robbery. David learns that they plan on attacking his family the same evening. Knowing that neither family has a chance for defense, he cleverly uses the lightning from a storm to disguise his starting a fire in the cotton fields. The panicked African-American and white families immediately join together to save the crop which is the livelihood for all of them. Since one-quarter of the Logan crop is ruined, no one questions David. Once again, we learn to understand David through his courageous action which gives context to the title *Roll of Thunder, Hear My Cry.*

Children's perceptions of their father also determine the positiveness of the image. David Logan clearly loves his children and they love him. Whenever he returns home, all four children run to greet him. He holds the two younger while the two older crowd around him. When asked what he is doing home, he easily says, "Just had to come home and see 'bout my babies."[28]

Cassie further fleshes out our picture of David. She misses her father and she makes frequent references to her father's characteristics. When she meets Mr. Jamison, a white lawyer in Strawberry, she comments, "In his way he was like Papa: Ask him a question and he would give it to you straight with none of this pussyfooting around business. I liked that."[29] Cassie appreciates David's directness and honesty. Moreover, she says that he listens to her.[30] When he is home, she knows that she can tell him of her visit to Strawberry with her grandmother and the humiliations of the day. He then advises her that she must learn to decide for herself what she can live with and what she cannot. He nurtures her self-esteem by adding, "You have to demand respect in this world, ain't nobody just going to hand it to you. How you carry yourself, what you stand for—that's how you gain respect. But little one, ain't nobody's respect worth more than your own."[31]

David continues to nurture Cassie's self-esteem in *Let the Circle Be Unbroken*. He counsels an older Cassie about boys and white boys in particular. While Cassie has no interest in boys except as friends, she listens to what he says about slave times and his white grandfather. He explains that at least in these times, white men look down on black women and want to use them. She must remember to respect herself. In *The Road to Memphis*, he finds a seventeen-year-old Cassie, and calls her just in time to save her from a car with three white boys who were bothering her as she walks a dirt road alone.

David Logan's watchful protection also extends to Stacey, Cassie's oldest brother. Because Stacey is the oldest, he wants to help with their financial difficulties. In *Let the Circle Be Unbroken*, a naive Stacey runs away to cut sugar cane in Louisiana. After many months, David and his brother find Stacey sick in jail and bring him home. David Logan protects the family members and maintains the circle. Once again, his action provides the context for the title of the book.

David Logan loves his wife and this feeling is evident to their children when he comes home. He picks her up, swings her around, and kisses her. Despite terrible troubles, they find moments to banter as if still courting. "Sometimes, David Logan, I wonder why I didn't marry sweet, quiet Ronald Carter or nice, mild Harold Davis." "Because woman," Papa said, putting his arm around her, "you took one look at big, handsome me and no one else would do."[32] When Mama gets fired from teaching because a student she has failed describes how radical she is, Papa shows his solid support. He tells the children that their mama was born to be a teacher and that her parents wanted her to be a teacher. He describes the sacrifices her parents went through to send her to the teacher training school in Jackson. He reminds them that she is a strong, fine woman, but the loss of teaching is a terrible blow. He cautions them all to be extra thoughtful in the next few days. David Logan is a sensitive, demonstrative husband and father who nurtures family members and preserves the family group in terrible circumstances.

Mildred Taylor's portrayal of David is full-bodied. We understand David clearly through his actions and words and the perceptions of the family members. His portrait is an emotional one in contrast to Virginia Hamilton's intellectual William Small.

WILLIAM SMALL

William Small is a historian who moves his family from North Carolina to Ohio so that he can teach in a small college town in *The House of Dies Drear*. He is the only member of his family to have visited the Ohio town where they are to live. William has rented and, through his readings, fallen in love with the secluded house of the famous abolitionist, Dies Drear. As the family drives from North

Carolina, he provides the history of the house. His son, Thomas, becomes as fascinated as his father with the house and its mysterious tunnels, false walls, and sliding mirrors once used to conceal escaping slaves in the underground railroad. Dies Drear also hid the exquisite tapestries, glassware, carpets, and china from his house in a secret cavern. The search for the cavern and the solution to the vendetta between the caretaker of the house and a family of townspeople become the adventure of a lifetime for this father and son team.

William Small indoctrinates his son in his profession as well as the upcoming adventure. At the beginning of the book, for Thomas' birthday, he gives Thomas a leather-bound book about the Civil War, the Underground Railroad, and slaves. Thomas loves the smell of real leather and rubs the book beneath his nose. He silently plans to read it aloud to his twin baby brothers, thereby passing on their father's love of history farther along into the family. Thomas observes his father casually encouraging the local gas station owner to talk more about the caretaker's feud with a family of townspeople. In this way, Thomas learns how to do fieldwork and even suggests a trip to the county seat to study family records and kinship relations. After they discover the treasures, Thomas sees his father, sick with a cold, furiously cataloguing each item. As the book ends, Thomas sits quietly and watches his father enraptured by his work, and waits until he asks for help. William Small models and teaches Thomas a passion for learning and pleasure that comes with a life in which intellect is the focus.

This father and son team have the adventure in common and they clearly like each other. William Small suggests that they have lunch in the college cafeteria until Thomas has so many friends he won't have time to have lunch with his father. Thomas replies with consideration that even when he has many friends, he will come with two or three friends once a week to eat with his father. However, Thomas is not always happy with his father. Angry that no one talked to the family in a welcoming way after their first Sunday in church, Thomas blames his father for the move to Ohio. His father insists that they all give the town some time, and then he and Thomas are immediately lost in the next clue. Thomas' anger is short-lived and sacrified to the mystery.

The caretaker's son talks about his own father at the end of the book, and contrasts him to William Small. Thomas replies that he likes his father and that even though he gets angry at him, he has a "powerful brain." The caretaker's son agrees that the townspeople know they can never fool William Small the way they fooled the caretaker.

> They'll fear your father in a way they never feared mine. They'll fear him not as a devil but as a man. He will have the right to say who can pass here and who cannot. Yes, they'll be afraid of him and the law he won't hesitate to use against them.[33]

His prophesy comes true in Virginia Hamilton's sequel to *The House of Dies Drear*.

William Small uses his powerful brain in *The Mystery of Drear House* to find a disposition for the treasure with which they can all live. The caretaker of the house, who guards the cavern with Dies Drear's treasures, is becoming too weak to protect the cavern from the Darrows, the family with whom he has a feud. The mother of the Darrow clan is mentally ill and wanders the tunnels around the house. Cleverly, William Small publicizes that Mrs. Darrow helped the caretaker discover the cavern with the treasures. The historical foundation which owns the Drear property then offers both the caretaker and the Darrow family rewards for their discovery. Thomas praises his father saying, "The best place to keep a secret safe is to bring it and the enemy of it out in the open. That way there can't be harm in either of them ever again."[34] When Thomas later resents the Darrows coming up in the world because of the reward, he questions his father about what he got from the treasure. After talking about the cataloguing, his work with the foundation, and the rehabilitation of an enemy, his father responds, "Son, I'm a historian. I'm happy to save a great discovery from its worst enemies—time and greed."[35] William Small reaffirms his professionalism and ultimately convinces Thomas that life is best lived with goals other than money. However, this world view is the luxury of a professional man.

CEPHUS (CRAB) LITTLE

In contrast, Crab Little in Walter Dean Myers' *Somewhere in the Darkness* is a man at a place in life where he has to worry about money. He has escaped from a prison hospital and is dying of kidney failure. He has no thought other than to find his son and convince him that while he is a thief, he is no murderer. When Jimmy tells him that he is nothing to him and he doesn't love him, Crab tells Jimmy that his words hurt but it is all right. He understands. By accepting Jimmy's feelings, Crab has an opportunity to express his own feelings and to establish a relationship with his son. He gives his perspective concerning the lack of contact between them:

> I tried writing to you and nothing came out right. Nothing came out right and it made me feel like nothing. Just like you said. I ain't nothing and that's how I felt. I tried to think about my father. I used to say that my father couldn't give us much but at least I loved him. You can't say that. You don't even know me.[36]

Crab explains his powerlessness when Jimmy asks why he didn't prove that he hadn't killed the guard. "Because I didn't give them a reason to believe what I was saying, that's why. They knew I was a thief. They knew I didn't have an education. All they saw was another black man they had to pass judgment on."[37] Through his honesty, Jimmy learns to understand his father and to avoid his example. Crab empowers Jimmy by expressing his feelings.

Crab also gives Jimmy a past. "His father had come from somewhere, some place, from some time when his mother had been alive, and when he had either been a baby or not yet born."[38] He is the man with his mother in his grandmother's photo albums. He tells Jimmy that he looks like his mother. He tells him that when Jimmy was little, he used to put him on top of the refrigerator. He says he half expected to do it again. Although Jimmy wishes that he didn't care, he wonders if Crab likes him.

Crab and Jimmy Little set out on an adventure. However, unlike William and Thomas Small, the adventure is secondary to their relationship. Crab wants to show Jimmy where he has lived and vainly hopes to now make a living. They start their drive to Chicago and then to Arkansas to find Crab's cohort who can clear Crab. They begin their journey however, with little understanding of each other and end with too little time to put their dreams together to make a common life. Finally, Crab tells Jimmy that he is all he has in this world that means anything. If Jimmy can't mean anything to him, his life has no meaning. Jimmy protests that all this traveling is so that Crab has meaning in his life, and Crab responds, "I wanted you to listen and maybe hear something you wanted to hear."[39] Jimmy confronts him with the truth that he does not know how to be a father. When the police catch up with Crab, in agony he apologizes to Jimmy who responds, "I know, Daddy. I know."[40] Crab and Jimmy have tried to reach each other somewhere in the darkness that existed between them. They have shared Jimmy's dream of ". . . something special that could never be forgotten" after all.[41]

PHANTOM FATHERS

Jimmy Little lived fourteen years with no father. This experience does not mean that he has never thought about his father or having a father.

> He had often wondered what it would be like to have a father, like some kids. For some reason he had always imagined a father as somebody who told him to come home at a certain time or who got mad when he didn't do his homework. He had imagined them going to baseball games together or maybe for walks in the park.[42]

Jimmy's ideal has not existed for him, and since his mother is dead, there is no possibility of a stepfather. However, Jimmy's image of a father can merge with the extent of Crab's caring for him. Jimmy can become the kind of father he wishes he had.

Sheema Hadley in Virginia Hamilton's *A Little Love* is consumed by thoughts of her missing father. Her mother died in childbirth and her father left her with her maternal grandparents. Despite their love for her, the emptiness within prompts her to overeat, and her insecurity causes her to worry about the bomb which may destroy the world. She feels her father would give her the security she needs and a little love. When she learns that from time to time her father has sent her grandparents money to take care of her, her father hunger makes her push her boyfriend Forrest to drive her south to find him.

Following Hadley's last return address on an envelope and his style of signpainting, they locate him in Georgia teaching a class in a building behind a big white house with a woman gardening and two babies in a sandbox. While Sheema sits and sobs, her father explains that he meant to keep in touch with her. He never did because he wanted to forget about that part of his life. To forget her mother's death, he married too soon after leaving and divorced quickly. He explains that he now has a new life. He has been married four years and has two children. He offers to continue to send her money for her education, but he clearly does not want his new life to include her. As Sheema and Forrest leave, her boyfriend looks around and sees her father in a glass door watching them. "He hadn't known men like Hadley, who were so closed, deep in themselves. The saddest eyes he'd ever seen. Forrest had not come upon circumstances that made a man give up one thing for another. He hoped he never would."[43]

Sheema is much like Jimmy Little in that the dream of her father has not matched his reality.

> Funny, you think you love somebody. But what you been lovin is the idea of somebody . . . a great big dad that's gone to care about you like nobody else, that's gone to do for you—But you don't really love someone unless he's there.[44]

Sheema's meeting with her father, much like Jimmy Little's with his father, causes her to lose her illusions about her father. She finally begins to take charge of herself and to get on with her life. For both Sheema and Jimmy, their confrontations with the realities of their fathers and their subsequent loss of the illusions about their fathers free them to work on their own lives.

Mr. Williams in Walter Dean Myers' *Fast Sam, Cool Clyde, and Stuff* is a real father who may as well be a phantom. He is so much in the background of the narrator Stuff's life that we can only guess at his name from a passing reference to his wife.

When the three boys retrieve a stolen pocketbook for a woman, they are arrested as criminals. The police rough them up and put them in a line up. An eyewitness tells the police they are not the thieves and they get busfare home. Stuff tells his father about the misadventure, and his father says that he is learning what the world is all about. Stuff disagrees because he feels his friends and his parents are not that mean. When Stuff is later arrested for associating with drug dealers, his father insists on going with him to the police station:

> All the way down to the police station my father had his arm around me. He said that no matter what happened he was on my side. I told him that I didn't do anything and he said, "Good." I don't ever remember him putting his arm around me like that before.[45]

His father's support is worth all the times he has lectured Stuff about coming home late, not doing a good job cleaning the bathroom, and fighting with his sister. Instead Stuff remembers that when he wanted a new mouthpiece for his saxophone, his father matched his savings from his job at the A & P. While Stuff's story is clearly about a group of friends growing up on 116th Street in New York City, Stuff always feels his father's presence in the background of his life.

BEING THERE

Mr. Williams and William Small are two fathers who are always in the kinship group and in the family's residence. Mr. Williams is a silhouette moving in Stuff's life. He is there not only when his son is in difficulty, but also when he has to nag, prod, and stay up if Stuff is late. William Small is the obvious leading player in Thomas' life. He determines the family's move to Ohio, understands the contexts for the clues in the mystery, and eventually finds a solution to the mystery.

At the beginning of their stories, Stuff and Thomas have both just moved. Stuff's peer group in his urban neighborhood immediately begins to dominate his life. Thomas has just moved to a rural area where his rented house is isolated from town and the natives are not welcoming. Uprooted from his previous life and with no peer group, he stays near his father. His father willingly keeps him close to help solve the Dies Drear mystery. Jimmy Little is also uprooted from his past life, but his dying father does not have a clear place in mind to take him.

Crab Little enters Jimmy's life and presses for closeness with frightening intensity. Crab could never find the words to write Jimmy from prison while Jimmy could only imagine what having a father might be like. Yet if Crab had not entered Jimmy's life, Jimmy would never have known the truth about his father's crime nor how much his father loved him. Their encounter changes Jimmy's life for the better, and he is able to be with Crab when he dies.

Hamilton's Cruze Hadley is physically alive but emotionally dead. Sheema's father is a sad figure of a former son-in-law still beloved by his inlaws and still in love with his first wife. To survive her death and to continue his life, he determines to isolate himself from their daughter. While he helps to maintain Sheema physically through long distance financial support, he will never be there for her emotionally.

In contrast, David Logan is a solid upright father who always provides emotional support for the members of his family. However, to provide financially for them, he cannot always be physically present. Yet the family's life is better whenever he is around. He is nurturing, protective, and loving. Even as he comes and goes, he maintains his family as a unit.

These men create a spectrum in their performance of the role of father. We have fathers who are always physically present (Mr. Williams and William Small), occasionally present (David Logan), suddenly present (Crab Little), or never present (Cruze Hadley). Emotionally, the fathers' involvement with their children follows as wide a range. We have intense involvement (Crab Little), interested involvement (Mr. Williams, William Small, David Logan), and avoidance (Cruze Hadley). At the core, these men are good fathers. They care about their children. However, they care in very different ways. If literature is a reflection of life, then young adult literature reflects the variability it sees in the fathers in our society.

This variability supports the anthropologists' previous claim that there has always been diversity in how American families are organized. To base an ideal family structure on an intact nuclear model is as false for African-Americans as it is for white Americans or any other Americans. In this instance, we would do better in life to follow the example of literature. We can then understand families and the roles of their members from a more realistic and a more humane perspective.

NOTES

1. Elmer P. Martin and Joanne Mitchell Martin, *The Black Extended Family* (Chicago, IL: The University of Chicago Press, 1976), 93.
2. Ibid., 94.
3. Earl Ofari Hutchinson, *Black Fatherhood* (Inglewood, CA: IMPACT Publications, 1992), 15.
4. Ibid.
5. W.E.B. DuBois, *The Philadelphia Negro: A Social Study* (New York: Atheneum, 1976), 207.
6. Ibid.
7. Hutchinson, 15.
8. Anna Lou Dehavenon, "An Etic Model for the Scientific Study of the Causes of Matrifocality," in *Where Did All the Men Go?* ed. Joan Mencher and Anne Okongwu (Boulder, CO: Westview Press, 1993), 62.
9. Hutchinson, 15.

10. Herbert G. Gutman, *The Black Family in Slavery and Freedom 1750–1925* (New York: Pantheon Books, 1976), 14.

11. Anne Okongwu, *Different Realities: A Comparative Study of Nineteen Black and White Single Parents* (Ann Arbor, MI: University Microfilms International, 1986), 23.

12. Ibid.

13. Dehavenon, 60.

14. Ibid., 62.

15. Hutchinson, 69.

16. Dehavenon, 63.

17. Hutchinson, 35.

18. McAllister, Bill, "The Plight of Young Black Men in America," *Washington Post National Weekly Edition*, 12–18 February 1990, 6.

19. Dehavenon, 63.

20. Hutchinson, 62.

21. Dehavenon, 63.

22. Anne Okongwu, "Some Conceptual Issues: Female Single-Parent Families in the United States," in *Where Did All the Men Go?* ed. Joan Mencher and Anne Okongwu (Boulder, CO: Westview Press, 1993), 108.

23. United States Bureau of the Census, Current Population Reports, Consumer Income Series, P–60, No. 60, *Poverty in the U.S.: 1986* (Washington, DC: U.S. Government Printing Office, 1986), 43.

24. Hutchinson, 17.

25. Ibid., 18.

26. Mildred D. Taylor, *Roll of Thunder, Hear My Cry* (New York: Dial Books, 1976), ii.

27. Ibid., 8.

28. Ibid., 34.

29. Ibid., 107.

30. Ibid., 118.

31. Ibid., 176.

32. Ibid., 208.

33. Virginia Hamilton, *The House of Dies Drear* (New York: Macmillan Publishing Company, Incorporated, 1968), 239.

34. Virginia Hamilton, *The Mystery of Drear House* (New York: Greenwillow Books, 1987), 188.

35. Ibid., 210.

36. Walter D. Myers, *Somewhere in the Darkness* (New York: Scholastic, 1992), 50.

37. Ibid., 50.

38. Ibid., 71.

39. Ibid., 155.

40. Ibid., 161.
41. Ibid., 153.
42. Ibid., 39.
43. Virginia Hamilton, *A Little Love* (New York: Philomel Books, 1984), 199.
44. Ibid., 201.
45. Walter Dean Myers, *Fast Sam, Cool Clyde, and Stuff* (New York: Viking Press, 1975), 169.

REFERENCES

Clark-Lewis, Elizabeth. *This Work Has No End*. Working Paper #2, Center for Research on Women. Memphis, TN: Memphis State University, 1985.

Dehavenon, Anna Lou. "An Etic Model for the Scientific Study of the Causes of Matrifocality." In *Where Did All the Men Go?* ed. Joan Mencher and Anne Okongwu, 51–69. Boulder, CO: Westview Press, 1993.

DuBois, W.E.B. *The Philadelphia Negro: A Social Study*. New York: Atheneum, 1976.

Gutman, Herbert G. *The Black Family in Slavery and Freedom 1750–1925*. New York: Pantheon Books, 1976.

Hamilton, Virginia. *The House of Dies Drear*. New York: Macmillan Publishing Company, Incorporated, 1968.

_____. *A Little Love*. New York: Philomel Books, 1984.

_____. *The Mystery of Drear House*. New York: Greenwillow Books, 1987.

Hannerz, Uls. *Soulside: Inquiries Into Ghetto Culture and Community*. New York: Columbia University Press, 1969.

Hare, Nathan and Julia Hare. *The Endangered Black Family*. San Francisco, CA: Black Think Tank, 1984.

Harris, Peter J. "Heroic Fathers." *Essence* (October 1988): 162.

Hutchinson, Earl Ofari. *Black Fatherhood*. Inglewood, CA: IMPACT Publications, 1992.

Leacock, Eleanor. *The Culture of Poverty*. New York: Simon and Schuster, 1971.

Leacock, Eleanor and Helen Safa, ed. *Women's Work: Development and the Division of Labor by Gender*. Hadley, MA: Bergin and Garvey Publishing Incorporated, 1986.

Leibow, Elliot. *Tally's Corner*. Boston, MA: Little, Brown, and Company, 1967.

Martin, Elmer P. and Joanne Mitchell Martin. *The Black Extended Family*. Chicago, IL: The University of Chicago Press, 1976.

McAllister, Bill. "The Plight of Young Black Men in America." *Washington Post National Weekly Edition*, 12–18 February 1990, 6–7.

Meier, August and Elliott Rudwick. *From Plantation to Ghetto*. New York: Hill and Wang, 1976.

Meier, August and Elliott Rudwick. "Black Men in Agarian America: Slavery and the Plantation." In *From Plantation to Ghetto*, ed. August Meier and Elliott Rudwick. New York: Hill and Wang, 1976, 27–86.

____. "Black Men in the Urban Age: The Rise of the Ghetto." In *From Plantation to Ghetto*, ed. August Meier and Elliott Rudwick. New York: Hill and Wang, 1976, 232–270.

Mencher, Joan and Anne Okongwu. *Where Did All the Men Go?* Boulder, CO: Westview Press, 1993.

Moynihan, Daniel P. *The Negro Family: A Case for National Action*. Washington, DC: Office of Policy Planning and Research, U.S. Department of Labor, 1965.

Myers, Walter Dean. *Fast Sam, Cool Clyde, and Stuff*. New York: Viking Press, 1975.

____. *Somewhere in the Darkness*. New York: Scholastic, 1992.

Okongwu, Anne. *Different Realities: A Comparative Study of Nineteen Black and White Single Parents*. Ann Arbor, MI: University Microfilms International, 1986.

____. "Some Conceptual Issues: Female Single-Parent Families in the United States." In *Where Did All the Men Go?* ed. Joan Mencher and Anne Okongwu, 107–129. Boulder, CO: Westview Press, 1993.

Powell, Gregory. "I'm a Witness to the Fact That Good Black Fathers Are Not Extinct." *Essence* (March 1987): 10.

Stack, Carol B. *All Our Kin: Strategies for Survival in a Black Community*. New York: Harper and Row, 1975.

Taylor, Mildred D. *Let the Circle Be Unbroken*. New York: Dial Press, 1981.

____. *The Road to Memphis*. New York: Dial Press, 1990.

____. *Roll of Thunder, Hear My Cry*. New York: Dial Press, 1976.

____. *Song of the Trees*. New York: Dial Press, 1975.

United States Bureau of the Census, Current Population Reports, Consumer Income Series, P–60, No. 60, *Poverty in the U.S.: 1986*. Washington, DC: U.S. Government Printing Office, 1986.

Valentine, Charles. *Culture and Poverty*. Chicago, IL: The University of Chicago Press, 1968.

NINE

A Chronicle of Family Honor: Balancing Rage and Triumph in the Novels of Mildred D. Taylor

Karen Patricia Smith

Mildred D. Taylor is considered to be a major voice in African-American children's and young adult literature. Her books span both segments of youth genre, but given their depth and applicability to gaining an understanding of the historical role participated in by African-Americans, are particularly appropriate for the middle school (grade six through eight) young adult. Praised for the consistency of her writing style, her singular method of conveying the spirit, personality, and heartfelt convictions of a united African-American family, Taylor has been the recipient of numerous honors for her work. In 1977 she won the John Newbery Award for *Roll of Thunder, Hear My Cry* (1976), a work which was also named as a National Book Award finalist as well as a Boston Globe-Horn Book Honor Book, and the Coretta Scott King Award for *Let the Circle Be Unbroken* (1982). She has had the distinction of having her work *Song of the Trees* (1975) named as a *New York Times* Outstanding Book of the Year for 1975, a book which in novella form had also previously won the Council on Interracial Books Award in 1973. In 1988, *The Friendship* (1987) was awarded both the Boston Globe-Horn Book and the Coretta Scott King awards, with the latter also being awarded to *Road to Memphis* (1990) in 1991. Taylor's work is informed by historical verification, personal biographical, reflection and literary artistry. With the exception of *The Gold Cadillac* (written in 1987 and not part of the Logan family chronicle), winner of the Christopher Award, her work is set against the backdrop of Depression day Mississippi, a particularly perilous time for African-Americans.

One of the unique aspects of Taylor's work is her focus upon a strong, upwardly mobile family unit which consistently, and also realistically, manages to meet "head-on" the social challenges of racism and disfranchisement without projection of a self-conscious perspective. In the Mississippi of the 1930s and 1940s, African-American success was uneasily measured by African-Americans not only by one's general ability to survive economically but also more specifically, by ownership of land and one's capacity to retain that ownership. All manifestations of success had to be accomplished without attracting, to any great degree, the negative attention of discontented whites who, themselves struggling, directed their energies towards ensuring that the black standard of living not progress beyond a bare subsistence level. The most extreme forms of danger lay ahead for those blacks who were too "flamboyant" in their achievements.

The politics of family survival sustained by a strong spiritual and moral base serves as Taylor's most prominent theme, in what might be termed her "chronicle" of the Logan family. Taylor has stated that in great part, her Logan family stories are based upon personal experience:

> Through David Logan have come the words of my father, and through the Logan family the love of my own family. If people are touched by the warmth of the Logans, it is because I had the warmth of my own youthful years from which to draw. If the Logans seem real, it is because I had my own family upon which to base characterizations. And if people believe the book to be biographical, it is because I have tried to distill the essence of Black life, so familiar to most Black families, to make the Logans an embodiment of that spiritual heritage; for, contrary to what the media relate to us, all Black families are not fatherless or disintegrating. Certainly my family was not.[1]

Such a factual basis for storytelling serves to underscore the reality stated above by Taylor, that many African-American families have in the past, despite the most oppressive of circumstances, succeeded in surmounting potentially overwhelming odds, and have done so *as a nuclear family*. Such a focus assists in illustrating to young people the positive and liberating possibilities, borne of that glorious combination of dreams and unabated hard work, that *can* await those who have the fortitude to prevail.

This does not mean that the hardships endured by a person of color should be submerged within a sea of optimism and certainly, Taylor does not do this. It also does not mean that one will not, or should not be entitled to experience a certain rage at injustices rendered. But what it does mean is that a youthful and also adult audience needs (and indéed *deserves*) to have the opportunity to see the good that can come of *not giving up and not giving in*; that there is the possibility of *triumph* at the end of adversity. In their study *Children of the Dream: The Psychology of Black Success*, Edwards and Polite state:

> A focus on pathology, however, tends to disturb rather than illuminate. Our contention . . . is that it is much more useful to focus on the success stories within the black race to identify the special strengths and skills it takes to prevail in the face of persistent racism.[2]

Taylor reminds us that her family model flies in the face of stereotype. What is also evident upon further scrutiny, is the presence of *balance*, or as the Roman Horace referred to it, "the Golden Mean"; used here to indicate a mediating force which, when present within the most adverse of circumstances, has the ability to offset a potentially destructive course of events. Balance, of a spiritual, social, economic, and political nature, in as much as the key players are able to "juggle" the internal mechanisms of each of the components (rather than one element against another), may be seen to be the key to the survival of the Logan family. These elements then, will be the focus of discussion in this chapter, and are deemed to be the mechanisms through which Taylor works through the problem of balancing rage and triumph.

An analysis of Taylor's fictional family saga, one which we are reminded is informed by factual accounts, also serves to highlight through the literary vehicle, similar experiences of other African-American families of the era, and hopefully serves as a possible archetype for those contemporary African-American families for whom the dream still has not been realized.

IN GOD WE TRUST

In his comprehensive look at the institution of slavery during the seventeenth and eighteenth centuries, Peter Kolchin points out that plantation owners, often taking an ironically paternalistic point of view towards the people they had subjugated, included as part of their domain the responsibility of converting "their" people to Christianity. The conversion process however, was not to be as neatly accomplished as white plantation owners would have liked. Indeed, it was not until well into the eighteenth century that the influence of Christianity was to make itself felt in a widespread manner.[3] But, even then the slaves focused more upon the Christian message as a means for eventual spiritual release from bondage, rather than as a doctrine to help them become more "acculturated" to slave life. Christian belief was also combined with vestiges of African religions, which incorporated magic and folklore alien to Christian practices. Thus, side by side with faith in God and the teachings of Christ existed belief in stories, for example, that people might actually escape bondage by "flying" through the air.[4] This state, while it suggests the Christian ideal of the final rapture, is probably more directly related to the magical practices found in African religions.[5] In incorporating prior beliefs and practices within the framework of an imposed religious doctrine, African slaves were no different from the earlier Europeans who had subsumed aspects of pagan religions into Christian religious practice. This speaks to the human desire to *balance* that which is known and comfortable with the unknown and potentially volatile. The degree to which one is able to do this will determine the level of success with which one can co-exist with one's spiritual, physical, and social environment, in other words, one's ability to maintain an *implied* balance. In the case of the African slaves, the incorporation of liberating conceptions was absolutely essential for spiritual and emotional survival. It formed a way of internally and secretly regulating a system of existence (in the form of slavery) which defied self regulation. While for most under slavery, *balance* in the truest sense was an impossibility (indeed, the master-slave relationship is predicated upon *imbalance*), still this did not preclude the innate human yearning for this state. The struggle for balance in an environment which sought to maintain imbalance would characterize the condition of African-Americans in the century which followed.

Noticeable in Taylor's work is the strong ability of the Logan family to incorporate spiritual belief and practice into daily living, without sacrificing a certain necessary awareness of the worldly environment. The Logan family embraces a non-charismatic form of Christianity, generally devoid of the more energetic physical manifestations of faith. Their spirituality is demonstrated through the quality of their actions in everyday life as well as through interactions with others, an approach totally consistent with that of the New Testament. The family avoids being totally subsumed within a religious framework which might prevent them from coming to terms with a generally irreligious world view. The Logans are totally at ease with their spirituality; it is neither overlooked during their progress through the outside world, or over-emphasized in a self-alienating fashion. Thus, in this regard, the Logans achieve equilibrium.

The need for balance is a necessity and also a dilemma that will always pose a challenge and unique responsibility for Christians. In a recent Readers Opinion article within the Christian publication *Alliance Life: A Journal of Christian Life and Missions*," Jared F. Gerig has stated the following:

> Divine sovereignty must be balanced by human responsibility. The theological bias of many Christians centers around the overemphasis on one or the other of these biblical truths. The "whole counsel of God" demands that we give equal time to both, even though human wisdom has never probed the depths of either separately, or more so of both together. Our human inability to reconcile these great absolutes often causes us to intellectually and theologically ignore or annul one or the other.[6]

Often, rationalization is called for; a circumstance which can be quite disorienting and even upsetting for those attempting to regulate their lives through Christian principles. In *Roll of Thunder, Hear My Cry*, Cassie tells her father of the confrontation she has had with the contemptuous Lillie Jean, daughter of a racist white storekeeper:

> When I had explained the whole . . . business to Papa, he said slowly, "You know the Bible says you're s'pose to forgive these things."
> "Yessir," I agreed, waiting.
> "S'pose to turn the other cheek."
> "Yessir."
> Papa rubbed his moustache and looked up at the trees standing

like sentinels on the edge of the hollow, listening." But the way I see it, the Bible didn't mean for you to be no fool. Now one day, maybe I can forgive John Andersen for what he done to these trees, but I ain't gonna forget it. I figure forgiving is not letting something nag at you—rotting you out. Now if I hadn't done what I done, then I couldn't't've forgiven myself, and that's the truth of it."[7]

David Logan works out the problem in the presence of his daughter, fully cognizant of her impressionable nature and the fact that anything he says or does will leave a lasting effect upon her psyche. He is a man of pride who is not pride-filled. He attempts to follow biblical principles in thought and action. He does not wish to leave a legacy of hatred behind him for his children and also his oppressors; on the other hand, he will not allow his children to be humiliated. Logan however, acknowledges his own humanity and also the reality that in order to survive and survive successfully, he must find a way to balance the situation without contradicting biblical practices—a constant struggle for all believers.

David Logan's decision making process does not go unwitnessed. The text tells us that the very trees seem to quietly await his response. They provide a divine setting for this moment. After a brief pause, Mr. Logan renders his decision of reconciliation rather than vengeful action, acknowledging that absolute forgiveness, while eminently desirable and required by Christian principle, is often in human terms, a goal to be honestly worked towards rather than one which can in every case be assumed and immediately attained. Forgiveness in effect, involves *process*, an active state of becoming or growth (in some instances a faster or slower process, as the case may be) culminating in an eventual product. Realistically, forgiveness is not always possible on demand, though it remains an expectation.

The concept of nature bearing witness to momentous events is established in the previous *Song of the Trees*, in which David Logan's forest is threatened by his avaricious neighbors. As the Logan children play unknowingly amongst the trees, Mr. Andersen and his men plot, and begin to carry out their plan to cut down the Logan trees and sell them for profit, taking advantage of the fact that David Logan is away from home, working in another city. For Taylor, land and spirituality are inextricably bound with one another.

> On the ground lay countless trees. Trees that had once been such strong, tall things. So strong that I could fling my arms partially around one of them and feel safe and secure. So tall and leafy green that their boughs had formed a forest temple.[8]

The image of a temple formed by the trees is a powerful one. The forest is to be revered, not for its own sake but for its presence as a representation of the work of the creative Deity. A legacy of time is established; time which has stood witness to many things. Taylor goes on to say of the forest:

> And old.
> So old that Indians had once built fires at their feet and had sung happy songs of happy days. So old, they had hidden fleeing black men in the night and listened to their sad tales of a foreign land.
> In the cold of winter when the ground lay frozen, they had sung their frosty ballads of years gone by. Or on a muggy, sweat-drenched day, their leaves had rippled softly, lazily, like restless green fingers strumming at a guitar, echoing their epic tales.
> But now they would sing no more. They lay forever silent upon the ground.[9]

The inheritance of the Logan land is the major means through which the family is able to maintain its economic independence, thus curiously connecting spiritual matters with those of the world, in a way ironically similar to the statement "In God We Trust," which frames our coins. This appears to be a secularization of the most extreme form; and it is, if taken (pardon the expression), "at face value." How then can it be justified, or balanced? The answer I believe, for David Logan, lies in the fact that he believes that all things including the land which his family has been fortunate enough to own, come through the will of God, and as long as the origins of his ownership of this legacy are not forgotten, and the land is correctly worked, cared for, and utilized, the Logan family does not live in violation of their spiritual beliefs.

Living up to, or within ones beliefs, *totally*, is not always possible as we have pointed out. Sometimes belief codes are also violated through youthful ignorance or purposely put aside. Again, this is part of the human condition and representative of "balancing" of another type. In *Let the Circle Be Unbroken*, Cassie, Taylor's principal spokesperson in the Logan chronicles, covets Son-Boy's emerald-blue marble while in Sunday school, but feels no guilt about memorizing the Bible verse "Thou shalt not covet thy neighbor's house or anything that is thy neighbor's."[10] She plots to get that marble with incredible calculation and adolescent mindlessness. This ironic act is both indicative of her "innocence" (in not sensing a dichotomy between the memorizing of the verse and covetous desire) and simultaneously, what many would deem typical adolescent self-centeredness. But Cassie's subconscious balancing of what she has been *taught* with what she *wants*, represents the covetous side of human nature, and as such is separate and apart from the type of compromise required for "safe" living in the Mississippi of the 1930s.

Overshadowing the same story however, is the aura of fear and anxiety brought on by the incident of T. J. Avery, a sad soul of a young man who takes up with the disreputable Simms brothers. They are the sons of Charlie Simms who is also father to the Christ-like Jeremy and to Cassie's nemesis, the unbearable Lillie Jean. T. J. has been enticed into participating in a scheme to steal a gun. The two Simms brothers accompany him, but are surprised by the owner and his wife. One of the Simms brothers (in a mask) hits and kills Mr. Barnett with the flat of an ax. The two boys later claim it was T. J. Avery who committed the assault.

A lynching is only averted when David Logan and his trusted hired hand Mr. Morrison, purposefully set fire to the Logan land to provide a distraction. The Logan family is outraged at the injustice of T. J.'s situation; everyone knows who is responsible for the killing. David Logan, through his actions has taken the initiative to do what he can for T. J.—at the expense of risking his own land. However, even he realizes that there is only so much one can do before ones own safety and the safety of ones family is jeopardized. Even burning his own land does not stop the wheels of injustice from grinding out their inevitable verdict on T. J. Avery. Mrs. Logan, David's mother and the children's wise grandmother, realizes this as well. Her utterance and response: " 'Lord, Lord,' and [she] absently continued to stir the collards,"[11] is not indicative of an over preoccupation with cooking and a lack of interest in T. J.'s predicament. Rather, this response is an affirmation of the inevitability of T. J.'s situation, the belief that God does everything for a reason, and the acceptance of man's (and woman's) basic inability to understand His ways and also the villainy of human beings.

This same acceptance is indicative in Cassie's frustrated response to her parent's telling her that T. J.'s situation is almost hopeless.

> Still, though I knew they [Mama and Papa] believed what they told us, I couldn't help but wish that a miracle would happen and T. J. would go free. After all, the Bible was always talking about miracles. I figured that if Daniel could get out of the lion's den alive and Jonah could come up unharmed from the belly of a whale, then surely ole T. J. could get out of going to prison.[12]

Cassie's thoughts are framed within the context of youthful ignorance. As such, she fails to perceive a basic biblical truism, one that hints of a knowledge beyond what man can fathom.

> The spiritual man makes judgments about all things, but he himself is not subject to any man's judgment:
> "For who has known the mind of the Lord
> that he may instruct him?"[13]

A final powerful manifestation of "balancing" within the spiritual framework may be seen in the presentation of Taylor's most recent two books *The Road to Memphis* and *Mississippi Bridge*, both published in 1990. Here, the author takes the situation out of the hands of her characters and attempts to balance the scales in a larger, more overt fashion. Yet, the results are anything but "heavy-handed." The elements of vindication are skillfully interwoven in a starkly realistic manner. Though both books were published during the same year, according to the indications in the notes to *Mississippi Bridge*, *The Road to Memphis* was officially issued before *Mississippi Bridge*. If *The Road to Memphis* is Taylor's angriest book to date, *Mississippi Bridge* is her most actively retaliatory. The plot line in the former novel is unrelenting in the magnitude of the injustices she lays bare for her readers. The resolution in *Mississippi Bridge* seems designed as a horrible (and yet frighteningly justified) commentary on mankind's inhumanity to man. A cycle is initiated in *The Road to Memphis*, where the Logan children anxiously await the return of their brother Stacey from Jackson where he works in a box factory. When Stacey does arrive it is in a marvelous new car, a self-bestowed present bought out of frustration. After all of the passengers in Jackson had boarded the bus, the only seats left were those in the front; seats reserved for whites only. Given the choice of either standing during the entire bus ride or getting off of the bus, Stacey leaves in anger and then decides to solve his situation by buying a used car, something he has wanted to do for a long time.

This incident initiates a shiver of foreboding in the sunny, late fall afternoon. The shiver soon turns to a terrifying chill when a young friend of the Logan children, Harris is chased and hunted by three young white brothers as a prank, attended by a reluctant but silently participating cousin, Jeremy Simms, the young man who has befriended the Logan family throughout the earlier books of the series. This terrible "prank" in which a hunter becomes the hunted, results not only in emotional trauma for Harris, but a permanent, debilitating injury from which we are led to believe, he will not recover.

Taylor continues to add injuries to insults, which accumulate at times with almost unbearable rapidity but yet, her writing avoids the pitfall of appearing contrived or clichéd. Another friend of the Logan children, Moe is forced into a no-win confrontation with the same three young white youths who persecuted Harris earlier. Driven beyond endurance when one of them knocks the cap off of his head, Moe strikes out with a tire iron, seriously injuring all three. This incident causes Moe to have to flee town, aided by Cassie and Stacey, and in a strange paradox, Jeremy Simms, who hides Moe under a tarpaulin in his wagon. En route to Memphis, Cassie is denied the use of a ladies room at a gas station, and in a crushing and demoralizing blow, kicked by the gas station owner. Later, at a hospital, the children's friend Clarence is denied crucial medical care at a white hospital—and subsequently dies.

In so establishing an escalating hierarchy of insult, injury, and injustice, Taylor leads the audience toward a conclusion that something devastating beyond the individual novel must take place to "balance" the scales. That something involves divine intervention, the calling in of a power which has the ability to make a pronouncement and take action upon what has gone before, and what must come after. The pronouncement, and subsequent action comes in the form of the sequel *Mississippi Bridge*. Though Taylor chooses to set this novel approximately ten years earlier during the 1930s, at a time when the Logan children are in their youth, this chronological "interruption" complicates, but does not destroy the major premise. The reader is left with the feeling that spiritually, Taylor intended us to surmise that God seeks his own time and is present in every age as a mediating force. Time then, is not to be exclusively measured by chronological events, cause and effect, but rather by the overall condition of mankind. His imperfect nature was ordained before his imperfect actions were committed; therefore, divine responses are not necessarily "in tune" with individual acts.

On a day of a driving rainstorm, Jeremy Simms witnesses the humiliation of a black customer in the Wallace store, who is denied the right to try on a hat. He observes this incident and almost immediately after, the double standard treatment of a white woman, Miz Hattie, who comes into the store requesting the same, and is granted her request. Miz Hattie is a product of her environment. She would probably consider herself a God-fearing woman who has a healthy respect for the existing system of white superiority, but feels uncomfortable when its inequities are practiced before her. Yet, she is not above delivering a few insensitive statements of her own. In an acute irony, she makes fun of her driver, an elderly black man whose name is Uncle Moses, an action which can be taken as not only a "jest" at the expense of someone doing his best to "lead" Miz Hattie into town, but on another level, a spiritual insult to the biblical leader Moses (referred to as a "servant" in the Bible), whose task it was to lead the Israelites amidst adversity:

> "Well child, when Mr. McElroy was alive, we used to drive down all the time, but since he passed I just rather take the bus. I can't drive that car myself—my nerves are too bad—and Uncle Moses can't half see." She laughed. "As far as I would trust him to drive is from the house to this store and back. Believe me, it's a lot safer to take the bus."[14]

Outside the store, a group of people wait for that bus. Cassie Logan's grandmother is among them. Cassie innocently tries to direct Big Ma to a seat in the front and is shocked when she is told that these seats are reserved for whites only. Later, in a final outrage, all blacks are ordered off the bus when a white family with many children arrive on the scene. One young black man, Josias who had been previously humiliated inside the store, is physically thrown off the bus with his belongings when he dares to beg the driver to allow him to ride the bus, because he knows he has a job waiting for him in the next town.

On the way over the bridge out of town, the bus careens off of the bridge, sending everyone on board to their death. *Mississippi Bridge* is Taylor's most explicit portrayal of the rendering of divine justice. This is Old Testament law at work; a unique commentary on an accumulation of evils displayed throughout the saga of this family, but most vividly expressed in *The Road to Memphis*.

Yet, despite the chilling finality of this bus ride, we are offered hope. Taylor does not wish to leave us with the unredeeming message of revenge as the only conclusion to injustice. She reminds us that there is more to the story. For it is Josias, the wronged young black man who was forcibly removed from the bus, who is the first to go down into the cold waters of the Rosa Lee and try and save the passengers, though to no avail. Josias is linked spiritually with the Josias mentioned in the King James Version of the Bible (in other versions, "Josiah"), a very young king who sought to correct the evils of his forefathers by reinstating correct Judaic practice in worship of the Lord.

It is Taylor's Josias who unknowingly forecasts the bus accident, when he jokingly refers to Noah and his building of the ark, an act which biblically preceded human destruction—destruction that is, with the exception of a select few.

> He [Josias] seen me [Jeremy] and he smiled that wide-toothed grin of his. "Wet 'nough for ya?" he asked, stepping onto the porch. I asserted it was and he laughed. "Keep it up 'round here and we gonna hafta start building ourselves an ark, just like ole Noah!"[15]

When the devastating accident takes place, some in the reading audience will feel that Josias has every right to walk away from the bus passengers without attempting to aid them. After all, he has been wronged if not by each one of them personally, by the system collectively, which allows them to occupy the front seats on the bus or all of the seats on the bus. However, Taylor lets her audience know that there are other considerations of a higher order at work here. This is a story only in part about God's divine justice on those who have wronged others. The second level of the narration involves New Testament belief and man's ability, and indeed obligation to forgive, despite repressive and oppressive circumstances. Earlier, Josias has been forced to lie about going out of town to take a job because he is intimidated by Jeremy's father and friends who threateningly insist that no "nigger".

could possibly have a job when white men are out of work. And yet, Josias does not hesitate to risk his own life to go into the cold waters on, as it turns out, a fruitless mission to rescue those who have presented themselves as so undeserving. This is a Josias who has a higher mission to fulfill, one that he does without hesitation because it is his duty to do so. When asked by the horror stricken Jeremy why he thinks this terrible thing has come to pass, Josias replies:

> "Ain't for me t' know. Can't go questionin' the ways of the Lord. Onliest thing I know is that the good book, it say the Lord He work in mighty mysterious ways."[16]

Josias has fulfilled his unquestioning obligation to help those in need, thereby fulfilling his part of his personal covenant with God. In the end, he signifies not just the ordinary man who has been sorely served by white society, but all black men who suffer and yet, refuse to become victims of their suffering. The Bible says of Josias in 2 Kings 22:2:

> And he did *that which was* right in the sight of the Lord, and walked in all the way of David his father, and turned not aside to the right hand or to the left.[17]

And later:

> And like unto him was there no king before him, that turned to the Lord with all his heart, and with all his soul and with all his might, according to all the law of Moses; neither after him arose there *any* like him.[18]

Despite the fact that it is Jeremy who witnesses all events in this story, and that the narrative is told from his point of view, it is neither Jeremy, nor the Logan children who are the heroic figures. Josias emerges as a quiet, unsung hero, but one who, despite ill treatment and the potential if not inevitable loss of the job which he had waiting for him, can ironically be at peace with his actions.

Jeremy, on the other hand is in turmoil. His relatively passive role has cost him dearly. He is inert, unable to initiate, but rather merely to respond. This is in fact the state in which Jeremy Simms finds himself during most of the Taylor chronicle. After Josias sends him to ring the church bell and alert the townspeople about the tragedy, Jeremy verbalizes his inability to comprehend what he has witnessed:

> I run straight up to the church, straight up to the belfry and I rung
> that bell, rung that bell as hard as I could, and all the while I was
> crying 'cause I couldn't understand nothing about the day, about
> how come Miz Hattie and Grace-Anne was on that bus, and
> Josias, and Stacey's and them's grandmama and Rudine and her
> mama wasn't. Mysterious ways, Josias done said. Well, if the
> Lord was punishing, how come Grace-Anne and Miz Hattie?
> They ain't hurt nobody.[19]

Jeremy Simms' fate is to forever witness, internalize the wrongs
committed against blacks, and be an outcast among his own people
who accuse him of being "a nigger lover." He lacks the intellect to look
beyond the situation and conceptualize the larger issue. Culpability by
association eludes him; the punishing nature of collective guilt seems
too harsh a judgment for him. Yet, the reader comes to know, as does
indeed Josias, that the child Grace-Anne and her mother Miz Hattie are
participants in a larger social system. Upon being removed from the
water, Miz Hattie still wears the hat which she was able to try on and
buy while others were previously denied the same right. Taylor suggests that the injustices in this Mississippi of the 1930s are so overwhelming that no white person there can ever claim total innocence.
Perhaps the time shift between *The Road to Memphis* and *Mississippi
Bridge* serves also to underscore the inevitability of oppression and
response across the ages. The overall conception of Taylor's chronicle
may be seen however, as part of an elaborate Biblical commentary on
the nature of anger, human response and divine judgment. Through a
series of incidents within all of the stories, and the tragedy of *Mississippi Bridge* in particular, Taylor attempts to balance rage and injustice
with a deep sense of spirituality. While this may be seen to be the primary determinant in her stories, it is not only through spirituality that
Taylor attempts to balance the scales. Imposed social/political and economic factors consistently challenge the participants in her "factions"
but through Taylor's artistry and also her family's actual resilience,
become mechanisms through which the Logan family both copes and
triumphs.

COERCION AND CONTAINMENT:
WARY SHIPMATES IN A LEAKING VESSEL

When the Great Depression of October 1929 gripped the country, it imposed an almost unbearable burden upon the entire American populace. But for the black citizen, the Depression brought with it additional possibilities and often realities of white anger. Since Reconstruction, whites had wrestled uneasily and unsuccessfully with the black presence; at once, they deemed it essential to maintaining the economic viability of the southern income and simultaneously, wished the backbone of their economy to become invisible. The black "presence" could be tolerated in the most menial of jobs as long as most whites had one. Once the Depression struck, putting millions out of work, the oppressed, previously objects of ridicule and derision, became easy scapegoats for frustration and almost incongruously, targets of a dangerous envy.

A black man who achieved any manifestation of material success at all was best advised to not discuss or show his good fortune too freely amongst the white populace. In Neil R. McMillen's study *Dark Journey: Black Mississippians in the Age of Jim Crow*, the author states the following:

> In rural areas, prudent blacks did not smoke cigars in white company, wear dress clothes on weekdays, drive large or expensive cars, or otherwise carry an air of prosperity. Indeed, any deviation from the Sambo style could result in trouble. "There was a day when the average Negro householder was afraid to paint his house and fix up his premises because of the attitude of some white man," conservative Piney Woods schoolmaster Laurence Jones observed. Not every sign of black ambition was perceived as "being uppity," Jones added, "but the fact remains that a Negro did not always feel as safe in a neat cottage with attractive surroundings as he did in a tumbling-down shack."[20]

The "trouble" referred to by McMillen could come in a variety of horrific designs, the most terrifying of which was lynching, that extreme form of social control reserved almost entirely for blacks under countless circumstances. W. Fitzhugh Brundage has commented that the concept of lynching was not just the ultimate outrage resulting from white supremacist hatred, but rather was also the backlash emanating from complicated local conditions inherent within a given environment:

> Distinctive conditions, not some rigid notion of white supremacy, explain why mobs executed more blacks in central Georgia than

in the low country of South Carolina. Specific circumstances explain why mob violence persisted in Mississippi years after the practice had declined in North Carolina. That lynch mobs victimized blacks most often was an outgrowth of much more than just some sweeping white desire to "keep blacks in their place." At work stirring up mobs and focusing their wrath upon certain targets were social, economic, and political concerns rooted in the dramatic changes that the South underwent between 1865 and 1930. [21]

In 1929, the Annual Report of the National Association for the Advancement of Colored People stated optimistically a drop in the number of reported lynchings from one hundred in 1909 to twelve in 1929.[22] By 1933 however, during the height of the Depression, the Annual for that year reported:

> Lynchings during 1933 numbered almost three times those which occurred in 1932 when there were only ten. In 1933 there were twenty-eight known lynchings.[23]

Two of the lynchings occurred in Mississippi. Many explanations for the general increase are possible. Among them may be the fact that heightened anger and general discontent about the economic situation caused whites to seek out easily available targets upon which to vent their anger. Blacks readily fit this most unfortunate category.

Given the dark possibilities which awaited those who "stepped over the line," possibilities afforded a wink and a nod by the Mississippi legal justice system, black revolt over unbearable conditions was greatly delayed, postponed—but, as history has proven, not cancelled.

With a wary eye cast upon the present, but yet another turned towards the past, the Logan family adults in Taylor's series train their young people to live life as fully as possible, be a doormat for none, and to function and exist as the discerning protagonists of a cautionary tale: be prudent in what you say or do and never, never forget where you live. Taylor convincingly shares vignettes with her readers about her father which speak of his inner strength, fortitude and caring.

> He was warm and steadfast, a man whose principles would not bend, and he had within him a rare strength that sustained not only my sister and me and all the family but all those who sought his advice and leaned upon his wisdom.[24]

An existence in oppressive surroundings has the potential of becoming overwhelming, however. It is not surprising therefore, given his deep love and concern for his family's welfare, that Wilbert Taylor abruptly pulled up stakes and moved to Toledo, Ohio when Mildred was three months old as the result of his involvement in a racial incident which definitively convinced him of the precarious position of blacks in Mississippi.[25]

Taylor's Logan family chooses to stay in Mississippi, maintaining the balance of a prudent, yet uncompromising life style, a circumstance which is crucial to Taylor's integrity as a person, an African-American and as a writer:

> As I grew, and the writers of books and their publishers grew, I noticed a brave attempt to portray Black people with a white sense of dignity and pride. But even those books disturbed me, for the Black people shown were still subservient. Most often the Black characters were housekeepers and, though a source of love and strength to the white child whose story it was, they remained one-dimensional because the view of them was a white one. Books about Black families by white writers also left me feeling empty, not because a white person had attempted to write about a Black family, but because the writer had not, in my opinion, captured the warmth or love of the Black world and had failed to understand the principles upon which Black parents brought up their children and taught them survival.[26]

Surviving in the Mississippi of the 1930s, socially as well as politically, required delicate negotiations, mediations which are not always heeded by all of the participants in Taylor's chronicle. Those who fail to do so often meet harsh ends. Such circumstances come not as a result of didactic interference on the part of the author, but rather as the realistic, often tragic outcome of behaviors out of temperament with the times. Taylor's perception of the socio-political reasons for the condition of blacks during the 1930s is directly related to the racist viewpoint which she feels was held by most (though not all) white Mississippians of the time. This view was fueled by fear and, Taylor suggests, the underlying suspicion that given an opportunity, the black man might be able to best his white counterpart in the game of "one-upmanship." The white need to *accentuate* differences may well be based then, Taylor suggests, upon the frightening realization that there may be few differences among individuals at all beneath the surface of skin color. This is a revelation with which Jeremy Simms, in his supposed naiveté, was born. Jeremy undergoes no transformation of viewpoint in Taylor's stories; yet, he avoids the designation of a stereotyped character, a foil for his racist relatives, or even a true breath of fresh air for the Logan children. In fact, Jeremy is viewed by the Logan family with a careful eye, not because of what he individually represents, but because of what he has the power, in his innocence, to bring down upon the heads of any black child or adult whom he befriends. Jeremy's presence is a gadfly in the racist inheritance of his family; much of the time they seem angrily perplexed as to from where, Jeremy with his ability to accept people as people regardless of color, has come. After it is discovered that Jeremy has played a role in hiding Moe on his truck, "Mr. Simms emitted a horrendous scream and slammed his enormous fist into Jeremy's jaw."[27] Then later,

> Charlie Simms set a dead-eyed stare on his son. Then, in a voice as chill as well ice water and as low and quiet as a winter still night, he said, "Get outa my sight. Don't know where ya got it from, but you always was a nigger lover. Never thought I'd live to see the day I said that 'bout my own flesh, 'bout my own son, but it's so. I done tried to beat it outa you since you was knee-high, done tried to make ya see right, but you jus' had t' be 'round niggers. Well, ya might's well be one your ownself, 'cause you ain't white no more. Not after what you gone and done 'gainst your own kin. Your own blood, boy!"[28]

The Logan children stand witness to this public disownment of a son, a chilling phenomenon. After such an experience, Taylor suggests, only death can resolve the situation for this young man. Indeed, he goes off to enlist in the army soon after and, we are told, never returns.

An explanation of basic racial hatred for the injustices which occur however, is too simplistic a reason for Taylor to offer her readers, given the perceptive nature of the author. As Brundage suggests, there is more to the story. The onset of the Depression itself, fueled the situation faced by all of Taylor's characters. All must make a sometimes unconscious decision regarding whether or not to give in to despair, or struggle to cope and move on. Jeremy's family, and so many others like them, choose to given in, though ironically, they do not see it this way. They are, in effect, impotent in their abilities to move ahead both emotionally and physically. Paralyzed then, by their hatred, their static position in the social spectrum, and inner insecurities which reach deep into the recesses of their own souls as well as historically back to the subjugation of blacks whom whites fear might someday rise up in revolt, Taylor's white Mississippi populace, for the most part, are unable to balance their own rage. While they ironically see blacks as collectively representative of the uncivilized natural man incapable of learning, rationalizing, and projecting himself forward towards positive action, the Logans stand before white society as an entire family living the reality that many whites cannot attain. Therefore, when in *Mississippi Bridge*, Josias walks proudly into John Wallace's store, a kind of theater for the absurd, and announces the fact that he has a job waiting for him in a nearby town, he inadvertently and quite naively, (some might think foolishly) places oil on ever smoldering flames. Put another way, such a pronouncement is the equivalent of screaming fire in a crowded movie theatre; it simply cannot be ignored.

Such is also the case when the elderly Tom Bee in *The Friendship* insists upon calling John Wallace by his first name, flaunting the deferential treatment historically given to whites. Again, the action is set in a store, in which are featured a crowd of witnesses, a situation which cannot be ignored by John Wallace. Tom Bee steadily insists upon the familiarity of calling John Wallace, "John," such a little thing . . . this thing about a name,"[29] Cassie Logan muses. But even at her young age, and in her innocence, Cassie *senses* though she does not understand, the ancient power of "naming." In European folklore, the one who knew your name was also the one who would consequently have power to bend you to his will. An imbalance in naming designation then, brought with it the potential of a power relationship; one that did not favor the black individual. One cannot help think here of the old tale of Rumpelstiltskin. It will be remembered that he remained in the "driver's seat," until that is, the Miller's daughter discovered his name. This ruined the relationship and shifted the power base in her favor. Having "lost the edge," he stamped his foot and literally lost his position by falling through the floor, never to be seen again. The whites in Taylor's Mississippi dreamed the nightmare of becoming invisible in a state in which they were outnumbered. McMillen points out that blacks outnumbered whites in every Mississippi census from 1840 through 1930, with the situation changing beginning about 1940.[30] The power of "title" was one way that whites could psychologically maintain dominance over a numerically larger group of people; a group who, if they ever should decide to revolt—had a good chance of being successful..Cassie Logan views the issue of name designation as though it were one indicative of a childish sign of respect, one which she has been previously told, means nothing to her grandmother, who because of her advanced age, is referred to by white people as "auntie." These same individuals however, would never consider addressing the grandmother as "Mrs. Logan," the ultimate sign of respect. Yet, Cassie notes her older brother Stacey's words:

> Papa say white folks set an awful store 'bout names and such. He say they get awful riled 'bout them names too. Say they can do some terrible things when they get riled. Say anybody call a white man straight out by his name just lookin' for trouble.[31]

Tom Bee agrees with Mr. Logan's assessment, but refuses to accede, dismissing the practice of calling white people "mister," as "foolishness." He feels this unjustified deference keenly since he has in years past, on two occasions, saved John Wallace's life. In return for these two incidents of embarrassing intimacy, John Wallace told Tom Bee that he considered him a friend and that consequently, Tom could always call him by his "Christian" name. But, for no explained reason other than perhaps perversity and old age, Tom has for years avoided the privilege of calling John Wallace "John." It is only recently, much to Wallace's anger that Bee now insists upon doing this.

The Logan children then, have two models before them. One, consisting of the words of an elderly man who now refuses to bow to none, and secondly, the advice of a loving father, whose discernment and strength are unifying forces for his family. The children sense that if they are being warned against such familiarity—even though they cannot immediately comprehend why, there must be a reason. The fate which befalls Tom Bee, shocking though it is, is perhaps one which comes as not so much of a surprise to the horrified children. It is also perhaps a fate which Tom Bee never expected or, on the other hand, perhaps it is. After Bee's repeated utterings of what John Wallace calls his "Christian name," Wallace shoots Tom Bee in the leg, giving a horribly ironic twist to the concept of "friendship." Tom Bee is ultimately a tragic-heroic figure, dragging himself away down the street still shrieking "John! John!," as the story closes.

TURBULENT SEAS; COSTLY VOYAGE:
THE POLITICS OF INEQUITABILITY

The disfranchisement of African-Americans so thoroughly accomplished by the 1930s came about partly as the result of custom emanating from the days of slavery, but also through legal maneuvers which in many instances held within their wording a "gentleman's agreement" as to exactly whom would be affected by their enactment. Following Reconstruction, some gains had been made politically by African-Americans, including the initial registration of freedmen under military authority in 1867.[32] However, by the establishment of the Second Mississippi constitution of 1890, the elements of exclusion had been all but codified. The Raymond *Gazette* was to report in 1890 that the convention was called "for the purpose of divising means by which negroes can be constitutionally eliminated from politics."[33] When the convention was over, the new constitution included among other components a poll tax and, a clause of "understanding." This last was the vehicle through which legalized discrimination would take place, for the individual who would vote would first have to prove to the satisfaction of the examiners that he could read or be able to understand any part of the state constitution. Such a requirement opened wide the door for allowing illiterate whites to gain access to the ballot, while effectively keeping blacks away. Denial of access to voting therefore, was the key to disfranchisement. Once "legalized," denial of the right to vote would be an issue upon which whites would confront blacks through threats, intimidation, and physical punishment.

When sixty-four-year-old Mrs. Lee Annie announces to Big Ma and Cassie in *Let the Circle Be Unbroken*, "I thinks I wants to vote,"[34] she sets into action a chain of events which have resounding effects for the Logan family. Once over the shock of the announcement, the Logans make a decision to help Mrs. Annie study for the literacy test. This she does amidst warnings from her friends and relatives who tell her stories of dire happenings to other blacks who tried—and failed. Mrs. Annie is unmoved. Helping her prepare for the test becomes a family project, though each member is aware of the possible dangers ahead for Mrs. Annie and for anyone who is suspected of having assisted her. The Logans take a strong stand against injustice in making this decision. They choose to fight the system by coaching her in its rules. In the end, Mrs. Annie successfully learns all of the two hundred eighty-five sections of the Constitution and its fifteen amendments.

The Logan family goes a step further in showing their support for Mrs. Annie's project. David Logan allows his wife and Cassie to be with her during her appearance for the registration process. (He does not attend due to the fact that the male presence will be perceived as being more threatening.) Such a decision represents a major sacrifice and great potential personal risk. In making this choice, David Logan balances personal ideals and the opportunity to fight the system *through* the system in whatever small way he and his family can, against possible personal dangers. Nonetheless, his decision is not made irrespective of precautions for his family's safety; he realizes that were he to go to the courthouse, his presence alone might be enough to turn this encounter with "justice" into an immediate tragedy for all concerned. Therefore, David "bends" and refrains from being present during the event. The Logan children have grown through the experience of learning about the Constitution. They have gained first hand knowledge of the document that reflects the law of the state and the sections and articles designed to protect rights—and also the knowledge that in selective cases, those rights are not granted.

When in the end Mrs. Annie is denied the right to register, and tragically she and her relatives are thrown off the land which they tenant farm, the lesson becomes a harsh one indeed. But Mrs. Annie has successfully challenged the system, and the reader having the advantage of historical hindsight, acknowledges the fact that such brave acts laid the groundwork for successful voter registrations decades later. It is an acute historical irony that in devoting their attention to customizing racial hatred, and misusing the power vested in codified law, white Mississippians ultimately protected nothing and left themselves open to useless expenditures of energy, antagonism, and violence which might better have been used in uniting to re-build a shattered economy.

When Mrs. Logan accompanies Mrs. Annie to the courthouse, she is confronted by Harlan Granger, a plantation owner of some 6,000 acres, an unscrupulous man of considerable power and influence. Seeing her standing there, he attempts to intimidate her:

> ". . . Thought I'd stopped you from messing in what you got no business."
> "You stopped me from teaching at Great Faith."
> "Look like I ain't stopped nothing else."[35]

Granger is referring to an incident in an earlier book, *Roll of Thunder, Hear My Cry* in which Mrs. Logan loses her job as a result of Granger's interference. Infuriated at Mrs. Logan's role in helping organize a boycott of the Wallace store which is located on Granger's property, he arranges to have her fired. The immediate reason given is that Mrs. Logan has "destroyed" school property, referring to some school books in which she pasted over the ownership record which listed the race of black students as "nigra." More importantly, Granger witnesses a lesson taught on the subject of slavery, a topic which does not appear in the assigned history book. These "infractions" remind him that Mrs. Logan is a person to be reckoned with, a clear threat. He attempts to eliminate that threat by taking her job, but as he discovers, the Logans are not to be so easily dispatched. Different from most families, they maintain their quiet strength, make their protests against the system in reserved, yet meaningful ways and force a certain respect from the white people around them. Large plantation owners like Granger, wielded tremendous power. Granger is on the school board, involved with voter registration and seemingly, just about every activity that involves money and power.

When one considers Granger's position on the one hand, and the Logan's on the other, it is clear that despite the fact that they are well thought of in the community, politically, there is no comparison to be made. The scale is tipped severely in Mr. Granger's favor. However, this is in terms of things which can be measured. What really infuriates Mr. Granger is the *weight of the intangible*, weight *not* tipped in his favor. He is aware of the dignity and the strength possessed by this family who, because they own the land they live on, are owned by no one. The Logan elders possess an "elegance of approach," a self-confidence of which no white person has been able to rob them. Even when forced to accede to the formalities of "address," and to all of the elements attendant to racist policy and custom, somehow the Logans still maintain their dignity and their stature in the black community. Further, greatly against their individual wills, whites are forced to admire them as well, and in so doing, to some extent, they *fear* the Logan elders. Harlan Granger is aware of this and longs to bring them to their knees, but thus far, he has not been successful. He is aware that he has been successful in hurting the family peripherally in causing Mrs. Logan to lose her job, but he is also cognizant of the fact that he has not truly robbed the family of their total well being. He longs to see

Mrs. Logan run down the street begging him to change his mind, as he has the sadistic pleasure of seeing Mrs. Ellis do after he has ordered her and her family off his land:

> "Lordy, no, Mr. Granger!" Mrs. Ellis cried, running into the street to plead with him. "Mr. Granger, no!" Mr. Granger saw her coming, but disdainfully he gassed the Packard and sped away, leaving Mrs. Ellis desperately yelling after him. And I [Cassie] knew even as she stood there crying out for mercy, Harlan Granger would not change his mind. He had gotten what he wanted.[36]

But he suspects that he will never have the "pleasure" of seeing Mrs. Logan do so. While the Logan family pays a high price for each challenge delivered, they manage to do so—and survive.

Mr. Wade Jamison, an attorney, offers the Logan family political support of a kind which is invaluable. Mr. Jamison stands alone as the only white adult who extends to the Logan family unconditional trust and assistance. Yet, ironically, he is not a friend. The barriers between true white and black friendship preclude such a relationship, Taylor lets us know. But, what Mr. Jamison has to offer is by far more valuable. His profession and position in the community make him a formidable adversary among whites. He also possesses tremendous common sense as well. Furthermore, since he is white, he has available to him the resources of the white community; he knows the people, how they think, how they will react. He can weigh the law on the one side, and human emotions and response on the other. He is a most valuable contact, *and* he is loyal.

> There was a mutual respect and, because the years had proven it justified, a mutual trust; but there was no socialization other than the amenities. Neither he nor we would have felt comfortable in such a situation, for the unwritten laws of the society frowned upon such fraternization, and the trust and respect were valued and needed more than the socializing.[37]

It is Mr. Jamison who defends T. J. Avery against murder charges in *Let the Circle Be Unbroken*, though to no avail. It is also Mr. Jamison who in *Roll of Thunder, Hear My Cry*, the earlier book, states his intention to David Logan to keep mention of the Logan children's assistance given to T. J. out of T. J.'s trial, and is later successful in doing so. And Mr. Jamison shares the deadly Logan secret, that in fact it was David

Logan who purposely started the fire to distract the Night Riders and keep them from lynching T. J. for the assault on Jim Lee Barnett, the storekeeper. Through his actions, Mr. Jamison plays a not insignificant role in the lives of the Logans as an ally who can offer an equilibrium during times which are dangerously unbalanced.

MAINTAINING THE INHERITANCE; PRESERVING THE LEGACY

At the heart of the Logan family's relative economic and social well being is their inheritance of land, 400 acres purchased by Big Ma's father between 1887 and 1918. This legacy allows the Logan adults to function as true breadwinners, rather than as tenants subject to the cruel turns and twists of fate so often delivered by plantation owners. Black ownership of land in the 1930s was an uncommon occurrence. In 1930 only 26.3% of land owners were black; while in 1940, this percentage had fallen to 24.1%.[38] Tenant farming kept the black populace in servitude, forever at the mercy of the white landowner. The black individual who owned his land, had a leverage that was denied others. It is not surprising then, that such ownership could place a family at risk—if it were not managed correctly. Too much flaunting of ones good fortune, particularly during Depression times, could result in tragedy. The Logan family realizes the difficulties inherent in their situation. Their children are trained to be prudent and to exercise good judgement, to not shun risks but to take them on when the fight is worth fighting and when it is in the best interest of the family as a unit.

Having the land as an economic base allows the family to be relatively self-sufficient, even though David Logan is still forced to go north for a portion of each year to work so that he can bring in extra income.

> I [Cassie] asked him once why he had to go away, why the land was so important. He took my hand and said in his quiet way: "Look out there, Cassie girl. All that belongs to you. You ain't never had to live on nobody's place but your own and long as I live and the family survives, you'll never have to. That's important."[39]

Though David Logan must go north each year to earn extra income, he successfully manages to keep his family together, avoiding the divisive effects that such actions had upon many families. In so doing, he is able to support his family, even though there is often very little left over for "extras." In his study *Fatherhood in America: A History*, Griswold states:

> Constrained by Jim Crow laws and racist attitudes, most black fathers found it extraordinarily difficult to support their families. In the South, the crop-lien system and the collapse of Reconstruction left black men economically marginalized and politically vulnerable, and these liabilities often dashed their hopes of supporting their families by farming.[40]

Despite the fact that they, like many others, must struggle, owning land allows the Logans to consider the possibilities of upward mobility, something that others can only dream about. The Logan parents do not lecture their young excessively about the rewards of education, but when the children appear confused, angry, or victimized by the designs of white society around them, the Logan elders communicate to them the need for self-control, forbearance, and pride—and the future possibilities that education could afford them. In particular, Mrs. Logan's interest in education, models for the children the benefits that may attend the educated. Big Ma further reinforces the necessity of schooling as a legitimate way of making ones mark on society. As she tells Little Man:

> "One day you'll have a plenty of clothes and maybe even a car of yo' own to ride 'round in, so don't you pay no mind to them ignorant white folks. You jus' keep on studyin' and get yo'self a good education and you'll be all right."[41]

Owning land also affords one the self confidence which allows one to take what may be perceived as necessary risks. The risks may be formidable. The Logans consider joining union efforts to organize tenant farmers and sharecroppers. As the organizers explain it, David Logan's endorsement will encourage others to join, since he is so highly thought of. Mr. Logan weighs his responsibility against the inherent dangers involved; he makes no commitment. Shortly thereafter, the agent who had approached him is found beaten up in his car. David Logan's decision to not become actively involved ultimately, turns out to be a good one. Later, another man involved in union business is found burned to death. In the final scene of *Let the Circle Be*

Unbroken, union efforts are broken amidst gunfire and terror in the town center. David Logan's discernment in this matter saves his family from a possibly tragic involvement in this movement. This dilemma however, decided after a considered weighing of possible risks and probable outcomes, is one which could not have been seriously considered were it not for the reality of ownership of the land.

CONCLUSION

At an American Library Association Conference session in June, 1987 Mildred Taylor inscribed the following in my copy of *Let the Circle Be Unbroken*:

> The Logans are very special to me and I hope they will be special to you too.

In writing her chronicle of the Logan family, Mildred Taylor has indeed communicated a rare and special family relationship which has not lost its significance with time. Rather, she has offered her readers clear and compelling vignettes of a family whose spirituality, love, unity, and vision enable them to survive successfully despite overwhelming social, political and economic obstacles. Contemporary readers are offered the real possibilities of what *can be* despite the efforts of others to construct a negative and repressive reality. Taylor offers her audience the motivating gift of a message of positive action, one which while acknowledging history and memory, seeks to inspire a people with the ability to progress beyond a condition of oppression.

NOTES

1. Mildred Taylor, "Newbery Award Acceptance," *The Horn Book Magazine* (August 1977), 402.
2. Audrey Edwards and Dr. Craig K. Polite, *Children of the Dream: The Psychology of Black Success* (New York: Anchor Books, 1992), 4.
3. Peter Kolchin, *American Slavery: 1619–1877* (New York: Hill and Wang, 1993), 143.
4. See Virginia Hamilton's "The People Could Fly," and accompanying notes in *The People Could Fly: American Black Folktales* (New York: Alfred A. Knopf, 1985).
5. See Virginia Hamilton's "Jack and the Devil," and "Better Wait Till

Martin Comes," in her collection *The People Could Fly; American Black Folktales* as examples of stories which incorporate Christian spiritual beliefs within folklore tradition.

6. Jared F. Gerig, "Readers Opinion—The Biblical Balance," *Alliance Life: A Journal of Christian Life and Missions* 128, no. 17 (September 29, 1993): 13.
7. Mildred D. Taylor, *Roll of Thunder, Hear My Cry* (New York: The Dial Press, 1976), 174.
8. Mildred D. Taylor, *Song of the Trees* (New York: Dial Press, 1975), 31.
9. Ibid., 31–34.
10. Mildred D. Taylor, *Let the Circle Be Unbroken* (New York: The Dial Press, 1981), 17.
11. Ibid., 30.
12. Ibid., 41.
13. 1 Cor. 2: 15–16 NIV (New International Version).
14. Mildred D. Taylor, *Mississippi Bridge* (New York: Dial Books for Young Readers, 1990), 12–13.
15. Ibid., 16.
16. Ibid., 60.
17. 2 Kings 22:2.
18. Ibid., verse 25.
19. Taylor, *Mississippi Bridge*, 61.
20. Neil R. McMillen, *Dark Journey: Black Mississippians in the Age of Jim Crow* (Urbana and Chicago, IL: University of Illinois Press, 1989), 24–25.
21. F. Fitzhugh Brundage, *Lynching in the New South: Georgia and Virginia, 1880–1930* (Urbana and Chicago, IL: University of Illinois Press, 1993), 13.
22. *Twentieth Annual Report of the National Association for the Advancement of Colored People for 1929: A Summary of Work and an Accounting* (New York: National Association for the Advancement of Colored People, 1930), 4.
23. *Twenty-fourth Annual Report of the National Association for the Advancement of Colored People for 1933: A Summary of Work and an Accounting* (New York: National Association for the Advancement of Colored People, 1934), 20.
24. Mildred D. Taylor, *Roll of Thunder, Hear My Cry*, Author's Note.
25. Phyllis J. Fogelman, "Mildred D. Taylor," *The Horn Book Magazine* (August 1977): 411.
26. Mildred D. Taylor, "Newbery Award Acceptance," *The Horn Book Magazine* (August 1977): 405.
27. Mildred Taylor, *The Road to Memphis* (New York: Dial Books, 1990), 274.

28. Ibid., 275.
29. Mildred Taylor, *The Friendship* (New York: Dial Books for Young Readers, 1987), 29.
30. McMillen, 152–153.
31. Taylor, *The Friendship*, 37.
32. McMillen, 35.
33. McMillen, 40.
34. Taylor, *Let the Circle Be Unbroken*, 193.
35. Ibid., 358.
36. Ibid., 379.
37. Ibid., 37.
38. McMillen, 113.
39. Taylor, *Roll of Thunder, Hear My Cry*, 7.
40. Robert L. Griswold, *Fatherhood in America: A History* (New York: Basic Books, 1993), 52.
41. Taylor, *Roll of Thunder, Hear My Cry*, 45.

REFERENCES

Brundage, F. Fitzhugh. *Lynching in the New South: Georgia and Virginia, 1880–1930*. Urbana and Chicago, IL: University of Illinois Press, 1993.

Edwards, Audrey and Dr. Craig K. Polite. In *Children of the Dream: The Psychology of Black Success*. New York: Anchor Books, 1992.

Fogelman, Phyllis J. "Mildred D. Taylor," *The Horn Book Magazine*. (August 1977): 411–414.

Gerig, Jared F. "Readers Opinion—The Biblical Balance," *Alliance Life: A Journal of Christian Life and Missions*, 128, no. 17 (September 29, 1993): 13–15.

Griswold, Robert L. *Fatherhood in America: A History*. New York: Basic Books, 1993.

Hamilton, Virginia. *The People Could Fly: American Black Folktales*. New York: Alfred A. Knopf, 1985.

The Holy Bible, 2 Kings 22:2 and 25.

Kolchin, Peter. *American Slavery: 1619–1877*. New York: Hill and Wang, 1993.

McMillen, Neil R. *Dark Journey: Black Mississippians in the Age of Jim Crow*. Urbana and Chicago, IL: University of Illinois Press, 1989.

The NIV Study Bible, 1 Cor. 2:15.

Taylor, Mildred. *The Friendship*. New York: Dial Books for Young Readers, 1987.

_____. *The Gold Cadillac*. New York: Dial Books for Young Readers, 1987.

_____. *Let the Circle Be Unbroken*. New York: The Dial Press, 1981.

_____. *Mississippi Bridge*. New York: Dial Books for Young Readers, 1990.

_____. "Newbery Award Acceptance," *The Horn Book Magazine* (August 1977): 401–409.

_____. *The Road to Memphis*. New York: Dial Books, 1990.

_____. *Roll of Thunder, Hear My Cry*. New York: The Dial Press, 1976.

_____. *Song of the Trees*. New York: Dial Press, 1975.

Twentieth Annual Report of the National Association for the Advancement of Colored People for 1929: A Summary of Work and an Accounting. New York: National Association for the Advancement of Colored People, 1930.

Twenty-fourth Annual Report of the National Association for the Advancement of Colored People for 1933: A Summary of Work and an Accounting. New York: National Association for the Advancement of Colored People, 1934.

TEN

Children of the Diaspora: Four Novels About the African-Caribbean Journey

Lucille H. Gregory

> *". . . who block off de paff an*
> *rip up de*
> *kite when it pitch down? where de pond*
> *water gone wid de frogs*
> *an de mornin*
> *stars? who fence in de gully wid cat*
> *wire? who put up dat sign*
> *sayin*
> *KEEP OUT"*
>
> Edward Kamau Brathwaite[1]

The journey which began when Africans were wrenched from their native lands and forced into "New World" slavery has been presented to children primarily from the perspective of African-Americans in the United States. The experience of the Caribbean diaspora is often misunderstood or trivialized. For Caribbean African-Americans traveling the journey toward adulthood, the path is often cluttered with multiple obstacles which appear to threaten their very survival as human beings. These young people, who are confused by the same baffling problems as other children traveling toward adulthood, find their particular experiences largely ignored by institutions such as the popular press and the children's book publishing industry. These institutions, for the most part, find it appropriate to represent the whole of the adolescent experience as a monocultural one, thereby invalidating the richness and the variety of experiences of millions of young adults.

The paucity of books for children of color in the Caribbean diaspora is compounded by the "relative neglect of criticism on the subject by the general reading public."[2] According to Samuel Pickering, it is through the reading and writing of criticism that "hard thinking" is produced, and it is that thinking which can potentially reveal the connections between society and history.

The virtual absence of social recognition, may lead the black Caribbean child to believe that he/she is alone in the universe, and render him or her unable to relate or identify with the rest of humanity. Why else, the child might reason, would the Caribbean African-American experience be ignored? If Caribbean children are only allowed to peer into the lives of others without any sense of participation, the reading experience offers them only a "zero image of themselves." Carolyn Gerald captures the impact of such "invisibility."

> . . . we cannot judge ourselves unless we see a continuity of ourselves in other people and in things and concepts. We question our very right to exist without other existences like our own. . . . The black child growing into adulthood . . . seeing white protagonists constantly before him projecting the whole gamut of human experience, is . . . persuaded that he too must be white, or (what is more likely), he experiences manhood by proxy and someone else's image. He sees . . . a zero image of himself.[3]

Since Gerald penned these lines in the 1960s, a few Caribbean-related novels have been published. Those discussed below, Rosa Guy's *The Friends* (1973), Joyce Hansen's *Home Boy* (1982), Jamaica Kincaid's *Annie John* (1983), and Jacqueline Roy's *Soul Daddy* (1990), join the Caribbean world to life in the United States and Great Britain, and all are what can be termed "problem novels." The importance of these works lies in their inclusion of the Caribbean black experience, in their insights into adolescence, and preadolescence, and in their depictions of the child in a problem-afflicted world.

Children of the Caribbean diaspora can find positive image-making experiences in these books, novels written by black women with a Caribbean connection.

THE FRIENDS

The "problem novel," as the name implies, is typically about the myriad of emotional, physical, and psychological conflicts that children deal with on the road toward emotional maturity.

In Rosa Guy's novel *The Friends*, Phyllisia, a fourteen-year-old girl recently arrived in Harlem (New York) from the West Indies (possibly Trinidad), discovers that fitting into the alien world of hostile adults and unsympathetic peers is a daunting task. Mocked at school for her "funny" accent and her love of learning, Phyllisia recognizes soon enough that the students do not like her.

> "They mocked my West Indian accent, called me names—'monkey' was one of the nicer ones."[4]

The children are alluding to notions of climbing trees and eating coconuts, which they fantasize is what everyone does on an island and which they also associate with animalistic behavior. These associations do not spring out of nothingness. They are the images reinforced by white society and in this instance verbalized by their white teacher, Miss Lass. She addresses the class:

> "Let me tell *you* what people—decent people—call you," she screeched . . .[5]

emphasizing the difference between the school children and decent people. She delineates just what makes the difference in this way:

> "The way most of you come to school I wouldn't think that any of you had any mothers. You come to school like pigs! Greasy, oily, filthy pigs! The filth in your streets shows what kind of people you are!"[6]

Miss Lass also contributes to the animosity the other black children feel towards Phyllisia by playing them against one another. As a recent arrival in the school, Phyllisia has not yet learned the rules by which Miss Lass is operating. She comes from an environment where learning is considered important and children have been encouraged to demonstrate their knowledge. The children here, however, resent her contributions in class and it is little wonder, given the words of Miss Lass.

> "If some of you would follow Phyllisia's example and study your books, then perhaps the intelligence rate in this room might zoom up to zero."[7]

Phyllisia is dismayed by the apparent lack of good judgement from someone who should have known better. She feels the tension in the room and suddenly realizes that this was exactly what the teacher intended:

> "I knew it suddenly . . . Miss Lass was afraid! . . . She was afraid and she was using me to keep the hatred of the children away from her. I was the natural choice because I was a stranger and I was proud."[8]

Later, when Phyllisia refuses to be a pawn in the game any longer, Miss Lass turns on her:

> "Come, my brainy one," she taunted. "What has become of your intelligence? Has it gone to the bottom of your feet? Or are you sitting on it?"[9]

The image that Miss Lass has of her black students acts as an unbreachable barrier between her and the students.

The concept of psychological warfare is not unusual in the "problem novel." Writing about this literary subgenre, Sheila Egoff notes that the "problem novel" includes such recognizable points as the following:

1. Problem novels have to do with externals, with how things look rather than how they are.

2. The protagonist is laden with grievances and anxieties that grow out of some form of alienation from the adult world, to which he or she is usually hostile.[10]

In Phyllisia's story, the child's teacher as well as her father are at the center of her anxious and alienated existence. How, then, can she turn to them for guidance when faced with a serious problem that requires adult intervention?

When Phyllisia's best friend, Edith, is left alone to care for her younger siblings after the death of her mother and the disappearance of her father, Phyllisia is trapped between loyalty toward Edith and the adults who may misunderstand the dimensions of Edith's problem. Phyllisia's father, Calvin, has bought into the white model of success and is determined to make it work for him. Wanting only the best for his two daughters, he works day and night to bring them economic opportunity. This was his reason for bringing them out of the Island to New York City. Here he could own a business and be important. He does not want to be a "fool," which is what losers are in his view. He sees Edith as part of that world which he wants no part of, as a "ragamuffin" similar to the impoverished people on the Island and the customers in his restaurant—the very ones who enable him to make a living. Holding himself above them allows him to feel in control of a world he *can't* control.

Calvin is trapped by his parental need to ensure the safety of his daughters and tries to accomplish this by restricting their freedom and not allowing them to associate with any but the "upwardly bound." They are under orders to leave the apartment only when going to school. New York is not a safe place for young, unsupervised girls and he is not available to supervise them because of his work. This is his survival strategy, but because it is misguided, it proves ineffective. His inflexibility only serves to alienate his daughters and renders him unworthy of Phyllisia's trust.

The cost of the silence Edith and Phyllisia have pledged regarding Edith's new "parental" role is high. Edith's baby sister dies, and the horror of what appears to have been an unnecessary death forces Phyllisia to view her life in a more mature manner. She sees the connection between her father's misguided, although well-intentioned discipline, and her own actions. She tells him:

> "[Edith's] baby sister died because of you . . . because I was afraid of you . . . you hated her and called her a ragamuffin. You chased her out of the house and it didn't matter that she was decent and good, because she was poor . . . I let you chase her out of the house . . . because I really believed that I was better than she . . . I didn't know then that you made your living off poor people." [11]

Refusing to accept any blame, Calvin attempts to justify his actions:

> "What I got to do with some girl dying because I run my house
> the way I want to run it? . . . I ain't make no living off poor peo-
> ple. I make a living off people! . . . I'm a hard-working man. I
> work night and day to take care of you . . . I can't do that and
> have to worry about where you are and what you doing night and
> day. New York is a big city, too big to have my worries walking
> around it."[12]

Phyllisia's new mature stance, however, forces Calvin to look at
her finally as an individual, apart from himself. This in turn allows him
to envision an alternative to his inflexibility. He is still confused, but
becomes a more accepting person, recognizing that he doesn't have to
have all the answers but that he does need to listen. His confusion can
be understood if we consider the contrast between the Western definition of parental responsibility and the West Indian model, as Heidi
Safia Mirza notes in *Young, Female, and Black*:

> The strong emphasis on discipline and doing "what was
> expected of you" in the West Indian household was acknowl-
> edged . . . to be part of [West Indian] culture and ultimately prac-
> ticed by parents in [the child's] best interests.[13]

The approach to discipline in the West Indies can vary between a
passive role and a disciplinarian one and is determined by the ability to
rely "heavily on trust between parent and child. . . ."[14]

In Phyllisia's case, the trust factor is non-existent, thereby forcing her father into a disciplinarian role. This sense of discipline is not
just arbitrary manipulation, however, but tied into the West Indian parent's understanding of the racism the family must face and combat. As
Mirza explains:

> Despite their disciplinarian values . . . parents were aware of the
> political issues involved.[15]

Failure of an author to portray the delicate strands of the web of
issues that surround Calvin would lead to a misunderstanding of the
complexity of his experience and the effect it has upon his children.
Instead of presenting a stereotypical portrayal of a "problem parent,"
Rosa Guy has revealed the deeper layers of character that lead to
understanding.

Guy's interpretation of the particularities of African-American experience enables us to develop a deeper understanding of a black character's special dilemmas. She follows the broad outlines of the generic "problem novel," and also emphasizes features that are characteristic of black novels for adolescents. Martha F. Booth in "Black Ghetto Life Portrayal in Novels for the Adolescent" has taken note of the following content areas in such fiction:

1. Home and family relationships.

2. Peer relationships.

3. The attitudes toward the authority of police, welfare and whites.

4. The attitudes toward the educational system.[16]

Guy has elaborated upon issues of home and education, while novelist Joyce Hansen in *Home Boy* highlights police and educational systems.

HOME BOY

Home Boy, by Joyce Hansen, presents the adolescent "problem" from a different view. The story evolves around Marcus, a fifteen-year-old from St. Cruz, Virgin Islands, and his difficulty in adjusting to the foreign world of the South Bronx. Through the use of flashbacks, Hansen weaves the story of his experience over a two year time span.

Marcus encounters a world that does not recognize him as a valuable individual. In the eyes of his high school classmates, he is merely "Jamaica" because of his accent and because that "seemed to be the only island Americans knew about."[17]

Worse than his unrecognizable identity among his friends is the absolute condescension with which he is treated at school by his teachers. In one instance he is given a mathematics placement test to determine his achievement level, and Marcus thinks:

> He wanted to tell her that shopkeepers never cheated him because he knew how to add, subtract and multiply. He used to tell his friends in school, "What else you need to know? You go' fill your head with some algebra and you ain't know when the people giving you the wrong change."[18]

This pragmatic approach to mathematics was beyond his teacher's comprehension. She views him as impoverished and in need of remediation:

> Marcus watched the teacher's expression as she marked the test. .
> . . She twisted her lips, shook her head, sighed, and walked over
> to him looking as if someone had just died. She spoke very softly
> in funereal tones, "Marcus, you have to be put in a special mathe-
> matics class. Did you study math at all where you came from?"[19]

It takes him a few moments to absorb the impact of her insult and then he pierces the bubble of her assumption with an exaggerated, mocking response:

> "No Miss. Me ain't study nutting a'tall. Me just play in de trees
> all day."[20]

He gets placed in a remedial class where he is only required to add and subtract in single digits. When he attempts to explain that he really can do this activity, the teacher's response is:

> "Young man, I wish I had a dollar for every student in this school
> who thinks he knows so much."[21]

The school is in Harlem, the students referred to are black, and the remedial class is where students who come from the Islands are immediately dumped. The educational institution is treating him as inferior because of his race and sees no reason to provide him with the encouragement and support that would enable him to succeed in school and eventually the "real world." Hansen places his reality in perspective by offering us contrasting images of how he is viewed, how he sees his reality, and how his extended family comes together to offer an alternative to the dead end existence the white establishment would reserve for him.

This is not the first time Marcus's resistance to education has gotten him into trouble. Back home when he was bored by the passivity of "book learning," when he would much rather be at the beach with his friends, he is called to task by his Aunty:

> "You have to do something about the fire in you, Marcus. Else
> you go' spend the rest of your life sorry about something. . . .
> You going to the States after cane season . . . you promised . . . to
> go to the Professor. . . . Don't burn in your own fire."[22]

Marcus does not understand what his Aunty has internalized, that if he is going to escape the life of menial labor in the sugar cane fields, he can only do so through education. But the fire that burns in Marcus is the desire to find meaning in his existence as a black man. The books that teach him do not make any sense to him, and even his Professor will not quench his thirst for understanding. He asks his Cruzan professor (who is teaching him from an outdated textbook which is apparently what this U.S. territory receives from the Department of Education) to explain his history:

> "How do we come to be in this place? Is we Africans? Is we black?" [23]

In his response the Professor shows his own lack of understanding about the diaspora and the brotherhood of all people of color. He lacks what the African-American writer/critic Julian Mayfield calls the "collective memory," the

> unshakable knowledge of who we are, . . . [people] who have leaped out of the loins of all those slaves and semi-slaves, who survived so that we might survive. [24]

The Professor tells Marcus:

> "You are no African. You are a St. Cruzan. It was just a couple of Africans they brought here and they quickly mixed up with the Indians so you couldn't really tell who was who. And anyway, the few Africans they bring to the islands was like kings and chiefs and princes. They sent the riffraff Africans to the United States."

> "But what about being black?" [insists Marcus.]

> "Marcus I just tell you, we St. Cruzans." [25]

Eventually Marcus' "fire" leads him to a Rastafarian, a member of a religious sect whose members believe in Africa, especially Ethiopia, as the promised land. This man, James, enlightens Marcus by explaining to him that he is indeed of African heritage and a member of an oppressed people.

When Marcus arrives in the states, questions concerning the heritage of his people are burning within him. The answers he finds are the ones that clip wings and crush hope. Instead of freedom and opportunity, he finds oppression and is robbed of the promise of a new life by the racist society he encounters. Feeling trapped, he fights to defend the one thing he has left—his pride, and eventually stabs a classmate who has unmercifully tormented him since his arrival.

Marcus learns from his father that this kind of pride—foolish pride—is not the good kind to have. Good pride is the one that recognizes and seeks to protect the treasures found in family ties that bind with love. How different Marcus' experience would have been if he had found an accepting society that allowed him to blossom in his new surroundings. James Berry writes about this feeling in his poem "Black Kid in a New Place":

> I stretch myself, I see
> I'm like a migrant bird
> who will not return from here.
>
> I shake out colorful wings.
> I set up a palmtree bluesky
> here, where winter mists were.[26]

ANNIE JOHN

"For a short while during the year I was ten, I thought only people I did not know died."[27] With the opening line in *Annie John*, Jamaica Kincaid embarks on a revelatory journey of the adolescent female experience. Her heroine, Annie John, a young woman coming of age in Antigua, negotiates the rugged terrain from oneness to separateness with a candor and honesty that embraces all who share in the reading experience. "The feelings are . . . autobiographical" says Kincaid in an interview and it is her ability to describe those feelings that makes this novel one that almost any young adult can connect with.[28]

Annie is the beloved, intellectually precocious child of her father and her mother, Annie Senior. Her experience with the father, while not insignificant, is mostly peripheral. Annie's emotional bond is with the mother, and it is from that bond that she must disentangle herself if she is to emerge whole and independent. The gentle unhurriedness with which Annie Senior raises her child and her constant availability conveys an image of the paradise world of which Annie feels herself to be a part. At the same time, Kincaid confronts the stereotypes of black mothers—stereotypes that imply inferior parenting styles.

In an essay that Annie has written at school, she describes some of the child-loved intimacies with her mother:

> When I was a small child, my mother and I used to go down to Rat Island on Sundays right after church, so that I could bathe in the sea. . . . My mother was a superior swimmer. . . . I on the other hand could not swim at all. . . . The only way I could go into the water was if I was on my mother's back, my arms clasped tightly around her neck, and she would then swim around not too far from shore.[29]

Annie does not fool herself and in turn, is not fooled by others. Her instincts are not dulled by sugar coated fairy tale explanations about life and its complexities. This is not to say that she has all the answers. She does have the necessary questions that arise in adolescence about life.

Annie encounters her beginning menses for example, with an acceptance of this significant rite of passage that is untainted by any feelings of shame or inhibition . . .

> . . . at recess, among the tombstones, I of course had to exhibit and demonstrate. None of the others were menstruating yet. I wished instead that one of the other girls were in my place and that I were just sitting there in amazement. How nice they all were, though, rallying to my side, offering shoulders on which to lean, laps in which to rest my weary, aching head, and kisses that really did soothe.[30]

Similarly, the conflicting emotions that Annie experiences in witnessing her transformation into a young "lady" are of universal application; some aspects of this transformation she finds difficult to cope with.

> . . . I stood naked in front of a mirror and looked at myself from head to toe. . . . I tried to push my unruly hair down against my head so that it would lie flat, but as soon as I let it go it bounced up again . . . and then I got a good look at my nose. It had suddenly spread across my face, almost blotting out my cheeks, taking up my whole face, so that if I didn't know I was me standing there, I would have wondered about that strange girl—and to think that only so recently my nose had been a small thing, the size of a rosebud.[31]

In reading *Annie John*, young adults are exposed to beautiful writing, strong women as viable role models, and an uncompromised view of the transition between childhood and adulthood. Moreover, by experiencing this adventure through the lens of the Caribbean diaspora, young adults in the U.S. are learning to see themselves through the eyes of the "other"—the political and social outsider.

In a chapter about Columbus ("Columbus in Chains"), Annie recounts her experience after writing "The Great Man can no longer get up and go" under a picture of Christopher Columbus in shackles in one of her school books. Miss Edward, her English teacher, is shocked.

> . . . Her whole face was on fire. Her eyes were bulging out of her head. I was sure that any minute they would land at my feet and roll away. . . .[32]

Miss Edward cannot accept what she perceives to be a "defaming" of a great hero.

Kincaid has created a book that fills in some of the conventional gaps in social history. And she makes this offering to all children, whether of the Caribbean or mainstream America.

SOUL DADDY

Unlike the other novels discussed, Jacqueline Roy's *Soul Daddy* is set in a predominantly white London suburb. The experience of fifteen-year-old Hannah Curren, the protagonist, is very similar to those of the protagonists in the other stories, thus illustrating a certain commonality of experience. Hannah is the product of a bi-racial union: a white mother and a black father. Her mostly peaceful life with her twin sister, Rosie, and their mother, Isabel, is abruptly thrust into turmoil upon the arrival of Joe, her long absent father, and a half sister, Nicola. The greatest challenge for all three girls, however, is to come to terms with their black identity.

For Hannah and Rosie, who grew up with their white mother in a white neighborhood, thinking of themselves as black is a new experience. They were raised with that knowledge, a quiet fact of their background. Their curly hair and golden skin did not stand out as noticeably as Nicola's skin and hair type or Joe's black skin.

All the girls are at an age when how one looks to others is of great importance. Hannah asks Rosie:

> "Rosie, how do you think we look to other people?"
> "Character-wise or physically?"
> "Physically, of course."[33]

Being different is not what a teenager seeking validation from an adult world desires. This is especially the case if that difference is considered "less than" desirable. Nicola faces a major adjustment as she is now forced to deal with a white world which does not approve of her color. As the daughter of a famous Reggae singer, Nicola has been sheltered from rejection, and the world she has inhabited has been primarily black. She had been comfortable with her image. Now things are different:

> She could never belong here. It was an alien world that she could never fit into. . . . She and Joe and Hannah and Rosie seemed to be the only black faces on the streets. Sometimes when she went to the shops or to the park, she felt heads turn to look at her. . . . They seemed puzzled by her presence. She represented something new, a disruption to their neatly organized, safe world. Nicola gained a sense of herself as an infiltrator.[34]

The girls grapple with a myriad of troubles connected with their search for understanding their "new" identities, and eventually they begin to look to their father and his music for clues and direction. The lyrics of one of his songs provides a sense of direction for the girls, as well as an understanding of Joe's own worldview:

> They will always judge you
> By the color of your skin—
> Remember you're a black boy
> Or we can never win.
> Don't turn your back
> On your brothers who are poor,
> If we don't stand together
> Black pride won't be no more.
> Black pride won't be no more.[35]

CONCLUSION

African-American young adult literature is to some extent a battleground where a revolution can and should be fought. The four books

I have reviewed constitute part of that revolution—the kind that bring new ideas and different perspectives to the wounding racism that permeates many of our institutions. When I read books like these, I come away with a fresh sense of hope, for I recognize that we have not heard it all, or tried everything or seen everything there is to see.

This revolution must become part of us on all fronts. Perhaps Rosario Morales has captured it best in her poem, "My Revolution":

> My revolution is not cut from a pattern, *I* designed it.
>
> It's homemade and handcrafted . . .
>
> My revolution is comfortable
> > hard-wearing
> > > long-lasting
> > > > versatile!
>
> My revolution fits,
> So well
> Sometimes
> I don't know I'm wearing it. . . .[36]

NOTES

1. Edward Kamau Brathwaite, "Noom," as quoted in "Clips (Poems)" *Callaloo* 11, no. 1 (1988): 61–63.
2. Samuel Pickering, Jr., "The Function of Criticism in Children's Literature," *Children's Literature in Education*, 13, no. 1 (Spring, 1982): 16.
3. Carolyn Gerald, "The Black Writer and His Role," in *The Black Aesthetic*, ed. A. Gayle (Garden City, NY: Anchor Press, 1972), 352.
4. Rosa Guy, *The Friends* (New York: Henry Holt and Company, 1973), 5.
5. Ibid., 46.
6. Ibid.
7. Ibid., 8.
8. Ibid.
9. Ibid., 46.
10. Sheila Egoff, "The Problem Novel," chap. in *Only Connect: Readings in Children's Literature*, 2nd ed., ed. Sheila Egoff, G. F. Stubbs, L. F. Ashley (New York: Oxford University Press, 1980), 357.
11. Guy, 199–200.
12. Ibid., 200–201.
13. Heidi Safia Mirza, *Young, Female, and Black* (London, England: Routledge, 1992), 183.

14. Ibid., 176.
15. Ibid., 178.
16. Martha Booth, "Black Ghetto Life Portrayal in Novels for the Adolescent" (Ph.D. diss., University of Iowa, 1971).
17. Joyce Hansen, *Home Boy* (New York: Clarion, 1982), 1.
18. Ibid., 18.
19. Ibid., 18–19.
20. Ibid., 19.
21. Ibid., 21.
22. Ibid., 151.
23. Ibid., 145.
24. Julian Mayfield, "You Touch My Black Aesthetic and I'll Touch Yours," in *The Black Aesthetic*, ed. A. Gayle (Garden City, NY: Anchor Press, 1972), 26–27.
25. Hansen, 145.
26. James Berry, "Black Kid in a New Place," in *When I Dance*, by James Berry (New York: Harcourt Brace Jovanovich, 1992), 42.
27. Jamaica Kincaid, *Annie John* (New York: A Plume Book, 1986), 3. (Originally published by Farrar, Straus & Giroux, Inc., 1983.)
28. Selwyn R. Cudjoe, ed. *Caribbean Women Writers: Essays From the First International Conference* (Wellesley, MA: Calaloux Publications, 1990), 220.
29. Kincaid, 41–42.
30. Ibid., 52.
31. Ibid., 26–27.
32. Ibid., 81–82.
33. Jacqueline Roy, *Soul Daddy* (San Diego, CA: Harcourt Brace Jovanovich, 1990), 129.
34. Ibid., 48–49.
35. Ibid., 134.
36. Rosario Morales, "My Revolution," in *Puerto Rican Writers at Home in the USA*, ed. Faythe Turner (Seattle, WA: Open Hand Publishing, 1991), 293.

REFERENCES

Berry, James. "Black Kid in a New Place." In *When I Dance*. New York: Harcourt Brace Jovanovich, 1992.

Booth, Martha. "Black Ghetto Life Portrayal in Novels for the Adolescent." Ph.D. diss., University of Iowa, 1971.

Brathwaite, Edward Kamau. "Noom," as quoted in "Clips (Poems)," *Callaloo* 11, no. 1 (1988): 61–63.

Cudjoe, Selwyn R., ed. *Caribbean Women Writers: Essays from the First International Conference.* Wellesley, MA: Calaloux Publications, 1990.

Egoff, Sheila, "The Problem Novel." In *Only Connect: Readings in Children's Literature.* 2nd edition, ed. Sheila Egoff, G. F. Stubbs and L. F. Ashley, 356–369. New York: Oxford University Press, 1980.

Gerald, Carolyn. "The Black Writer and His Role." In *The Black Aesthetic*, ed. A. Gayle, 349–356. Garden City, NY: Anchor Press, 1972.

Guy, Rosa. *The Friends.* New York: Henry Holt and Company, 1973.

Hansen, Joyce. *Home Boy.* New York: Clarion, 1982.

Kincaid, Jamaica. *Annie John.* New York: A Plume Book, 1986. (Originally published by Farrar, Straus & Giroux, Inc., 1983.)

Mayfield, Julian. "You Touch My Black Aesthetic and I'll Touch Yours." In *The Black Aesthetic*, ed. A. Gayle, 23–30. Garden City, NY: Anchor Press, 1972.

Mirza, Heidi Safia. *Young, Female, and Black.* London, England: Routledge, 1992.

Morales, Rosario. "My Revolution." In *Puerto Rican Writers at Home in the USA*, ed. Faythe Turner, 292–294. Seattle, WA: Open Hand Publishing, 1991.

Pickering, Samuel, Jr. "The Function of Criticism in Children's Literature." *Children's Literature in Education* 13, no. 1 (Spring 1982): 13–18.

Roy, Jacqueline. *Soul Daddy.* San Diego, CA: Harcourt Brace Jovanovich, 1990.

Eleven

Virginia Hamilton's Justice Trilogy: Exploring the Frontiers of Consciousness

Millicent Lenz

Virginia Hamilton's *Justice* trilogy, comprised of *Justice and Her Brothers* (1978), *Dustland* (1980), and *The Gathering* (1981), is perhaps her most challenging creation for young readers, exploring as it does the outermost edges of traditional concepts of space and time. The most in-depth critical discussion to date is Janice Hartwick Dressel's "The Legacy of Ralph Ellison in Virginia Hamilton's *Justice* Trilogy," which appeared in 1984, an essay noteworthy for carving out an important niche for Hamilton in mainstream American literary tradition. Both Dressel's article and Kirby Farrell's "Virginia Hamilton's *Sweet Whispers, Brother Rush* and the Case for a Radical Existential Criticism," which brings existential philosophy and feminist theory to bear upon the novel published a year after the last book in the *Justice* trilogy, are evidence that Hamilton's work is drawing long overdue, sustained critical attention.

A number of critics—and indeed Hamilton herself—have linked her achievements as a writer to her recurring theme of "survival" and her creation of "cultural consciousness": Rudine Sims, in *Shadow and Substance: Afro-American Experience in Contemporary Children's Fiction*, has characterized Hamilton's works as "culturally conscious" narratives, reflecting both the uniqueness and the universally human in Afro-American experience from an Afro-American perspective. She also draws a contrast between the culturally conscious books and those she terms works of "social conscience," written by white authors about black characters in an effort to help primarily white readers understand the condition of their fellow humans, and proceeds to identify a third type of book, termed "melting pot" literature, written by both blacks and whites for both black and white children, and intended to show non-white and white as alike except for their skin colors. Teresa Kleibrink Aggen, analyzing the survival themes in six novels, demonstrates Hamilton's belief that barriers of race, culture, and gender threaten human survival, a concept illustrated in *Dustland* both by the unit's interpendency and its dependence upon the survival of other intelligent beings radically unlike human beings of today.[1] At the first Virginia Hamilton Conference (then called the Virginia Hamilton Lectureship on Minority Group Experiences in Children's Literature) at Kent State University in April of 1985, Anita Moss praised Hamilton's "use of space as a metaphor for her characters' inner space, places where miraculous transformations and new possibilities may occur,"[2] a remark which applies well to Hamilton's highly original settings in the *Justice* trilogy. Another of Hamilton's contributions is her concept of "parallel cultures," a term she uses to describe a perspective she prefers to a "narrower view" of America as a land of the majority surrounded by minorities; "parallel peoples" create "a significant literature out of their own unique yet universal qualities."[3] Her vision of the United States, expressed in "A Toiler, A Teller," is one of a "multicultural, polycentric, pluralistic" member of "the world village where we must enter into the bond of learning and understanding together, in community," and she believes strongly in "liberation literature"—books that take readers through the liberating process of "reading about the suffering and tribulation of others," so "our spirits fly free,"[4] enabling us to relate as strong individuals to the unit of society.

Significantly, and perhaps paradoxically, Hamilton declares in "Ah, Sweet Rememory!" (written shortly after the completion of the *Justice* books), that race in the trilogy has "nothing whatever to do with plot and the outcome for the characters"; the children's powers—extrasensory perception, telepathy, telekinesis—far from being "peculiarities" are rather a representation of "a majestic change in the human race" through the unleashing of "new gene information," giving them psychic powers and the ability to visit the future. They time-travel as a unit and "only as a unit are they able to return to the present." Earlier in the essay she speaks of finding a sense of continuity and a "narrative source" for her writing in "the progress of a people across the hope-scape of America," and also notes that "My fictions for young people derive from the progress of Black adults and their children across the American hopescape . . . [against the background of] the dream of freedom tantalizingly out of reach."[5] Her marvelous coining, "hope-scape," suggests the metaphor of the frontier so pervasive in American literature, though Hamilton gives it her own psychological and spiritual twist. As I shall endeavor to show in my analysis of the *Justice* trilogy, the American Myth of the Frontier, the related idea of a special mission (epitomized in the belief in a "manifest destiny"), and faith in "progress," can illuminate Hamilton's narrative and add to the reader's appreciation of the theme of evolution of consciousness towards the state Hamilton terms a "majestic change in the human race." My analysis will draw upon some of the concepts put forward in the aforementioned essays by Dressel and Farrell, a variety of critical writings about the frontier archetype in American literature, and some of the key ideas expressed by current thinkers in the field of consciousness evolution.

First a brief reprise of the main characters and events of the three novels. Justice Douglas, also called Ticy or Tice, is an eleven-year-old of lively sensibilities who initially feels overshadowed by her thirteen-year-old twin brothers, Thomas and Levi, "mirror" twins: "The boys were as identical as two peas in a pod, and . . . as different as night from day. . . . Levi liked books and would read anything he could get his hands on. He loved music and poetry." In contrast, the domineering Thomas bosses the other kids around, though his unpleasantness is off-set by his strong talents in rhythm and drumming. He suffers from "a terrible stutter."[6]

The twins differ markedly in their treatment of Justice, as Marilyn F. Apseloff notes: "Levi is kind and considerate, especially of Justice, but Thomas goes out of his way to confound her, even to attempt bodily harm. Moreover, Thomas is able to control Levi's mind. . . ."[7] This power to control Levi's mind, which Thomas misuses in sometimes sadistic ways, is the most frightening aspect of Thomas's character and sets him into opposition with Justice (whose name reflects her judicious handling of her own psychic gifts). Yet all of the youngsters share the human qualities of " 'Kids,' " the final word of the novel: they love bike-racing, light-hearted games, competition.

All of the Douglas children, and a thirteen-year-old neighbor boy, Dorian Jefferson, possess psychic gifts to greater or lesser degrees.

Thomas is the "Magician" who can cloud minds with marvelous, sometimes terrible illusions, as well as a gifted drummer; Levi is the caring, kind brother, the one who suffers for them all; Dorian is the Healer.

JUSTICE AND HER BROTHERS— "PEOPLE OF THE PARENTHESIS"[8]

The first novel in the trilogy introduces us to the main characters, establishes Justice's strength in the rivalry with Thomas, and prepares the reader for the "unit"—the combined intelligences of the four youngsters—whose time-transcending adventures in a bleak, strange future realm are the material for *Dustland*. The final novel in the trilogy, *The Gathering*, relates how the unit, now established as harbingers of a new kind of human being with extraordinary powers, returns to Dustland to overcome Mal, the evil force that has kept the Dustlanders in thrall.

The first novel explores in detail the process of Justice's growth in awareness of her unusual endowment and her success in coming to terms with her "difference" from others; her growth from adolescence to adulthood is complicated by her recognition that she is the Watcher. Dorian's mother, a "sensitive" or psychic herself, guides Justice to an understanding and acceptance of her dawning gifts. The Watcher first appears to Justice in a dream, entering into her consciousness.[9] But earlier in the novel Justice has had intimations of her psychic nature; she loves "Cottonwoman," the great tree which is alive to her imagination, and speaks to her as a person,[10] and on entering the Jefferson's living room, she shows receptivity to communications from the plants: they "welcomed her . . . they understood her as they did Dorian and his mother."[11] Thus Hamilton prepares the reader for the full blossoming of Justice's psychic powers.

Justice's realization of her gift is tinged with pain: "She knew anguish. She understood the source and destiny of herself, Justice, the Watcher."[12] Late in the novel she reflects at length on the responsibility her mysterious psychic gift entails: "She was set free in a space-time inner universe, at the heart of which was the Watcher of her power." She hears Thomas's voice, questioning, "Who are we?" and she knows the answer, "We four are the first unit. I'm the Watcher." Thomas persists in questioning, "Why us?" and she replies that there must always be a "first." They are the first of a new kind of human being (what scholars of consciousness evolution call the *homo noeticus*, to be defined below):

> Their alteration must have been an accident. The difference in one chromosome was enough to alter a few inherited characteristics. Into existence could come sensory and physical changes, the release of genetic information far beyond the ordinary.
> Sentience. Telepathy. Telekinesis—motion produced without the use of force. And clairvoyance—ability to see objects or actions beyond the natural range. The four of them each had one or more of these capacities. But Justice's power was exotic, giving her the energy to combine these forces.
> *"Our place isn't here*, Justice traced. *Our time isn't now, but in the future, . . .* [and] *The way to the future has to be learned. . . . That will take time."*[13]

Justice and her brothers, together with Dorian, correspond to what psychiatrist Jean Houston has called "the people of the parenthesis"—a transitional kind of human being living in "the era between the old, limited consciousness and the not-yet-quite-born era of Second Genesis."[14] As such, they are harbingers of a new kind of human being, what J. White refers to as *homo noeticus*, the "emerging form of humanity." "Noetics" means the study of consciousness, and this pursuit is one of the primary activities of the new humans; they are characterized by "deepened awareness and self-understanding," a "changed psychology" based on "expression of feeling, not suppression. Their motivation is cooperative and loving, not competitive and aggressive. Their logic is multi-level/integrated/simultaneous, not linear/sequential/either-or. Their sense of identity is embracing-collective, not isolated-individual. Their psychic abilities are used for benevolent and ethical purposes, not harmful and immoral ones."[15]

Human beings, Hamilton implies, are evolving to a new kind of consciousness; we are about to cross a psychological-spiritual frontier the nature of which is only hinted at in the "hopescape" metaphor she has at times employed. What is the connection between the hopescape and the frontier of the American Myth? In what sense may Justice be an American Eve figure, parallel to the American Adam? Janice Hartwick Dressel, in showing how Ralph Ellison's literary legacy is reflected in the *Justice* trilogy, has laid some of the basic groundwork for showing the connections of Hamilton's novels to the large, traditional American mythology.

To recount the main parallels Dressel finds between *Justice* and *The Invisible Man*, there are the thematic concerns: the "journey toward identity, the growth from innocence to experience, and the themes of survival, social responsibility, and basic optimism." Further, there are stylistic parallels in the use of language, folklore, and tradition. Importantly for my purposes, Dressel has explored how Hamilton retains Ellison's motif of "double consciousness," which W.E.B. DuBois called "inherent in being black in America."[16] Dressel defines double consciousness as "the need to assume 'differing identities,'" finally becoming "invisible," but Hamilton "makes the protagonist powerful rather than powerless. Her four adolescent protagonists are each well-developed characters, who can choose to join their separate identities into one powerful entity known as the 'unit.'" Further, Hamilton's characters, unlike the Invisible Man, are not stripped of their identities, not at the mercy of others; the four, united, are in control and can increasingly appreciate their "communal power."[17] I would add that Hamilton's "unit" possesses not just "double consciousness" but entirely new, more highly evolved powers of mind.

Justice's exploration into her identity, a process typical of adolescence, is crucial to the development of the theme of "frontier" consciousness. It incorporates a fundamental mythic or archetypal pattern in American literature—the exploration of the unknown that lies tantalizingly unseen, over the horizon. As David Mogen demonstrates, the pervasive "Dream" of the frontier as the line beyond which one could enjoy freedom from existing social and political restraints shifted in emphasis to a symbolic drama charting a shift in consciousness. Mogen sees how critics, following the lead of D. H. Lawrence's *Studies in Classic American Literature* (among them R.W.B. Lewis in *The American Adam*, Henry Nash Smith in *Virgin Land*, Leslie Fiedler in *Love and Death in the American Novel* and *The Return of the Vanishing American*, Leo Marx in *The Machine in the Garden*), have interpreted the symbolic drama of the American consciousness as (in Lawrence's words) "shifting over from the old psyche to something new."[18] Because Justice is female, however, and the Myth of the Frontier is as Linda Ben-Zvi points out, a patriarchal one, Hamilton's version of the myth takes a different form from the usual one. The frontier myth is, as Ben-Zvi recognizes, "gender related . . . *his* story, since the conquest of the continent has been encoded as a male adventure," and consequently, when "he" is replaced by a "she," the values associated with the male are reinscribed: she becomes "as if" a he. Thus, Ben-Zvi continues, the frontier myth is not only the story of conquest but "also the psychological tale of masculine individuation, separation, and schism."[19] This may indeed be the case in most narratives where "he" is replaced by "she" [Ben-Zvi cites Annette Kolodny, *The Lay of the Land: Metaphor as Experience and History in American Life and Letters* (1975) and the same author's *The Land Before Her: Fantasy and Experience of the American Frontier, 1630–1860* (1984), in support of her statement], but Hamilton's Justice is another case altogether, for her developmental process is anything but a tale of "schism." When asked about her portrayal of female characters in an interview with Marilyn F. Apseloff, Hamilton said "The males in my family were very dominant. . . . The women were not as strong; it was a very traditional household"; she added that she was beginning to see "other ways," and trying to "speak to that, although it's very difficult because I'm always busy at having the females win out."[20] Justice does "win out," despite Thomas's strong resistance to her greater psychic gifts, but she does so without becoming a "female man."

A perfect metaphor for Justice's way of winning can be seen in how she triumphs in the Great Snake Race (significantly, with Levi's help, for it is he who releases her snake when she hesitates to do so). Although Thomas treacherously has allowed her to believe the contest is a "race" involving swiftness, when winning it is actually based upon having the greatest number of snakes, Justice's pregnant snake gives birth at the opportune moment, giving her the victory, much to Thomas's dismay.[21] Thus, it is the natural, inherent female power of fertility that triumphs. Moreover, Justice's psychological development is characteristically feminine, seeking affiliation (as obvious in the "unit" formation); and the "heroic paradigm" Hamilton expresses through Justice corresponds to what Kirby Farrell, speaking of heroic paradigms in general, has called a "generative" one, nurturant, and bestowing meaning,[22] not the destructive (overtly selfish) one of some patriarchal frontier narratives. It should be noted, however, that Farrell's analysis of *Sweet Whispers, Brother Rush* finds certain flaws in Hamilton's heroic paradigm in that book, where "black males meekly perish and women bravely endure until idealized mates appear."[23] A critique of how Justice's process of individuation corresponds to and differs from the female developmental dilemmas described in Nancy Chodorow's *The Reproduction of Mothering: Psychoanalysis and the Sociology of Gender*, and how because of the difficulty of separating from a parent of the same sex girls are disposed to see themselves as less differentiated than boys (hence needing a greater degree of nurturance and attachment, persisting into their adult lives), is matter for another discussion. Here it must suffice to note that Justice's mother and father play a remarkably slight role in her maturation throughout the three novels; Mrs. Jefferson seems a surrogate parent, able to understand Justice's developing psychic power and giving her alternately the protection and the freedom she requires to exercise it wisely.

The symbolic importance of the Quinella Trace, with its weirdness and its consciousness-transforming function, in Justice's evolution of consciousness can hardly be overstated. For Justice, the Trace is a place of horror and fascination; the sight of its snakes arouses in her a sense of the sublime: "she divined the beginning, the primal urge which caused these ordinary snakes from the surrounding land to return again and again to this home of their ancient past. To mate and bear their young." Meditating on the snakes as primal animals, Justice's consciousness spans space and time; she feels the trace of "the long gone and dead." She feels "sudden sympathy: You creatures." And joy: She hugs the ground: [you creatures] "Finding holes and cracks deep down. You stay warm. You live. And never die out."[24] Part of the fascination stems from their apparent timelessness, their seeming immortality, their ability to win out over death. It is true, however, that Justice also fears the Trace and the snakes; in her nightmare early in the book, her jumprope metamorphosizes into a snake and pulls her into the Quinella River.[25] The phallic power symbolized by the serpents both attracts and repels Justice. If she is a budding American Eve figure (a case might be made for such an interpretation), she does not, like the biblical Eve, face the temptation to forbidden knowledge; rather, she must simply learn to acknowledge and exercise wisely the knowledge already inherent in her. (One may be reminded of the main characters of L. Frank Baum's *The Wizard of Oz*, who find they already have the gifts they have looked to the Wizard to provide.)

Dressel has commented on Justices's thought that "trace" means "to follow the lines, or to disappear leaving but a trace of a former existence, to become invisible," as another link to Ellison's *Invisible Man*. Moreover, as she adds, Justice feels a great affinity and compassion for the snake, the lowliest of creatures, always remembering its past, returning again and again to its place of origin, "who finds refuge underground, stays warm, lives, and never dies out. The parallel with the Invisible Man who sheds his skin upon emerging from hibernation is unavoidable."[26] The symbolic action of shedding skin, it goes without saying, also suggests the American Adam (or in this instance Eve) as a new creation, a new beginning for the human race.

DUSTLAND—SURVIVAL IN A HOSTILE FRONTIER

Dustland is arguably the least accessible of the three novels, possibly because of the oppressiveness of its suffocating, wasteland-like atmosphere of "Graylight" or "Nolight," and its scarcely lovable inhabitants, strange beings such as Worlmas (which move around even after they are dead, until they dry up), Slakers (with their outlandish physical characteristics), and Miacis (a furry, blind, telepathic, canine-like creature), whose name signifies the ancestor of the dog. It is also a realm where relationships are burdened with an uncommon amount of violence and hatred: Miacis despises the Slakers;[27] the male and female Slakers, physically differentiated in ways that promote hostility between the sexes, are intolerant of each other; and the Rollers, enormous storms, make survival extraordinarily difficult. In this unpleasant region—which symbolically is related, as already noted, to the wasteland (and for some readers may also suggest Dante's Inferno)—Thomas shows his wayward self-will, violently wrenching himself from the unit to go off on his own.[28] Neither he nor the unit can survive except as a whole; Justice sends Miacis out to find Thomas and bring him back, not knowing he has taken the real Levi with him (Levi's persona remains behind). When Dorian, the Healer, soothes Justice's headache and she remarks he must be a god, Dorian replies, "It's the unit that's the god . . . and you must be the Goddess Enormous," foreshadowing Justice's later projection of a huge image of herself on the horizon after the unit's Crossover and return to home.[30]

The details of life in Dustland are repulsive and full of carnivorous images: the Slaker males store blood and meat from a kill under their membranous skins and only grudgingly share leftover food with females; in the future, we are told, they are likely to refuse to share at all, causing the females, and then the species, to die out.[31] They have "lost their instinct for peace"[32] and only the females protect and nurture the young.[33] The only thing to admire in this blatantly sexist society is the persistent questing of the Slakers for an escape from the dust, and Justice realizes the role of the unit, and herself as the Watcher, will be to return to Dustland and help the Slakers in the completion of their Quest.[34] Mal, short for Malevolence, will do anything in its power to prevent the unit from fulfilling this compassionate goal; towards the close of the book, Justice must combat the presence of Mal, which has come "to strike fear so that the first unit will not return to Dustland"; this challenge, however, only crystallizes her determination that "the first unit will return."[35] Thomas undergoes some growth of character in this second book of the trilogy, using his Magician powers compassionately, to protect their parents from seeing the difference in Justice, whose temporary physical changes—reminiscent of the growth spurts of adolescence—make her eyes too small, eyesockets too large, and neck too thin.[36] It is also significant that Thomas loses his stutter in this future world,[37] suggesting he may outgrow it, as he does in the last novel at the point where he learns to control his hostility.

Dustland takes on added meaning when considered in the context of the Myth of the Frontier. It seems a vivid picture of the probable consequences, in a future steadily growing nearer, of the abuse of the environment occasioned by human folly, greed, pollution, over-industrialization, nuclear war, and nuclear winter, all in turn the consequence of a failure of awareness, a limitation of consciousness. Richard Slotkin, in *The Fatal Environment: The Myth of the Frontier in the Age of Industrialization, 1800–1890*, presents his formulation of "the Janus-faced role of mythology," which can on the one hand expand yet on the other limit and constrict the meanings of our experience. Mythology can turn history into cliché by oversimplifying it (into "icons" such as the landing of the Pilgrims, the rally of the Minutemen at Lexington, the attack on Pearl Harbor); but it also "transforms history into symbol, providing artists a meaningful medium with which to interpret our heritage and to give it new forms."[38] In Slotkin's earlier study, *Regeneration Through Violence*, he defines the major structural elements of myth: a protagonist or hero, with whom the audience will in some way identify; a universe in which the hero acts, which resembles the reader's concept of the world; and a narrative wherein the hero and the universe interact.[39] All these elements are present in *Dustland* and the *Justice* trilogy as a whole. There is a mythic setting, Dustland, which sets up an opposition between two worlds—the present one and the wasteland of the future; the hero, Justice, whose name has symbolic resonances, and who moves between the worlds; and a narrative dramatizing the "progress" of the hero as she moves through the conflicts between the present and future worlds and deals with a future nature turned hostile, a wilderness of a particularly repugnant kind, in need of her compassionate help. Her psychic metamorphosis is prior to the saving of the wasteland; spiritual change must precede the transformation of Mal from Malevolence to Benevolence. In terms of the Frontier myth, she is the revitalizing goddess, the New Eve who brings about, in the last book, *The Gathering*, a significant change and new life for the Dustlanders. First, however, she must "descend" into the "hell" of their scarcely bearable existence. Viewed in this light, the *Justice* trilogy seems to be aligned with the concepts of "perennial philosophy," which are at the heart of the great religions,[40] and which suggest as Roger Walsh has said, "that consciousness is central and its development is the primary goal of existence."[41]

An apocalyptic time such as the present may, in this framework of thought, give birth to an apotheosis of humanity. The change of consciousness accompanying the unit's time-travel to Dustland, while they leave their physical forms behind at the Quinella Trace, is analogous to the process of "play death" which Farrell applies to the interpretation of *Sweet Whispers, Brother Rush*. In that novel, selves are not annihilated by death, but "converted to ghosts, spirits, or angels."[42] Similarly, the four youngsters in the unit cannot be certain they have physical substance after entering Dustland; there, they have "bodies" that are not like their earthly ones. Farrell finds such fantasies of "death"-like states can be "freeing," enabling a person to relinquish conventional identity, experience reorganization and renewal, and break out of "defensive rigidity"; she compares the Gospel vision of salvation from slavery, so central a metaphor in Afro-American history.[43] Similarly, in the *Justice* trilogy the youngsters of the unit experience a kind of psychological emancipation as the outcome of their "near-death" experiences in Dustland.

Thus, Hamilton's trilogy reflects fundamental mythic patterns of thought in American culture—the American dream of unlimited potential (with all its ambivalence and ambiguity, for it has not minimized the violence in our history), the Myth of America as having a special mission (given flesh in Justice), the idea of the evolution of the heroic role, and the expansion of human consciousness.

THE GATHERING—
A CELEBRATION OF DELIVERANCE

· All of this is borne out in *The Gathering*, wherein the unit brings help to Duster and his people, delivering them from the enmity of Mal and ultimately freeing them from the conformity suffered by the clones manufactured by the cyborgs, represented by Celester. This comes about through Justice's gift of the Watcher to Colossus, the gigantic computer. Before this event, the astonishing history of the end of the world as we know it is recounted by Celester, who explains how thermonuclear catastrophies cause genetic destruction and generations of mutations;[44] the fertile earth turns to deserts, and the Starters, the greatest of the Seers (future descendants of the four children), realizing an impending end to life, try to prepare to save a remnant of people. Colossus is programmed to transport the Seers to a far planet to save them from impending destruction.[45] When Justice protests, "But I can't believe our . . . our kind . . . the seers, would save themselves and leave all the rest to die!" Celester cryptically answers, "Seers saved some—it was not that. . . . It was that seers left a dying earth."[46]

Colossus's memory says survivors "lived to hunt mythical greenspans said to thrive beneath the dust. . . . Greenspans, like waterholes, were the dreams and myths of survivors."[47] The resulting world of the domities (domes which shelter life), sterile and conformist, is as Dressel has noted a society without diversity, where all who differ (such as Duster and his friends) are branded "mutant" and banished to Dustland. Those within the domes are drugged to keep them under control; though this horrifies Justice, Celester rationalizes: the drug is only a mild synthetic one, less harmful, he claims, than coffee. He praises the "efficiency" of the practice.[48]

Dressel has observed that Justice's gift of the Watcher to Colossus, which makes Colossus whole, also enables the computer to "permit diversity and overcome Mal."[49] Mal, Dresser continues, the force embodying all evil, "whether that evil be white society, machine, slavery, or oppression," is "reminiscent of the machine used during the lobotomy in *Invisible Man*—a means of mind control, exerting a grip like that of a powerful alien personality invading any consciousness that comes within its grasp. If Mal is like the machine, Dressel argues, the Watcher is comparable to High John de Conquer of black folklore, invisible, yet a present source of strength.[50]

In drawing parallels between Ellison's *Invisible Man* and the *Justice* trilogy, Dressel illuminates the role of singing and music in Hamilton's narrative. Thomas's aggressive use of his kettledrums as "instruments of torture" to Justice has been alluded to above; in reaction, she perceives his "music" as noise.[51] However, with her change in consciousness and a secure sense of self, she comes to appreciate his drum-playing. Hamilton also uses music artfully in depicting how the children of Dustland communicate by "toning." In Dressel's words, the toning gives *The Gathering* "a melodic quality of timelessness, reflecting a present without beginning and without end, as well as a premonition of the fuure."[52] It is true that Duster and his "packen" are humanized and made more sympathetic as characters through their use of song and harmony. Thus, Justice's gift to them seems motivated and credible; they are presented as worthy of her compassion. What Justice does is clarified when Levi, after the unit's arrival back at home, "draws" their experience: his drawing graphically expresses how Colossus needed Mal to complete itself, for the Watcher fits into Colossus as "a rod of fuzzy, soft-blue light" which flows around the coils of the great computer, "illuminating complex dimensions of Colossus. A beautiful, perfectly round diamond crystal larger than a basketball balanced at one end of the Watcher rod of light." This is Mal, transformed, now generating "perpetual energy." Levi knows that "Watcher power had transformed it into Watcher treasure."[53] The picture is one of a final unity of opposites, a fittingly Jungian conclusion to Hamilton's universal drama of good versus evil. Appropriately, Justice is depicted in the closing lines as feeling love for "everything" —an optimal, even mystical state of expanded consciousness—and an "unusual energy."

CONCLUSION

What is Hamilton's achievement in the *Justice* trilogy, beyond spinning an absorbing tale? May the reader take comfort in believing humanity is destined for a "majestic change," with individuals such as Justice and the unit endowed with the ability to save humankind from the dire, dystopian fate depicted in Dustland? Can an expansion of our consciousness, a new way of thinking, prevent the pollution and corruption depicted in Celester's "history" from being actualized in our future? In what way is it possible to act upon the future, as Justice, her brothers, and Dorian do in these narratives, to alter human destiny for the better? These speculative questions remain unanswered and un-answerable. Hamilton's achievement lies in bringing attention to the seriousness of humanity's plight, the very real threats to survival from our failures in awareness, our need to see earth as alive (as Justice sees Cottonwoman) and recognize all sentient beings as meriting compassion; and she has done this in a story accessible to young readers. Through her narrative she suggests how the sources of our ills, whether social, political, economic, or personal, lie within our own consciousness. Yet the landscape is also a "hopescape," for within us also dwells the Watcher. We can choose to align ourselves with the Watcher's kind of consciousness, rather than with Mal. The choice is crucial, for it is a law of mind: that to which we give our attention will grow stronger in our lives.

NOTES

1. Teresa Kleibrink Aggen, "Character, Setting and Survival; The Development of the Survival Themes in Six Novels by Virginia Hamilton" (M.A. thesis, Stephen F. Austin State University, 1991), 15.
2. Quoted in "Foreword," *Many Faces, Many Voices: Multicultural Literary Experiences for Youth. The Virginia Hamilton Conference*, ed. Anthony L. Manna and Carolyn S. Brodie (Fort Atkinson, WI: Highsmith Press, 1992), xviii.
3. Ibid., xii–xiii.
4. Virginia Hamilton, "A Toiler, A Teller," in *Many Faces, Many Voices*, 4 and 7.
5. Virginia Hamilton, "Ah, Sweet Rememory," *The Horn Book Magazine* 57 (December1981): 639–40, 635, 638.
6. Virginia Hamilton, *Justice and Her Brothers* (New York: Greenwillow, 1978), 16.
7. Glenn E. Estes, ed., *Dictionary of Literary Biography*, vol. 52, (Detroit, MI: Gale Research Co., 1986), "Virginia Hamilton," by Marilyn F. Apseloff, 180.
8. Jean Houston, *The Possible Human: A Course in Extending Your Physical, Mental, and Creative Abilities* (Los Angeles, CA: Tarcher, 1982), xiv, 213.
9. Hamilton, *Justice and Her Brothers*, 135.
10. Ibid., 23–24.
11. Ibid., 94.
12. Ibid., 206.

13. Ibid., 210–211.
14. I have discussed this concept in *Nuclear Age Literature for Youth: The Quest for a Life-Affirming Ethic* (Chicago, IL: American Library Association, 1990), 226 ff. See also Jean Houston, *The Possible Human: A Course in Extending Your Physical, Mental, and Creative Abilities* (Los Angeles, CA: Tarcher, 1982), xiv, 213.
15. J. White, quoted in Kenneth Ring, "Near-Death Experiences: Implications for Human Evolution and Planetary Transformation," in *Human Survival and Consciousness Evolution*, ed. Stanislav Grof with the assistance of Marjorie Livingston Valier. (Albany, NY: State University of New York Press, 1988), 267.
16. W.E.B. DuBois, *The Souls of Black Folk* (New York: New American Library, reprinted 1969) in Janice Hartwick Dressel, "The Legacy of Ralph Ellison in Virginia Hamilton's *Justice* Trilogy," *English Journal* 73 (November 1984): 45.
17. Janice Hartwick Dressel, "The Legacy of Ralph Ellison in Virginia Hamilton's *Justice* Trilogy," *English Journal* 73 (November 1984): 45.
18. David Mogen, "The Frontier Archetype and the Myth of America: Patterns That Shape the American Dream," in *The Frontier Experience and the American Dream: Essays on American Literature*, ed. David Mogen, Mark Busby, and Paul Bryant (College Station, TX: Texas A & M University Press, 1989), 29. Lawrence's statement occurs in D. H. Lawrence, *Studies in American Literature* (1923; reprinted New York: Viking Press, 1966), 1.
19. Linda Ben-Zvi, " 'Home Sweet Home': Deconstructing the Masculine Myth of the Frontier in Modern American Drama," in *The Frontier Experience and the American Dream*, 219.
20. Marilyn F. Apseloff, "A Conversation with Virginia Hamilton," *Children's Literature in Education* 14 (Winter 1983): 210.
21. Hamilton, *Justice and Her Brothers*, 188.
22. Kirby Farrell, "Virginia Hamilton's *Sweet Whispers, Brother Rush* and the Case for a Radical Existential Criticism," *Contemporary Literature* 31 (Summer 1990): 173.
23. Ibid., 169.
24. Hamilton, *Justice and Her Brothers*, 156.
25. Ibid., 71.
26. Dressel, 45.
27. Virginia Hamilton, *Dustland* (New York: Greenwillow, 1980), 30.
28. Ibid., 25.
29. Ibid., 44.
30. Ibid., 148.
31. Ibid., 63.

32. Ibid., 61.
33. Ibid., 100.
34. Ibid., 126.
35. Ibid., 162–163.
36. Ibid., 163.
37. Ibid., 173.
38. Quoted by Mark Busby, David Mogen, and Paul Bryant, "Introduction: Frontier Writing as a 'Great Tradition' of American Literature," in *The Frontier Experience and the American Dream*, 4.
39. Quoted by David Mogen, "The Frontier Archetype and the Myth of America," in *The Frontier Experience and the American Dream*, 23.
40. See Aldous Huxley, *The Perennial Philosophy* (New York: Harper and Row, 1944).
41. Roger Walsh, "Human Survival: A Psycho-Evolutionary Analysis," in *Human Survival and Consciousness Evolution*, ed. Stanislav Grof with the assistance of Marjorie Livingston Valier (Albany, NY: State University of New York Press, 1988), 5.
42. Farrell, 170.
43. Ibid.
44. Virginia Hamilton, *The Gathering* (New York: Greenwillow, 1981), 104.
45. Ibid., 105–108.
46. Ibid., 108.
47. Ibid., 106.
48. Ibid., 109.
49. Dressel, 47.
50. Ibid., 46.
51. William Irwin Thompson's insight that "teenagers who go to rock concerts understand that noise is the new form of identification with the group" would seem to have no application to Justice, though it might help to explain the behavior of the boys who follow Thomas. See his "Pacific Shift: The Philosophical and Political Movement from the Atlantic to the Pacific" in *Human Survival and Consciousness Evolution*, 236.
52. Dressel, 47.
53. Hamilton, *The Gathering*, 176.

REFERENCES

Aggen, Teresa Kleibrink. Unpublished M.A. thesis, "Character, Setting, and Survival: The Development of the Survival Themes in Six Novels by Virginia Hamilton." Stephen F. Austin State University, August, 1991.

Apseloff, Marilyn F. "A Conversation with Virginia Hamilton." *Children's Literature in Education* 14 (Winter 1983): 204–214.

____. "Virginia Hamilton." *Dictionary of Literary Biography*, Volume 52, ed. Glenn E. Estes. Detroit, MI: Gale Research Co., 1986.

Ben-Zvi, Linda. " 'Home Sweet Home': Deconstructing the Masculine Myth of the Frontier in Modern American Drama." In *The Frontier Experience and the American Dream: Essays on American Literature*, ed. David Mogen, Mark Busby, and Paul Bryant, 217–225. College Station, TX: Texas A & M University Press, 1989.

Busby, Mark, David Mogen, and Paul Bryant. "Introduction: Frontier Writing as a 'Great Tradition' of American Literature." In *The Frontier Experience and the American Dream: Essays on American Literature*, ed. David Mogen, Mark Busby, and Paul Bryant, 3–12. College Station, TX: Texas A & M University Press, 1989.

Chodorow, Nancy. *The Reproduction of Motherhood: Psychoanalysis and the Sociology of Gender*. Berkeley, CA: University of California Press, 1978.

Dressel, Janice Hartwick. "The Legacy of Ralph Ellison in Virginia Hamilton's *Justice* Trilogy." *English Journal* 73 (November 1984): 42–48.

DuBois, W.E.B. *The Souls of Black Folk*. New York: New American Library, reprinted 1969.

Ellison, Ralph. *Invisible Man*. New York: Vintage, 1972. (Originally published 1947.)

Farrell, Kirby. "Virginia Hamilton's *Sweet Whispers, Brother Rush* and the Case for a Radical Existential Criticism," *Contemporary Literature* 31 (Summer 1990): 161–176.

Grof, Stanislav, ed., with the assistance of Marjorie Livingston Valier. *Human Survival and Consciousness Evolution*. Albany, NY: State University of New York Press, 1988.

Hamilton, Virginia. *Justice and Her Brothers*. New York: Greenwillow, 1978.

____. *Dustland*. New York: Greenwillow, 1980.

____. *The Gathering*. New York: Greenwillow, 1981.

____. "Ah, Sweet Rememory!" *The Horn Book Magazine*, 57, no. 6 (December 1981): 635–640.

____. "A Toiler, A Teller." In *Many Faces, Many Voices: Multicultural Literary Experiences for Youth: The Virginia Hamilton Conference*, ed. Anthony L. Manna and Carolyn S. Brodie, 1–7. Fort Atkinson, WI: Highsmith Press, 1992.

Houston, Jean. *The Possible Human: A Course in Extending Your Physical, Mental, and Creative Abilities*. Los Angeles, CA: J. P. Tarcher, 1982.

Huxley, Aldous. *The Perennial Philosophy*. New York: Harper and Row, 1944.

Lawrence, D. H. *Studies in American Literature*. 1923. Reprinted, New York: Viking, 1966.

Lenz, Millicent. *Nuclear Age Literature for Youth: The Quest for a Life-*

Affirming Ethic. Chicago, IL: American Library Association, 1990.

Manna, Anthony L. and Carolyn S. Brodie, eds. *Many Faces, Many Voices: Multicultural Literary Experiences for Youth: The Virginia Hamilton Conference*. Fort Atkinson, WI: Highsmith Press, 1992.

Mogen, David. "The Frontier Archetype and the Myth of America: Patterns That Shape the American Dream." In *The Frontier Experience and the American Dream: Essays on American Literature*, ed. David Mogen, Mark Busby, and Paul Bryant, 15–30. College Station, TX: Texas A & M University Press, 1989.

Mogen, David, Mark Busby, and Paul Bryant, eds. *The Frontier Experience and the American Dream: Essays on American Literature*. College Station, TX: Texas A & M University Press, 1989.

Ring, Kenneth. "Near-Death Experiences: Implications for Human Evolution and Planetary Transformation." In *Human Survival and Consciousness Evolution*, ed. Stanislav Grof with the assistance of Marjorie Livingston Valier, 251–270. Albany, NY: State University of New York Press, 1988.

Sims, Rudine. *Shadow and Substance: Afro-American Experience in Contemporary Children's Fiction*. Urbana, IL: National Council of Teachers of English, 1982.

Slotkin, Richard. *Regeneration Through Violence*. Middletown, CT: Wesleyan University Press, 1973.

____. *The Fatal Environment: The Myth of the Frontier in the Age of Industrialization, 1800–1890*. New York: Atheneum, 1985.

Thompson, William Irwin. "Pacific Shift: The Philosophical and Political Movement from the Atlantic to the Pacific." In *Human Survival and Consciousness Evolution*, ed. Stanislav Grof with the assistance of Marjorie Livingston Valier, 218–238. Albany, NY: State University of New York Press, 1988.

Walsh, Roger. "Human Survival: A Psycho-Evolutionary Analysis." In *Human Survival and Consciousness Evolution*, ed. Stanislav Grof with the assistance of Marjorie Livingston Valier, 1–8. Albany, NY: State University of New York Press, 1988.

TWELVE

Octavia E. Butler: New Designs for a Challenging Future

Janice Antczak

For many readers, Octavia E. Butler represents the premiere African-American woman's voice in science fiction. She has achieved cult status as an author whose works speak to a diverse audience who respond to her inclusion of issues of race and feminism in provocative and exciting science fiction. Although Butler is not a "YA" author, she began writing her science fiction as an adolescent. Very significantly, her work has found a readership among young adults, and her books are reviewed and discussed in the journals concerned with young adult literature.

Butler's own adolescent interest in science fiction and her appeal to YA readers may find their origins in the very typical adolescent concern with the outsider, the misfit who does not quite find a niche in the peer group. Butler was raised in the Baptist home of her mother and grandmother, where strict tenets forbade dancing and other activities that customarily interest many young adults. Butler was shy and found it difficult to gain acceptance among those her own age. She turned to books and writing. "I began writing when I was about ten years old for the same reason many people begin reading—to escape loneliness and boredom."[1] She began to write science fiction "simply because I liked to read it," and wrote the "first version of her first published novel, *Patternmaster*, when she was twelve. At thirteen, she began submitting her work to science fiction magazines."[2] This adolescent beginning has grown into a body of work that has gained recognition and respect. This recognition includes the Nebula Award in 1985 and two Hugo Awards, one in 1984 and the other in 1985.

Belden and Beckman write that Butler's fiction "should appeal to idealistic teenagers impatient to build a better society."[3] Her nine novels develop patterns and themes that would encourage YA readers to speculate about what such a goal could encompass. Yet, her novels are not simple blueprints for building a better future. Perhaps because she describes herself as "pessimist, if I'm not careful";[4] Butler's writings do not provide easy answers. Rather, she explores issues and ideas that young adults face, not in an imaginative distant future, but rather, in their daily lives.

Butler's works provoke and challenge. The strong language of the novels may deter some from including her works in their collections. Yet, her use of such language, while offensive to some, is not gratuitous; for it reflects the nature of her characters and their settings and situations. Many are outcasts or loners seeking power and their language connotes their status. The "outlaw car family" in *Clay's Ark* speak in a manner befitting their degenerate lifestyle, and even Doro, the powerful protagonist of many of the Patternist novels, uses scatological language as part of his strategy of intimidation.

Butler's use of frank vocabulary is matched by her provocative use of sexuality. She explores and employs all aspects of the sexual. Butler incorporates strong but not necessarily graphic sexual scenes in the novels. Both heterosexual and homosexual encounters are presented, and some of these are of a violent nature. Rape is a common occurrence, again indicative of the breakdown of society or of the attempt to prove one's power over another. In some of her works, Butler challenges readers with exotic ideas of sexuality. Her alien characters practice a sexuality quite different from an earthly norm. The Oankali in the Xenogenesis trilogy engage in sexual triads, and while accepting alien notions of sexuality may not be too provocative on its own terms, the inclusion of humans in these "menage a trois" may be troubling to some readers. Such strange sexual patterns are not uncommon in adult science fiction because they are but another look at alien beings' biology and culture; they are part of sophisticated explorations of new worlds and their inhabitants. While some may feel such frank language and presentations do not belong in young adult collections, the inclusion of this provocative material is very much a part of the concerns which Butler so strongly addresses in her work.

Butler's themes revolve around issues of personal and societal concern. Her novels treat these concerns in imaginative ways, but Butler frequently addresses them, as well, in essays and interviews which help to clarify her work. When asked to describe herself, Butler responds that she is "black" and a "feminist," and these two words comprise and illuminate much of what she has written. Butler writes of racism and sexism, but does not always focus upon the negative impact of these patterns in society. She also presents the positive aspects of racial and sexual differences. Her major characters are most often strong, black women who survive and even triumph in the difficulties of their time and place. She emphasizes issues of power and the power struggle. Sometimes this exploration of the domination and exploitation of the powerless by the powerful takes on a violent cast in her novels, but it is precisely this theme that provides the most provocative reading. The issue of power encompasses the themes of race, gender, and otherness that challenge readers in her fictional and the real worlds.

Race, gender, power—these are challenging words and issues, and they comprise the patterns that appear repeatedly in Butler's novels. Her nine novels include two series: the "Patternist" series of *Patternmaster* (1976), *Mind of My Mind* (1977), *Survivor* (1978), *Wild Seed* (1980), and *Clay's Ark* (1984); and the "Xenogenesis" trilogy which includes *Dawn* (1987), *Adulthood Rites* (1988), and *Imago* (1989). Another novel, *Kindred* (1979), stands alone. Throughout these works the themes that concern Butler appear again and again in variations that fascinate readers.

EXPANDING THE LIMITS OF
MIND AND MATTER: THE PATTERNISTS

(The publication order of the Patternist novels does not follow the sequence of events that occur within the books. To facilitate an appreciation of the use of Butler's themes and patterns, this discussion will follow the novels in order of events.)

Butler began work on the Patternist books when she was twelve years old. In an interview with Larry McCaffrey, she said that when she was in her teens and was asked about her hopes and dreams, about what she would do if she could do anything she wanted—she answered that she wanted "to live forever and breed people. . . ."[5] Butler stopped believing in an afterlife when she was twelve years old, but became fascinated by the powers of the mind, the psi phenomena. Therefore, during early adolescence, she began to weave these two strands into the pattern that would become her novels; for the Patternist novels do use forms of immortality and psionic powers to explore her themes of race, gender, and power from times past to times future.

Butler creates characters and situations that reflect and embody her major themes. She asks readers to question why power so often resides in the male hierarchy, in which men scramble over each other to be dominant and women are left at the bottom, raped and powerless. In her novels Butler depicts patterns of male dominance over centuries, but challenges the inevitability of this gendered social order by creating strong female challengers in characters such as Anyanwu, Amber, Mary, and Alanna. Butler also ties in the issue of race to complete the triad of concerns. While her strongest female characters are women of color, she comes to show that strength and power reside at the core of one's self and are beyond race. All of this challenges readers with questions such as: Where does ultimate power reside? How far can manipulation of the mind proceed? How ethical is this manipulation? If one has the power to do so, should one be allowed to breed a super-race? Are women ultimately breeders? Are women in power more nurturing? Can humans get beyond color and accept diversity in all its glory? Is there a future for the human race as it now exists? Or must we evolve or be shaped by others into another mode of thinking and being to survive?

Race, gender, and power are at the core of this series of novels and at the core of the character of Doro. Doro is a 4,000-year-old Nubian whose name is Nubian for "the direction from which the sun comes."[6] He survives through the ages as a predator who kills others to assume their bodies. Assuming male and female forms, he has been all races. Doro breeds people. His mission is to create a super-race of humans with psi powers. It is in *Wild Seed*, the prequel to the series, that his lives begin to unfold. *Wild Seed* is a hybrid science fiction/historical fiction novel, covering the years 1690–1840. It traverses geographical space, as well as time, as the characters appear in Europe, Africa, Colonial and pre-Civil War America.

Butler's settings are fully developed to convey a sense of time and place, and the people who live there. The Africa of the days of the slave trade is depicted as a land of almost idyllic, unique tribal villages whose way of life is periodically shattered by the forays of the slavers. Life there seems suffused with the power of nature, particularly the sun. This contrasts strongly with the images of colonial New York, with its crowds and buildings, and a "civilized" code based on externals, like mode of dress. This is a world in which nature seems less powerful, a world which men seek to control. The pre-Civil War period as described by Butler is truly a world on the verge of chaos, where good and evil seem to have been turned upside-down. The lush landscape of the southland seems to barely hide the uncontrollable power which seeks to destroy that which stands in its way. Butler has selected eras of history which are powerful icons—the idyllic cradle of life in Africa, the birth of a new nation, and the sundering of that nation in a war between brothers. These powerful epochs are appropriate choices for these stories.

Wild Seed begins the story of the struggle for power between immortals, a struggle that begins in Africa, 1690. Doro's breeding project had been proceeding for centuries without contest. As he tours his "seed villages" in Africa, conflicts begin to surface. Slavers have decimated his villages, prime descendants are captured and herded to the coast, and Doro finds himself being drawn by a strong "mental undertow."[7] This strong force is Anyanwu (whose name means "sun"), the woman who will be his equal in the struggle for power and immortality. She is the wild seed, "descended from people whose abnormally long lives, resistance to disease, and budding special abilities made them very important to him. People, who like so many others, had fallen victim to slavers or tribal enemies."[8] Anyanwu is a healer, a shape-shifter, a jumper of rivers, an oracle to her people. She believes "It is better to be a master than to be a slave."[9] She has known power and is not going to relinquish it quickly. To Anyanwu, who has had several husbands over time, even marriage holds threats to her power. Woman's role and place in society plays a dominant role in the life of Anyanwu. She has never met a man with the spirit and power of Doro, and there is mutual attraction, yet simultaneously revulsion.

Doro's seed villages are not immune to danger and destruction. He often loses prime descendants, so he travels gathering those with promise to new places where he can provide protection. Doro has placed loyal, disciplined men in strategic places around the world, ready to serve his needs. One such character is Daly, a white man working for the Royal African Company, a slaver, who tests each slave to determine if any have Doro's inbred powers. Such slaves are saved for Doro, a black man who will use even an institution like slavery to serve his ends.

Doro has enough of his people gathered to fill a "slave" ship. It is captained and crewed by his own people. During the voyage, Doro's powerful sons work the ship and sail it through calm and storm. Each with his own specialty and with their combined powers, the sons save the ship and passengers. Thus they echo African folklore in which Anansi the spider and his sons all use their remarkable powers to help themselves and the people. In these early pages of the series, the emphasis on African myth and lore is strong and brings power and resonance to the books.

Butler again raises the issue of slavery when Doro explains a real slave ship to Anyanwu and contrasts it to his slaver.

> In the benign atmosphere of the ship, all the slaves were recovering from their invariably harsh homeland experiences. Some of them had been kidnapped from their villages. Some had been sold for witchcraft or for other crimes of which they were usually not guilty. Some had been born slaves. Some had been enslaved during war. All had been treated harshly at some time during their captivity.[10]

During the voyage, Doro continues his breeding program, making sure appropriate pairs are matched. So the issues of what is slavery and what is freedom resonate through the novel, as Doro rescues people from the "slavers" and ironically and purposefully enslaves them in his breeding program.

Anyanwu learns more about her shape-shifting abilities as she assumes the bodies of sea creatures like the dolphin. She learns or acquires the special abilities of those she helped or entered, and she is able to hide from Doro in the assumed animal forms. Doro does not take on the unique attributes of those bodies he assumes. He kills to inhabit those bodies and discards them when they are no longer useful to him.

Doro takes his slave ship to an American town in New York called Wheatley. (Butler often uses names associated with African-American heritage or having biblical "echoes" in this series. Wheatley, Doro's village, is homage to colonial poet Phillis Wheatley. While Isaac is Doro's favored son, Thomas is the doubting outcast. Mary becomes mother to the Pattern, and the Missionary colony is called Canaan, the promised land. Butler's use of such names causes a confrontation with readers. Such time-honored names call up images from the past of piety and purity, but she asks readers to see in a new way what it means to be a loyal son or the mother of a people.) Here all races mingle as Doro continues his breeding. "Wheatley is Doro's American village. He dumps all the people he can't find places for in his pure families on us. Mix and stir. No one can afford to worry about what anyone else looks like. They don't know who Doro might mate them with—or what their own children might look like."[11]

Anyanwu is eager to find her place. She discusses African and Wheatley ways with Doro's son Isaac. Isaac feels social mores are all relative and tells her, "Civilization is the way one's own people live. Savagery is the way foreigner's live."[12] Yet Anyanwu is wise to changing mores. She "lived in enough different towns through her various marriages to know the necessity of learning to behave as others did."[13] Anyanwu is a survivor.

The novel passes through time as well as place as it moves to the year 1741. Anyanwu is now a major figure in Wheatley for she has given Doro eight children and Isaac five in the breeding program. Her portrait resembles a black Madonna, but race prejudice is growing in the colonies and some people of Wheatley find the portrait offensive.

Doro continues his breeding work and expands to the Native-American tribes. He feels that "Indians were rich in untapped wild seed that they tended to tolerate, or even revere rather than destroy. Eventually, they would learn to be civilized and to understand as the whites understood that the hearing of voices, the seeing of visions . . . were evil or dangerous, or at the very least imaginary."[14]

In this section of the novel, Butler's characters frequently comment on race. Doro himself seems not to be concerned with race, but other characters reveal their own prejudice or that of their time and place. Doro takes Anyanwu south to mate with Thomas a white who lives as a wild man. Doro, himself an African, says cruelly to her, ". . . she should not mind the way he lived, since she was from Africa where people swing through the trees and went naked like animals."[15] Thomas, who lives in squalor, curses her blackness and asks if she can turn white. In an echo of slavery he tells her, she is here for breeding and nothing more. Thomas is an anomaly in Doro's program. "Was he really so concerned about her color? Usually Doro's people were not.

Most of them had backgrounds too thoroughly mixed for them to sneer at anyone."[16] Those in Doro's breeding program are in virtual slavery to their master and his own designs.

Anyanwu is a survivor who claims, "If I have to be white to survive, I will be white. . . ."[17] As the novel moves to 1840, Anyanwu assumes many other forms to survive—a black dog, a dolphin, a leopard, and an old white man. She now lives on a Louisiana plantation and Doro tracks her there. She, in the form of a white man, is master of the plantation and purchases slaves at auction, especially those who reveal some power. Doro wants to continue his breeding and bring mates for Anyanwu's people.

Death and destruction follow as Butler begins to show how Doro's people may be born with special gifts, but must first survive a transition period before they can be used. As Doro and Anyanwu wage war against each other through their children, the nation's Civil War is about to begin. They agree to a peaceful coexistence. He will no longer try to command her nor interfere with her children. To escape the hostilities between North and South, Anyanwu moves her people to California and takes the name Emma, the grandmother or ancestress. She is the survivor and no one's slave—a powerful black woman with her own destiny and dynasty. Emma Anyanwu represents Butler's heroic female characters, compelling and fascinating to readers.

Emma Anyanwu also appears in the next title of the series, *Mind of My Mind*. Here her role is secondary, that of the wise old woman, the matriarch who guides her extended family in the California city of Forsyth. (The southern California setting, replete with racism, drug addiction, alcoholism, prostitution, and child abuse approximates contemporary times.) Emma presents herself most often as the old grandmother, but her shape-shifting powers still work to her advantage when needed. She and Doro continue their relationship through the centuries—they are still lovers and co-conspirators in his breeding program. While Emma Anyanwu appears in this novel, it is her granddaughter Mary who is the central character.

Mary's skin is "a kind of light coffee, . . . gifts from the white man's body that Doro was wearing when he got Rina pregnant."[18] Doro brings Mary to live with Emma, to spare her the abusive situation at home with her mother, an alcoholic prostitute. Doro also recognizes the strength of Mary's psionic powers. She may prove to be the capstone of his breeding program, so he wants Emma to oversee her transition. The novel becomes Mary's story, much of it told in first person, allowing the reader to truly enter Mary's mind.

Other portions of the book are related in third person, as when the stories of other characters unfold or Patternist phenomena are explained. The description of the results of Doro's breeding program makes up a large portion of the novel. Much attention is paid to the rite-of-passage called "transition." This momentous event in the life of Patternists occurs in young adulthood. Those born in the breeding program who show some psionic potential are called "latents." Transition into adulthood with a full flowering of telepathic abilities creates "actives" in the Patternist society. Latents who do not successfully complete this phase often go mad, become violent, die, or must be killed to remove the threat they pose to the Pattern and others. Those characters without any powers or potential are called "mutes." Mutes become the lowest class in the Pattern hierarchy. At one point in the novel Butler describes them as "ordinary people," but their lower class status is made evident when Emma Anyanwu says the word mute "means nigger."[19] Here she is not speaking of race, but rather the perception of roles participated in, within Patternist society.

Racism does become an issue in the novel as characters discuss color and racial diversity. Doro's African roots are chronicled, but he hopes to breed a new "race" through his eugenic program. Mary questions Doro about his origins; and when she learns he is a Nubian from the Nile Valley, she exclaims:

> "Black people!"
> "Yes," replies Doro.
> "God! You're white so much of the time, I never thought you might have been born black."
> "It doesn't matter."
> "What do you mean, 'It doesn't matter'? It matters to me."
> "It doesn't matter because I haven't been any color at all for about four thousand years. Or you could say I've been every color. But either way, I don't have anything more in common with black people—Nubian or otherwise—than I do with whites or Asians."
> "You mean you don't want to admit you have anything in common with us. But if you were born black, you *are* black. Still black, no matter what color you take on."
> . . . "You can believe that if it makes you feel better."[20]

To Doro, powers of mind supercede all issues of race. His four thousand years on Earth have been filled with a single purpose, the creation of his "master race." All other issues are secondary. In fact, Doro views racial diversity as a positive part of his plan. He has been bringing his most promising offspring from all over the world to North America for hundreds of years for "He had decided then that the North American continent was big enough to give them room to avoid each other and that it would be racially diverse enough to absorb them all."[21] Doro is beyond color. To him strength and power reside in other facets of one's being.

Doro's quest for power culminates in Mary. Like Emma Anyanwu before her, Mary will be a challenge for Doro. She is his greatest creation; and like her grandmother, she proves to be Doro's equal and more. Mary's difficult transition succeeds. Her emergence as an active Patternist gives her power and strength rivaling Doro's, but she is also a nurturing woman in the tradition of her grandmother. It is this nurturing inclination which prompts Mary to gather others to her, especially those young people whose gifts cause them to clash with their parents and who need fostering in other homes. She is not willing to allow gifted young people to be lost in the painful rite-of-passage, even those for whom the process is long and dangerous. Thus Mary begins to enlarge the Pattern.

Mary's own psionic powers are prodigious. She can get beyond others defenses and shields. She is able to gather other actives and bind them to her without killing them as Doro would have. Mary uses her ability to continue to enlarge the pattern; she is building a true network in a community of active telepaths. She is one who has a sense of community and whose activities distress Doro, the loner and the breeder. "Together, the 'Patternists' were growing into something that he could observe, hamper, or destroy, but not something he could join. They were his goal, half accomplished. He watched them with carefully concealed emotions of suspicion and envy."[22] Doro's creation is growing beyond him after four thousand years of endeavor.

Doro's resentment of his daughter grows and he seeks to stop her expansionist plans. He wishes no more latents to be brought through transition and wants the Patternists to grow only through births, thereby stressing that he does have an interest in continued breeding efforts. He still feels very much the "master" and intends to kill Mary, if necessary, to continue his plans. Mary realizes that her father now hates her for her individual ability to handle the Pattern. He resents the fact that his children have grown up and don't need him anymore.

Mary and Doro will have to fight for supremacy of the Pattern in the archetypal battle more often seen between father and son. The issue of gender now emerges fully as Doro comes to resent and despise his female offspring for achieving more than he. The conflict between father and daughter draws in and threatens all actives in the net. Mary and Doro both use all their powers, but ultimately, it is Mary's ability to draw additional power from her community of actives that brings her to victory. Mary's use of female nurturance vanquishes her father's macho individualism. With Doro's death, Mary is now the undisputed power of the Pattern. Her position is secure, for Emma Anyanwu dies when she hears of Doro's demise. Doro's dominant world view leads to a lethal trap and downfall. Mary is the new woman of power, another representative of Butler's vision of strong, black women leading the way to a new order.

Another book in the Patternist series, *Clay's Ark*, follows a different path, as it does not deal directly with the Patternists. The novel, set in a near future time from *Mind of My Mind*, chronicles the disaster that befalls Earth and sets the stage for the subsequent novels of the series. The chapters of *Clay's Ark* alternate between the past and the present of the novel and tell of the invasion of an alien plague and its aftermath.

The story begins with the science fiction convention of a space ship returning from a mission in which things have gone awry. The sole survivor of the ship knows things are desperately wrong, but he seeks food, water, and human companionship. The chapters concerning the past chronicle how the extraterrestrial plague established itself on Earth. Eli had been a geologist on the mission to Proxima Centauri. He knows he carries the organism that killed fourteen crew members and that it drives him to seek:

> out new hosts for the alien microorganisms that had made themselves such fundamental parts of his body. Their purpose was now his purpose, and their only purpose was to survive and multiply. All his increased strength, speed, coordination, and sensory ability was to keep him alive and mobile, able to find new hosts or beget them.[23]

Anyone he touches might die; but if a person survived the infection it gave him/her the same heightened sense and functions.

Eli seeks food and water at a ranch near the re-entry site and is driven to infect everyone there. Here, alien invasion mixes with racial issues for Eli is a black man. The white ranch family takes him in and one brother remarks to his sister, "If that guy were white, I'd tell you to marry him."[24] Eli becomes part of the family as the issue of plague containment supercedes those of race.

Those who survive begin to change: they can see in the dark, and they prefer to eat live prey. Eli makes the ranch his colony and harem and they remain aloof from the rest of the world. Their children are mutations, born to look like "a gray, hairless monkey."[25] These children are intellectually precocious, and become brown quadrupeds who run with great speed. They resemble the sphinx. This result of the plague could bring about the end of humanity, as it had been known, for these mutants are the future, "the sporangia of the dominant life form of Proxi Two."[26] Those on the ranch are careful about limiting contact with the outside world to minimize the spread of Clay Ark disease.

The alternate chapters set in the present time of the novel focus on the journey of Blake Martin and his two teenage daughters from the sheltered world of the privileged in southern California through the desert to visit grandparents. They drive an "armored, high-suspension Jeep Wagoneer . . . relic of an earlier, oil-extravagant era."[27] Sixteen-year-old Keira has leukemia and is not responding to treatment. They are attacked on the road and taken to the ranch. Life on the ranch resembles that of the nineteenth century, primitive and alien to Blake Martin and his family, for "Like most enclave parents, Blake had done all he could to recreate the safe world of perhaps sixty years past for his children."[28] Through contact with the ranch family, Martin and his daughters are infected and now the ranchers try to keep them in isolation. Martin and his daughters notice the strange, mutant children and feel they must escape this madness.

They flee the ranch family, but are captured by an "outlaw car family," and so Clay Ark disease spreads. They do escape the car family, but Martin is killed in the process. Thus the novel relates the premise of the origin of the Clay Arks who become enemies of the Patternists later in the series.

In addition to developing the concept of the Clay Arks, Butler uses this novel to comment on social issues. The interracial marriage of

Blake Martin and his wife Jorah divides her family who

> "did not like her interest in him. They were people who had
> worked themselves out of one of the worst cesspools in the south-
> land. They had nurtured Jorah's social conscience too long to let
> it fall victim to a white man who had never suffered a day in his
> life and who thought social causes were passé."[29]

While daughter Keira felt she had learned a great deal about life "walking down a city street between her mother and father . . ."[30] Butler's
extrapolation takes contemporary prejudice and racial tension into the
Los Angeles of 2021. She also projects a worsening of societal ills in
the future: illegal drugs and weapons, water and fuel shortages, lawless
economic ghettos, and worse.

Butler depicts as well, a society's futile effort to fight these ills
through religious fanaticism at the turn of the century, even Eli the
astronaut had been a child preacher. Car gang members spend time
watching videos of this era about the second coming of Christ in which
God is a woman, or a dolphin, or a throwaway child, or an alien. Yet, all
these ills pale in the face of the crisis of Clay Ark disease described in
the epilogue. Cities are burning—San Francisco, Los Angeles, San
Diego. Texas oil refineries are in flames. Louisiana residents are shooting strangers, especially if they're black, brown, or Asian. Doctors and
nurses are spreading the disease. Some feel it is the end of the world or
the beginning of a new order where human beings will be obsolete.
Clay's Ark is a conventional science fiction story of alien invasion and
apocalypse, but Butler uses the novel to voice concern over contemporary issues of racial prejudice, economic class war, depletion of the
environment, and degradation of life. All this will have an impact on
the Patternists.

Patternmaster is set in an even more distant future. Civilization
has been ravaged. Patternists are living in enclaves called Houses.
Clayarks threaten their existence in what resembles a guerrilla war, and
the struggle for power in the Pattern continues.

The hierarchy of the Pattern has been maintained, perhaps it has
become even more stratified. The leaders of the Pattern, Rayal and his
wife Jansee, are worshiped as gods, and mutes are truly slaves. In
between there are housemasters, apprentices, outsiders, and indepen-
dents. It is indeed a complex Pattern. "The Pattern was a vast network
of mental links that joined every Patternist with the Patternmaster."[31]

The mutes who once led and developed a mechanized society are in eclipse, while the Patternists have ascended to power and a war with the Clayarks. The Clayarks have no telepathic powers and the Patternists cannot enter their minds. Each believes the others are "Not people" and so the warfare goes on and on. When the Clayarks attack Rayal and kill his lead wife Jansee, the conflict reaches a new phase. Rayal is injured and contracts Clay Ark disease. His diminished strength hampers his leadership.

The novel employs the archetype of the competition of two brothers battling to assume their aging father's powers. Young Teray, just finished his schooling, is now a threat to his older brother Coransee. Teray wants his own House, not to be an outsider, a permanent servant to those in power. Coransee expects to assume control of the Pattern when Rayal dies. His manipulations make Teray his servant and a muteherd.

Teray does not have the strength to fight Coransee alone. Here Butler creates another strong female character—Amber, an independent healer. She is a strong, brown woman (as her name suggests), who has made her own way through this dangerous world. Amber has much to teach Teray; she guides him on his quest. Amber provides most of the interesting facets of character in the novel. She is a Houseless wanderer, but has valued skill as a healer that makes her less vulnerable in the violent world. She fights the abuse of women in the Houses. She has had to kill to preserve her independence. She rejects marriage and is bisexual. She is a nurturer, a teacher. Amber is a woman who knows her own strengths, her needs and desires, and who is not afraid to work toward her own goals. She is in sharp contrast to Iray, who had hoped to marry Teray right after graduation, but who is just as happy to be with Coransee if he can offer security and worldly comfort. In Amber, Butler provides a feminist character whom many readers cheer. Although Teray eventually prevails against his older brother, he is the hero because a strong woman taught him healing and compassion as a complement to his ability to rule and kill when necessary.

The last of the Patternist novels, *Survivor*, is set in outer space at a Mission Colony called Canaan. The story is told in alternate chapters by Alanna, a colonist from Earth, and Diut, a native of the planet. Connections are made to the past and to Patternist history, although this is a story of mutes. Alanna's parents had been killed by Clayarks when she was eight years old and she was left to forage for herself. She became a wild human, but was drawn back into society when she was caught stealing a cow. The Missionaries Jules and Neila Verrick adopted her to fill the gap of the loss of their own children to Clay Ark disease. The Missionaries were a religious sect who believe the human shape was sacred while the sphinx-like form of the Clayarks was the work of the devil. The Missionaries took to space to escape the Clay Ark plague and to spread their idea of the sacred human form to another world.

Jules and Neila had been mute slaves of the Patternists in Forsyth for twenty-five years before they left to become Missionaries. It was the Patternists of Forsyth who built the starship, using the concept of the "Dana Drive,"[33] which had powered the Clay Ark starship. This combination of particle physics and psionics used human psi powers to fuel and guide the spacecraft. People with strong psychokinetic abilities could not use the Dana Drive for they overcontrolled it. The Missionaries' ship had been powered by a deformed young man, who died in the process. When they journey to Canaan, the Missionaries leave behind the Patternists and Clayarks to try to give human life one last chance.

The Missionaries bring the human form to a new world, but they also bring the seemingly ever present human problems. Racial discrimination again becomes a theme. Many of the Missionaries, who quote scripture and preach strong moral values, still have a difficulty with skin color. When the Verricks adopt Alanna, who is Afro-Asian, the other Missionaries never really accept her. Even the children taunt and fight with her. A contingent led by Beatrice Stamp feels the races should not mix and that Alanna should live "with her own kind."[34] Although the Verricks protect her from the less tolerant members, Alanna never really becomes one of the Missionaries. She is always the outsider, who mouths their words in return for food and shelter.

The colony of Canaan lands in the middle of a war between different tribes of the Kohns, the inhabitants of the planet. The two tribes, Garkohns and Tehkohns, struggle for power in a manner that echoes the war between the Patternists and Clayarks on Earth. In an additional irony, the two tribes engage in a form of racial discrimination, for to them one's color establishes one's role and worth in society. The Kohns are chameleon-like and a rainbow of colors is represented among their people. The Kohns' greatest weapon is their fur, "fine thick alive stuff that changed color and seemed to change texture. It permitted the natives to blend invisibly into their surroundings whenever they wished."[35] The Missionaries see them as "strangely colored, furred caricatures of human beings."[36] The Missionaries' religion allows them to regard the Kohns as lower creatures.

To the Kohns the rainbow of colors comprise their social hierarchy. Bright green are the farmers. Golden green are the artisans (although some are pure yellow). Deep green or blue green are the hunters, while deep blue are the judges and the Hao, the sacred leader. In addition to a basic color, Kohns also express emotion by a temporary change in color. All old Kohns have yellow age spots. Butler does not attempt to resolve the problems color presents for the Kohns, rather she describes it as a fact of Kohn life.

In another echo of Earthly concerns, Butler raises the issue of slavery. The mutes were slaves of the Patternists in Forsyth. They went to a new world secure in their feeling of superiority in carrying the sacred image of the human race to begin a new dynasty. In another ironic touch, the Missionaries side with the Garkohn in the tribal war, thinking they are allies. Yet, the Garkohn use the Missionaries for their own ends, first addicting them to meklah, a yellow fruit of the planet, and then enslaving them and using some in their own breeding program.

Alanna, another of Butler's women of power, grows beyond all this hatred and subterfuge. Since she was never truly accepted by the Missionaries, she has never adopted their intolerance and bigotry. She wants to learn all she can about Kohn culture, both Garkohn and Tehkohn. Alanna becomes a pawn and a prisoner in it all. Her opportunity to learn about Tehkohn culture increases when she is taken prisoner by them.

She alone survives the withdrawal from meklah that the Tehkohn require of all prisoners. This allows her to truly learn and become part of Tehkohn life and culture. After surviving the cleansing from meklah, Alanna lives with Gehnahteh, a green-gold woman and her husband Choh, who is more yellow in color. They are artisans and with them Alanna begins to learn Tehkohn ways. Although Alanna can have no rank in the Tehkohn hierarchy because she has none of their coloring, she is accepted by them in a way which was impossible with the Missionaries. Alanna learns their language so well, she begins to speak English with a Tehkohn accent. She proves she can hunt, be artistic, and exhibit the wisdom of a judge—all without the expected Kohn coloring. Eventually she marries Diut, the Tehkohn Hao, the man of highest rank in that culture. Diut had at first been repulsed and attracted by Alanna's exotic differences. She bears him a child, a daughter colored a dark shade of green, but with Alanna's round eyes and long hands and feet. Alanna, like Emma Anyanwu before her, has learned to adopt and adapt to the customs of others to survive and yet she is able to remain true to herself and to discover even more of her powers and abilities.

As the Kohn war accelerates, Alanna becomes even more powerful and important to the Missionaries and to the Tehkohn. Alanna and the Tehkohn return to Canaan, where Alanna is damned for her marriage to Diut and her bearing of a half-breed child. Despite her final rejection by the Missionaries, Alanna uses her strength to show them how to withdraw from meklah addiction, join the fight to throw off the oppression of Garkohn slavery, and to find a new life in a valley where no meklah grows. She helps the human colony to survive as thanks to the Verricks. She says, "For a while, I was your daughter. Thanks for that anyway."[37] Unlike the Missionaries and Garkohn who are defeated by their false sense of superiority and intolerance of differences, Alanna and the Tehkohn find true power in their acceptance and celebration of differences.

The entire Patternist series moves through time and space and explores the manifestation and consequences of racial issues. Butler provides no easy answers to questions of race, but her novels in this series suggest that cultures that persist in believing in intolerance come to a dead end, while those that embrace difference flourish. In so addressing these issues, Butler provides the reader with a personal challenge regarding bias and individual response to bias.

In addition, Butler's depiction of the woman of power who is instrumental in spearheading societal change allows for the consideration of a range of feminist ideas. Anyanwu, Mary, Amber, and Alanna are memorable characters, women who establish a new order where females contribute in equal or greater quantities and abilities than males. When Butler declares she is black and a feminist, she does so not only in interviews, but through her fiction as well.

A TIMELESS BOND;
A RADICAL ALLIANCE: *KINDRED*

The "stand alone" novel *Kindred* treats the issue of racial intolerance and slavery in an historical context. Butler originally intended this novel to be a part of the Patternist series; but she said "it didn't seem to fit, probably because I wanted to be more realistic."[38] She said she wanted to take "a middle-class black—and put him in the ante-bellum South to see how well he stood up" and "I developed an abused female character who was dangerous but who wasn't perceived as being so dangerous that she would have to be killed."[39] Butler's *Kindred* is a science fiction/historical fiction hybrid that uses the conventions of time travel to explore themes of racism and sexism.

Butler's heroic character is Dana, a young black woman, a writer living in southern California, who takes temporary jobs to support herself while she writes. (This aspect of the character is autobiographical.) Dana tells this story and her first person account provides the reader with total immersion into the personal experience of racism and sexism.

Dana and her husband Kevin, a white man, are unpacking books when she is called back in time. Dana is gone only ten to fifteen seconds but during that brief interval she rescues a white boy from drowning in a river. She is almost killed by his parents who don't quite understand what she has done. Thus begins the series of time shifts that draw Dana from 1976 Los Angeles to the Weylin plantation in antebellum Maryland. Through these time jumps, Dana and her husband come to experience directly the impact of slavery on black and white, male and female.

Dana becomes a pawn of time, beckoned to the past when Rufus, her white ancestor, finds his life in danger. Once more Butler uses the theme of the mix of races to demonstrate the irony of racial prejudice. Here also, she uses the science fiction convention of the paradox of encountering one's ancestors in past time and in that meeting affecting one's own existence. Dana realizes she is in the past "Not only to insure the survival of one accident-prone small boy, but to insure my family's survival, my own birth," for "if others were to live, he must live. I didn't dare test the paradox."[40]

Dana is called to the past each time red-haired Rufus's life is in danger, and she remains in the past until her life in turn is endangered. When Kevin is with her, he, too, is drawn from present to past and back again. Slavery becomes for them not a distanced historical institution but a fact of everyday life. Harsh reality strikes with a vengeance. Rufus calls Dana a nigger and she tries to explain to him that he should refer to her as "a black woman."[41] Dana is accused of not knowing her place. Rufus tells her, "You think you're white. You don't know your place any better than a wild animal."[43] Even Alice, another black woman, tells her, "You ought to be ashamed of yourself, whining and crying after some poor white trash of a man, black as you are. You always try to act so white. White nigger, turning against your own people."[44] Dana is made to work in the fields; she is also whipped. Kevin suffers as he tries to help runaway slaves escape to the North. Both Dana and Kevin learn "Slavery was a long slow process of dulling."[45]

Dana is a woman of talent and confidence, educated and published; and while these attributes work to her advantage in 1976 Los Angeles, they are a liability in the Old South. Here she meets slave women with some power of their own, who may not read or write; but who are able to hold things together in the grip of a double-edged oppression, especially Alice, the free black woman and Dana's ancestor, who loves with power until driven to hang herself by the effects of slavery and Rufus's lust, but not before her daughter Hagar, Dana's great-grandmother is born.

While the slaves suffer from the most obvious hardships and harshness, Butler writes of the effects of slavery on the white slave owners. Rufus has been whipped by his father with the same whip his father "whips niggers and horses with."[46] The Weylins live in fear of their thirty-eight slaves and in ignorance in a home where the whites feel reading is a waste of time. Margaret Weylin, the wife of the slave owner, is nervous and frustrated, jealous of the slave women who might attract the attentions of her husband. The system of slavery benefits no one, except perhaps economically. All spirits are blighted by the racist and sexist patterns.

Dana never really knows what power draws her to Rufus. All she knows is that she "was the worst possible guardian for him—a black to watch over him in a society that considered blacks subhuman, a woman to watch over him in a society that considered women perennial children."[47] Dana knows her sojourns to the past have altered her physically and spiritually. She bears the scars of slavery and has left a part of herself in the 1800s—part of her spirit and part of her arm—literally caught in slavery's grip as Rufus refuses to let go. Kevin, too, carries his scars—on his lined, aged face and in his feeling that life in contemporary Los Angeles was all too soft and easy. Dana and Kevin are caught between two worlds in many ways. The contrasts between past and present are made clear to them both, as they learn how powerless blacks and women were in the ante-bellum South. Yet, they also come to appreciate the similarities of the two times, as they see how people are still held in the bondage of racism and sexism. Butler takes her readers on the trip through time and place to better appreciate the impact of these persistent patterns in all lives—black, white, male, or female; and once again she uses a strong, African-American woman as the character to do so.

SURVIVING DIFFERENCES IN A BIAS-TEMPEST: XENOGENESIS

Butler's themes and patterns of racial and feminist issues continue to weave their way in her latest series, the Xenogenesis trilogy. These novels, *Dawn*, *Adulthood Rites*, and *Imago*, explore the fate of humanity in a post-holocaust setting. Butler, the self-described pessimist, confronts her readers with the notion that when faced with the ultimate devastation of ecological disaster and the almost certain destruction of the human race, that most humans will still cling to long held prejudice and fear of those who are different. As in her work in *Survivor*, Butler again uses an alien race to provoke humans to confront these issues and to accept dependence on others for continued survival.

In addition to the continued exploration of themes of race and gender, Butler raises even more provocative ideas. The alien Oankali have observed the human race and discovered that a barrier to successful survival lies in two incompatible characteristics. One is intelligence. "That's the newer of the two characteristics, and the one you might have to put to work to save yourselves. You are potentially one of the most intelligent species we've found. . . . You are hierarchical. That's the older and more entrenched characteristic."[48] Too often these two characteristics are combined in a manner that leads to destruction.

The Oankali are fascinated by what they find in the human race. Their research into human sociobiology finds not only the "mismatched pair of genetic characteristics"[49] of intelligence and hierarchy, but also the compelling "genetic inclination" in many humans "to grow cancers."[50] The Oankali regard cancer as a unique gift, while to humans it has been a scourge. The Oankali are able to stop the disease from harming humans, while harnessing its properties for work in the regeneration of tissue, as in growing replacement limbs. The Oankali see humans as a remarkable array of incongruities; and as genetic engineers and gene traders, the Oankali find humans a good investment. So much so that it is they who have saved the surviving humans from a dying Earth by placing them in a drugged sleep for centuries while they healed the plant Earth and fortified humans against disease. The Oankali want to bring humans back to Earth, but as traders they exact a price.

In *Dawn*, the process begins as Lilith (another first woman) is awakened from her sleep to the beginning of a new life on a ship orbiting Earth. Lilith is dark skinned, smart and strong, and the Oankali use her to select those humans who will be Awakened for this phase of their experiment. Lilith will be the first "mother" and teacher of the new human race. She is like Emma Anyanwu and Alanna in this role. Genetic engineering Oankali have made her pregnant with the first child of a new Earth, a daughter who is a genetic mix of Lilith, a man named Joseph, and two Oankali. For this is the price the gene traders exact for survival—interbreeding. Humans, including Lilith, will have more to learn, especially what it means to be human. The Oankali mixture will make notions of hierarchy, of superiority of one human to another obsolete. There will be no pure race.

The second novel in the series, *Adulthood Rites*, continues the saga of the regeneration of Earth. This novel is the story of the "constructs," the children born of the human-Oankali mixture. The Awakened humans still have difficulty in dealing with the aliens. They value human-looking babies, but still resent the fact that they are not fully human. They see the constructs as a threat to the old, pure human race. "Families will change. . . . A complete construct family will be a female, an ooloi, and children. Males will come and go as they wish and as they find welcome."[53] This new construct race can look different from the human form, especially after adolescent metamorphosis. Margit, a young construct, is angry at the old humans. She declares, "They blame me for not looking like them. They can't help doing it, and I can't help resenting it. I don't know which is worse—the ones who cringe if I touch them or the ones who pretend it's all right while they cringe inside."[54] Butler continues to explore the human tendency toward racism and xenophobia within this new context. The future here serves as a mirror for our contemporary society.

Many of the old human settlers of Earth cling to old ways and ideas. They try to build villages and towns to resemble the past as much as possible. Those who reject the Oankali will die out with their old ways, for almost all humans are infertile without Oankali genetic intervention. The old humans view Lilith and her construct trading village as traitors to the human race. "Human beings fear difference. Oankali crave difference. Humans persecute their different ones, yet they need them to give themselves definition and status."[55]

Akin, the adolescent son of Lilith, dead Joseph, and the Oankali, becomes the hero of the novel. He journeys between construct and human villages and feels he can be an envoy of peace and understanding. He is an idealistic youth, but he finds that his travels have made him unable to find a true bond with either constructs or old humans. He plans for the old humans to try a new settlement on Mars, leaving Earth for the constructs. "Humans would carry their dislike with them to be shut up together on Mars."[56] Perhaps working through the harsh environment there, humans would have to abandon their tendency to self-destruct. Akin is a true hero—the idealist willing to sacrifice a life with those most dear to him in order to carry out his mission to provide a self-destructive race with yet another chance for survival. The work is his rite of passage, as well as, hopefully, that of the human race.

The last novel in the trilogy, *Imago*, is told in first person by Jodahs, the first construct to become ooloi. Jodahs is an unknown factor which could cause pain and death. Without mature control, it could heal and yet, unknowingly, cause cancer. Jodahs, like all ooloi, can manipulate DNA within its body, earning the names "Life Trader" or "Weaver."[57] Since Jodahs is an unknown factor, it must return to the mothership for observation or go into exile on Earth. Jodahs and its family choose Earthly exile.

Jodahs's metamorphosis is not an easy one. It shape shifts from man to frog, to woman. It cures two humans, Tomas and Jesusa, of tumors. Jodahs finds these humans are fertile and as an ooloi it wants to mate with them. Their village of old humans would reject this. This new construct family has a strong will to survive and to help Aaor, another construct ooloi to complete metamorphosis and mate.

More construct ooloi are developing. They are a new species. When the old humans of Pascual, an Hispanic village, realize the ooloi can cure them, they welcome them. More families mate with Oankali, and thus more trader villages develop on Earth. The human-Oankali constructs have inherited the Earth. Issues of race and gender will become obsolete, as the notion of what it means to be human is transformed.

ON THE VALUE OF THE GENRE
TO AFRICAN-AMERICANS

Butler's science fiction has been described as "a literature of survival," with the basic premise "that black people survive the present and participate in shaping the future."[58] Yet, Butler says she is often asked by other blacks, "What good is science fiction to Black people?" Her answer:

> "What good is science fiction's thinking about the present, the future, and the past? What good is its tendency to warn or to consider alternative ways of thinking and doing? What good is its examination of the possible effects of science and technology, of social organization and political direction? At its best, science fiction stimulates imagination and creativity. It gets reader and writer off the beaten track, off the narrow, narrow footpath of what 'everyone' is saying, doing, thinking—whoever 'everyone' happens to be this year.
> And what good is all this to Black people."[59]

To all readers, and especially to young adults, Butler's ability to make the less travelled path exciting, to make readers see what it could mean to be truly human, to escape from the "beaten track" of racism and sexism, of trying to be bigger and better in the hierarchy, is a gift to be relished and pondered. Butler weaves strong patterns throughout her novels in which women of color assume power to challenge the established hierarchical thinking concerning race, gender, and the outsider. These are issues of importance which appeal to the adolescent reader, and they make Butler's novels an important contribution to the genre.

NOTES

1. "Octavia E. Butler," *Contemporary Authors*, ed. Frances Carol Locker (Detroit, MI: Gale Research, 1978), 73–76:104.
2. Sherley Anne Williams, "Sherley Anne Williams on Octavia E. Butler," *Ms.*, March 1986, 72.
3. Elizabeth A. Belden and Judith M. Beckman, "Extraordinary Viewpoints," *English Journal* 77 (April 1988): 78.
4. Williams, 70.
5. Octavia E. Butler, interview by Larry McCaffrey, in *Across the Wounded*

Galaxy: Interviews with Contemporary American Science Fiction Writers, ed. Larry McCaffrey (Urbana, IL: University of Illinois Press, 1990), 61–62.
6. Ibid., 67.
7. Octavia E. Butler, *Wild Seed* (Garden City, NY: Doubleday, 1980), 3.
8. Ibid., 8.
9. Ibid., 9.
10. Ibid., 60.
11. Ibid., 91.
12. Ibid.
13. Ibid., 98.
14. Ibid., 133.
15. Ibid., 141.
16. Ibid., 147.
17. Ibid.
18. Octavia E. Butler, *Mind of My Mind* (Garden City, NY: Doubleday, 1977), 7.
19. Ibid., 117.
20. Ibid., 60–61.
21. Ibid., 141.
22. Ibid., 113.
23. Octavia E. Butler, *Clay's Ark* (New York: St. Martin's Press, 1984), 30.
24. Ibid., 57.
25. Ibid., 156.
26. Ibid., 181.
27. Ibid., 5.
28. Ibid., 32.
29. Ibid., 160.
30. Ibid., 114.
31. Octavia E. Butler, *Patternmaster* (Garden City, NY: Doubleday, 1976), 17.
32. Ibid., 111.
33. Butler, *Clay's Ark*, 153.
34. Octavia E. Butler, *Survivor* (Garden City, NY: Doubleday, 1978), 31.
35. Ibid., 6.
36. Ibid., 5.
37. Ibid., 185.
38. McCaffrey, 65.
39. Ibid., 65.
40. Octavia E. Butler, *Kindred* (Garden City, NY: Doubleday, 1979), 29.
41. Ibid., 25.
42. Ibid., 163.

43. Ibid., 164.
44. Ibid., 165.
45. Ibid., 183.
46. Ibid., 26.
47. Ibid., 68.
48. Octavia E. Butler, *Dawn* (New York: Time Warner, 1987), 37.
49. Ibid., 36.
50. Ibid., 29.
51. Ibid., 11.
52. Ibid., 247.
53. Octavia E. Butler, *Adulthood Rites* (New York: Warner Books, 1988), 11.
54. Ibid., 15.
55. Ibid., 80.
56. Ibid., 276.
57. Octavia E. Butler, *Imago* (New York: Warner Books, 1989), 6.
58. Williams, 72.
59. Octavia E. Butler, "Birth of a Writer," *Essence*, May 1989, 134.

REFERENCES

Belden, Elizabeth A. and Judith M. Beckman. "Extraordinary Viewpoints." *English Journal* 77 (April 1988): 78–79.

Blauden, Nellie. "Otherworldly Women: Six All-Star Science Fiction Novelists." *Life*, July 1984, 112–117.

Bogstad, Janice. "Octavia E. Butler and Power Relationships." *Janus* 4 (Winter 1978–79): 28–29.

Butler, Octavia E. *Adulthood Rites*. New York: Warner Books, 1988.

____. "Birth of a Writer." *Essence*, May 1989, 74–79, 132–134.

____. *Clay's Ark*. New York: St. Martin's Press, 1984.

____. *Dawn*. New York: Time Warner, 1987.

____. *Imago*. New York: Warner Books, 1989.

____. Interview by Larry McCaffrey. In *Across the Wounded Galaxy: Interviews with Contemporary American Science Fiction Writers*, ed. Larry McCaffrey. Urbana, IL: University of Illinois Press, 1990, 61–62.

____. *Kindred*. Garden City, NY: Doubleday, 1979.

____. *Mind of My Mind*. Garden City, NY: Doubleday, 1977.

____. *Patternmaster*. Garden City, NY: Doubleday, 1976.

____. *Survivor*. Garden City, NY: Doubleday, 1978.

____. *Wild Seed*. Garden City, NY: Doubleday, 1980.

Davidson, Carolyn S. "The Science Fiction of Octavia Butler." *Salaga* (1981): 35.

Davis, Thadious M. and Trudier Harris, eds. "Octavia E. Butler." In *Dictionary of Literary Biography*, vol. 33, *Afro-American Fiction Writers After 1955.* Detroit: Gale Research, 1984.

Foster, Frances Smith. "Octavia Butler's Black Female Future Fiction." *Extrapolation* 23 (Spring 1982): 37–49.

Govan, Sandra Y. "Connections, Links, and Extended Networks: Patterns in Octavia Butler's Science Fiction." *Black American Literature Forum* 18 (1984): 12–15.

Lefanu, Sarah. *Feminism and Science Fiction.* Bloomington, IN: Indiana University Press, 1988.

Locker, Frances Carol, ed. "Octavia E. Butler." In *Contemporary Authors*, vol. 73–76. Detroit, MI: Gale Research, 1978.

Marowski, Daniel G., ed. "Octavia E. Butler." In *Contemporary Literary Criticism*, vol. 38. Detroit, MI: Gale Research, 1986.

Mixon, Veronica. "Futurist Woman: Octavia Butler." *Essence*, April 1979, 82–87.

Salvaggio, Ruth. "Octavia Butler and the Black Science-Fiction Heroine." *Black American Literature Forum* 18 (1984): 78–81.

Weixlmann, Joe. "An Octavia E. Butler Bibliography." *Black American Literature Forum* 18 (1984): 88–89.

Williams, Sherley Anne. "Sherley Anne Williams on Octavia E. Butler." *Ms.*, March 1986, 70–72.

THIRTEEN

Voodoo Visions: Supernatural African Themes in Horror Literature

Cosette N. Kies[1]

Most teenagers love horror in books and movies. One has only to visit any bookstore with a young adult (YA) section to see how many titles would be classified as horror, or more generally, thrillers. Although the adult horror fiction market was declared to be somewhat soft after the popularity of the genre during the 1970s and 1980s, teenagers continued to read and buy horror books enthusiastically. The publishing trends support this. In fact, some publishers started new YA horror lines in the 1990s, and authors who had previously worked in the adult field now try their hands at writing for teens, for example Charles L. Grant (also known as Simon Lake). Some titles from the early 1980s, such as those in the Twilight Series by Dell, were brought back into print as some authors gained a reputation in the horror field, such as Richie Tankersley Cusick. Some authors, traditionally thought of as YA thriller writers, for example, Lois Duncan, found their books continuing to sell well years after original publication.

Horror books have not been the favorite selection of most librarians and teachers who work with teenagers. As a result, many libraries did not stock a large selection of horror titles during the past few decades, and it has only been recently that the acknowledgement of the popularity of the horror genre with YAs has brought these adults to pay more attention to the books that young persons love to read for chills and thrills. Teachers and librarians have come to recognize that many teens will read horror books—if no others—including those written for adults, such as the massive, vocabulary-stretching works of Stephen King.

Young adults love the horror genre for a variety of reasons. A primary one is simply its shock value for "proper" adults, such as teachers, librarians, and parents. Also, teens enjoy the fantasy element of horror because it is manageable. You can close the book, or leave the movie, if fear becomes uncomfortable. In a modern world where teenagers can't control much of the real horror of society, having power over this one small area is rather appealing. It enables them to test their bravery levels, sort of like playing chicken with peers. "How much grossness can *you* take?" And those who endure and are truly scared reading a horror book or watching a horror movie are rewarded soon after with a positive emotional rush because the story wasn't real.

There are many popular horror themes, and teenagers seem to enjoy all of them—indestructible Freddy Krueger from Elm Street who "lives" to slice teenagers with his razor fingernails, seductive vampires, pathetic werewolves, man-made monsters, and haunted houses of unspeakable evil. Among these many popular themes are some with African origins that have become entrenched in American horror literature.

AFRICAN-AMERICAN HORROR THEMES

There are some African-American horror themes which cannot be considered uniquely African because they are present in a number of different cultures, such as shapechanging and the allure of unknown lands and lost civilizations. There is, however, an exclusive major theme from Africa that has inspired horror writers for generations, that of voodoo. Voodoo has its roots in African religions, religions that include a pantheon of gods and goddesses as complicated as the better-known classical mythological characters. Voodoo—sometimes termed "voudoun," "obeah," and "hoodoo"—acquired different aspects in the Western Hemisphere where African slaves disguised their own beliefs with an overlay of the Christian religion insisted upon by their European masters and adopted some aspects of Native American beliefs. Voodoo came to the Western Hemisphere early, dispersed widely to many different places, including America, and took on a variety of attributes. It was called by different names in different places, such as santería in Cuba and macumba in Brazil. The secrecy involving voodoo contributed to its mystique as well as laws forbidding its practice; certainly it was considered to be evil, yet fascinating, by European-Americans who knew little about it. Voodoo, as described by Zora Neale Hurston in *Tell My Horse*, is ". . . a religion of creation and life. It is the worship of the sun, the water and other natural forces, but the symbolism is no better understood than that of other religions and consequently is taken too literally."[2]

A number of scholarly and more popular works have been written about various aspects of voodoo. In the multivolume reference work, *Man, Myth & Magic: The Illustrated Encyclopedia of Mythology, Religion and the Unknown*, Francis Huxley includes a brief bibliography of scholarly works at the end of his article on voodoo. These include his own *The Invisibles*, plus one by Maya Deren, *Divine Horsemen: The Voodoo Gods* and another by Alfred Metraux, *Voodoo in Haiti*. These works approach voodoo primarily as a mythological and/or anthropological subject. The article and bibliography do not mention the work of Zora Neale Hurston. A more recent, personalized work by Migene González-Wippler, *The Santería Experience: A Journey into the Miraculous*, focuses on the sociological and psychological benefits of santería practice. The longer bibliography in this last work does include Hurston, but does not include the three scholarly works by Deren, Huxley, and Metraux. Clearly, a two-pronged approach is necessary for those interested in researching all aspects of voodoo. Primary emphasis in this essay will be on fictional works that include aspects of voodoo. The major topics covered include:

- The Gothic Tradition
- Mysteries
- Fantasy Influences
- Men's Adventures
- Mainstream Horror
- Zombies
- YA Thrillers
- Lost Lands and Legends
- Contemporary Legends

In earlier centuries in America voodoo was better known in certain locations, such as New Orleans, but it had an impact in other places in the colonies, such as Salem. The exotic tales of Tituba, the slave woman from the West Indies, were blamed for setting the devil loose in 1692 in Massachusetts and written about in YA books such as *The Devil's Shadow* by Clifford Lindsey Alderman and *A Break with Charity* by Ann Rinaldi. The transport of the devil from the tropics to cold New England produces changes, however, as explained by Tituba in Arthur Miller's play, *The Crucible*: "Oh, it be no Hell in Barbados. Devil, him be pleasureman in Barbados, him be singin' and dancin' in Barbados. It's you folks—you riles him up 'round here; it be too cold 'round here for that Old Boy. He freeze his soul in Massachusetts."[3] Tituba continues to intrigue writers, as evidenced in a new novel for adults, Maryse Conde's *I Tituba, Black Witch of Salem*, which reconstructs the life story of Tituba.

Voodoo was considered to be primitive by European-Americans into the twentieth century, when anthropological studies, including those by African-American folklorist and author Zora Neale Hurston, sparked public fascination for this now-syncretic belief system. Bestseller works, such as *The Magic Island* by W. B. Seabrook, contributed to a new interest in voodoo as well. The film industry made horror movies with voodoo themes; unfortunately, most were not as elegant as Val Lewton's *I Walked with a Zombie* (1943). Voodoo became a more popular theme in literature, and its legend as a mysterious power continued to grow. It is interesting to note that with growing sensitivity to racial issues starting in the 1960s, some European-American authors apparently became reluctant to use voodoo themes. It is also worth noticing the transformation of voodoo's zombie into a new, atomically-created shambling cannibal—a more American figure—from the simple, souless, living-dead creature. However, the old-style zombie returned again with another anthropological study, Wade Davis' bestselling *The Serpent and the Rainbow* in 1985.

THE GOTHIC TRADITION

In general, all horror literature had its start with the birth of gothic fiction in the eighteenth century. Gothic fiction was deplored by critics from the very beginning, with despair expressed over its excesses and overly dramatic episodes, not to mention the supernatural elements and romantic plots. Gothic literature has never really achieved respectability in the field of literature, but that has never affected its popularity with the public. The readership of gothic fiction is usually female, and in this century in America, its popularity can be clearly traced. The gothic's greatest popularity was in the 1960s and 1970s in the U.S. Original paperback gothics adorned bookstore shelves, most featuring a standardized cover with a fragile, beautiful heroine fleeing in distress from a gloomy mansion in the background. In many ways, this cover art summed up the appeal of gothics for many, for they provided readers with romance, mystery, and often a few inexplicable, supernatural thrills. It was during this period that a popular gothic, day-time soap opera appeared, "The House of Dark Shadows" featuring the life and loves of Barnabas Collins, a vampire.

Some of the original paperback gothics from this time included those with voodoo themes. These may be located occasionally in secondhand paperback stores, although most are now out of print. An examination of some of these titles provides useful clues concerning the authors' use of voodoo themes. Most of the authors are European-American, and although they appear to be all women, some of the books, such as those written by W.E.D. Ross under his other name of "Marilyn Ross," were written by men.

Ten gothic stories with voodoo themes were examined for this chapter. They are typical titles in gothic genre, with the chief protagonist being a lovely young woman, generally with no close family, who finds herself in a threatening, mysterious situation. Ultimately, the mystery is resolved with the assistance of at least one fascinating man, and the book ends happily. The books with voodoo themes, however, present some interesting aspects beyond this basic plot.

The most obvious commonality of the voodoo gothics is location. The heroine generally finds herself, for various reasons, in a new place. In the ten books examined, the most popular spot was Haiti, with five taking place in this locale famous for voodoo (*Dark Island* by Dorothy Daniels, *Drums of Darkness* by Marion Zimmer Bradley, *The Haiti Circle* by Marilyn Ross, *Haitian Legacy* by Sharon Wagner, and *Phantom of the Swamp*, also by Marilyn Ross). Three are set on other vaguely described Caribbean Islands (*Dark Talisman* by Anne-Marie Bretonne, *Isle of the Undead* by Virginia Coffman, and one by Dorothy Daniels based on the short-lived television serial "Strange Paradise," *Raxl, Voodoo Priestess*). One (*Voodoo Drums* by Veronica Leigh) is set in Louisiana bayou country. The last title, one considered an important work by many critics and originally published in hardback, (*Wide*

Sargasso Sea by Jean Rhys) is set partly in Jamaica and Dominica.

The heroines of the voodoo gothics arrive in the exotic locations for a variety of reasons: inheritance of a plantation, vacation and/or need to recuperate after illness or death in the family, escape from pursuing gangsters, a job, and in the case of *Wide Sargasso Sea*, the island has always been home.

Wide Sargasso Sea is the story of Bertha, Mr. Rochester's first wife, who upsets the wedding plans of Jane Eyre in Charlotte Brontë's classic. As an aside, it can be noted that *Jane Eyre* as a novel has had a great impact on gothic literature. In the ten gothics examined here, there are even two in which the heroines undertake the charge of young girls, a la little Adele in *Jane Eyre*.

Of the ten books under discussion, only this one, *Wide Sargasso Sea*, has achieved critical literary success and is the only one to end on a sad note. As Francis Wyndham says in his introductory notes:

> For many years, Jean Rhys has been haunted by the figure of the first Mrs. Rochester—the mad wife in *Jane Eyre*. The present novel—completed at last after much revision and agonized rejection of earlier versions—is her story. Not, of course, literally so: it is in no sense a pastiche of Charlotte Brontë and exists in its own right, quite independent of *Jane Eyre*. But the Brontë book provided the initial inspiration for an imaginative feat almost uncanny in its vivid intensity. From her personal knowledge of the West Indies, and her reading of their history, Miss Rhys knew about the mad Creole heiresses in the early nineteenth century, whose dowries were only an additional burden to them: products of an inbred, decadent, expatriate society, resented by the recently freed slaves whose superstitions they shared, they languished uneasily in the oppressive beauty of their tropical surroundings, ripe for exploitation.[4]

Another critic, Peter Hollindale, suggests in the *Times Literary Supplement* that the book ". . . is also a classic in its own right. Racial and feminist contexts are readily available here, too, but can more easily subvert a reading than assist it. This is not a novel about wronged identity, either racial or sexual, but something worse still. It is about deprivation of identity, about the horror and the madness that come from not knowing, on any level, who you are."[5]

The above comments are not meant to imply that superior novels can be found readily in the gothic genre. Most titles in this genre tend to be a bit silly. Even the voodoo gothic by Marion Zimmer Bradley, now a respected fantasy and science fiction writer, can best be described as a pedestrian romantic thriller, standing out from the crowd only because the heroine is African-American. It is not helped by being in an astrological series which includes horoscope analyses of the major characters by Sydney Omarr. Some titles by other writers, such as W.E.D. Ross, were obviously cranked out in haste with heavy emphasis on dramatic sensationalism, such as this beginning to *The Haiti Circle*:

> Voodoo!
> Until that moonlit night when she had first seen the ghostly white mansion rising up from a cliff on shore north of Port-au-Prince in Haiti, Agnes Woodridge had not paid any attention to the African cult which was said to have the exotic Caribbean island in its grip. She had experienced an eerie feeling at her first glimpse of the great house known as Seacrest, but she had never guessed what weird adventures waited for her in its shadowed corridors and rooms. Nor had she known that within its walls she would lose her heart to a man branded by many as a murderer![6]

These are hardly the words to inspire excitement in a Pulitzer Prize committee, but they admittedly reach out and grab readers who like the gothic genre. The passage, however, suffers in comparison with these opening words of *Wide Sargasso Sea*:

> They say when trouble comes close ranks, and so the white people did. But we were not in their ranks. The Jamaican ladies had never approved of my mother, ". . . because she pretty like pretty self" Christophine said.
> She was my father's second wife, far too young for him they thought, and worse still, a Martinique girl. When I asked him why so few people came to see us, he told me that the road from Spanish Town to Coulibri Estate where we lived was very bad and that road repairing was now a thing of the past.[7]

Other than the similarity of the first person narrative, very common in gothics, Ross and Rhys illustrate well the idea that although the gothic genre has the potential for creating fine books, most often the narrative is indicative of quick plotting and fast writing. Only one of the ten voodoo gothic titles considered here is still in print—*Wide Sargasso Sea*. The 1993 release of a film based on the book will no doubt produce renewed interest in the novel.

A gothic novel generally includes a mystery, so it is not surprising that there cannot be a firm line drawn between gothics and mysteries employing supernatural themes. Also, elements of fantasy provide grounds for including titles in the fantasy genre, as well. An example is Karen Blixen's (Isak Dinesen) gothic mystery written under the pseudonym of Pierre Andrezel. In *The Angelic Avengers* Olympia, a servant from Santo Domingo, practices voodoo and saves the young heroines through her skills.

MYSTERIES

Closely related to the gothics discussed above, are those more clearly mysteries. These stories place the emphasis on the puzzle that must be solved rather than the romance of the hapless heroine. These books are traditionally constructed mysteries, but with the overlay of supernatural implications. They are not mainstream horror, although some of these—to be discussed later—do employ the structure of mysteries in their plotting.

These mysteries show one strong common trait. Quickly examined here are three written by John Dickson Carr (noted author of mysteries), Norah Lofts (writer of gothics and historical novels), and Margot Arnold (mystery writer and author of a fictionalized biography of New Orleans voodoo queen, Marie Laveau).

Carr's *Papa La-Bas* offers a plot set in antebellum New Orleans. The hero, an English diplomat, becomes involved in solving a mystery and murder which leads to secret scandals and hints of voodoo activity. Lofts' book, *The Claw*, is set in twentieth-century England, where death and mystery include references to African herbal work and a secret Leopard Man cult. Margot Arnold's *Death of a Voodoo Doll* is one of the Penny Spring and Toby Glendower mysteries. The English scholars find mystery and murder, as well as sinister voodoo practices, in New Orleans during Mardi Gras.

These mysteries, and other similar titles, use supernatural touches to provide exotic touches to traditional English-style mysteries. In almost all cases, the supernatural is explained away, although the reader with imagination is usually left wondering if the rational explanation is the only one.

FANTASY INFLUENCES

A number of voodoo books can be classed in what many would consider to be the fantasy category. Many traditional ghost stories, hauntings, and folk legends, such as those incorporated in books like Charles Chesnutt's *The Conjure Woman*, are often considered fantasy.

Fritz Leiber's *Conjure Wife*, first published in 1953 and made into a number of movie versions, can be used as an example. The plot involves a college professor's wife, Tansy, who has acquired voodoo skills while accompanying her anthropological husband to research sites. Her husband is horrified to discover Tansy using her spells to advance his career at his college. Tansy reluctantly agrees to stop, but her husband, Norman, then discovers that the wives of some college administrators are also using magic. Without Tansy's supernatural protection, Norman's career seems doomed, and the vindictive administrative wives steal Tansy's soul. In order to get it back, Norman must use magic himself. It should be noted that for women readers especially, an extra dash of horror is created by Leiber in his premise that all women are witches with special magical powers.

Another earlier fantasy work useful to consider for its influence on the sub-field of voodoo fiction is A. [Abraham] Merritt's *Burn Witch Burn*, first published in 1933. The plot concerns the evil Madam Mandelip, a witch who steals souls which she uses to animate dolls to do her nefarious bidding. Only human love is a strong enough weapon to thwart her. Merritt was prolific. A final work, finished after his death by Hannes Bok, can be considered more mainstream horror than fantasy. In *The Black Wheel* terrible ghostly zombie-like subhumans are discovered to be the descendants of brutally murdered African slaves. They are out for revenge and kill anyone who comes near their Caribbean home.

By now it has probably been noticed that most of the titles discussed thus far were written primarily for an adult audience, although they have been read by YAs as well. Voodoo themes, in particular, seem to be avoided by YA authors, although some examples can be found.

For example, *Seven Spells to Sunday* by Andre Norton and

Phyllis Miller includes a voodoo doll (albeit a paper one) as one of the seven spells of the title. This book for very young teenagers does not have an evil voodoo doll or even dwell on the use to which such artifacts are usually put; instead the "voo-don't" paperdoll gives the protagonist, Monnie, a chance to improve people around her and bestow intangible gifts, such as small improvements for her classmates.

Another book to consider in the fantasy voodoo category, is Patricia Geary's *Strange Toys*, the tale of Pet who seeks her eccentric older sister Deane, a practitioner of voodoo. In the end Pet is able to put her sister to rest, but not until she has undertaken a bizarre search to discover herself, as well as Deane.

A more recent book dealing with the supernatural as fantasy is Barbara Hood Burgess' *Oren Bell*. As with Virginia Hamilton's *The House of Dies Drear*, the supernatural touches are not voodoo inspired but deal rather with the more universal concept of ghosts.

Twelve-year-old Oren Bell lives in Detroit with his twin sister, take-charge Latonya; younger sister Brenda, single working mother, and grandfather Bill Bell, a retired, drunken jazz musician. The Bells live in an old house with a ghost in one of the bedrooms and a deserted mansion next door full of unsavory characters and shady dealings. All the major characters in the book are African-American.

Some other books for YAs with fantasy-supernatural touches include *The Bridges of Summer* by Brenda Seabrooke, *Trouble's Child* by Mildred Pitts Walter, and *The Cay* by Theodore Taylor. These titles have aged African-American characters who cling to old traditions, containing such elements as conjure medicine.

MEN'S ADVENTURES

Another type of fiction has contributed to mainstream horror literature which for lack of a better term is sometimes described as men's adventure stories. In the past these books by authors such as Edgar Rice Burroughs and Christopher Percival Wren, were not limited exclusively to male readership, but the current publications seem to be more gender directed than in the past. Rather than the gentlemanly soldiers-of-fortune in older fiction, today's protagonists in men's adventure stories are often mercenaries, sometimes Vietnam veterans, who are very interested in dishing out their own brand of justice. There are a number of men's adventure series which include titles with voodoo themes.

Barry Sadler, probably best known as the writer of "The Green Berets" song, before his death authored a series of books about Casca, Roman legionnaire present at the crucifixion of Christ and cursed to roam the earth until the second coming. Casca spends most of his endless time as an adventuring mercenary participating in wars throughout the centuries. Number twelve in the series, *Casca: The African Mercenary*, finds Casca at somewhat loose ends after the end of the Vietnamese War. He is hired to assassinate a black African dictator in a racially tense area of Africa. The dictator, Matthew Dzhombe, is depicted as a follower of the old ways, and his excesses are supposedly sufficient to enlist the reader's support of Casca who is nothing more than a hired killer. The basic set-up is rather like an episode of the old television serial, "Mission Impossible," a common plot structure of books in the men's adventures.

Another title, *Cult War*, number forty-eight in the Able Team series by Dick Stivers, finds the Able Team in New Orleans fighting zombies. Similar is *Hellfire in Haiti*, number six in Jim Case's Cody's Army series. Cody leads his buddies on a rescue mission to save one of their members who has been captured by voodoo practitioners determined to turn Rufe into a zombie.

These books tend to have explicit sex and violence galore, but the ultra-masculine protagonists can always be counted on to complete their missions successfully. Earlier superheroes, such as Doc Savage, could also be depended on to dispatch villains as needed, but generally they treated women more gallantly than today's adventurers. These books often include sympathetic African-American characters, but they despise voodoo as much as the European-Americans.

Somewhat related to these stories, are historical novels which employ gratuitous sex and violence. *Mandingo* clones and variations can be found, such as *Voodoo Slave* by Norman Daniels and *Slavers* by C. C. Parx. Voodoo practices are sometimes alluded to in these books, but the main attraction is sex and violence.

MAINSTREAM HORROR

Fiction classified as horror has certain distinct features, although the elements of other kinds of fiction noted earlier, are included. Horror is earned as a classification when the author deliberately writes a story that will scare the reader. It has been suggested by a number of critics that the better horror tales create the more "refined" emotion of terror, particularly by implying awful things rather than laying the nastiness on with a trowel. Today's popular authors, exemplified by Stephen King, tend to settle for horror, rather than terror, and apparently today's teenagers like reading it just fine! Subtlety is generally not a quality to be found in the majority of contemporary horror fiction.

It should be noted that the majority of mainstream horror writers are European-American males. This tradition can be seen clearly in the short stories often created for pulp magazines, such as *Weird Tales* in the 1920s and 1930s and later collected in anthologies, stories such as "Mother of Serpents" by Robert Bloch, "Eyes of the Serpent" by August Derleth and Mark Schorer, and "Black Terror" by Henry S. Whitehead.

One of the horror writers who has often employed voodoo themes in his writing is Hugh B. Cave. Cave lived in the Caribbean for some time, witnessed various voodoo rites, and has written about voodoo in a number of books, including *Disciples of Dread*, *The Evil*, *Legion of the Dead*, *The Lower Deep*, *Lucifer's Eye*, and *Shades of Evil*.[8] Cave has also written a few YA books, but these do not deal with supernatural themes and are straightforward adventure stories in the tradition of Robb White. Cave's voodoo books written for adults and also read by young adults are traditional, employing the talking drums used for communication and summoning the ancient gods, voodoo rituals, magic, spells, and zombies. They include typical elements, such as a quest, romance, menacing supernatural horror, and a relatively happy ending after scary episodes and dangerous adventures. The stories stress the negative applications of voodoo and seldom consider any benefits, such as being able to seek, and sometimes receive, help from the gods.

Any number of mainstream horror writers have used voodoo themes, although none as extensively as Cave. Stephen King has not used voodoo as a major theme, but another best selling horror author, Dean Koontz, has written *Deadfall* dealing with a foul voodoo practitioner who summons up evil beasties. Only the police detective's little daughter, Penny, seems to know instinctively from the very beginning that something beyond accepted reality is killing people in the city. Two other authors who have used the detective story plot structure for voodoo horror are Bill Pronzini in *Masques* and Jonathan Wolfe in *Killer See, Killer Do*. Jeffery Wilds Deaver goes to the Caribbean in *Voodoo*, as do Martin James in *Zombie House*, Peter Tremayne in *Zombie*, and James Farber in *Blood Island*. Lisa Cantrell in *Boneman* mixes voodoo with drug dealing in North Carolina.

These stories typically tell of innocent, hapless, basically decent people who find themselves involved with horrible supernatural events they cannot control. Most horror novels are built on this basic premise: Can the puny abilities of humans be a match for the seemingly overwhelming power of supernatural evil?

There are many voodoo-inspired horror novels. These include *The Coven* and *Diabolus* by E. Howard Hunt under the pseudonym of David St. John, *Infernal Idol* by Henry Seymour, *Covenant at Coldwater* by John Osier, and *Night-Child* by John Meyer. One, *The Steeds of Satan* by Peter Leslie, capitalizes on the 1970s popularity of exorcism as a horror theme by sending a priest—hero of an exorcism series, Father Hayes—to do battle with Brazilian macumba practitioners. Most mainstream horror books are generally not remarkable in any way, but they provide a fast, scary read for those who enjoy the genre.

A book that received positive reviews on its publication in 1978 was William Hjortsberg's *Falling Angel*. It enjoyed renewed popularity with the film of 1987 staring Mickey Rourke, Robert De Niro, and Lisa Bonet. As with some other voodoo novels, voodoo *per se* is not separated from European-based supernatural beliefs: for example, Dennis Wheatley's *Strange Conflict*. An underlying premise of many supernatural horror stories is the idea that there is basically one good and one evil in our universe, and there are various paths to use in reaching heaven or hell. It is possible to sell one's soul to a European-inspired Satan, or an African-inspired Dambullah, the most powerful god of voodoo. As explained by African-American author Ishmael Reed in his "Neo-HooDoo Manifesto":

> HooDoo is the strange and beautiful "fits" the Black slave Tituba gave the children of Salem. (Notice the arm waving ecstatic females seemingly possessed at the "Pentecostal," "Baptist," and "Rock Festival," [all fronts for Neo-HooDoo]). The reason that HooDoo isn't given the credit it deserves in influencing American Culture is because the students of that culture both "overground" and "underground" are uptight closet Jeho-vah

revisionists. They would assert the American and East Indian and Chinese thing before they would the Black thing. Their spiritual leaders Ezra Pound and T. S. Eliot hated Africa and "Darkies." In Theodore Roszak's book—*The Making of a Counter Culture*—there is barely any mention of the Black influence on the culture even though its members dress like Blacks talk like Blacks walk like Blacks, gesture like Blacks wear Afros and indulge in Black music and dance (Neo-HooDoo).[9]

Another horror book that should be noted here, not due to the superior literary quality of the novel itself, but rather for its associated notoriety is *The Religion* by Nicholas Condé published in 1982. An anthropologist newly arrived in New York City with his young son discovers voodoo all over the place. The son is selected for human sacrifice by a santería cult which is trying to stop some sort of cataclysmic disaster. The book was made into a movie, retitled *The Believers* (1987) and starred Martin Sheen. In 1989, news broadcasts informed the public that sinister cult murders had taken place in Matamoros, Mexico, across the border from Brownsville, Texas. A number of individuals, including American student Mark Kilroy, had apparently been sacrificed in order to enhance the power of a drug ring cult. Investigations brought forth the information that one of the leaders of the group, Sara Maria Aldrete Villareal, had insisted that initiates to the cult watch the film, *The Believers*, for orientation. A number of quickly written true crime books confirm this detail.[10]

ZOMBIES

A subgenre of voodoo horror fiction involves the zombie. According to Zora Neale Hurston in *Tell My Horse*, zombies are:

> . . . bodies without souls. The living dead. Once they were dead, and after that they were called back to life again. . . . But to them [upper class Haitians] also it is a horrible possibility. Think of the fiendishness of the thing. It is not good for a person who has lived all his life surrounded by a degree of fastidious culture, loved to his last breath by family and friends, to contemplate the probability of his resurrected body being dragged from the vault—the best that love and means could provide, and set to toiling ceaselessly in the banana fields, working like a beast, unclothed like a beast, and like a brute crouching in some foul

den in the few hours allowed for rest and food. From an educated, intelligent being to an unthinking, unknown beast. Then there is the helplessness of the situation. Family and friends cannot rescue the victim because they do not know. They think the loved one is sleeping peacefully in his grave. They may motor past the plantation where the Zombie who was once dear to them is held captive often and again and its soulless eyes may have fallen upon them without thought or recognition.[11]

The traditional zombie of folklore and older fiction is a zonked-out, soulless being pulled back from the grave after death for purposes of revenge or labor. As Hurston's description explains, many zombies were automatons, beasts of burden, who were called from the grave by evil bokars simply to be unpaid laborers. Others were resurrected for reasons of revenge. In either case, the legend has had its desired effect, for the idea that even death cannot guarantee a final rest and peace is frightening.

In horror fiction, traditional zombies have been present, but they have not been a dominant theme; it is the threat of being turned into a zombie that is more fearful than the pitiable, shambling zombies themselves. These poor creatures have appeared in movies and books, such as Jay Callahan's *Footprints of the Dead* in the YA Twilight series. In this typical gothic plot, the heroine Danielle runs afoul of a zombie:

> The drumbeat altered its pattern and began delivering its message to the zombie. He withdrew the machete from his waistband and held it aloft. The moonlight glittered on its silver surface. Slowly, the zombie began circling Danielle. At the drum's insistence, he began slicing the deadly instrument though the air, creating a sound like the hissing of snakes. He brought it lower and lower until the breeze from the blade stirred Danielle's hair. Then he poised the machete above her. The razor-sharp tip rested lightly, delicately, on the flesh of her bare throat.[12]

This zombie is a little more threatening than most traditional zombies who generally clomp about stupidly with little purpose other than doing what they are ordered to do. *Doonesbury* character, devious Uncle Duke, even suggests during his brief stint as a zombie, "It's not a bad life. You don't have to take responsibility for any of your actions, but I miss the danger, the adrenaline, the sense of being right out there on the edge. . . ."[13]

The zombie character is often more pathetic than terrifying. Some variations have appeared, including Stephen King's Micmac Indian legend inspired zombies in *Pet Sematary* which features first a decidedly rotten pet cat returned from the grave followed by the demonic version of a once-lovable child. Here the zombies are full of evil, rather than being devoid of feeling.

In 1968 a new zombie was constructed with the now legendary horror movie, *The Night of the Living Dead*, created by George Romero and John Russo. As John Russo explains:

> *Night of the Living Dead* was a movie concept that took some old themes and old concepts and bent them into a brand-new shape. When we made that picture, zombie movies had been made before, but none of them had been smash hits. Zombies weren't considered heavyweight fright material like Frankenstein, Dracula, and the Wolfman. The zombies in the old horror movies didn't really do much other than walk as if they were in a trance and occasionally strangle somebody or heave somebody against a wall. They moved so slowly you could easily get away from one of them if you were out in the open instead of trapped in a locked room.
>
> What we did was give the old zombie legend a new twist. We made our zombies into cannibals—eaters of human flesh. Suddenly they were way more dangerous, way more terrifying. If a zombie bit you and your brain wasn't destroyed, you *became* one of them. And in our movie there were *lots* of them. They were weak and slow-moving as individuals, but they had strength of numbers on their side.
>
> These new slants struck at some primal fears that exist in people the world over. One of the strongest fears that people have is the fear of death—and the living dead, the zombies, are the fear of death magnified, because they represent death that never ends, and a "life after death" that nobody really wishes to have.[14]

Romero and Russo also changed the origin of their "new" zombies. Rather than having the dead resurrected by voodoo hougans, atomic testing is blamed for bringing a rebirth of sorts to corpses. The original movie inspired a number of sequels, with the cannibal zombies marching anywhere they want, even into that beloved teenage site, the mall. Russo has authored the novelizations of some of these films.

Russo has also used the more traditional zombie with the film and novelization, *Voodoo Dawn*, later expanded into a full-length horror novel, *Living Things*. In this opus, an evil hougan, or bokar, practitioner of Haitian voodoo, moves his venue from the island to the mainland U.S. In most horror novels it takes people awhile to catch on to what is really happening, and when the suggestion of the supernatural is made, it is usually pooh-poohed. In *Living Things*, a police lieutenant reacts, "I don't know, man," Jones said, as tongue-in-cheek as his partner. "If God can make folks who've been rotting in their graves for hundreds of years rise up whole on Judgement Day, maybe some kind of voodoo spell could animate those suckers even if they were all cut up in little pieces." [15]

Another variation on the old zombie theme was used by Hollywood in *Dead & Buried*, with novelization by Chelsea Quinn Yarbro. Here zombies don't know who—or what—they are. A small town sheriff finds it bad enough to finally realize he is dealing with murdering zombies, but is horrified to discover in the end that he, too, is a zombie.

YA THRILLERS

Many of the horror titles that adults and young adults like to read fall into the general category of thrillers and a newly named subgenre called "dark suspense." They are generally not as gruesome as mainstream horror and the supernatural is at a minimum or even nonexistant, but they still provide plenty of scares for those preferring a milder form of reading entertainment.

Lois Duncan has written a number of thrillers for teens. The last one she wrote with supernatural elements was *Locked in Time*, published in 1985. The teenage heroine, Nore, is spending the summer in Louisiana with her father's new family; mysterious Lisette and her two children, Gabe and Josie. Nore figures out immediately that something is not right in the decaying old mansion, but it takes time to deduce what is really going on there. It turns out that Lisette has resorted to a voodoo spell to provide eternal life for her and her children. Since Nore discovers the secret, her life is in danger. Nore eventually triumphs, and Lisette and Gabe are killed in a car accident. (The spell did not block death by accident.) Nore is left with thirteen-year-old Josie who will be her responsibility for the rest of Nore's life.

There are only a few voodoo details provided in *Locked in Time*.

In Duncan's hands, the obeah ceremony giving Lisette eternal life is so sanitized it seems more like a pagan Druid rite than the actualities of voodoo.

A title in the YA Twilight series, *Evil on the Bayou* by Richie Tankersley Cusick, is typical of the series by alluding to evil magic, in this case possible voodoo with lots of snakes slithering about, but there are few details regarding actual beliefs and practices. Again, a rotten old woman has bought into the bad side for eternal youth, but in this book the teenage heroine must sacrifice her own youth, and ultimately her life, for the old woman to succeed.

Another YA book using voodoo is *Swamp Witch* by Laurie Bridges and Paul Alexander in the Dark Forces series. The plot is less original than Duncan's, and is a teenage gothic. The heroine, Linda, is spending the summer with her best friend, Heather, in South Carolina. Heather's old mammy, Tubelle—a dreadfully stereotyped African-American—is determined that her precious Heather must have the best of everything, including Linda's boyfriend. If it means Linda must be totally eliminated, Tubelle is not averse to using some voodoo spells. In desperation, Tubelle uses a poisonous snake in an attempt to dispatch her intended victim, but Linda avoids death, and the snake gets Tubelle instead.

In *Journey*, a YA novel by Joyce Carol Thomas, an attractive African-American teenager, Meggie Alexander, runs into some medical horror. Teenagers are being murdered for their healthy, young body parts, replacements for the worn-out organs of three wicked old men. In an odd, mystical prologue, Meggie as a baby communicates with a spider that is closer in spirit to E. B. White's Charlotte than the creepy crawlies so many people fear. In the end, Meggie is saved by her spider friends.

LOST LANDS AND LEGENDS

The theme of seeking great treasures and awesome secrets in unknown lands is not limited only to Africa, but that continent has long appealed to writers as a mysterious place where strange and wonderous things may be found. Perhaps dinosaurs can be discovered in the dark jungles, as in the movie *Baby* and the comic book *The Punisher Wolverine—African Saga*. Precious jewels are always a draw, as in Haggard's *King Solomon's Mines*. Adventure is heightened when such a marvelous locale is used.

Over a century ago, H. Rider Haggard, a British author, used Africa as the setting for the story of *She*, a mysterious white goddess who can live forever. *She* inspired films and sequels, and one contemporary writer, Richard Monaco, incorporates Haggard himself in a sequel, *Journey to the Flame*.

A mainstream American horror author, John Farris, has used Haggard's idea of *She* in *All Heads Turn When the Hunt Goes By*. Farris' plot concerns a wealthy Arkansas family during the early 1940s. Horrible, savage crazes descend on the family members, until only the central character, Nhora, is left. She is the cause of it all, and perhaps she is "She" herself, a goddess with great powers, the Ai-da Wedo. "The Ai-da Wedo is serpent, goddess of the moon and wife of the sun. In Africa she's called Mawu, in Haiti Erzulie—she's dark, and as beautiful as the queen of Sheba. Those who want to change their fortunes, their station in life, invoke her. But there's a danger in that, as you already know." [16] Another character in the book speculates about her identity as well:

> Stories about Gen Loussaint were always fantastic and frequently chilling. One met old-timers, traders who were on the river long before the turn of the century, and some insisted they had dealt with her. In her prime she was said to be very beautiful—what else?—but inhumanly cruel, unequaled in wickedness, a priestess of butchery among savages infamous for their blood dealings with other tribes. Her cruelty so pleased the evil spirits of the forest that she was given the power to change her shape, to vanish in a twinkling and reappear miles away. Familiar rubbish. She became—reptilian, after the fashion of the Ajimba gods, but not less beautiful. Her other-worldly self was a kind of succubus, common in African folklore. [17]

Farris also uses Africa for another mainstream horror book, *Catacombs*. Mysterious red diamonds with a secret formula etched on them are rumored to be in the area of Mt. Killmanjaro. An international espionage struggle to find the formula ensues, with a great deal of blood and guts spilled. A tribe of cat people gives a bit of punch, as well. Another, milder book, *Stickmen* by Seth Pfefferle, in which ancient Africans are resurrected, also involves political intrigue in its plot.

No discussion of Africa's mysterious geography, however brief, would be complete without mention of Joseph Conrad's *Heart of Darkness*. A true classic of English literature, the book is complex and beautiful. The hero's quest upriver to find Kurtz is full of meaning and metaphor. Kurtz's final words, "The horror! The horror!" do not provide any easy clues to deciphering the multiple themes of the novella. "Horror" in this context is not the superficial horror of leisure reading fiction, it is a cry questioning the meaning of life and death—the purpose of existence itself.

CONTEMPORARY LEGENDS

Modern society has provided additional meaning to the more traditional themes to be found in African-American horror fiction. One can look at the terrors of recent history and discover more horror than can be dreamed up in the head of a novelist. In Frances Temple's *A Taste of Salt* the reader is presented with a story of modern Haiti. Djo, a teenage boy, is suffering from burns in a hospital, the result of fighting to rid his country of the hated dictator, Duvalier, who relied on voodoo traditions to terrorize the country. The taste of salt of the title refers to a voodoo legend. Djo explains why the teacher, Pe Pierre, calls his books Taste of Salt:

> But there is one little trick that can save the zombie. Do you remember what it is Jeremie? Did your mama tell you this?
>
> If the zombie can get a taste of salt, he will understand. He will open his true eyes and see that he has been made a zombie. And he will turn against his master. He will obey him no longer. He will make himself free.
>
> I am not so quick, Jeremie. Among us boys, Lally is the smart one. I use these books with Pe Pierre and not thinking anything about the title. Then one day I see why the books be called Taste Salt. It is because that is what being able to read and write is like. You understand things you didn't before.[18]

A different kind of contemporary horror is described in one of English writer Clive Barker's Books of Blood stories, "The Forbidden." Here is the idea that belief can create reality. If kids believe strongly enough in a hook-handed boogyman, he will come. In "The Forbidden"—used as the basis for the film *Candyman* set in Chicago—the boogyman appears to the heroine, sociologist Helen, in a housing project:

> "Don't kill me," she breathed.
> "Do you believe in me?" he said.
> She nodded minutely. "How can I not?" she said.
> "Then why do you want to live?"
> . . .
>
> "If you would learn," the fiend said, "just a *little* from me . . . you would not beg to live." His voice had dropped to a whisper. "I am rumor," he sang in her ear. "It's a blessed condition, believe me. To live in people's dreams; to be whispered at street corners, but not have to *be*. Do you understand?"
> . . .
>
> "I won't force it upon you," he replied, the perfect gentleman. "I won't oblige you to die. But think; *think*. If I unhook you . . . think how they would mark this place with their talk . . . point it out as they passed by and say, 'She died there, the woman with the green eyes.' Your death would be a parable to frighten children with. Lovers would use it as an excuse to cling closer together." [19]

Other new, American-style zombies have turned up in modern settings as well. In Nina Nikki Hoffman's short story, "Zombies for Jesus," zombies are the followers of the supernatural "Rev," surely a wicked commentary on some of today's evangelists and their followers. Other zombie stories appear in anthologies edited by John Skipp and Craig Spector, *Book of the Dead* and *Book of the Dead 2: Still Dead*.

Another contemporary folklore legend concerns secret formulas for gaining prowess on the football field, no doubt inspired by the real-life medical horror stories of steroid use by athletes. In David Morrell's short story, "Mumbo Jumbo," a coach uses an ancient idol for locker room rites to inspire the team to win. Without the rite, things don't go well on the gridiron.

In *De Mojo Blues* by A. R. Flowers, a Vietnam veteran who returns to his hometown of Memphis, Tennessee, becomes a sort of Robin Hood of hoodoo, using voodoo spells to help those in need—a combination of a traditional legend with the contemporary, enduring hope that there are many secret, yet-to-be-discovered cures for all human ills. Francine Prose in *Primitive People* uses voodoo as a symbol in a novel about contemporary society, relations between people, and attitudes.

Probably the most important author creating new voodoo images in his writing is African-American author Ishmael Reed. He is not a horror writer, but his influence on the creation of contemporary views about voodoo literature must be considered. Reed has described his concept of Neo-HooDoo in novels, including *Flight to Canada, The Free-Lance Pallbearers, The Last Days of Louisiana Red, Reckless Eyeball,* and *Yellow Back Radio Broke Down*: Reed's best known work is probably *Mumbo Jumbo,* a tongue-in-cheek scholarly account of a detective's efforts to combat the growth of an infamous dance, Jes Grew, which is sweeping the county:

> Jes Grew was going around in circles until the 1920s when it impregnated America's "hysteria." I was there, a private eye practicing in my Neo-HooDoo therapy center named by my critics Mumbo Jumbo Kathedral because I awarded the Asson to myself. Licensed myself. I was a jacklegged detective of the metaphysical who was on the case; and in 1920 there was a crucial case. In 1920 Jes Grew swept through this country and whether they like it or not Americans were confronted with the choices of whether to Eagle Rock or Buzzard Sweep, whether to join the contagion or quarantine it, whether to go with Jes Grew or remain loyal to the Atonist Path protected by the Wallflower Order, its administrative backbone, composed of grumblers and sourpusses. . . .[20]

POETRY

Poetry is occasionally used as a form for creating horror, telling a story, and creating a mood. Some of these poems use voodoo themes, and a few will be viewed briefly here. In Margaret Dunbar's "And through the Caribbean Sea," she creates images and contrasts similar to those of Ishmael Reed. Her use of colors—indigo and tangerine, particularly—is effective:

> The indigo sifted from its drum-like vein
> toward the blue of the sky that the Goths attained.
> The tangerine, became the orange of the tango, again.[21]

The poem culminates with:

Until, who questions whether we'd be prone to yearn
for a Louis Quinze frame, a voodoo fire,
Rococo, Baroque, an African mask or a Gothic spire
or any style of any age or any place or name.[22]

Another poem invoking the Caribbean is "Night Fishing on the Caribbean Littoral of the Mutant Rain Forest" by Robert Frazier and Bruce Boston. The piece begins:

Out beyond a humid sluggish slip of coast where
mangrove cays nose under like scuttled battleships,
beyond the corrugated tin hovels where Obeah ladies
stir their gruely brews of blue magic on to dawn,
beyond the hanging carcasses of loggerheads and crocs
yellowing to decay in the moon's carious light,
a patch of the Mutant Rain Forest shudders lifelike
in the way of a tropical squall, spooking the Caribs
who nightfish from a rickety stilt-legged pier,
causing them to blow their morning conches
and pipe a dire revelry to the dark wind above.[23]

Historical events also inspire poetry, and in her collection of African-American supernatural tales, *The Dark-Thirty*, Patricia C. McKissack uses an oral-history account to create the poem, "We Organized." The poem tells what happens when a cruel slave holder plans to sell Sally away from her husband, Lee, and does not free Corbella as he has promised. The slaves organize and hold a rite deep in the woods. They make a straw effigy of the master, and dance and chant all night. Before long, the master falls ill, and knowing what has happened, he frees all of his slaves in order to be rid of them.

HISTORICAL, ANTHROPOLOGICAL, AND FOLKLORIC INFLUENCES

Some mention should be made of nonfiction materials related to African-American horror themes. Most obvious is the influence of folktales on horror and related fiction. This influence has been mentioned before in this chapter, exemplified by Charles Chesnutt's work. As Gayle Jones comments in *Liberating Voices: Oral Tradition in African American Literature*, "The Chesnutt story is an example of the early uses of the folktale, essential to the story, but the landscape and imagination of the folktale is separate from the story proper. . . . The deeper texture and controlling values of oral tradition are often excluded from the interpretation."[24]

The oral tradition has been of critical importance in African-American literature. Earlier work in this century to capture narratives has been of crucial value. For example, the stories of still-living former slaves were collected by the Library of Congress during the American Depression, some of which have been included in *Bullwhip Days* edited by James Mellon. These reminiscences include this one by Lizzie Hughes:

> My young mistress was allus telling us ghost stories and trying to scare the niggers. She like to got killed at that business. She put a high chair on her shoulder, and kivvered herself with a sheet, and went out in the yard to scare my uncle, Allen. He was the blacksmith, and was going home from the shop carrying a big sledgehammer. When he seed "that tall white thin," he throwed the hammer at it, but missed and hit a big iron pot in the yard and busted it all to pieces.[25]

Oral accounts have been important to anthropologists who use this as a valued field research technique. Zora Neale Hurston, who had been a student of famous anthropologist Franz Boas at Barnard College in New York, researched and recorded first-hand information about American hoodoo and Haitian voodoo. Hurston's autobiography, *Dust Tracks on a Road*, as well as biographies published later for adults and young adults, such as *Zora Neale Hurston: A Storyteller's Life* by Janelle Yates and *Sorrow's Kitchen: The Life and Folklore of Zora Neale Hurston* by Mary E. Lyons, describe Hurston's life and research. As Hurston herself describes some of her work:

> In New Orleans, I delved into Hoodoo, or sympathetic magic. I studied with the Frizzly Rooster, and all of the other noted "doctors." I learned the routines for making and breaking marriages; driving off and punishing enemies; influencing the minds of judges and juries in favor of clients; killing by remote control and other things. In order to work with these "two-headed" doctors, I had to go through an initiation with each.[26]

One of the doctors Hurston studied with claimed to be the

nephew of the famous Marie Laveau, voodoo queen of New Orleans during the nineteenth century. Many legends have been told about this woman and her daughter, also called Marie. A European-American, Robert Tallent, a student of voodoo and Marie Laveau, produced a nonfiction work, *Voodoo in New Orleans*, and a fictionalized biography, *The Voodoo Queen*. Another fictionalized work about Marie was written by Francine Prose, and one about Marie's daughter, *Marie*, was written by Margot Arnold.

Other figures of legend and folklore may not be real as Marie Laveau, but their fame lives anyway. The tales of High John the Conquerer crop up frequently in African-American folktales, and he is included as a major figure in Virginia Hamilton's *The Magical Adventures of Pretty Pearl*.

Another common folklore figure is the trickster, often featured in African-American tales about Ananse, whose legend originated in Africa with the Akan. According to Christopher Vecsey in *Mythical Trickster Figures*, stories about Ananse are plentiful, some even giving him godlike status responsible for the creation of the world.[27]

There are many folktales and legends from Africa. Some changed in the western hemisphere. Some collections of folktales have been compiled and/or written by authors such as Roger D. Abrahams, Virginia Hamilton, Mary E. Lyons, and Patricia D. McKissack. Sometimes it is difficult to decide whether some characters are the creation of storytellers, and which have been derived from old traditions. Very often these mythic legends become intertwined. Just the simple and common use of the snake in contemporary horror fiction is based on religious belief. The voodoo gods have had a strong impact on various traditions. For example, from Hurston's *Tell My Horse*, "Damballah Quedo is the supreme Mystere and his signature is the serpent."[28] Other gods have symbolic attributes as well, and some of these have found their way into literature. It is easy to understand how various legends and traditions become combined and evolve through passage of time and place. All of this has produced a fruitful heritage and inspiration for stories by all kinds of authors for an enthusiastic diversified audience.

CONCLUSION

African-American culture has produced many rich and fascinating themes of interest to young adult readers of all backgrounds. Some of the African themes used by earlier European-American writers have been misunderstood and/or used simply for sensationalism and exotic touches. In more recent years, there has been a growing sensitivity on the part of European-American writers and even African-American writers to consider the positive values of the African cultures depicted negatively so often in the past—and, unfortunately, still today by some writers. Voodoo, in particular, has been treated as an unknown and primitive religion, but there seems to be an encouraging trend to treat modern santería practices with consideration for its positive values. This would seem to be somewhat parallel to the growing consideration for "fair treatment" of wicca, or white witchcraft, by contemporary authors. Increased understanding and appreciation of all cultures will ultimately bring about better and more truthful books for young adults, even in the area of the selectively accepted horror novels.

NOTES

1. The author thanks David Hagerman and Beverly Balster for their invaluable help in the preparation of this essay.
2. Zora Neale Hurston, *Tell My Horse* (Philadelphia, PA: J. B. Lippincott, 1938), 137.
3. Arthur Miller, *The Crucible* (New York: Viking, 1971), 122.
4. Francis Wyndham, foreword to *Wide Sargasso Sea* by Jean Rhys (New York: Norton, 1967), 12.
5. Peter Hollindale, "Wide Sargasso Sea," *Times Literary Supplement* (29 September 1989): 12.
6. Marilyn Ross, *The Haiti Circle* (New York: Popular Library, 1976), 5.
7. Jean Rhys, *Wide Sargasso Sea* (New York: Norton, 1967), 17.
8. "An Interview & Bibliography Featuring: Hugh B. Cave." *The Scream Factory* (Summer 1992), 53–4.
9. Ishmael Reed, "Neo-HooDoo Manifesto," poem in *New and Collected Poems* (New York: Atheneum, 1988), 20.
10. For example, see titles in References by Linedecker, Provost, and Schutze.
11. Hurston, 189–90.
12. Jay Callahan, *Footprints of the Dead* (New York: Dell, 1983), 132.
13. Garry B. Trudeau, *Action Figure! The Life and Times of Doonesbury's Uncle Duke* (Kansas City, MO: Andrews and McMeel, 1992), 117.
14. John Russo, *Scare Tactics: The Art, Craft, and Trade Secrets of Writing, Producing, and Directing Chillers and Thrillers* (New York: Dell, 1992), 11–12.

15. John Russo, *Living Things* (New York: Popular Library, 1988), 24.
16. John Farris, *All Heads Turn When the Hunt Goes By* (New York: Popular Library, 1977), 243.
17. Ibid., 266.
18. Frances Temple, *A Taste of Salt* (New York: Orchard Books, 1992), 26–7.
19. Clive Barker, "The Forbidden," story in *In the Flesh* (New York: Pocket Books, 1988), 139–40.
20. Ishmael Reed, *Mumbo Jumbo* (New York: Avon, 1978), 241–2.
21. Margaret Dunbar, "And Through the Caribbean Sea," poem in *The Black Poets*, ed. Dudley Randall (New York: Bantam, 1971), 152.
22. Ibid.
23. Robert Frazier and Bruce Boston, "Night Fishing on the Caribbean Littoral of the Mutant Rain Forest," poem in *Tropical Chills*, ed. Tim Sullivan (New York: Avon, 1988), 115.
24. Gayle Jones, *Liberating Voices: Oral Tradition in African American Literature* (New York: Penguin, 1991), 100–1.
25. James Mellon, ed., *Bullwhip Days: The Slaves Remember* (New York: Weidenfeld & Nicolson, 1988), 90.
26. Zora Neale Hurston, *Dust Tracks on a Road* (New York: HarperPerennial, 1991), 139.
27. Christopher Becsey, "The Exception Who Proves the Rules: Ananse the Akan Trickster," chapter in *Mythical Trickster Figures: Contours, Contexts and Criticism*, ed. William J. Hays and William G. Doty (Tuscaloosa, AL: University of Alabama Press, 1993), 112.
28. Hurston, *Tell My Horse*, 41.

REFERENCES

Abrahams, Roger D. *Afro-American Folktales*. New York: Pantheon Books, 1985.

Alderman, Clifford Lindsey. *The Devil's Shadow*. New York: Messner, 1967.

Andrezel, Pierre. [Blixen, Karen] *The Angelic Avengers*. New York: Random House, 1947.

Arnold, Margot. *Death of a Voodoo Doll*. New York: Jove, 1982.

_____. *Marie*. New York: Pocket Books, 1979.

Baby . . . Secret of the Lost Legend. Directed by B.W.L. Norton, 1985.

Barker, Clive. "The Forbidden." In *In the Flesh*. New York: Pocket Books, 1988.

The Believers. Directed by John Schlesinger, 1987.

Bloch, Robert. "Mother of Serpents." In *The Opener of the Way*. Sauk City, WI: Arkham House, 1966.

Bradley, Marion Zimmer. *Drums of Darkness*. New York: Ballantine/Zodiac Gothic, 1976.

Bretonne, Anne-Marie. *Dark Talisman*. New York: Popular Library, 1975.

Bridges, Laurie and Paul Alexander. *Swamp Witch*. New York: Bantam/Dark Forces, 1983.

Burgess, Barbara Hood. *Oren Bell*. New York: Delacorte, 1991.

Burn, Witch, Burn. Directed by Sidney Hayers, 1961.

Callahan, Jay. *Footprints of the Dead*. New York: Dell/Twilight, 1983.

Candyman. Directed by Bernard Rose, 1992.

Cantrell, Lisa W. *Boneman*. New York: Tor, 1992.

Carr, John Dickson. *Papa La-Bas*. New York: Carroll & Graft, 1989. (Orig. published in 1968.)

Case, Jim. *Cody's Army #6: Hellfire in Haiti*. New York: Berkley, 1988.

Cave, Hugh B. *Disciples of Dread*. New York: Tor, 1989.

_____. *The Evil*. New York: Ace/Charter, 1981.

_____. *Legion of the Dead*. New York: Avon, 1979.

_____. *The Lower Deep*. New York: Tor, 1990.

_____. *Lucifer's Eye*. New York: 1991.

_____. *Shades of Evil*. New York: Ave, 1982.

Chesnutt, Charles. *The Conjure Woman*. Boston, MA: Houghton Mifflin, 1899.

Coffman, Virginia. *Isle of the Undead*. New York: Lancer, 1969.

Conde, Maryse. *I, Tituba, Black Witch of Salem*. Charlottesville, VA: University Press of Virginia, 1992.

Condé, Nicholas. *The Religion*. New York: Signet, 1983.

Conrad, Joseph. *The Heart of Darkness*. London, England: J. M. Dent & Sons, 1902.

The Crucible. Directed by Raymond Rouleau, 1957.

Cusick, Richie Tankersley. *Evil on the Bayou*. New York: Dell/Twilight, 1984.

Daniels, Dorothy. *Dark Island*. New York: Paperback Library, 1972.

_____. *Raxl, Voodoo Priestess*. New York: Paperback Library, 1970.

Daniels, Norman. *Voodoo Slave*. New York: Paperback Library, 1970.

Davis, Wade. *The Serpent and the Rainbow*. New York: Warner, 1987.

Dead & Buried. Directed by Gary Sherman, 1980

Deaver, Jeffery Wilds. *Voodoo*. Toronto: PaperJacks, 1988.

Deren, Maya. *Divine Horsemen: The Voodoo Gods*. New York: Delta, 1972.

Derleth, August and Mark Schorer. "Eyes of the Serpent." In *Colonel Markesan and Less Pleasant People*. Sauk City, WI: Arkham House, 1966.

Dunbar, Margaret. "And through the Caribbean Sea." In *The Black Poets*, edited by Dudley Randall. New York: Bantam, 1971.

Duncan, Lois. *Locked in Time*. Boston, MA: Little, Brown, 1971.

Farber, James. *Blood Island*. New York: Pocket Books, 1981.

Farris, John. *All Heads Turn When the Hunt Goes By*. New York: Popular Library, 1977.

_____. *Catacombs*. New York: Tor, 1987.

Flowers, A. R. *DeMojo Blues*. New York: Dutton, 1985.

Frazier, Robert and Bruce Boston. "Night Fishing on the Caribbean Littoral of the Mutant Rain Forest." In *Tropical Chills*, edited by Tim Sullivan. New York: Avon, 1988.

Geary, Patricia. *Strange Toys*. New York: Bantam/Spectra, 1987.

González-Wippler, Migene. *The Santería Experience: A Journey into the Miraculous*. Rev. Ed. St. Paul, MN: Llevellyn, 1992.

Haggard, H. Rider. *She*. London, England: McKinlay, Stone, & Mackenzie, 1886.

Hamilton, Virginia. *The Dark Way: Stories from the Spirit World*. New York: Harcourt Brace Jovanovich, 1990.

_____. *The House of Dies Drear*. New York: Macmillan, 1968.

_____. *The Magical Adventures of Pretty Pearl*. New York: Harper Collins, 1983.

Hays, William J. and William G. Doty, eds. *Mythical Trickster Figures: Contours, Contexts and Criticism*. Tuscaloosa, AL: University of Alabama Press, 1993.

Hjortsberg, William. *Falling Angel*. New York: Harcourt Brace Jovanovich, 1978.

Hoffman, Nina Kiriki. "Zombies for Jesus." *In The Year's Best Horror Stories XVIII*, edited by Karl Edward Wagner. New York: Daw, 1990.

Hunt, E. Howard (pscud., David St. John). *The Coven*. New York: Weybright & Talley, 1972.

Hurston, Zora Neale. *Dust Tracks on a Road*. New York: Harper Perennial, 1991.

_____. *Men and Mules*. Philadelphia, PA: J. B. Lippincott, 1935.

_____. *Tell My Horse*. Philadelphia, PA: J. B. Lippincott, 1938.

Huxley, Francis. *The Invisibles*. New York: McGraw-Hill, 1966.

I Walked with a Zombie. Directed by Jacques Tourneur, 1943.

James, Martin. [Kiser, James] *Zombie House*. New York: Pinnacle, 1990.

Jones, Gayle. *Liberating Voices: Oral Tradition in African American Literature*. New York: Penguin, 1991.

King, Stephen. *Pet Sematary*. New York: Doubleday, 1983.

Koontz, Dean. *Darkfall*. New York: W. M. Allen, 1984.

Lee, Edward. *Ghouls*. New York: Pinnacle, 1988.

Leiber, Fritz. *Conjure Wife*. New York: Twayne, 1953.

Leigh, Veronica. *Voodoo Drums*. New York: Award Books, 1976.

Leslie, Peter. *The Steeds of Satan*. New York: Zebra, 1976.

Linedecker, Clifford L. *Hell Ranch*. New York: Tor, 1990.

Lofts, Norah. *The Claw*. New York: Tor, 1984.

Lyons, Mary E. *Sorrow's Kitchen: The Life and Folklore of Zora Neale Hurston*. New York: Charles Scribner's Sons, 1990.

_____, ed. *Raw Head, Bloody Bones: African-American Tales of the Super-*

natural. New York: Charles Scribner's Sons, 1987.

Man, Myth, & Magic: The Illustrated Encyclopedia of Mythology, Religion, and the Unknown, 12 Volumes. "Voodoo." New York: Marshall Cavendish, 1983.

McKissack, Patricia C. *The Dark-Thirty: Southern Tales of the Supernatural*. New York: Knopf, 1992.

_____. "We Organized." In *The Dark-Thirty: Southern Tales of the Supernatural*. New York: Knopf, 1992.

Mellon, James, ed. *Bullwhip Days: The Slaves Remember*. New York: Weidenfeld & Nicolson, 1988.

Merrit, Abe. *Burn Witch Burn*. London, England: Neville Spearman, 1955.

Merrit, Abe and Hannes Bok. *The Black Wheel*. New York: New Collectors' Group, 1947.

Metraux, Alfred. *Voodoo in Haiti*. New York: Oxford University Press, 1959.

Meyer, John. *Night-child*. New York: Pocket Books, 1978.

Miller, Arthur. *The Crucible*. New York: Viking, 1971.

Monaco, Richard. *Journey to the Flame*. New York: Bantam, 1985.

Morrell, David. "Mumbo Jumbo." In *Night Visions: Dead Images*, edited by Charles L. Grant. New York: Berkley, 1985.

Night of the Living Dead. Directed by George A. Romero, 1968.

Night of the Living Dead. Directed by Tom Savini, 1990.

Norton, Andre and Phyllis Miller. *Seven Spells to Sunday*. New York: Archway, 1980.

Osier, John. *Covenant at Coldwater*. New York: Ballantine, 1986.

Parx, C. C. *Slavers*. New York: Charter, 1980.

Pfefferle, Seth. *Stickman*. New York: Tor, 1987.

Potts, Carl. *The Punisher Wolverine: African Saga*. New York: Marvel, 1988.

Pronzini, Bill. *Masques*. New York: Arbor House, 1981.

Prose, Francine. *Marie Laveau*. New York: Berkley, 1978.

_____. *Primitive People*. New York: Ivy, 1993.

Provost, Gary. *Across the Border*. New York: Pocket Books, 1989.

Reed, Ishmael. *Flight to Canada*. New York: Random House, 1976.

_____. *The Free-Lance Pall Bearers*. Garden City, NY: Doubleday, 1967.

_____. *The Last Days of Louisiana Red*. New York: Random House, 1974.

_____. *Mumbo Jumbo*. New York: Avon, 1978.

_____. "Neo-HooDoo Manifesto." In *New and Collected Poems*. New York: Atheneum, 1988.

_____. *Reckless Eyeballing*. New York: St. Martin's Press, 1986.

_____. *The Terrible Twos*. New York: Atheneum, 1989.

Return of the Living Dead. Directed by Dan O'Bannon, 1985.

Return of the Living Dead Part II. Directed by Ken Wiederhorn, 1988.

Rhys, Jean. *Wide Sargasso Sea*. New York: Norton, 1967.

Rinaldi, Ann. *A Break with Charity*. New York: Harcourt Brace Jovanovich/

Gulliver Books, 1992.

Ross, Marilyn. *The Haiti Circle*. New York: Popular Library, 1976.

____. *Phantom of the Swamp*. New York: Paperback Library, 1972.

Russo, John. *Living Things*. New York: Popular Library, 1988.

____. *Night of the Living Dead*. New York: Pocket Books, 1981.

____. *Return of the Living Dead*. New York: Avon, 1978.

____. *Scare Tactics: The Art, Craft, and Trade Secrets of Writing, Producing, and Directing Chillers and Thrillers*. New York: Dell, 1992.

____. *Voodoo Dawn*. Pittsburgh, PA: Imagine, 1987.

Sadler, Barry. *Casca: The African Mercenary*. New York: Charter, 1984.

St. John, David. [E. Howard Hunt] *Diabolus*. New York: Fawcett Crest, 1971.

Schutze, Jim. *Cauldron of Blood: The Matamoros Cult Killings*. New York: Avon, 1989.

Seabrook, Brenda. *The Bridges of Summer*. New York: Cobblehill, Dutton, 1992.

Seabrook, William. *The Magic Island*. New York: Literary Guild, 1929.

Seymour, Henry. *Infernal Idol*. New York: Avon, 1969.

She. Directed by Irving Pichel and Lansing C. Holden, 1935.

She. Directed by Robert Day, 1965.

Skipp, John and Craig Spector, eds. *Book of the Dead*. New York: Bantam, 1989.

____, eds. *Book of the Dead 2: Still Dead*. New York: Bantam, 1992.

Stiver, Dick. *Able Team: Cult War*. Toronto: Gold Eagle, 1990.

Tallant, Robert. *Voodoo in New Orleans*. New York: Collier, 1962.

____. *The Voodoo Queen*. New York: Putnam, 1956.

Taylor, Theodore. *The Cay*. New York: Avon/Flare, 1970.

Temple, Frances. *A Taste of Salt*. New York: Orchard Books, 1992.

Thomas, Joyce Carol. *Journey*. New York: Scholastic, 1988.

Tremayne, Peter. *Zombie!* New York: St. Martin's Press, 1987.

Trudeau, Garry B. *Action Figure! The Life and Times of Doonesbury's Uncle Duke*. Kansas City, MO: Andrews and McMeel, 1992.

Voodoo Dawn. Directed by Steven Fierberg, 1991.

Wagner, Sharon. *Haitian Legacy*. New York: Avon, 1974.

Weird Woman. Directed by Reginald LeBorge, 1944.

Wheatley, Dennis. *Strange Conflict*. London: Hutchinson, 1941.

Whitehead, Henry S. "Black Terror." In *West India Lights*. Sauk City, WI: Arkham House, 1946.

Wide Sargasso Sea. Directed by Lee Duigan, 1993.

Witches' Brew. Directed by Richard Shorr and Herbert L. Strock, 1980.

Wolfe, Jonathan. *Killer See, Killer Do*. New York: Leisure Books, 1977.

Yarbro, Chelsea Quinn. *Dead & Buried*. New York: Warner, 1980.

Yates, Janelle. *Zora Neale Hurston: A Storyteller's Life*. New York: Ward Hill, 1991.

FOURTEEN

An Exploratory Study: Using On-Line Databases to Analyze the Dispersion of Contemporary African-American Young Adult Literature

Edna Reid

Kenneth Donelson and Aileen Nilsen define young adult literature as materials that "readers between the approximate ages of twelve and twenty choose to read."[1] In particular, African-American young adult literature focuses on the African-American experience as seen from an African-American perspective.[2] Rudine Sims categorizes it as culturally conscious literature that reflects, with varying success, the social and cultural traditions associated with growing up black in the United States.[3] Although many authors have examined the concepts, themes, and plots depicted in African-American young adult literature, what is the current stage of growth and development of this literature?

This chapter reports an exploratory study which uses an integrated methodology to document the dispersion of African-American young adult literature and to analyze the development of this emerging specialization. Dispersion in this type of study means an examination of patterns and trends in the publications of a given author or authors within a specific discipline as revealed over a specific time span. In studying the dispersion of this literature, different on-line bibliographical databases were searched to identify a scattering map of African-

American young adult literature and to determine patterns of appearances and influences of this literature. This unconventional application of data from on-line databases has been used by several researchers, among them, Paul McGhee and F. Wolf Lancaster, to perform trend analysis on different topics and, in addition, to track the growth in cognitive development research and acid rain literature.[4]

This study goes beyond these earlier investigations in demonstrating how the results of on-line database searches may be used to provide a broader picture of the development of a specialty. By focusing on the amount of publication activity, the communication, dissemination and dispersion activities, and the influences on future literature and critical research, it is possible for even a nonspecialist to analyze a specialty, in this instance, African-American young adult literature. This investigation permitted further application of an integrated methodology, developed in earlier studies by the author, for analyzing the dissemination, communication, and dispersion activities that occur in a discipline and how such activities lead to the development of an emerging specialty.

As an exploratory case study, this research investigates such essential questions, as: What are the major characteristics of this literature? What dispersion patterns are revealed in relation to authors of African-American young adult literature? How do these authors interact with other knowledge producers (e.g., other authors, researchers, publishers) to construct, maintain, and modify the ideas associated with young adult literature? What does the future portend for African-American young adult literature?

METHODOLOGY

The development of contemporary African-American young adult literature is explored using a model developed by the author for analyzing how a specialized community evolves and influences future growth. The theoretical contexts for this methodology are the work of Derek DeSolla Price, Diane Crane, Leah Lievrow, and Peter Haas.[5] The model (see Figure 1) presents a snapshot of an integration of quantitative research strategies used to investigate how a specialty evolves, how its ideas are dispersed and marketed, and finally, how they are integrated into future works. It uses several research techniques such as on-line bibliometrics, citation analysis, and tracing.

FIGURE 1. A Model of Evolution of Knowledge and Influence on Decision-Making

Phase I Measure Size of Science in Specialty	Phase II Measure Dispersion of Works	Phase III Measure Impact on Growth of Knowledge
A. Identify major members of a community B. Identify and measure their related works, research and publications C. Outline their communication, dissemination and funding activities	A. Identify dispersion patterns of their works, etc. B. Trace the dissemination of their works and associated ideas C. Identify the dispersion patterns of the common beliefs and processes by which communities package their ideas	A. Identify how the community's ideas are marketed and promoted B. Trace how the works seem to influence the broad assumptions and beliefs underlying programs and policies C. Identify the community's communication activities linking the retrieval and integration of ideas D. Conduct trend analysis and make projections about impact future works/publications

The model has been applied in an analysis of the development of contemporary political terrorism.[6] The results of that study identified how the research area of political terrorism developed and what multifaceted activities impacted on the specialty and the diffusion of ideas about political terrorism. On-line bibliometrics involves conducting searches in different on-line databases and then performing a bibliometric analysis on the critical features of the retrieved publications. Such features include the number of authors, publishers, copyright dates, types of materials, types of authorship, and number of reviews. Bibliometric analysis is the application of mathematics and statistical methods to books and other media of communication.[7] In order to apply bibliometric analysis to this investigation, first, a group of African-American young adult authors had to be identified and, second, a bibliography of their publications compiled. Once the bibliography was available, the publications were searched in different on-line databases to identify the frequency of publications within different databases, or the increasing/decreasing frequency of databases listing the topic. This was used to determine how widespread the topic is, and its patterns of appearances. The topic, in this instance, was African-American young adult literature and the focus is on each of the authors identified in the sample. Therefore, the initial steps in Phase I were to identify a sample of major members of the specialized community as well as their related works and subject them to an on-line bibliometric analysis.

IDENTIFICATION OF MAJOR MEMBERS OF THE COMMUNITY

The initial issue in the design of this study was the selection of major members of the African-American young adult literature community. Prior works on other research fronts pointed the way.[8] In identifying major authors, lists compiled by Carolyn Corson, Rosalie Kiah, and Jane Anne Hannigan were consulted.[9] In addition, the Coretta Scott King award list was used.[10] Any authors that appeared on at least two lists were used to compile the cluster studied. Table 1 lists the 18 authors who comprise this sample. The authors selected are writers of poetry, plays, fiction, and nonfiction publications for young adults.

TABLE 1.
List of Authors of African-American Young Adult Literature

Alice Childress	Sharon Bell Mathis
Eloise Greenfield	Dindga McCannon
Rosa Guy	Patricia McKissack
Virginia Hamilton	Walter Dean Myers
Joyce Hansen	Ntozake Shange
James Haskins	Mildred D. Taylor
Kristin Hunter	Joyce Carol Thomas
Belinda Hurmence	Mildred Pitts Walter
June Jordan	Brenda Wilkinson

IDENTIFICATION OF RELEVANT WORKS

A bibliography of young adult publications was compiled for each author in the sample. Using Donald Hawkins' procedure to perform searches for on-line bibliometric analysis and the *DIALOG* Information Services, Inc., on-line searches were conducted.[11] But before searching *DIALOG*, the *Subject Guide to DIALOG Databases* was consulted to identify relevant databases in the subject categories of Language and Linguistics, Library and Information Science, and

Education.[12] Initially, ten databases were selected and searched including *Books in Print,* Library of Congress's *LC MARC, Book Review Index, LISA, SOCIAL SCISEARCH, Dissertation Abstracts, Magazine Index, National Newspaper Index,* and *ERIC.*

In addition to exploring the on-line databases on the *DIALOG* system, author searches were conducted on the *OCLC's EPIC* system (Union Catalog database), the *NEXIS* system, and *WILSONLINE: Library Literature, Book Review Digest* and *MLA* databases. The *OCLC's Union Catalog* and the *DIALOG's AV Online* databases were useful in identifying young adult nonprint media materials. Since the *OCLC's Union Catalog* has worldwide holdings of library collections, it is a valuable source of information for assessing the number and types of libraries that have purchased African-American young adult literature written by the sample authors. Table 2 provides a matrix of the specialized usages of on-line databases.

TABLE 2. On-line Databases and Their Specialized Applications

	AWARDS	CITATIONS	CONFER./LECT.	DISSERTATIONS	GRADE LEVEL	INTERVIEWS	LIBRARY HOLDINGS	NONPRINT MATERIALS	PURCHASING DATA	REVIEWS	TV/RADIO TRANSCRIP./SUM.
Arts & Humanities Search		X								X	
AV ONLINE						X		X			
Book Review Digest					X					X	
Book Review Index					X					X	
Books in Print					X				X	X	
Dissertation Abstract				X							
Education Index			X							X	
ERIC	X		X								
LC Marc			X						X		
Library Literature	X									X	
LISA											
Magazine Index	X		X			X				X	
MLA	X		X	X							
National Newspaper Index	X		X			X				X	
Newspaper Abstract	X		X			X				X	X
NEXIS	X		X			X					X
Newspaper & Periodicals	X		X			X				X	
OCLC's UNION CATALOG			X				X	X			X
SOCIAL SCISEARCH		X								X	

For the purposes of this study, a publication was classified as young adult literature if the grade level was higher than sixth grade or the intellectual level indicated "Young Adult." The grade and/or intellectual levels were included in the *Books in Print, Book Review Digest,* and *Book Review Index* databases. Altogether 202 young adult publications including books, anthology chapters, collections of poetry, and plays were identified for the period 1964–1993.

Bibliographical data about the publications were supplemented with information from the *LC MARC* database, and authors' biographical data was identified in the *Contemporary Authors. Children's Books Awards and Prizes* and selected author's publications provided additional data. The information was used to create the publication and author files for the *dBASE III Plus* database management system. For the publication file, bibliographical and other descriptive data for the 202 sample publications were included. Most of the data was collected from the on-line database searches. The publication file contained fields such as publication title, copyright date, number of reviews, type of authorship communication pattern, and the LC subject headings and classification codes. For example, some fields associated with Kristin Hunter's publication are as follows:

Kristin Hunter's *Soul Brothers and Sister Lou*[13]

Copyright date	1968
Number of Reviews	17
Number of Authors	1
LC Subject Heading	Afro-American Social Conditions
Dewey Call Number	Fiction

IDENTIFICATION OF DISPERSION AND MARKETING PATTERN

The major steps in Phase II and III of the study are to identify and trace the dispersion of authors' works. The process for outlining systematically the dispersion and communication activities is to identify the following: literary reviews of author's works, awards, nonprint resources, participation in conferences and special lectures, coverage in the popular press (mass media), and impact on intellectual content (other's research). To compile this information, additional on-line searches were conducted in several databases. But it must be clearly understood that no attempt was made in this exploratory study to refine the data, so that entry duplications were not controlled and, therefore, not always eliminated.

The information was used to generate a tracing matrix which included the type of awards, conference presentation, citation data, publisher, type of resources produced about the author, and any change in subject coverage. It identified how far publications had diffused throughout the popular and research literatures and which authors had received the most awards, participated in specialized projects and media broadcasts.

FINDINGS OF THE EXPLORATORY STUDY

The growth in African-American young adult literature area as evidenced by the 202 publications was organized into four periods. The first period, spanning 1964–1969, is characterized with a sprinkling of publications generated by such authors as Kristin Hunter, Rosa Guy, and Virginia Hamilton. The second period, 1970–1979, showed increased growth in the latter part of the 1970s while the third period spanning 1980–1989, demonstrated increased publication growth and eventual doubling of the rate of the previous decade. The fourth period, although only a four-year time period, spanning 1990–1993 experienced a slight increase in publications except during 1991. The rate of growth over this thirty-year period shows 47% of the sampled literature was produced during the third period. To understand the implications of this growth pattern, analyses of the size of the sample literature and the associated dispersion activities are presented in the following section.

GROWTH OF THE LITERATURE BY TIME PERIODS

1964–1969

The first period, 1964–1969, is characterized by a few publications produced during the era of the civil rights movement and what Donelson and Nilsen and Sims describe as a time of growing social consciousness.[14] Table 3 presents a summary of the size of the sample literature. The publications produced during this period of social consciousness were the first young adult books written by the following

TABLE 3. Summary of Size of the Literature and Selected Author's Frequency

PERIOD	TOTAL NO. OF PUBLICATIONS	AUTHOR GREATEST NO. OF PUBLICATIONS	TOTAL NO. OF REVIEWS	AUTHOR GREATEST NO. OF REVIEWS	TOTAL NO. OF AWARDS	AUTHOR GREATEST NO. OF AWARDS	TOTAL NO. PUBLISHERS Per Period	AUTHOR GREATEST NO. PUBLISHERS
1964–69	7	Hamilton 2	56	Hamilton 34	4	Hamilton 3	5	
1970–79	54	Haskins 18	675	Haskins 130	8	Hamilton 7	23	Haskins 10
1980–89	96	Haskins 24	1099	Hamilton 261	16	Hamilton 8	36	Haskins 16
1990–93	45	Haskins 10 Myers 10	313	Myers 76	8	Taylor 3	22	Haskins 8
TOTAL	202		2143		36		86	

five authors who all lived or worked in New York City: Kristin Hunter, Rosa Guy, Virginia Hamilton, Jim Haskins, and June Jordan. Harlem is the setting for Hunter's *God Bless the Child*, Guy's *Bird at My Window*, and Haskins' *Diary of a Harlem Schoolteacher*.[15] Their publications are influenced greatly by their backgrounds. For example, during the 1960s Haskins taught at Public School 92 in Harlem. As a result of those experiences, he wrote a realistic portrayal of disadvantaged children struggling to get an education in Harlem. Later, he was approached by major publishing companies about writing other books for young adults.[16] *Bird at My Window*, Guy's first novel, is often considered an adult book on forces that hamper blacks in a society that is racist. Guy was concerned about reactions to the civil rights movement and to the series of terrible assassinations. She asked young people (ages 13–23) to write about their feelings and these writings she edited as *Children of Longing*.[17] For Hamilton, her first novel was based on a short story that she had written in college and later, with the help of editors at Macmillan, turned it into a novel entitled *Zeely*.[18] This novel was placed on the American Library Association's Notable Children's Book List and also won the Nancy Block Memorial Award. In 1969, Hamilton published *The House of Dies Drear* which won the Edgar Allan Poe Award for a juvenile mystery, and it also won the Ohioana Book Award in the Juvenile (or Young Adult) Book Category.[19]

All of these authors explored and expressed black consciousness and a sense of verification about everyday living in African-American communities. Based on Donelson's and Nilsen's classification, all of the publications except Jordan's can be characterized as examples of realistic problem novels for young adults.[20] Although Jordan is a poet, Jordan's *Who Look at Me* was the only poetry identified in this period.[21] This poem and the accompanying paintings are a testimony on black identity. Although designed for young readers, this book has a universal appeal. The above authors constituted an emerging cadre of new image-makers with Hamilton becoming one of the foremost image-makers for African-American young adult literature.[22]

This cadre was evolving during the time of increased awareness of the need for quality in African-American children's and young adult books. According to Karen Patricia Smith's study of the progress made in African-American literature,[23] two literary awards for new African-American books were announced. The Council on Interracial Books for Children established an annual search for the best new book on

African-American issues. In 1969, the Social Responsibilities Round Table of the American Library Association established the Coretta Scott King Award described below:

> The award (or awards), given to a black author and to a black illustrator for an outstandingly inspirational and educational contribution, is designed to commemorate the life and work of the late Dr. Martin Luther King, Jr., and to honor Mrs. Coretta Scott King for her courage and determination in continuing to work for peace and world brotherhood. Book(s) must be published one year prior to year of award presentation.[24]

1970–1979

During the second period, 1970–1979, the number of authors and publications increased. Seventy-two percent of the sampled authors had joined the research area. The majority of the titles produced during this period can be classified as realistic fiction and they reflected some of the issues in society such as concerns with family relationships, drugs, and alcoholism. According to their Library of Congress subject headings, 20% of the publications were cataloged with subject headings such as family problems, family life, brothers and sisters, or fathers and sons, while 19% were identified as biographies. Table 3 lists Haskins as the most prolific author. His books on black history and biographies of black people followed the theme of presenting realistic experiences for young adults to understand the larger world. In 1977 he won the Coretta Scott King Award for *The Story of Stevie Wonder*.[25] These themes are in agreement with Donelson's and Nilsen's characterization of young adult literature in the 1970s.[26]

Also, this period was a major turning point in the recognition of the contributions of African-American authors. Table 3 indicates that Hamilton has received more awards than any other sampled author. *The Planet of Junior Brown* was named a Newbery Honor book in 1972.[27] In 1975, Hamilton's *M. C. Higgins, the Great*,[28] was the recipient of several awards, including the prestigious Newbery Medal. In addition, it was the first work to also win the National Book Award. This book also won the Boston Globe-Horn Book Award.

Sharon Bell Mathis won the 1974 Coretta Scott King Award for *Ray Charles* and, in 1976, her *The Hundred Penny Box* was a Newbery Honor Book.[29] In 1977, Mildred D. Taylor won the Newbery Award for her brilliant *Roll of Thunder, Hear My Cry*. In the introduction, Taylor writes:

> I learned a history not then written in books but one passed from generation to generation on the steps of moonlit porches and beside dying fires in one-room houses, a history of great-grand-parents and of slavery and of the days following slavery; of those who lived still not free, yet who would not let their spirits be enslaved. From my father the storyteller I learned to respect the past, to respect my own heritage and myself.[30]

When Cassie Logan's mother is fired because she chooses to teach her students black pride, Taylor sets the stage for an exploration during this bitter year of young Cassie's life. The Logan family would go on in other books but always with a connection of strong family relationships.

Eloise Greenfield received the Jane Addams Children's Book Award and the Jane Addams Peace Association Award in 1976 for *Paul Robeson*.[31] Greenfield is eager to help young people find themselves and to survive in a difficult world and her poetry, novels, and biographies all work to that end. Ntozake Shange achieved outstanding success with her poem/play *for colored girls who have considered suicide/ when the rainbow is enuf* written in 1974 and winner of the Obie Award in 1976.[32]

1980–1989

The third period, 1980–1989, is characterized as a stage of almost doubling the growth of titles and an increase in the number of authors. Although 10% of the publications are biographies, in this period a broader range of subject coverage and a tendency towards more historical fiction is indicated. The subjects revealed that the works are not parochial in coverage but included the Caribbean Islands, Cuba, Vietnam, India, Spain, and South Africa. The most frequently cited subjects were family relationships (9%), race relations (7%), and mysteries (6%). Table 4 summarizes the publication growth and identifies Hamilton as the most frequently reviewed author. In 1988, her *Anthony Burns: The Defeat and Triumph of a Fugitive Slave* won the Boston Globe-Horn Book Award and in 1989 it won the Coretta Scott King Award.[33] Also, she is the author of the most frequently reviewed title

The People Could Fly: American Black Folktales.[34] In 1989, *In the Beginning: Creation Stories from Around the World* was named a Newbery Honor book.[35] Walter Dean Myers won several awards for his novels portraying the lives of young Harlem blacks. Before becoming a free-lance writer, Myers was a book editor at a major publishing company in New York.[36] His *Fallen Angels*[37] won the Coretta Scott King Award and the South Carolina Young Adult Book Award. Dianne Johnson writes about *Fallen Angels:*

> But just like Walter Dean Myers, who continually returns to the city streets through the pages of his many powerful novels, Richie [the protagonist in *Fallen Angels*] continually returns to the streets as he analyzes his wartime experience. The army proves to be the environment in which he poignantly reexamines his many questions rather than running away from them. Throughout his story, he draws connections, both physical and psychological, between the gang warfare of Harlem and Chicago streets and the Vietnam fields of war.[38]

Myers wrote *Scorpions*[39] in 1988 and it was named a Newbery Honor book in 1989. Carol Collins writes as follows about *Scorpions*:

> *Scorpions* describes real problems, and the reader of these pages will immediately see this. The reader will also recognize Jamal's lack of direction as well as the absolute powerlessness of the schools to help students who are most in need of help. Myers offers no solutions, but he does show that innocence, conscience, and responsibility still are important, even in the ghetto.[40]

Joyce Hansen, Belinda Hurmence, Patricia McKissack, and Mildred Walter are the new authors identified in this period. McKissack, a former book editor, has won two awards, the Coretta Scott King Award and The Jane Addams Award, for *The Long Hard Journey: The Story of the Pullman Porter.*[41] A picture book, *Mirandy and Brother Wind*[42] was a 1989 Caldecott Honor book, indicative of her impact in the literary community. McKissack, Hurmence, Hansen, and Walter wrote historical fiction, but both Hansen and McKissack gave direct credit to their students as their source of inspiration for their novels.[43] Joyce Hansen opens the question of a troubled teenager in *Home Boy.*[44] Hansen then chose to go on to write historical fiction that is set in the time of the Civil War and post Civil War. She received an honorable

TABLE 4. Publication of African-American Books

	1985	1986	1987	1988	1989	1990	1991	1992	1993
Total number of children's and Young Adult books by African-Americans	18	18	30	39	48	51	70	*	*
Total number of African-American Young Adult books written by the 18 sampled authors	9	8	11	13	7	13	3	19	10

* Numbers were not available.

mention in the Coretta Scott King Award for *Which Way Freedom?* in 1987.[45] Belinda Hurmence's *Tancy* won the Golden Kite Award and the North Carolina Literary and Historical Association Award.[46] Set in the time of Emancipation, Tancy leaves the plantation to search for her own black mother from whom she has been separated as a young child. Hurmence used slave narratives to help evoke the period successfully; and in the protagonist, Tancy, she is able to recreate the personal emancipation of Tancy in the period of a larger political emancipation. Mildred Pitts Walter won the Coretta Scott King Award in 1987 for *Justin and the Best Biscuits in the World.*[47] Dindga McCannon wrote of Harlem and the mid 60s dream of following an art career in *Wilhemina Jones, Future Star*[48] which continues her interest in art as a career which began in *Peaches.*[49] Joyce Carol Thomas was the recipient of many awards and honors for *Marked By Fire*[50] and the Coretta Scott King Award for its sequel *Bright Shadow.*[51] Thomas characteristically brings authenticity to her novels. Thomas wrote in her essay in *Something About the Author* as follows:

> If I had to give advice to young people, it would be that whatever your career choice, prepare yourself to do it well. Quality takes talent and time. Believe in your dreams. Have faith in yourself. Keep working and enjoying today even as you reach for tomorrow. If you choose to write, value your experiences. And color them in the indelible ink of your own background.[52]

1990–1993

Although the fourth period includes only four years, 1990–1993, the growth in publications is almost as much (83%) as the total publications produced during the decade of the 70s. This growth in young adult literature is in contrast to the projected growth in children's literature. According to an issue raised by Dianne Johnson, less black children's literature is being published in the 1990s than was published in the 1970s.[53] Yet, this data revealed that the 1990s has started with growth in African-American young adult literature that, if continued, should triple the growth over that of the 1980s. Table 4 compares this data with Horning's statistics of the publication of African-American children and young adult literature.[54]

During the 1990s, biographies (26%) continued to prevail in the subject coverage of African-American young adult literature. Other subjects included civil rights (18%), slavery (11%), and family relation-ships (8%). This is in agreement with the current reemergence of the need to better understand African heritage and the challenges of being an African-American. Brenda Wilkinson wrote on Jesse Jackson and the civil rights movement.[55] She also wrote *Definitely Cool* in 1993 which is a novel on the move from a middle school to a junior high school in an upper-class area.[56] This might be compared to *Maizon at Blue Hill* by Jacqueline Woodson who addresses a similar question.[57] Also during this period, Myers who is recognized as one of modern young adult literature's premier authors of fiction about African-American experiences, emerged as one of the most prolific authors.

Table 3 indicates that both Haskins and Myers were prolific authors. In fact, maybe there is some validity to Myers' unique writing schedule of producing ten pages of a novel per day.[58] Both Myers and Haskins are associated with a wide range of major publishers and their works are frequently reviewed. In this four year period, Myers has writ-ten for six publishers, been reviewed 76 times and received two awards while Haskins has written for ten publishers, been reviewed 63 times and received an award. Myers was the most frequently reviewed author for the 1990s.

Of the total number of publications identified in this study, Haskins, Myers, and Hamilton authored 108 publications. Therefore, 17% of the sample authors wrote over half of the 202 publications. This distribution of publications is consistent with social science research studies which validated that a small proportion of the authors con-tribute most publications.[59] This implies that even in African-American young adult literature, a sub-specialty of young adult literature, there is little deviation from the main scientific pattern of a few highly produc-tive authors who produce the majority of works in a specialty. If this is the pattern for African-American literature, what about the entire spe-cialty of young adult literature?

DISPERSION ACTIVITIES

Although the analysis of the growth of the literature identifies some of the major members in the African-American young adult literature community, what roles did they play in the dispersion and communication of ideas about their literature? According to James Smith's study of how ideas are marketed to decision makers, ideas are promoted so that they spark talk and further writings in reviews, editorials, broadcast interviews, op-ed pieces and are eventually heard in legislative testimonies, briefings, and lectures.[60] A similar pattern holds true for young adult literature because the works were dispersed by the generation of secondary materials about the novels such as literary reviews, nonprint materials, awards, interviews, coverage in the popular press, conference and lecture presentations, and literary research. Table 5 summarizes the sample authors involvement in these activities. The databases used to identify the dispersion activities are listed in Table 2.

REVIEWS OF BOOKS BY AUTHORS

Since Hamilton has received more reviews, literary awards, interviews, and nonprint resources based on her literature, she was examined in an analysis of the scattering of African-American young adult literature through review publications. Hamilton, one of the most highly respected and established young adult authors, has received 443 reviews of 24 publications over a thirty year period. According to the Book Review Index database, the reviews were indexed in 74 different publications. In a comparison with Donelson and Nilsen's list of reviewing sources for young adult books, she has been reviewed by every major reviewing publisher.[61] Both *Publishers Weekly* (ranked #2) and *Kirkus Reviews* (ranked #6) review the majority of new books from the larger publishers two or three months before their publication dates. *School Library Journal* (ranked #4) and *Booklist* (ranked #1) often review books before publication and are the major reviewing services for the library market. Once the book is available on the market then a major reviewing source is the *New York Times Book Review*. Although Gerald Howard, an editor for W. W. Norton, describes the *New York Times Book Review* as the most fully staffed book reviewing supplement in American journalism, this is not true in relation to the reviewing of the literature of the youth field.[62]

The *New York Times Book Review* has about 80,000 subscribers and ranked number three in reviewing Hamilton's books. In addition to the wide distribution of reviewing sources, it is indexed in many print and on-line abstracting and indexing systems. For example, *Booklist* is indexed in twelve systems such as *Legal Information Management Index, Library Literature, Children's Book Review Index,* and *Micro-*

TABLE 5. Dispersion Activities

AUTHOR	NO. OF YOUNG ADULT PUBLICATIONS	NO. OF CONFERENCES AND LECTURES IDENTIFIED IN THE DATABASE SEARCH	NO. OF INTERVIEWS IDENTIFIED IN DATABASE SEARCH	NO. NONPRINT YOUNG ADULT MATERIALS IDENTIFIED IN DATABASE SEARCH	NO. OF OTHER ARTICLES/SPEECHES ON YOUNG ADULT LITERATURE	NO. RESEARCH ABOUT THE AUTHOR IDENTIFIED IN DATABASE SEARCH	NO. LITERARY REVIEWS IDENTIFIED IN DATABASE SEARCH	NO. AWARDS RECEIVED BY AUTHOR (BASED ON DATABASE SEARCH)
Childress	6	2	1	4	5	26	73	4
Greenfield	6	2	3	2	25	7	72	10
Guy	13	1	0	3	6	10	217	2
Hamilton	24	5	7	17	19	24	443	19
Hansen	6	0	1	0	5	0	57	0
Haskins	53	1	1	2	9	0	367	12
Hunter	6	0	1	2	4	3	58	5
Hurmence	4	0	1	1	0	0	40	0
Jordan	5	0	3	0	13	12	3	0
Mathis	2	0	1	2	2	5	47	2
McCannon	2	0	1	0	0	0	11	0
McKissack	11	0	1	0	2	2	55	4
Myers	31	0	4	5	7	3	292	13
Shange	4	0	1	0	12	42	62	0
Taylor	7	1	1	7	0	14	159	13
Thomas	7	0	1	0	3	0	62	5
Walter	7	2	1	1	5	3	67	0
Wilkinson	6	0	1	0	2	0	58	2
TOTAL	200	14	30	46	119	151	2143	91

computer Index. The reviews are major instruments in the marketing and dispersion of information about young adult literature.

AWARDS TO THE AUTHORS IN THE STUDY

Awards are an important mechanism for recognizing literary excellence in any area. In addition to the two awards in African-American children's and young adult literature, there are numerous literary awards such as the John Newbery Medal and Boston Globe-Horn Book Award. Virginia Hamilton has received nineteen awards including the Coretta Scott King Award and the John Newbery Medal. Early in her career, she received recognition and visibility for the quality of her work. The collegial recognition (in itself reinforcing) attracted additional resources that facilitated future young adult books. Hamilton has published twenty-four books with ten publishing houses and has seventeen nonprint resources such as a film, videocassette, audiocassette, and filmstrip of *M. C. Higgins the Great.*[63] This book was also named to the International Board of Books for Young People (IBBY) Honor List. The *House of Dies Drear* was adapted for the Public Broadcasting System (PBS) series "Wonderworks" in 1984. In 1992, Virginia Hamilton reached a high point in her career with winning the international Hans Christian Andersen Medal for the body of her work.

Most prolific authors may use many publishing companies. For example, Jim Haskins has published with 26 different publishers and Walter Dean Myers with ten. By working with different publishing companies, an author can tailor the selection of the publishing houses to the type of work that he/she is planning and can maintain a vigorous schedule for completion. Hamilton's early recognition had a causal link with consistently high productivity, financial support, and wide distribution of African-American publications. The early recognition was a positive reinforcement and the winning of many awards over three decades is consistent with the theory of accumulative advantages among scientists. This is similar to the reward structure in most universities where the act of publishing signals professional accomplishments, rewards, more publications, and recognition. This is also in agreement with studies of scientific productivity and the reward structure of science. For example, Reskin analyzed chemists to test the relationships between early productivity, recognition and productivity at the end of the decade. She confirmed the importance of positive reinforcement among professionals. Positive reinforcements have had major impact on the development of African-American young adult literature. The 1990s appear to be similar to the 1970s, a decade of positive reinforcements for African-American literature.

AUTHORS AS THE SUBJECT OF RESEARCH

The works of the sample author's have been the subject of various research studies. Table 5 indicates that there have been 151 publications that focused on their work. In addition, there were twenty-five dissertations on the following authors: Shange (9), Hamilton (4), Childress (3), Hunter (3), Guy (2), Jordan (2), and Myers (1). Shange, a poet and writer of both adult and young adult fiction, has been the subject of dissertations that examined African-American women writers. The sample of dissertations appears to confirm Donelson's and Nilsen's assertion that the majority of the dissertations focused on pedagogical or social issues.[64]

The citation patterns of selected publications were analyzed using the results of searches in the *Arts and Humanities Search* and the *SOCIAL SCISEARCH* databases. More relevant publications were identified in the latter database. The *Arts and Humanities Search* database yielded fewer results. *Arts and Humanities* citation database tracks the references appearing in 1,300 of the world's leading arts and humanities journals and about 5,000 social and natural sciences journals.[65] The searches identified the dispersion of African-American young adult literature in the literary and research areas. For example, the results of a search about Alice Childress', *A Hero Ain't Nothin' But A Sandwich*, shows that the publication is cited 39 times.[66] Reference to Childress was made in several psychiatry articles on the developments in understanding drug abuse.[67] The subject ranges of the citing journals include law (10 citing articles), psychology (7 citing articles), and education (5 citing articles). It is no wonder that this novel merits such attention. No one offers Benjie any easy solutions and, in fact, the treatment of drug use is strong and the responses of other characters to Benjie's addiction is realistic. Although written in 1973, this Childress novel still reaches young people.

CONCLUSIONS

The implications of this exploratory study are several. At least a number of the young adult authors examined in this study had reached into alternative discipline research. Many authors in the exploratory study have received awards for their work, and a number of the authors have been the subject of critical articles. The authors selected for this study have been reviewed a number of times. At the same time, there are a number of concerns that arise from such an investigation. First, there is the concern about accuracy of names in database searching. For instance, in searching Virginia Hamilton in LC-MARC one uncovers the existence of Virginia [van der Veer] Hamilton who is a historian. Second, a number of the databases used in such a search strategy do not include large numbers of journals in youth literature; and, therefore, not all the findings may be as representative as the reality. Third, to choose only one database for a search may severely limit the findings since, for example, reviews from newspapers such as *The Washington Post* and *The Los Angeles Times* are not included in *Book Review Index* but rather in *NEXIS*.

A model was used in this exploratory case study of African-American young adult literature in order to analyze the growth and dispersion activities that occur in an emerging specialty. The activities of the sample authors of contemporary African-American young adult literature were multifaceted. These authors produced many social consciousness books that provided realistic portrayals of the experiences of African-Americans. The model provided a framework of quantitative procedures to characterize the specialty and even to compare it with growth trends in the social sciences. In fact, the growth pattern was similar to other areas in the social sciences where a few authors produced most of the publications. The publications of these authors were widely dispersed by the generation of many secondary materials such as nonprint resources, literary reviews, and interviews. These secondary resources were easily identified and indexed heavily in on-line bibliographic and full-text databases. Selected authors who received early recognition and visibility in their careers published frequently and with many different publishing houses. This early recognition, financial support, and high productivity are consistent with studies of scientific productivity and the reward structure in science. In addition, the works of the sample authors have advanced the study of young adult literature and these selected authors have been the subject of various research studies to analyze the pedagogical aspects of this literature.

Since the model presented a series of measures for analyzing the publication, dissemination, and dispersion activities, it permitted a broader picture of the development of African-American young adult literature. However, this broader examination might be followed with additional research addressing the following:

> What impact might this study have on educators and their use and understanding of African-American literature for young adults?
>
> Might the dissemination of ideas about African-American literature change the way adults interpret this specialty?
>
> How might this type of analysis influence the overall study of young adult literature?
>
> How might African-American young adult literature impact on the global marketplace?

A major significance of this investigation is the confirmation that African-American young adult literature is an emerging specialty worthy of scholarly research. Exploratory studies of this kind help to validate the model proposed in this paper and help to demonstrate and confirm relationships that might not appear as obvious without such investigations.

NOTES

1. Kenneth L. Donelson and Aileen Pace Nilsen, *Literature for Today's Young Adults* (Glenview, IL: Scott, Foresman & Co, 1989), 13.
2. Carol J. Collins, "A Tool for Change: Young Adult Literature in the Lives of Young Adult African-Americans," *Library Trends* 41 (Winter 1993): 380.
3. Rudine Sims, *Shadow and Substance* (Urbana, IL: National Council of Teachers of English, 1982), 49.
4. Paul E. McGhee and others, "Using Online Databases to Study Current Research Trends: An Online Bibliometric Study," *Library & Information Science Research* 9 (1987): 285–291; W. Lancaster and J. L. Lee. "Bibliometric Techniques Applied to Issues Management: A Case Study," *Journal of the American Society for Information Science* 36 (1985): 389–397.
5. Derek J. DeSolla Price, *Little Science, Big Science* (New York: Columbia

University Press, 1963); Diane Crane. "Social Structure in a Group of Scientists: A Test of the 'Invisible College' Hypothesis," *American Sociological Review* 34 (1969): 335–352; Leah A. Lievrouw and others. "Triangulation as a Research Strategy for Identifying Invisible Colleges Among Biomedical Scientists," *Social Networks* 9 (1987): 217–248 and P. M. Haas, "Introduction: Epistemic Communities and International Policy Coordination," *International Organization* 46 (1992): 1–35.

6. Edna O. F. Reid, "Terrorism Research and the Diffusion of Ideas," *Knowledge and Policy* 6 (1993).

7. A. Pritchard, "Statistical Bibliography or Bibliometrics," *Journal of Documentation* 25 (1969): 348.

8. Diane Crane, "Social Structure in a Group of Scientists." Kenneth Donelson and Aileen Nilsen, *Literature for Today's Young Adults*, 562; and Edna O. F. Reid, "An Analysis of Terrorism Literature: A Bibliometric and Content Analysis Study" (Dissertation, University of Southern California, May 1983), 67.

9. Carolyn M. Corson, "YA Afro-American Fiction: An Update for Teachers," *English Journal* 76 (April 1987) 25–27; Rosalie B. Kiah, "Black Women Writers of Adolescent Literature," *Educational Horizons* 65 (Summer 1987): 176; Jane Hannigan, Informal Conversation in May 1993.

10. Social Responsibilities Round Table, *Coretta Scott King Award List* (Chicago, IL: American Library Association, 1993).

11. Donald T. Hawkins, "Unconventional Uses of On-Line Information Retrieval Systems: On-Line Bibliometric Studies," *Journal of the American Society for Information Science* 28 (1977): 13–18.

12. *Subject Guide to DIALOG Databases* (Palo Alto, CA: DIALOG Information Services, Inc., 1992).

13. Kristin Hunter, *Soul Brothers and Sister Lou* (New York: Charles Scribner, 1968).

14. Kenneth Donelson and Aileen Nilsen, *Literature for Today's Young Adults*, 56 and Rudine Sims, *Shadow and Substance*, 49.

15. Kristin Hunter, *God Bless the Child* (New York: Scribner, 1964); Rosa Guy, *Bird At My Window* (New York: Lippincott, 1966); and James Haskins, *Diary of a Harlem Schoolteacher* (New York: Grove Press, 1969).

16. "James Haskins," *Contemporary Authors*, 188.

17. Rosa Guy, ed. *Children of Longing* (New York: Holt, 1971).

18. Virginia Hamilton, *Zeely* (New York: Aladdin Books, 1967).

19. Virginia Hamilton, *The House of Dies Drear* (New York: Macmillan, 1968).

20. Kenneth Donelson and Aileen Nilsen 86.

21. June Jordan, *Who Look At Me* (New York: Crowell, 1969).

22. "Virginia Hamilton," *Contemporary Authors*. New Revision Series 20 (1987): 207.

23. Karen Patricia Smith, "The Multicultural Ethic and Connections to Literature for Children and Young Adults," *Library Trends* 41 (Winter 1993): 340–353.

24. American Library Association, *ALA Handbook of Organization 1993/ 1994* (Chicago, IL: American Library Association, 1993), 125.

25. James Haskins, *The Story of Stevie Wonder* (New York: Doubleday, 1976).

26. Kenneth Donelson and Aileen Nilsen, 54.

27. Virginia Hamilton, *The Planet of Junior Brown* (New York: Macmillan, 1971).

28. Virginia Hamilton, *M. C. Higgins the Great* (New York: Macmillan, 1974).

29. Sharon Bell Mathis, *Ray Charles* (New York: Crowell, 1973); and *The Hundred Penny Box* (New York: Viking, 1975).

30. Mildred D. Taylor, *Roll of Thunder, Hear My Cry* (New York: Dial, 1976), Author's Note.

31. Eloise Greenfield, *Paul Robeson* (New York: Harper & Row, 1975).

32. Ntozake Shange, *for colored girls who have considered suicide/ when the rainbow is enuf* (New York: Macmillan, 1977).

33. Virginia Hamilton, *Anthony Burns: The Defeat and Triumph of a Fugitive Slave* (New York: Knopf, 1988).

34. Virginia Hamilton. *The People Could Fly: American Black Folktales* (New York: Knopf, 1985).

35. Virginia Hamilton, *In the Beginning: Creation Stories from Around the World* (New York: Harcourt, 1988).

36. "Walter Dean Myers," *Contemporary Authors*, 325.

37. Walter Dean Myers, *Fallen Angels* (New York: Scholastic, 1988).

38. Dianne Johnson, *Telling Tales: The Pedagogy and Promise of African American Literature for Youth* (New York: Greenwood Press, 1990), 76.

39. Walter Dean Myers, *Scorpions* (New York: Harper & Row, 1988).

40. Carol Collins, 390.

41. Patricia McKissack and Frederick McKissack, *A Long Hard Journey: The Story of the Pullman Porter* (New York: Walker, 1989).

42. Patricia McKissack, *Mirandy and Brother Wind* (New York: Knopf, 1988).

43. "Joyce Hansen," *Contemporary Authors*, 202.

44. Joyce Hansen, *Home Boy* (Boston, MA: Houghton Mifflin, 1982).

45. Joyce Hansen, *Which Way Freedom?* (New York: Walker, 1986).

46. Belinda Hurmence, *Tancy* (New York: Clarion, 1984).

47. Mildred Pitts Walter, *Justin and the Best Biscuits in the World* (New York: Lothrop, 1986).
48. Dindga McCannon, *Wilhemina Jones, Future Star: A Novel* (New York: Delacorte, 1980).
49. Dindga McCannon, *Peaches* (New York: Lothrop, Lee & Shepard, 1974).
50. Joyce Carol Thomas, *Marked By Fire* (New York: Avon, 1982).
51. Joyce Carol Thomas, *Bright Shadow* (New York: Avon, 1983).
52. Joyce Carol Thomas, "Essay," in *Something About the Author Autobiography Series* Volume 7 (Detroit, MI: Gale), 299–311.
53. Dianne Johnson, 12.
54. Kathleen T. Horning, "Contributions of Alternative Press Publishers to Multicultural Literature for Children," *Library Trends* 41 (Winter 1993) 528.
55. Brenda Wilkinson, *Jesse Jackson: Still Fighting for the Dream* (Morristown, NJ: Silver Burdett, 1990).
56. Brenda Wilkinson, *Definitely Cool* (New York: Scholastic, 1993).
57. Jacqueline Woodson, *Maizon at Blue Hill* (New York: Delacorte, 1992).
58. "Walter Dean Myers," *Contemporary Authors*, 329.
59. Derek De Solla Price and Donald D. Beaver, "Collaboration in an Invisible College," *American Psychologist* 21 (November 1966), 45; Diane Crane, "The Nature of Scientific Communication and Influence," *International Social Science Journal* 22 (1970), 40; and Barbara Reskin, "Scientific Productivity and the Reward Structure of Science," *American Sociological Review* 42 (June 1977), 496.
60. James Allen Smith, *Idea Brokers: Think Tanks and the Rise of the New Policy Elite* (New York: Free Press, 1991), 193.
61. Kenneth Donelson and Aileen Nilsen, 34.
62. Gerald Howard, "Cultural Ecology of Book Reviewing," *Media Studies Journal* 6 (Summer 1992), 96.
63. *M. C. Higgins the Great*, Newbery Video Collection, Random House Video, 1986; *M. C. Higgins the Great*, Cassettes. Recorded Books, Prince Fredericks, MD, 1993; and *M. C. Higgins the Great*, 2 filmstrips. Random House School Division, MD, 1980.
64. Kenneth Donelson and Aileen Nilsen, 344.
65. *Dialog Database Catalog* (Palo Alto, CA: Dialog Information Service, Inc., 1992), 16.
66. Alice Childress, *A Hero Ain't Nothin' But A Sandwich* (New York: Coward, McCann & Geoghegan, 1973).
67. E. Kaufman and J. P. McNaul, "Recent Developments in Understanding and Treating Drug-Abuse and Dependence," *Hospital and Community Psychiatry* 43 (March 1992): 223–235 and J. E. Rose and E. D. Levin, "Concurrent Agonist-Antagonist Administration for the Analysis and

Treatment of Drug-Dependence," *Pharmacology Biochemistry and Behavior* 41 (January 1992): 219–226.

REFERENCES

American Library Association. *ALA Handbook of Organization 1993/1994.* Chicago, IL: American Library Association, 1993.

Childress, Alice. *A Hero Ain't Nothin' But a Sandwich.* New York: Coward, McCann & Geoghegan, 1973.

Collins, Carol J. "A Tool for Change: Young Adult Literature in the Lives of Young Adult African-Americans." *Library Trends* 41 (Winter 1993): 378–392.

Contemporary Authors, New Revision Series. Detroit, MI: Gale Research, 1987–.

Corson, Carolyn M. "YA Afro-American Fiction: an Update for Teachers." *English Journal* 76 (April 1987): 24–27.

Crane, Diane. "Nature of Scientific Communication and Influence." *International Social Science Journal* 22 (1970): 28–41.

_____. "Social Structure in a Group of Scientists: A Test of the 'Invisible College' Hypothesis." *American Sociological Review* 34 (1969): 335–352.

DIALOG Information Services, Inc. *Subject Guide to DIALOG Databases.* Palo Alto, CA: DIALOG, 1992.

_____. *DIALOG Database Catalog.* Palo Alto, CA: DIALOG, 1992.

Donelson, Kenneth L. and Nilsen, Aileen P. *Literature for Today's Young Adults.* 3rd ed., Glenview, IL: Scott, Foresman & Co., 1989.

Garcia, Jesus and Pugh, Sharon L. "Children's Nonfiction Multicultural Literature: Some Promises and Disappointments." *Equity and Excellence* 25 (Winter 1992): 151–155.

Greenfield, Eloise. *Paul Robeson.* New York: Harper & Row, 1975.

Guy, Rosa. *Bird at My Window.* New York: Lippincott, 1966.

_____, ed. *Children of Longing.* New York: Holt, 1971.

Haas, P. M. "Introduction: Epistemic Communities and International Policy Coordination," *International Organization* 46 (1992): 1–35.

Hamilton, Virginia. *Anthony Burns: The Defeat and Triumph of a Fugitive Slave.* New York: Knopf, 1988.

_____. *The House of Dies Drear.* New York: Macmillan, 1968.

_____. *In the Beginning: Creation Stories from Around the World.* New York: Harcourt, 1988.

_____. *M. C. Higgins, the Great.* New York: Macmillan, 1974.

_____. *The People Could Fly: American Black Folktales.* New York: Knopf, 1985.

_____. *The Planet of Junior Brown*. New York: Macmillan, 1971.

_____. *Zeely*. New York: Aladdin Books, 1967.

Hansen, Joyce. *Home Boy*. Boston, MA: Houghton Mifflin, 1982.

_____. *Which Way Freedom?* New York: Walker, 1986.

Harris, Violet J. "Multicultural Curriculum: African American Children's Literature." *Young Children* 46 (January 1991): 37–44.

Haskins, James D. *Diary of a Harlem Schoolteacher*. New York: Grove Press, 1969.

_____. *The Story of Stevie Wonder*. New York: Doubleday, 1976.

Hawkins, Donald T. "Unconventional Uses of On-line Information Retrieval Systems: On-line Bibliometric Studies." *Journal of the American Society for Information Science* 28 (1977): 13–18.

Horning, Kathleen T. "Contributions of Alternative Press Publishers to Multicultural Literature for Children." *Library Trends* 41 (Winter 1993): 524–540.

Howard, Gerald. "Cultural Ecology of Book Reviewing." *Media Studies Journal* 6 (Summer 1992): 90–110.

Hunter, Kristin. *God Bless the Child*. New York: Scribner, 1964.

_____. *Soul Brothers and Sister Lou*. New York: Scribner, 1968.

Hurmence, Belinda. *Tancy*. New York: Clarion, 1984.

Johnson, Dianne. *Telling Tales: The Pedagogy and Promise of African American Literature for Youth*. New York: Greenwood, 1990.

Jordan, June. *Who Look At Me*. New York: Crowell, 1969.

Kaufman, E. and McNaul, J. P. "Developments in Understanding and Treating Drug-Abuse and Dependence." *Hospital and Community Psychiatry* 43 (March 1992): 223–236.

Kiah, Rosalie B. "Black Women Writers of Adolescent Literature." *Educational Horizons* 65 (Summer 1987): 174–176.

Lancaster, W. and Lee, J. L. "Bibliometric Techniques Applied to Issues Management: A Case Study." *Journal of the American Society for Information Science* 36 (1985): 389–397.

Lievrouw, Leah A. and others. "Triangulation as a Research Strategy for Identifying Invisible Colleges Among Biomedical Scientists." *Social Networks* 9 (1987): 217–248.

Mathis, Sharon Bell. *The Hundred Penny Box*. New York: Viking, 1975.

_____. *Ray Charles*. New York: Crowell, 1973.

McCannon, Dindga. *Wilhemina Jones, Future Star: A Novel*. New York: Delacorte, 1980.

_____. *Peaches*. New York: Lothrop, Lee & Shepard, 1974.

McGhee, Paul E. and others. "Using Online Databases to Study Current Research Trends: An Online Bibliometric Study." *Library & Information Science Research* 9 (1987): 285–291.

M. C. Higgins, the Great. Cassettes. Prince Frederick: Recorded Books, 1993.
———. Filmstrips. Newbery Award Series. MD: Random House School Division, 1980.
_____. Newbery Video Collection. New York: Random House Video, 1986.
McKissack, Patricia. *Mirandy and Brother Wind*. New York: Knopf, 1988.
McKissack, Patricia and McKissack, Frederick. *A Long Hard Journey: the Story of the Pullman Porter*. New York: Walker, 1989.
Myers, Walter Dean. *Fallen Angels*. New York: Scholastic, 1988.
_____. *Scorpions*. New York: Harper & Row, 1988.
Price, Derek J. DeSolla. *Little Science, Big Science*. New York: Columbia University Press, 1963.
Price, Derek J. DeSolla and Beaver, Donald D. "Collaboration in an Invisible College." *American Psychologist* 21 (November 1966): 1011–1018.
Pritchard, A. "Statistical Bibliography or Bibliometrics." *Journal of Documentation* 25 (1969): 348–349.
Reid, Edna O. "An Analysis of Terrorism Literature: a Bibliometric and Content Analysis Study." Doctoral dissertation, University of Southern California, 1983.
_____. "Terrorism Research and the Diffusion of Ideas." *Knowledge and Policy* 6 (1993).
Reskin, Barbara F. "Scientific Productivity and the Reward Structure of Science." *American Sociological Review* 42 (June 1977): 491–504.
Rose, J. E. and Levin, E. D. "Concurrent Agonist-Antagonist Administration for the Analysis and Treatment of Drug-Dependence." *Pharmacology Biochemistry and Behavior* 41 (January 1992): 219–226.
Scholl, Kathleen. "Black Traditions in *M. C. Higgins, the Great*." *Language Arts* 57 (April 1980): 420–424.
Shange, Ntozake. *for colored girls who have considered suicide/ when the rainbow is enuf*. New York: Macmillan, 1977.
Sims, Rudine. *Shadow and Substance*. Urbana, IL: National Council of Teachers of English, 1982.
Slade, Leonard A., Jr. "Growing Up as a Minority in America: Four African-American Writers Testimony." *ALAN Review* 8 (Spring 1991): 9–11.
Smith, Karen Patricia. "Multicultural Ethic and Connections to Literature for Children and Young Adults." *Library Trends* 41 (Winter 1993): 340–353.
Smith, James Allen. *Idea Brokers: Think Tanks and the Rise of the New Policy Elite*. New York: Free Press, 1991.
Social Responsibilities Roundtable. *Coretta Scott King Award List*. Chicago, IL: American Library Association, 1993.
Taylor, Mildred D. *Roll of Thunder, Hear My Cry*. New York: Dial, 1976.
Thomas, Joyce Carol. *Bright Shadow*. New York: Avon, 1983.
_____. *Marked By Fire*. New York: Avon, 1982.

Walter, Mildred Pitts. *Justin and the Best Biscuits in the World*. New York: Lothrop, 1986.

Wilkinson, Brenda. *Definitely Cool*. New York: Scholastic, 1993.

_____. *Jesse Jackson: Still Fighting For the Dream*. Morristown, NJ: Silver Burdett, 1990.

Woodson, Jacqueline. *Maizon at Blue Hill*. New York: Delacorte, 1992.

Index

---

* An asterisk denotes a fictional character. There is no inversion of the name.
When any portion of a poem is quoted, that poem is indexed under its title.